LONELY COLONSAY

Island at the Edge

KEVIN BYRNE

LONELY COLONSAY

Island at the Edge

KEVIN BYRNE

Cover photograph "The Equipoise" by Brian Hindmarch;
all other photographs by the author.

British Library Cataloguing in Publication Data
A catalogue record of this book is available from the British Library

ISBN 978-1-904817-07-9

Typeset by XL Publishing Services, Tiverton
Printed and bound in Great Britain by,
CPI Antony Rowe, Chippenham and Eastbourne
Isle of Colonsay, Argyll PA61 7YR

CONTENTS

PLATES

between pages 136 and 137

PREFACE

This book is intended to be both useful and stimulating. An effort has been made to give precise directions and descriptions, and to be accurate in respect of known facts or historical information.

On the other hand, some facts are uncertain and many traditional tales might be difficult to corroborate. Clearly, that makes them no less significant, because they colour the life and nature of the island and its inhabitants. I am particularly grateful to those many islanders who have shared such information with me over the years and can only regret that as time moves on I can no longer thank them all in person.

It is hoped that readers will enjoy reading about various parts of the island and then exploring for themselves – perhaps to make new discoveries, or perhaps to shed new light where it is needed. With this in mind, and so that information can be shared, a Readers' Forum will be provided by the publishers via www.houseoflochar.com

This is a practical guide – it is envisaged that the user might read through a given chapter in advance of following the suggested walks, and then refer back to the route itself "in the field". For this reason, the text of some chapters might include more than one reference to a particular site of interest – the second one is just a gentle reminder.

Please do not think of using the "maps" provided for actual navigation – they are only provided to form a link between the text and the latest edition of the Ordnance Survey.

Kevin Byrne, April 2010

COLONSAY and ORONSAY
Based upon a map by
Symington Greave

COLONSAY

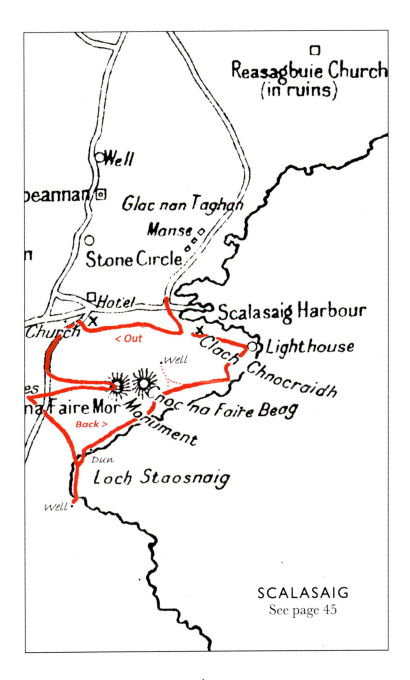

SCALASAIG
See page 45

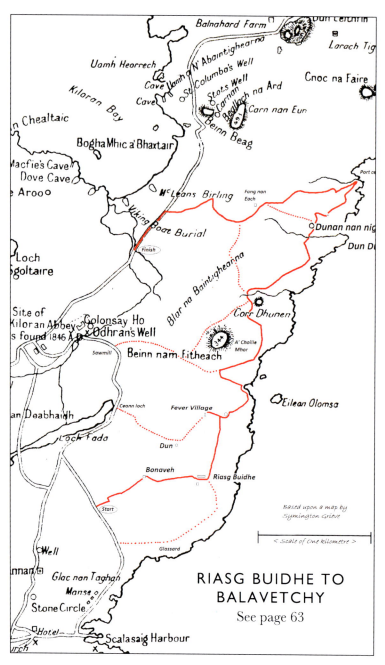

Balnahard Farm

Dun Cenchrin

Larach Tig

Uamh Heorrech

Uamh N' Abaintighearna

St Columba's Well

Stot's Well

Cnoc na Faire

Kiloran Bay

Cave

Cave

Carnan

Bealach na Ard

Carn nan Eun

n Chealtaic

Beinn Beag

Bogha Mhic a'Bhaxtair

Macfie's Cave

Dove Cave

Port ce

e Arooo

MᶜLeans Birling

Fang nan Each

Viking Boat Burial

Dunan nan nig

Dun D

Finish

Loch Sgoltaire

Blar na Baintighearna

Corr Dhunen

Site of Kiloran Abbey

Colonsay Ho

Odhran's Well

s found 1846 A D

A' Choille Mhor

Sawmill

Beinn nam Fitheach

Eilean Olomsa

an Deabhaidh

Ceann loch

Fever Village

Loch Fada

Dun

Bonaveh

Riasg Buidhe

Based upon a map by Symington Grieve

Start

< Scale of One kilometre >

Well

Glassard

nnan

Glac nan Taghan

Manse

RIASG BUIDHE TO BALAVETCHY

Stone Circle

Hotel

See page 63

urch

Scalasaig Harbour

X

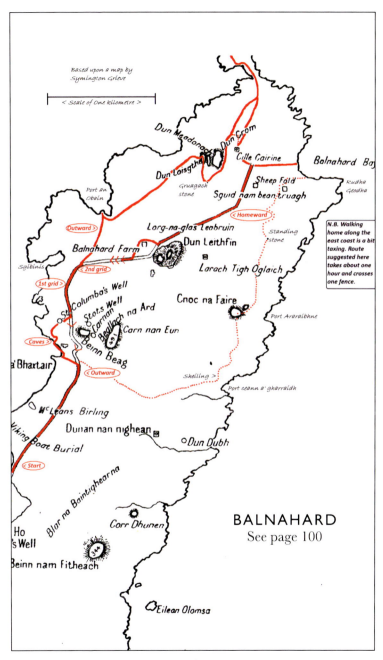

Based upon a map by
Symington Grieve

< Scale of One kilometre >

Dun Meadonach
Dun Crom
Cille Cairine
Balnahard Bay
Dun Loisgthe
Gruagach stone
Port an Obain
Sheep Fold
Sguid nam bean truagh
Rudha Geodha
< Homeward >
Outward >
Lorg-na-glas leabruin
Dun Leithfin
Standing stone
Balnahard Farm
Sgibinis
< 2nd grid >
Larach Tigh Oglaich

N.B. Walking home along the east coast is a bit taxing. Route suggested here takes about one hour and crosses one fence.

1st grid >
St Columba's Well
Stots Well
Carnan
Beallach na Ard
Cnoc na Faire
Port Araraibhne
Carn nan Eun
Caves >
Beinn Beag
a' Bhaxtair
< Outward >
Sheiling >
Port ceann a' gharraidh

McLeans Birling
Dunan nan nighean
Dun Dubh
Viking Boat Burial
< Start

Blar na Baintighearna

Ho
's Well
Corr Dhunan

BALNAHARD
See page 100

Beinn nam Fitheach

Eilean Olomsa

xi

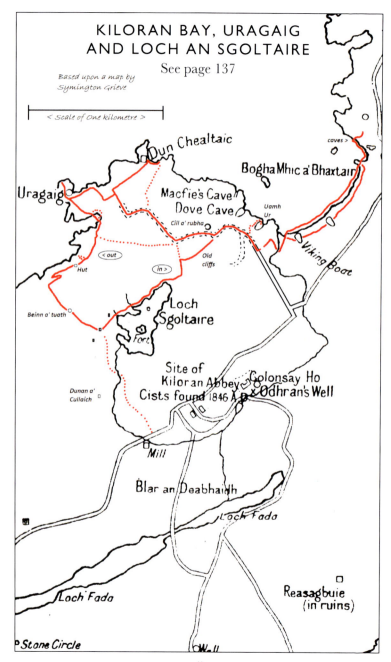

KILORAN BAY, URAGAIG AND LOCH AN SGOLTAIRE

See page 137

Based upon a map by Symington Grieve

< Scale of One kilometre >

Dun Chealtaic

caves >

Bogha Mhic a' Bhaxtair

Uragaig

Macfie's Cave
Dove Cave

Uamh Ur

Cill a' rubha

< out

in >

Old cliffs

Viking Boat

Hut

Beinn a' tuath

Loch Sgoltaire

Fort

Site of
Kiloran Abbey
Cists found 1846 A.D.

Colonsay Ho
Odhran's Well

Dunan a' Cullaich

Mill

Blar an Deabhaidh

Loch Fada

Loch Fada

Reasagbuie
(in ruins)

Stone Circle

W. II

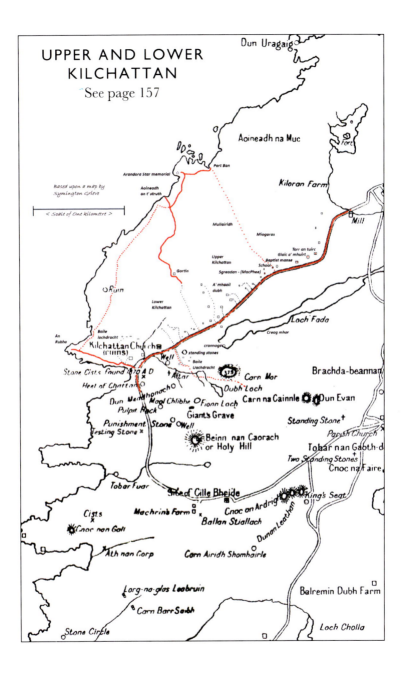

UPPER AND LOWER KILCHATTAN

See page 157

Based upon a map by Symington Grieve

< Scale of One kilometre >

Dun Uragaig

Aoineadh na Muc

Fort

Port Ban

Arandora Star memorial

Aoineadh on t' struth

Kiloran Farm

Mill

Mullairidh

Miogaras

Upper Kilchattan

Torr an tuirc

Glaic a' mhuirt

Baptist manse

School

Sgreadan - (MacPhee)

Gortin

A' mhaoil dubh

Lower Kilchattan

Loch Fada

An Rubha

Baile Iochdracht

Creag mhor

Ruin

Kilchattan Church (ruins)

cranmogs

Well

standing stones

Baile Uachdracht

Stone Cists found 1870 A D

Altar

379

Carn Mor

Brachda-beannan

Heel of Chattan

Dubh Loch

Dun Meinmhonacho

Maol Chlibhe Fionn Loch

Carn na Cainnle Dun Evan

Pulpit Rock

Giant's Grave

Standing Stone

Punishment Stone Well

Parish Church

Testing Stone

Beinn nan Caorach or Holy Hill

Tobar nan Gaoth-d

Two Standing Stones

Cnoc na Faire

Tobar Fuar

Site of Cille Bheide

King's Seat

Machrins Farm

Cnoc on Ardrig

Cists

Cnoc nan Gall

Ballan Stiallach

Dunan Leathan

Ath nan Corp

Carn Airidh Shomhairle

Lorg-na-glas Leabruin

Balremin Dubh Farm

Carn Barr Sebh

Stone Circle

Loch Cholla

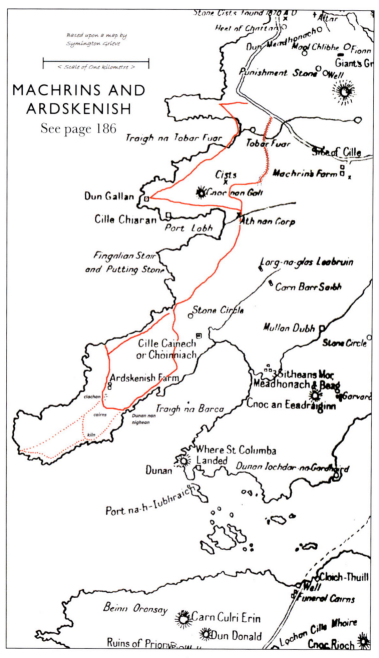

MACHRINS AND
ARDSKENISH

See page 186

Based upon a map by
Symington Grieve

< Scale of One kilometre >

Stone Cists found 1870 A D
Heel of Charran
Altar
Dun Meird
Maol Chlibhe
O Fionn
Giant's Gr
Punishment Stone
Well
Traigh na Tobar Fuar
Tobar Fuar
Side of Cille
Cists
Machrins Farm
Dun Gallan
Cnoc nan Gall
Cille Chiaran
Port Lobh
Ath nan Corp
Fingalian Stair
and Putting Stone
Lorg-na-glas Leabruin
Carn Barr Saibh
Stone Circle
Mullan Dubh
Cille Cainech
or Choinniach
Stone Circle
Ardskenish Farm
Sitheans Mor
Meadhonach & Beag
clachan
Garvard
cairns
Dunan nan
nighean
Cnoc an Eeadraiginn
Traigh na Barca
kiln
Where St Columba
Landed
Dunan
Dunan Iochdar na Gardherd
Port na-h-Iubhraich
Cloich-Thuill
Well
Funeral Cairns
Beinn Oronsay
Carn Culri Erin
Dun Donald
Lochan Cille Mhoire
Ruins of Priory
Cnoc Rioch

xiv

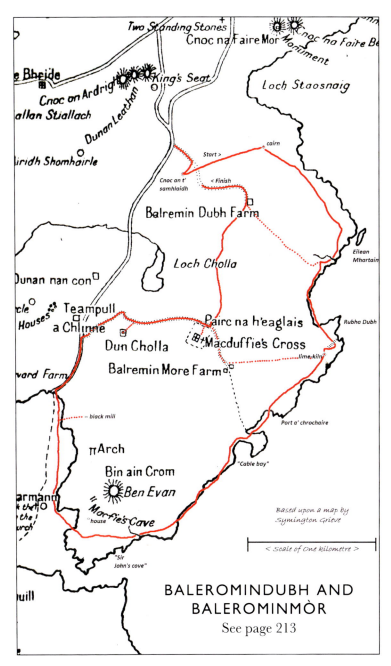

Two Standing Stones

Cnoc na Faire Mor

Cnoc na Faire Be

Monument

Loch Staosnaig

e Bheide

Cnoc on Ardrig

King's Seat

allan Stiallach

Dunan Leachan

iridh Shomhairle

Start >

cairn

Cnoc an t' samhlaidh

< Finish

Balremin Dubh Farm

Eilean Mhartain

Loch Cholla

Dunan nan con

Teampull a Chlinne

Houses

cle

Pairc na h'eaglais

Rubha Dubh

Dun Cholla

Macduffie's Cross

lime kiln

Balremin More Farm

vard Farm

Port a' chrochaire

black mill

πArch

"Cable bay"

Bin ain Crom

Ben Evan

armann

k the

the

urch

"Morfie's Cave

house

"Sir John's cove"

uill

BALEROMINDUBH AND BALEROMINMÒR

See page 213

Based upon a map by Symington Grieve

< Scale of One kilometre >

GARVARD & TEAMPULL A' GHLINNE See page 235

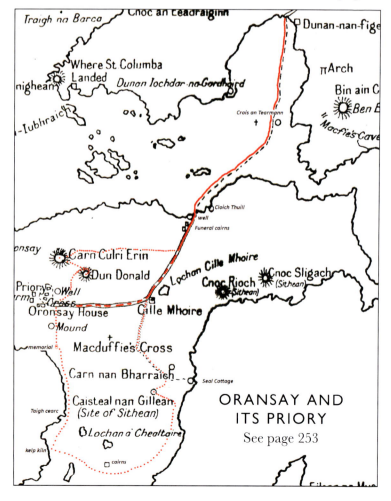

ORANSAY AND
ITS PRIORY

See page 253

INTRODUCTION

"Lonely Colonsay"

This epithet was coined by Sir Walter Scott and adopted by Professor Mackinnon, the first Chair of Celtic Studies at Edinburgh University, who from 1883 used the words to symbolise his beloved island home. Donald Mackinnon was a crofter's son who had succeeded in his career through his own merits and application, bringing great credit to his community. He was born in 1839 into a substantial population of almost one thousand souls, at a time when the islanders were already in a stricken condition and, unknowingly, on the point of a yet-more calamitous decline.

It seems strange that Colonsay should have fallen into such a condition, because its very landscape carries clear signs of successful occupation from the earliest times. Although the true antiquity of the most ancient monuments was perhaps unclear, place names indicate that the local population was aware of the importance of the great Mesolithic midden sites, which even by the 1880s were a subject of archaeological study. The story of a rich and varied past lies in every ridge and hollow of the island's landscape, and was one with which the inhabitants were intimately familiar.

For over a thousand years, Colonsay had controlled access to a vital seaway, the Sound of Islay. The island was the postern gate to the Dalriadic territories of the early *Scottii*, and a vital stepping-stone for St. Columba and other early missionaries. In due course it became an important Viking stronghold, and came to be held by the powerful Jarl Gilli, whose direct descendant, Somerled, was to achieve such prominence. Certainly it was no coincidence if it was from Colonsay that Somerled planned and launched his ambush against the King of Man. From this event, in 1156, one can trace the origins of Clan Donald and the Lordship of the Isles.

The Lords of the Isles held court in Colonsay, and even after the Forfeiture of 1493 the island retained its strategic importance. It played its part in the turmoil of the seventeenth century and, in July 1647, Colla "Ciotach" MacDonald of Colonsay was the last accredited Royalist commander to remain in the field. At the age of seventy seven, this famous hero accepted and held the King's commission long after Montrose had withdrawn to France, and even after Huntly had been routed from his positions. Even later, in January 1760, when Captain Thurot used Colonsay's lee to cover a surprise French raid into Islay, there are persuasive hints that he had a Colonsay pilot.

So throughout recorded history, Colonsay had had a significance which belied its size and it has been at the hub of vital seaways. Unfortunately, and no doubt inevitably, times had changed. After the '45 a fever of agricultural reform had swept the land as money rents became the measure of prosperity and success, and Colonsay was not exempt. As farms were re-organised and let to the highest bidder, the old systems of tacksmen and runrig were abolished.

The resultant pressures had forced some 20% of the population into exile in 1791, when they were shipped out direct from Colonsay to North Carolina aboard the "*General Washington*", in the bare clothes in which they stood. By 1806, although the emigration was by then consensual, a further 20% departed for Prince Edward Island aboard the "*Spencer*". The outward flow continued, but for forty years was countered by declining infant mortality and inward migration from neighbouring islands, further assisted by an additional food source, the potato.

These should have been years of reasonable prosperity, when the Peninsular and Napoleonic wars had created a demand for Colonsay's produce; John Loder, author of "*Colonsay and Oronsay in the Isles of Argyll*", admired "The Old Laird", John McNeill (1767–1846) and wrote: "… by his efforts, Colonsay was in a better state than any other island in the Hebrides to face the years of depression that lay ahead. Mercifully for him, he did not live to see the misery and distress that afflicted the Isles during the next half century".

We now know rather better – whatever prosperity there was did not extend to the local inhabitants, but was strictly preserved for the landlord and the mainland speculators who had taken on the leases of the remodelled farms. The following report appeared in "*The Times*":

House of Commons, Tuesday April 4 1837

"Mr Hume presented a petition from the Island of Colonsay, relating to the distress which prevails in the highlands and Islands of Scotland. The petitioners stated that the amount of distress had been becoming greater every year, and they prayed that the house would adopt such steps as would enable them to emigrate. Of the 84 persons who joined in the petition, 48 could only make their mark. That their education had been so neglected, he considered disgraceful to Scotland."

A fortnight later, the same newspaper highlighted the distress in a Leader. Elsewhere we read of glittering society balls being held in London, and of Mrs. McNeill graciously accepting small sums of money towards the relief of her peasantry.

So, when the future Professor Donald Mackinnon was born in 1839 the island was already in a parlous condition although, in the census of 1841, a population of 979 inhabitants is recorded; unhappily, such was their condition that they were ill-prepared for the desperate days of famine and disease that were to follow.

Some of these problems were common to the nation at large – famously, one thinks of the Famine Years in Ireland and one can also cite the death of over 30,000 in London alone in 1871, victims of Scarlet Fever. Yet, taken within its narrow confines, the catalogue of disasters which fell upon Colonsay in such bewildering succession came to assume almost Biblical proportions. The vital potato crop was affected by blight, there were epidemics of smallpox and scarlatina, even cholera; a nascent fishing industry was destroyed by the advent of steam trawlers and the disappearance of the herring, cottiers were flooded out in "the night of the big wind" – it just went on and on. Meanwhile, opportunity of a sort beckoned elsewhere – industrial expansion in the cities, the wars in South Africa, the development of Canada and Australia. The results were inevitable – the population was decimated time and again throughout the years of Professor Mackinnon's youth. By the turn of the century it fell to 313 inhabitants, and only one of the original crofting families had survived the upheavals.

Colonsay had always been isolated by definition, but now it began to seem as if it had been abandoned by the world. In 1904 the last of the McNeill lairds died and was succeeded by an immensely successful and vigorous incomer, "Labrador Smith", the first Baron Strathcona; in truth it made little difference. For over half a century, and during a critical period, Colonsay was little more than a holiday home for the proprietors and their friends, and it was then that the inhabitants began to think of themselves as "Lonely", the inhabitants of a beautiful but increasingly irrelevant place.

"Island at the Edge"

Perhaps the wheel has turned again. During the twentieth century, the population decline continued but it became more measured and eventually it bottomed-out. By the 1970s the population had stabilised at about one hundred and today it is much the same (usually between 115 and 130 since 2000).

There are hints of a spirit of optimism, as the community starts to rebuild itself. There are large, comfortable and reliable car-ferries, there is mains electricity and water. Mobile telephones, email and internet access means that communications are first class – the successful oyster-farm was a pioneering enterprise, a small publishing company was established in 1995 and other modern businesses have been created in recent years, including a highly-acclaimed micro-brewery. A licensed aerodrome has replaced the former airstrip, with scheduled services and special "scholars' flights" to permit the schoolchildren to come home for the week-ends. A small but vigorous team launched an annual Folk Festival *"Ceol Colasa"* in 2008, and the Colonsay and Oronsay Heritage Trust is gathering materials and funds in preparation for a permanent centre.

Following extensive audits of local potential, the community has taken on certain economic functions in its own right, through a Community Development Company – crucially, the supply of coal, gas, diesel and petrol. For some years, the Development Company partnered Colonsay Estate in a *Rhododendron ponticum* eradication project, and on another front the company has purchased some 80 hectares of land with a view to creating additional crofts for incoming residents. The realms of agriculture and fishing are boosted by honey production and the oyster-farm; Oransay has become a reserve for the Royal Society for the Protection of Birds, and large areas of farmland in Colonsay are carefully managed to enhance the flora and birdlife.

The 200 year-old, 18 hole golf course has been rejuvenated and offers unlimited play for £20 per year; the brown trout first introduced by the mediaeval monks for their table now tempt visiting fly-fishermen who pay but a modest fee. The famous gardens of Colonsay House are opened to the public, and there has been a frenzy of building to meet the demand for early retirement and second-homes.

In 1609, the provisions of the Statutes of Iona had led to an obligation to establish inns throughout the islands or "*ordanit certane oist-lairis to be set doun in the maist convenient placeis within every Ile*". Nowadays the ever-popular 250 year old hotel has central heating, double glazing and all bedrooms with *en suite* bathrooms; traditional cottages and purpose built self-catering accommodation offers a range of options up to four-star quality. There is a well-appointed back-packers' Lodge, and two or three houses offer guest house or B&B facilities.

The population is justly proud of its heritage. The Royal Commissioners for the Ancient and Historic Monuments of Scotland were persuaded to produce a special volume for Colonsay and Oronsay, "*Extracts*" from Volume V of their magisterial work, and this means that everyone is well-informed and can act as a custodian. Some individuals offer guided walks and talks, covering flora, birdlife, placenames, archaeological and historic sites. The island has a thriving website www.colonsay.org.uk which includes a fort-nightly newspaper, "*The Corncrake*". Over 1,500 people read each issue, and many of them are engaged in family research… the website offers assistance to more than 1,000,000 individuals who can claim a Colonsay connection.

So, although Colonsay maintains its "Lonely" status, it is an island whose population nowadays has a very real understanding of its unique qualities and attractions. In providing a genuine welcome and high-quality facilities to visitors, islanders hope that they are laying the foundations for a thriving community in the generations to come. On the other hand, of course, the resident community has teetered "at the edge" for many years and its average age is now increasing rapidly – the situation continues to be a cliff-hanger.

Acknowledgements

This book is for Christa, who loves the island and knows every inch of the suggested routes – with grateful thanks for patience, encouragement and picnics… and the loan of Coco, our faithful hound.

I am also most grateful to the many people who have given me information over the years, and also to those who have kindly given me specific help and guidance for this publication. Particular thanks are due to Christa Byrne, John and Diane Clark, John and Pamela Clarke, Dr. Richard Gulliver, David Hobhouse, Georgina Hobhouse, Hon. Alex Howard, Duncan "Sandy" McAllister, Melanie McKellar, Donald "Gibbie" MacNeill, Donald "Pedie"

MacNeill, Flora MacNeill, Eleanor McNeill, Jessie McNeill, Seamus McNeill, Fran Patrick, Mike and Val Peacock, Alastair Scouller, Angela Skrimshire, Netta Titterton and Walter Williams.

Of course, none of the above are in any way responsible for the errors that persist, which are entirely mine.

Kevin Byrne

NOTE ON LOCAL PLACENAMES

"Colonsay" is the English version of "Colbhasa", and "Oransay" is the equivalent version of "Orasa"; in both cases the "-ay" suffix means "Isle of – " and therefore the purist might claim that such phrases as "Isle of Colonsay" are tautological. For practical purposes, the tautology is acceptable and has been widely adopted, since it means that in indices and other listings islands can be grouped together. Thus entries for "Isle of" Gigha, Iona, Islay, Jura, Scarba, Texa etc. will appear in proximity to "Isle of" Colonsay and Oronsay, rather than be scattered at random amongst mainland place-names.

Although the correct English spelling of "Orasa" is clearly "Oransay", an official spelling of "Oronsay" has been adopted by the Ordnance Survey and is now in the ascendant; nonetheless the alternative spelling of "Oransay" remains valid locally and is used randomly in this book.

For many years, it was accepted that the two islands were named in honour of St. Columba and St. Oran but the origins of the names as we now know them have been clarified. In modern Sweden, at Lake Vänern, one can visit the island of Kallåndsö (pronounced like "Colbhasa"), which was the site of the last battle ever fought in Scandinavia by Magnus Barelegs. "Kallåndsö" means "Island of Kallånd", "Kallånd" being the name of an adjoining hilly territory to which it belonged (therefore "Island of the Hilly District").

Kallåndsö has a smaller pendicle, Orensö (pronounced like "Orasa"), which in times of flooding becomes an island in its own right. "Orensö" means "Tidal Island" and is a very common name in both Scotland and Scandinavia. Several miles out into Lake Vänern is a large and uninhabited island, Djurö. "Djurö" means "Wild Animal Island" – the inhabitants of the area are very specific that although deer are included in the concept of wild animals, the name cannot be translated merely as "Deer Island".

So, whilst it is not hard to see how Colonsay, Oransay and Jura got their modern names, one might well wonder if Colonsay had an earlier and similar name. It is recorded in Adomnàn's *Life of St. Columba* that the sacred islands of "Hinba" and "Hinbina" lay on

the direct sea route from Iona to Ireland, that they were distinguished by a bag-shaped bay of the sea, and that they had a
particular significance to St. Columba himself. This matter has been
thoroughly researched, most recently in *Adomnàn of Iona: Life of St.
Columba*, by Richard Sharpe, and in *Jura, Island of Deer* by Peter
Youngson.

Perhaps Oransay and its islets may reasonably be identified with
Hinbina ("Inlet Isles"), and therefore, through its association with
the saint, Adomnàn's "Hinba" itself could perhaps have come to be
known by some variant of his name, meaning "St. Columba's Isle",
but sounding very like "Kallåndsö". An alternative and more likely
derivation, but with the same effect, might be from an old Gaelic
word "coll" giving "hazelwood island".

From his own writing, we know that Jura was called "Sainea
insula" by Adomnàn, which Donald McEachern (cited by
Youngson) suggests will have derived from the "Saponis" of the
Roman navigators, but this will have mattered little to the Vikings.
Men such as Magnus Barelegs will not have hesitated to use names
with which they were familiar and which seemed apt – if one of the
islands sounded like Kallåndsö, the others had effectively named
themselves. Thus "Sainea" just had to become Djurö and Hinbina
became Orensö, particularly when those names were so appropriate.

On a more parochial level, many local place-names in Colonsay
have varying spelling and pronunciation. Such diversity is attractive
and the present author has not attempted to impose a rigid orthog-
raphy, although he has tried to ensure that locations can be easily
associated with place-names used by the Ordnance Survey.

Farm acreages, transcribed from
Colonsay Estate Map, Wilson 1804

	Arable & Meadow A.R.P.	Pasture A.R.P	Totals A.R.P.
Balinahard	117.0.32	833.3.08	950.0.00
Keiloran	330.3.05	1132.3.16	1463.2.21
Dungallion	13.30.00	131.1.00	145.0.00
Risbuie	0.0.00	63.0.00	63.0.00
Glassert	12.1.30	154.2.10	167.0.00
Clunery	24.3.02	104.0.09	128.3.11
Kielhattans	155.1.11	612.0.00	767.1.11
Machrey more	230.3.22	540.3.38	771.0.00
Machrey beg	45.0.10	401.3.30	447.0.00
Scallasaig	66.3.25	582.3.38	649.3.23
Milbuie	21.0.16	40.2.00	61.2.16
Glebe	8.0.00	18.2.00	26.2.00
Merchant's croft	1.3.17	11.1.10	13.0.27
Baliramon dow	85.3.37	184.0.00	269.3.37
Baliramon more	43.2.05	488.2.01	532.0.06
Garvard	78.2.00	477.0.00	555.2.00
Ardskinish	70.3.30	429.0.00	500.0.00
Oransay	433.2.36	705.1.04	1139.0.0
Total Contents of Land	1740.2.38	6910.2.34	8650.1.32
Long Loch			124.0.00
Black Loch in Kiloran			27.0.00
Part of Strand fit for Growing kelp			131.2.08
			8933.0.06

Scots' Statute Measure *per* David Wilson

Notes:
1 The above figures are in Scots acres, and various boundary changes have occurred in the last two centuries; nonetheless these figures provide a useful framework for a study of this nature.

2   There are 40 Perches to the Rood and 4 roods to the acre.

3   1 Scots Acre = 1.3 Statute or English Acres, or 5000 square metres (0.5 hectares).

4   Thus one rood (Scots) = 125 square metres

5   Figures have not been altered (despite slight error at Machrey more); missing perch zeros have been inserted.

6   "Black Loch" refers to Loch an Sgoltaire; "Long Loch" is Loch Fada.

7   "Glebe" refers to the field and grazing opposite "The Quarry". The field is now part of Scalasaig farm and the grazing is part of Machrins.

8   "Merchant's Croft" was to the east of the Parish Church, and existed until the hotel was sold to K & C Byrne in 1978 but it was subsequently engrossed in Scalasaig farm.

Chapter 1

THE PREHISTORY OF COLONSAY

Even as one approaches Colonsay, particularly from the south, it is clear that it is well-favoured and fertile; there are certainly some extensive areas of heather and substantial rocky outcrops, but the island is far from barren. On closer inspection, one is immediately struck by the wide variety of landscapes and habitat, by the impressive machair areas of Oransay, Machrins, Kiloran and Balnahard, by the woodlands and by the sheltered pockets of tillage in every valley.

This compares strangely with the almost lunar landscape of Jura, the nearest neighbour to the east, or with the apparently endless rolling heaths of Islay, which are all that are visible from Colonsay or its approaches. Looking to the north, one can see the forbidding face of Mull, dominated by lofty peaks which jostle with Ben More itself. From a vantage point in Colonsay, one can see vast tracts of land in neighbouring islands, almost all of which are virtual desert, and one cannot help but wonder at the contrast.

The explanation is, quite simply, geological. Colonsay has little in common with Mull, Jura or eastern Islay, but everything in common with Islay's significant western wing, the Rhinns ("The Points" *i.e.* double promontory). Geologists tell us that the Great Glen faultline, bisecting Scotland from Inverness via Loch Ness, comes sweeping out into the Firth of Lorn but it divides northeast of Colonsay. The main arm runs off towards Donegal, passing between Colonsay and the Ross of Mull, and the other runs between Colonsay and Jura and then to the east of the Rhinns of Islay, along the lengths of Loch Gruinart and Loch Indaal. Thus Colonsay and the Rhinns of Islay are geologically very similar, and indeed some 60 miles away they have a tiny sibling, Inishtrahull ("Three-peaks Isle"), just a few miles off the fertile and desirable peninsula of Inishowen.

As soon as one has recognised that Colonsay is truly "isolated" from Mull and Jura, the rest of the topography falls into place. Glacial action has eroded the landscape from east to west, as is readily apparent to the eye. As the weight of the ice was removed, the inherent instability of the island permitted it to start to tilt, so that little by little the western side has risen almost 200 feet whilst the east side has acted as a hinge. In addition, but over a timescale of millions of years, there has been a further movement whereby the older sedimentary rocks are exposed in Oronsay and towards the south-west of Colonsay.

To see this at its best, go to the cattle grid 200 metres south of Port Mòr and look towards the north. On your right, there are impressive ancient sea cliffs and at the head of Port Mòr there are two distinct bands of shingle clearly visible in the field. These are raised beaches, one at about 15 metres and the other about 25 metres above modern datum. As you look a little higher, you will notice that the line of the fields of Drumclach ("Stony Ridge") runs out towards the west in a series of plateaux, all of which betray an ancient marine platform, some 45 metres above modern sea level. To the northwest, the impressive cliffs of Druim nam Faoileann ("Seagull Ridge") and Binnein Riabhach ("Brindled Peak") show the full extent of the post-glacial resurgence. This extraordinary sight is very rare within such a narrow compass, but it reflects faithfully the much greater picture whereby the English Channel and the North Sea were created.

Although the geology of Colonsay was dismissed as "extremely uninteresting" by Macculloch, ("*A Description of the Western Isles of Scotland*" 1819), other writers have been more measured. In July 1772, Pennant visited Colonsay and reported that: "I met with no very remarkable fossils. Black talc, the *mica Lamallata martia is nigra* of *Cronsted*, sect. 95, is found here, both in large detached flakes, and immersed in indurated clay. Also rock stone of glimmer and quartz. An imperfect granite is not unfrequent".

His account is both succinct and accurate. There are no fossils because the island is composed of very ancient but inert sedimentary deposits of silt and sand. These accumulated to a great depth and came under enormous pressure, before becoming folded and distorted and eventually thrust back to the surface to be exposed to millennia of erosion by ice, sea and weather.

The mica to which he refers occurs in an atypical monchiquite dyke at Lower Kilchattan, created about 270 million years ago. "The most striking peculiarity of the rock is the presence of large black phenocrysts of biotite, augite and hornblende, which make it a typical "lamprophyre"." (Geological Survey, 1911). This rock, which is mildly radioactive, is a great natural curiosity and attracted many visitors to the island in a more cerebral age.

Glimmer is an archaic term for "mica, glist, Muscovy glass" and suggests that the writer had noted its widespread presence in association with host rocks; very possibly he was thinking of the outcrop at the northern end of Kiloran Bay, where it is accompanied by quartz. The "imperfect" granite he mentions is mainly at Scalasaig, where it forms the largest igneous intrusion in the island, and which was subsequently described by Professor Geikie (1882) as a "coarsely crystalline rock of a very hard, tough, and durable character. It forms a handsomely-marked rock – the pale and dark-coloured minerals being in about equal proportions. For structures requiring great strength hardly a better stone could be desired, as its crushing power must be very considerable." This rock is a diorite (green stone), clearly to be seen on both sides of the road running from the pier to the hotel, and has been used in the construction of the retaining wall at the parish church.

The student of geology will have no difficulty in obtaining the numerous scientific papers which have been published in connection with Colonsay in recent years; for the convenience of others, some references are included in the bibliography. Most visitors to the island will be more concerned with the features which are readily apparent to the lay person, and in their implications for landscape and habitats.

The significant sedimentary deposits of which the island consists, perhaps to an original depth of some 1500 metres, are obviously resting upon some deeper surface, and in the case of Colonsay this base consists of Lewisian gneiss (*pron.* "nice"), one of the oldest rocks in the world. It gets its name from Lewis in the Outer Hebrides, and although Lewisian gneiss is uncommon in the Inner Hebrides it is not surprising that it also exists in the Rhinns of Islay, Colonsay's near relation. The locally important exposure of Lewisian gneiss is to be found at Balnahard, just beyond the northeastern edge of the sandy bay. Whilst in that vicinity, one should note the remarkable conglomerate deposit at Leac Buidhe, which adjoins the gneiss, in which coarse gravel and water-smoothed stones may be seen embedded in the living rock.

The sediments which now compose the island were, of course, originally deposited in even layers; but earth movements have folded these layers, and differential rates of erosion have further confused the picture. Even the gneiss does not appear as the lowest of a neat succession of later rocks, very possibly because it is at the centre of an anticline. The sedimentary rocks are all described as metamorphic ("changed"), which is to say that they have been subjected to processes that have altered their characteristics. These rocks have usually been dated as Torridonian (i.e. comparable with the geology of the Loch Torridon area), but it is perhaps sufficient to note that they are many millions of years old. Recent radiometric dating has suggested an origin in the Proterozoic age, when life first appeared on earth (1.8 thousand million years ago).

Any geological map will show the basic disposition of the sedimentary rocks of which the island is composed. At a much later date, igneous activity led to superheated material being forced to the surface. In some places it emerged through cracks and fissures and has created the very obvious (and attractive) dykes which are encountered widely. Elsewhere more significant outcrops of igneous or "Plutonic" material may be found, such as the diorite already mentioned at Scalasaig. Reference to such a map will show kentallanite at Balnahard, also syenite at the north end of Kiloran Bay.

The distribution of Colonsay's metamorphic sedimentary rocks is outlined clearly on geological maps and the succession can be traced readily over the ground by a determined walker. From Ardskenish farmhouse, one should follow a compass course to the north-east, crossing the northernmost tip of Traigh nam Barc and in due course running just to the north of Abhainn a' Ghlinne. Having crossed the road and the flank of Cnoc an t' Samlaidh, the line continues across Baleromindubh and down towards Loch Staosnaig. In that short span of 5 kilometres one will have crossed all the sedimentary exposures in ascending order, starting from the oldest.

Unfortunately, to the lay eye there is little direct correlation between the geological strata and the landscape that we see, beyond the basic profiles created by folding and tectonic distortion. Some of the best land and some of the worst will be found on exactly the same foundation, and it is clear that much later factors are at work. In truth, almost everything that affects the modern landscape is quite recent and, with the exception of the basic profile, Colonsay evolved within the last 10,000 years.

When the last glaciers receded, some 9,800 years ago, they left their mark upon the hills and valleys. The ice had travelled from east to west, and the tops of the hills and all their eastern flanks had been heavily scoured and eroded. As the ice melted, rocks and other material that had been carried within it were released in the melt, giving the entire landscape a basic covering from which soil would result, interspersed with rocks and boulders of varying sizes. Many of these rocks are obviously far from their native heath, and are identified as erratics – an example is the large piece of Loch Fyne granite just below the kissing-gate at Kiloran Bay. A few hundred metres to the east, where Abhainn a' Mhuilinn runs through the dunes, a very hard blue rock is exposed and bears unmistakable *striae*, the scratches left by ice-borne pebbles and rocks being dragged across an unyielding surface.

Since Colonsay and all its fault lines tends to run on an axis from southwest to northeast, many of the valleys were at right angles to the movement of the ice and the receding ice left more significant depths of moraine material in the lee of the hills. The valleys of Scalasaig and Balavetchy were scoured by the ice itself, and as the ice receded more slowly from these deeper thoroughfares so they gained a richer deposit of material. Although the landscape will have been raw, with precarious cliffs and teetering mounds of unsettled material, wind and weather will have taken little more than twenty years to create something less stark. Subsequently, climatic and geographical influences will have been profound.

The fertility of many areas is directly attributable to blown sands, as at Oronsay, Ardskenish, Machrins, Kiloran and Balnahard. Other areas have suffered through poor drainage – the area at the Black Gate (the junction between the main road and the spur leading towards Oronsay), the land at Miogaras, or in front of Gortin, or the central portion of Baleraomin ("Boggy Farm"). Peats and blanket bog indicate acid soils, and some of the land is shaded from the sun, whilst many of the hills remain scoured by the ice and devoid of any thickness of soil. Good soils have been created by freshwater alluvial deposits as at Phàirc Bhaile Mhaide, or marine deposits as at Drumclach and Homefield.

It was into this raw yet evolving landscape that Colonsay's earliest known inhabitants arrived some 8,700 years ago, almost on the heels of the receding ice. As far as is known, these Mesolithic ("Middle Stone-age") hunter-gatherers originally reached this country from the Scandinavian region, crossing on foot the area now occupied by the north sea. Sea levels were still changing, very possibly the English Channel did not yet exist, but here in Colonsay the sea level was somewhat higher than at present and created an extensive inter-tidal zone. The island was thus surrounded by valuable and easily-exploited colonies of shellfish and weed.

The Mesolithic occupation was evidently quite significant, and traces have been identified the full length of the island, from Balnahard to Oronsay. Our recent forefathers noticed the microliths (very small flint blades) that they had used and ascribed them to fairies; they tended to be found in the sheltered areas used for milking, and so were assumed to be the tips of tiny arrows used by malignant forces to work harm against the cows. The great midden mounds were called *sithean* (fairy knolls), and were their assumed dwelling places (*cf. bansith* "female fairy").

In 1881, an antiquarian named Symington Grieve excavated one of the larger middens, Caisteal nan Gillean in Oransay, and published his findings. He established that such mounds consisted of occupation waste and he collected a wide range of stone implements of varying sophistication; he noted the absence of pottery but wrongly concluded that the remains were Neolithic ("New Stone-age"). Symington Grieve was to retain a lifelong interest in Colonsay and his published work includes many details and references which are of great interest; curiously enough, his discoveries even included the skeleton of a Great Auk.

In 1913 the site was re-examined by Glasgow archaeologists and re-dated to the Mesolithic period, although with an over-generous age of up to 30,000 years. In the 1970s, Paul Mellars devoted six full seasons to a comprehensive study of the Oronsay remains and established that the sites had been used for seasonal occupation by small groups who had been exploiting the marine resources of the area. The total period of occupation had exceeded six hundred years, the sea level had been some seven metres higher than at present, and the inhabitants had enjoyed a rather finer climate than in modern times. Dr. Mellars and his collaborators used a wide variety of dating techniques and concluded that the occupation of those sites began about 6,000 years ago.

In the late 1980s, Steven Mithen launched the Inner Hebridean Mesolithic Study, and in the course of his work discovered extraordinary Mesolithic remains beside Loch Staosnaig, about 1 km south of Scalasaig. The complexity of the site, exceptionally difficult working conditions and the huge quantity of lithic finds all made for a daunting task, but every detail was recorded and every tiny piece of flint was examined and catalogued. For example, 6,707 finds in 1991 were divided into more than thirty categories, whilst the season of 1994 produced 61,217 further examples.

As time went by, the researchers identified and excavated a circular pit, 4.5m in diameter and a couple of feet deep; they also discovered stone settings and fireplaces. They found a "guitar-shaped" assemblage of stones which could have been an oven and flue, operating not by the direct application of fire but through the use of pre-heated stones; which, of course, would permit the more precise regulation of the cooking temperature.

No less than 113 "coarse stone" items were discovered, including 78 of the "limpet hammers" so often recorded in the past, now cata-logued as "elongated pebble tools". Other stone implements are described as anvils, hammerstones and pounders.

The research also uncovered a very large number of hazelnut shells, and established that this was an important resource. It seems that this one small site may have processed anything up to 300,000 cob-nuts, and there is evidence that crab-apples were also being dried and preserved. In addition, the tubers of lesser celandine were found in abundance, suggesting nutritional exploitation. Although this particular site may not have had lengthy use, it has added greatly to scientific knowledge. It has helped to support the current belief that plants may have contributed up to 40% of the protein content in the Mesolithic diet.

The Staosnaig occupation was dated to some 8,700 years ago, and that of Oronsay seems to have ended by about 5,000 years ago. Throughout that period, the climate was rather warmer than at present and the perceived temperature will have been further enhanced by much lower windspeeds. As the climate began to dete-riorate, it is found that traces of occupation dwindle and this absence of human activity has been confirmed by analysis of peat samples. In some places the peat is up to ten metres deep, and it is possible to extract cores that provide a timeline into the distant past. Analysis of pollen and other material – notably carbon – reveal much about the climate at any given time. Rainfall and temperature are reflected in the plant cover, and the mixture of vegetation and the effects of fire reflect human intervention. From all the evidence, the Mesolithic activity was followed by a lengthy period of dormancy during which Colonsay was uninhabited. By the time that human beings returned, the Neolithic period was almost at an end and it was the dawning of the Bronze Age (c.2500–600 BC).

By now, people were equipped with powerful stone axes, they had begun to practice agriculture, and their ability to make and use pottery revolutionised their cooking and storage practices. In one important site on Colonsay, Uaimh Ùr ("New Cave"), a pottery vessel was said to be still standing on a rock shelf when the site was first discovered. Barely a mile away, at Uaimh Shiorruidh ("Endless Cave") there are numerous cup-marks, examples of the distinctive art-work of the Bronze Age. The island is peppered with standing stones of this period, also cist ("chest") graves, burial cairns, cremations and other memorials. Because of its history and location, Colonsay has been spared from the excesses of intensive and sustained agricultural exploitation, and in consequence houses and field systems of the Bronze Age survive here in a remarkable state of preservation.

In future chapters, significant sites which have been mentioned in this introductory chapter will be mentioned again in their appropriate landscape context.

Chapter 2

HISTORIC TIMES – AT A CANTER

In the Introduction to this book, brief reference was made to Colonsay's position on a vital trading route, and the significance of this becomes apparent over time. During the Neolithic and Bronze Ages, Colonsay's location gave it convenient access to passing traders, as is evidenced by the fact that cultural developments kept pace with communities elsewhere. Such links continued during the Iron Age – a decorative bead from the Mediterranean region was found in Oransay, and there are innumerable examples of such linear contact elsewhere. An interesting DNA project http://clan-maclochlainn.com/leinster.htm has discovered patrilineal connections centred upon Leinster in south-east Ireland but extending from Spain into south-west Scotland, so it is worthwhile to stress the importance of this trade route.

One can imagine the trade routes which criss-crossed the Mediterranean, and continued around or across the Iberian peninsula. A seaborne trader would have little incentive to continue along the length of the English Channel, because that part of Europe was well-served by the great river routes of the Rhone, the Rhine, the Danube etc. Instead, he could enter the Irish Sea, trading with ancient inhabitants of modern Cornwall, Wales and Ireland for gold, silver, lead and tin; the sea-route would lead across or around the Mull of Kintyre and up the Sound of Islay. There would be good reason to avoid the aptly-named Cape Wrath and the Pentland Firth – instead, goods would be traded along the length of the Great Glen and thence across the North Seas into Scandinavia. Bearing this in mind, one can see that the North Channel (between Ireland and Scotland) developed an increasing significance, and that whoever controlled the Sound of Islay would have immense power. The only alternative routes involved an exposed open-sea passage around Cape Wrath, or else negotiation of the hazardous waters of the Sound of Jura, passing between Corrievreckan whirlpool and Dorus Mòr and onwards through the narrows at Belnahua.

Crucially, Colonsay was so sited as to exercise control over the Sound of Islay; in due course, this was to make it particularly attractive to the early Scots, to the Christian missionaries, to the Vikings and to the Lords of the Isles.

The advent of the Iron Age led rapidly to a more organised society, with an increase in trade and greater exposure to cultural developments. Better tools and weapons led inevitably to greater ambitions, hence the need for defensive structures – impressive fortresses of this period still dominate the Colonsay landscape. Dùn Cholla ("Colla's Fortress") has a commanding view of An Faoghail, the strand between Colonsay and Oransay, and is in line of site with Dùn Domhnaill on Oransay itself. Dùn Eibhinn is about 300 metres to the northwest of Scalasaig farmhouse, and Dùn Gallain is the mighty promontory fort at Machrins. These, and others which will be encountered, are often associated with good farming land and inevitably population centres will have grown up around them, but the locations are primarily strategic.

Pre-existing natural features of the landscape were modified to create these strongholds, and each fort has a good view of likely routes of attack. More significantly, it will be noticed that each fort is in plain sight of one or two others, greatly increasing their communal strength. Any attackers must necessarily have arrived by sea, and must become divided on arrival – if one party formed an expeditionary force, the other had to remain with the boats. As soon as any fort came under attack, the alarm would be passed to all the others, whereupon relief parties would be raised, presumably to prevent the raiders from regaining the sanctuary of their boats and so to annihilate them.

Of course, the system would not be proof against well-organised or coherent attack by a determined aggressor, but it would have been sufficient to deter casual raids. Unprotected crops and livestock were highly vulnerable, as were isolated individuals and their homes, but the raiders would very likely be identifiable and in due course reprisals could be arranged.

This Iron Age period (c. 600 BC – c. AD 400) was an heroic one, and the origins of some of our ancient stories can be traced to that period – the tales of the Fianna, of Ossian and Cuchulain. J.F. Campbell collected many such stories in the nineteenth century, one of which was entitled "*Murachadh MacBhroin*" (still readily available in print). He recorded that "this tale was taken down in May

1859, from the recitation of Donald Shaw… who was in the 42nd Highlanders at Waterloo. He said that he had learned it from one Duncan MacMillan, a Colonsay man, well advanced in years, about fifty years ago." (Possibly this was the Duncan MacMillan, married to Bell Currie, whose son Donald was christened February 2 1802).

The Iron Age tribes of Britain and Ireland were in close contact with one another, as is known from archaeological evidence as well as through the history of the Arthurian and Roman cultures. In the opening years of the Christian era, population pressures in Ireland led adventurous individuals to cross the narrow North Channel into Kintyre and the Southern Hebrides, where they began to settle; thus they gained control of the direct trading route linking Scandinavia with the Mediterranean. Their origins lay along the northern coast of Ireland, in an area known as Dál Riada ("The Route"), so called because it linked two prosperous areas in northern Antrim which were otherwise separated by difficult terrain. In the fullness of time, they became firmly established in their new territory, which came to be called Dalriada in its turn.

The area grew until its heartland could be broadly represented as encompassing modern Argyll, (Earraghàidheal, "the eastland of the Gaels"), the tribesmen themselves being known as "Scottii". Eventually, this tribe became pre-eminent and gave its name to the entire country, Scotland. In the early days these people were based at Dunadd, in Kintyre, but their area of influence was wide and included Colonsay on their northern border.

The annalists record that it was one Cairbre "Riata" who first established our Scottish Dalriada, and he had a remarkable pedigree – the son of Cormac, the brother-in-law of Fionn Mac Chumail, and the great-grandson of Conn of the Thousand Battles (d. c.173 AD). Cairbre had three sons, all of whom were called Colla, and all of whom lived for a time in Dalriada; the most influential of them all was Colla Uais ("Noble Colla") and by local tradition he had a special affection for Colonsay. Dùn Cholla is said by some to commemorate the name of Colla Uais, and to have been a stronghold of his powerful descendants.

Perhaps a century or so after the time of Colla Uais, c. 475 AD, three brothers again came to prominence in Dalriada – these were Lorn, Fergus and Angus, sons of King Erc of Dàl Riada in Ireland. They ("who had the blessing of St. Patrick") divided the territory between them, and from this time Colonsay is said to have belonged to Lorn, who held the northern portion and after whom the Firth of Lorn is named. Carn Fherguis ("Fergus' Cairn") is close to Dùn Cholla and may be a reminder of the brothers and of the death of Fergus (AD 501).

Traditional sources say that the sons of Erc had about 150 supporters, and it is believed that they organised the earlier-settled Scots into a family or clan system. The origins of Colonsay's ancient clan MacPhee may perhaps be traced to this later period, as an ongoing DNA project has already apparently confirmed its "Celtic" roots. All other local families can be traced back to the Scottii ("bandits"), usually to a branch of the mighty Uì Neill.

By now, Ireland was Christian as a result of Roman influence (Patrick = "patricius", patrician); the Irish missionaries followed hard on the heels of the sons of Erc, and began the conversion of the neighbouring Picts. Colonsay is associated with Saints Bridget, Mael Rubha, Kenneth, Oran, Catan, and Ciaran, but most famously with St. Columba himself. The traditions about them will be mentioned elsewhere *(see Chapter 12 for St. Columba)* but it worth noting that Colonsay was on the direct sea route from Ireland, and provided a convenient haven on the very borders of Pictland. There is every reason to believe that Colonsay and Oronsay were the "Hinba" and "Hinbina" recorded by Adomnàn in his "*Life of St. Columba*".

St. Columba probably arrived in Colonsay in AD 563, and within a year or two he had established his forward position in Iona. Interestingly, he very quickly made his way along the great sea-route to the other end of the Great Glen, so as to establish a working relationship with the Pictish ruler and so secure the valuable trading link. Even after his death in AD 597 the missionary work went on and, despite reverses, it was not until the first Viking raids of AD 794 that there would be any serious interruption. The insubstantial mud and wattle buildings of those early Christians have left little trace upon the ground, but the circular graveyard of Cill a' Rubha is delineated by bluebells in the springtime and the outlines of an early Celtic field system can be seen from the air at Garvard. Undoubtedly, our greatest treasure of the period is the incomparable Dealbh na Leisg, normally translated as the "Image of Sloth" although perhaps "indolence" or "indulgence" would be more meaningful. This is a "face cross" of c. AD 700 carved in local stone, and it was originally sited at the ancient graveyard of Riasg Buidh (nowadays it is at Colonsay House). One side of the work depicts a robed monkish figure, with a Celtic tonsure; the sleeves are whorled and the garment falls into the symbolic Christian fish-shape. By contrast, the obverse shows more than a hint of the *membrum virile*, perhaps an echo of ancient potency.

The early Christian era is well represented in local placenames (eight chapel dedications, four holy wells, many names such as Glaic na Aifrionn, "Mass Hollow" etc.), but there are many Viking names as well. The very word which gave them their name ("vig" or "aig", meaning "inlet" or "creek") is found in Scalasaig, Staoisnaig and Uragaig. Their ships are remembered in Port na Luinge Locharnaich and Sgibinis, and their way of life almost everywhere – Creag Eibhinne, Grunnd an Dùin, Holmfeld, Turnigil *etc*. The island is also rich in physical evidence of their presence, and contains more Viking graves than any comparable location, including the magnificent ship burial that was excavated at Kiloran.

Machrins was a major occupation site and the whole of the golf course area is of interest – the third tee is on a Viking site, Dùnan Gach Gaoithe ("Windy Homestead"), and the sixth is close to a Viking grave beside the ancient chapel of Cille Chiarain. On excavation, it was found that the deceased had been buried with his faithful friend, an aged dog riddled with arthritis but very like a modern Corgi. Some such sites are hard to spot, but nobody can miss such mighty forts as Dùn Ghallain ("Fort of the Stranger") or Dùn Eibhinn ("Eyvind's Fort" or more probably "Great Hall"). The latter, at Scalasaig, was originally an Iron Age fort which became a major Norse administrative centre and eventually the home of Earl Gilli, brother-in-law of Sigurd, Jarl of Orkney (*floruit* 990 AD).

Notice that by now Colonsay exercised comprehensive surveillance of all of the surrounding sea. Dùn Domhnuill in Oransay was an excellent viewpoint, and in sight of Dùn Ghallain; the west coast had a minor post at Meall Lamalum, no doubt supervised from Dùn Uragaig – which was itself in sight of the magnificently-located Dùn Meadhonach at Balnahard. The east coast had a chain of three watching-posts, each called Cnoc na Faire and each beside a sheltered natural harbour. With Dùn Cholla to protect the Strand and the harbour of Port a' Chrocaire, the entire chain could be controlled from Dùn Eibhinn ("Great Hall"). In addition there were lookout posts at Dùn Mara and An Dùnan, a signal post at Beinn nan Gùdairean and a relay post at Cnoc an t' Samhlaidh.

By this period, Colonsay is mentioned increasingly in the written
records. There are many references in the Norse sagas, and also in
the Irish and Manx chronicles. Earl Gilli is identified by some
scholars with Gilladomnan, whose son Gillebrede was the father of
Somerled, Gaeldom's greatest leader. Although the exact genealogy
is hazy, there is no doubt that Somerled had significant Norse
ancestry, yet was also a direct descendant of Fergus, son of Erc, and
that his grandfather lived in Colonsay's Dùn Eibhinn.

Somerled rose to power in the twelfth century and broke the
stranglehold of the Vikings when he defeated Godred of Man. The
actual battle (AD 1156) was fought at sea to the west of the Sound of
Islay, and Somerled very probably had assembled his fleet in the
privacy of Colonsay's secluded harbours. He died just eight years
afterwards at Paisley, murdered in his tent, but his dynasty gave us
the Lords of the Isles and he was the progenitor of the House of
MacDonald. Throughout the Lordship (which was eventually
forfeited in AD 1493), Colonsay retained its geographical significance and was as important as it had been throughout the Viking
and Celtic periods. There are Statutes extant from AD 1492, date-
lined Dùn Eibhinn in Colonsay and Dùn Domhnuill in Oransay, on
29 July and 1 August, less than twelve months before the Act of
Forfeiture.

Although initially moving constantly throughout his territories,
the Lord of the Isles eventually established a permanent base, at
Finlaggan Loch in Islay; this is dated to about AD 1220 and
explained in a Colonsay context by Symington Grieve, the nineteenth-century antiquarian. Seemingly Donald, son of Reginald,
had a lengthy rule AD 1207 – c. 1247 in the course of which he
supposedly re-fortified the eponymous Iron Age fort in Oransay,
Dùn Domhnuill, thus offending the sensibilities of the Church. A
pilgrimage of atonement was required and "when (Donald) arrived
in Rome, we are told, he was accompanied by seven priests. They
interpreted his confession to the Holy Father, who is said to have
asked him if he was willing to submit himself to any punishment he
might decree. Donald said he was; even to being boiled in a leaden
cauldron.

"Seeing his apparently sincere penitence, the Holy Father
granted him absolution. Donald had got a fright … When he
returned home he abandoned Dùn Domhnuill and removed the
chief seat of the clan to Finlaggan, Isla, but to maintain the prestige

of his family he is said to have conveyed, no doubt miraculously, from Colonsay to Isla a sacred well."

Whatever the truth of the matter, Colonsay remained at the heart of events. Since Finlaggan was on a main trading route with Ireland and is not upon the coast, communications were established by reverting to the old signalling system, adapted to the new circumstances. Using fires and mirrors, signals could be flashed within minutes from the fringes of the Lordship right to its heart at Finlaggan. From Dùn Eibhinn or Dùn Cholla or Cnoc na Faire in Colonsay, a message was transmitted via Cnoc an t-Samhlaidh ("Reflection Hill") at Baleromindubh to be received at the Cnoc an t-Samhlaidh above Finlaggan Loch, and relayed down to the Council Isle itself. Indeed, messages originating in the Sound of Islay could be relayed back to Finlaggan by way of the Colonsay system.

Although the last traces of the Abbey of Kiloran were swept away by the McNeill lairds when they built the mansion house, Colonsay is fortunate that other work has survived from the period. The nunnery at Balnahard is associated with the period of John the Good and his wife Amie, as are the earliest of the Priory buildings in Oransay (AD 1325–1353). The stone chapels of Kilchattan and An Gleann are both thought to date from the late fourteenth century. The gravestones and monumental masonry of Oransay span a much wider period, with the latest date given being AD 1539.

The Forfeiture of the Lordship in AD 1493 and the disruption caused by the Reformation of AD 1540 presaged two centuries of turbulence for Colonsay. As it happened, the island was a centre of both MacDonald resistance and of the Counter-Reformation, so that the tombstones and religious buildings here were spared the worst attentions of the zealots. The islanders themselves were less fortunate – they were deprived of traditional institutions and exposed to crude assault. Religious services became a rarity, marriages were conducted in Ireland or not at all, medical treatment had to be sought in Antrim, education was abandoned. For centuries Clan MacPhee of Colonsay had been the hereditary record keepers of the Lordship, and the hereditary Priors of Oransay; yet by AD 1609, when he witnessed the Statutes of Iona, the then chieftain was illiterate and had to make his mark with an "X".

There are traces of this period on the ground, most notably in the creation of the agricultural divisions that remain in use until the present day (Balnahard, Balavetchy, Kiloran etc.). Since times were dangerous, special arrangements were made to protect important assets – there is a concealed lairage on Beinn Bheag where cattle could be hidden away, and there were crannogs (artificial islands) in Loch Fada where seedcorn would be safe from fire or casual depredation. In this period, at least two entirely new farmsteads were created for the "twa Killoderans", Dùnan a' Chullaich ("Farm of the Boar") and Dùn Ghaillionn ("Mound of the Blizzard").

Dùn Ghaillionn obtained its name from its first tenant, and in curious circumstances. In 1541 the King had leased Colonsay to Archibald MacPhee and it seems that MacPhee had formed an alliance of some sort with MacNeill of Barra and had given a tenancy to one of his name. One winter's morn, a boat set out from Barra to Colonsay; presumably it was MacNeill's "flitting" or removals but certainly it was carrying MacNeill's wife and some livestock. Unfortunately the weather deteriorated and, as a blizzard came on, MacNeill's wife went into labour and was delivered of a son. The resourceful crew of the boat slaughtered a cow and gralloched it, to provide shelter within its warm carcass for the mother and her baby. They survived the journey and the son, who was raised at Dùn Ghaillionn, was known ever afterwards as Iain a' Chuain ("John of the Ocean"); he has numerous descendants living in Colonsay to the present day.

Colonsay's role in the history of seventeenth-century Scotland was remarkable and it is worth noting that it was Sir Alasdair MacDonald of Colonsay who empowered Montrose, and that it was his father, Colla Ciotach or "Colkitto", who was the last accredited Royalist commander to leave the field in Scotland, July 1647. Colkitto was hanged at Dunstaffnage by the Campbells, and is commemorated in Colonsay at the place where he kept his birlinn, now called Port a' Chrochaire ("Port of the Hangman's Victim").

After the Williamite accession ("The Glorious Revolution") in 1688, Colonsay slipped into a more conventional role. It became the property of a leading scion of the McNeills of the south, whose estate expanded at various times to include all of Gigha and the northern part of Jura. Colonsay and Oransay remained with that family until the death in 1904 of Major General Sir John Carstairs McNeill G.C.V.O., K.C.B., K.C.M.G., V.C., "Laird of Colonsay and Oransay and late of Gigha and Ardlussa, J.P. and D.L. for

Argyllshire, 27 years Equerry to H.M. Queen Victoria". The estate was then purchased by a family friend, Donald Smith, First Baron Strathcona. Most of the island of Colonsay is still owned by Donald Smith's descendants, the current generation of whom manage the estate and have developed a range of businesses to serve holiday visitors. Many agricultural tenants have exercised their rights to buy the freehold of their crofts, and in all there are now about 58 independent residential freeholders. The island of Oransay was sold in the 1970s and is now owned by Mrs. Frances Colburn, who has given an agricultural tenancy to the Royal Society for the Protection of Birds.

An unofficial but fairly accurate snapshot of the island on 15 March 2010 shows a population of 116 persons, including 62 females and 54 males living in 77 households. There are 3 empty residential properties, and the total of 77 includes 46 which are privately owned, 17 which are owned by Colonsay Estate and 14 which are in some form of public ownership. Of the residential properties, 13 may be said to be reserved for work-related occupation and there are an additional 20 properties which are second-homes of persons who live elsewhere. A total of 46 properties are available for holiday lets, 38 of which are part of island-based businesses; the remaining 8 include commercial usage of some additional second homes. The entire housing stock amounts to 143 units, of which 46 were constructed within the last twenty years; work has commenced on the sites of an additional 5 houses.

The resident population includes 19 persons whose full-time education is not yet complete, also 46 persons over 60 years of age. Residents include 6 who are in Colonsay in work-related postings and 22 who came to the island in retirement.

Chapter 3

FLORA AND FAUNA

We know that Colonsay's flora and fauna appeared within the last 10,000 years, following the retreat of the ice. It was once believed that there had been a land-bridge connecting neighbouring islands and the mainland, and that the range of species in any specific island reflected the length of time that its land-bridge had survived. This theory has now been largely discounted and I am grateful to Dr. Richard Gulliver for the following suggested mechanisms of colonisation as regards Colonsay:

1 "Positive natural colonisation", e.g. birds nesting.
2 "Accidental natural colonisation", e.g. insects and seeds carried on the wind.
3 "Accidental colonisation via the agency of man", e.g. small mammals arriving on boats, sometimes perhaps inside sacks of grain, bundles of hay etc.
4 "Deliberate colonisation by man", e.g. there is some evidence that red deer were deliberately introduced to the Inner Hebrides during the Mesolithic period.

Thus Colonsay supports a range of species that is in essence very similar to others in the Inner Hebrides, save that time, chance and the intervention of man has refined that range. The modern species list has a few obvious omissions – e.g. snakes, frogs, hedgehogs, weasels, stoats, badgers, hares, pine-martin, wildcat etc. Some of these creatures may never have reached Colonsay, but place-names and archaeological evidence suggest that others existed and became extinct locally. The Great Auk and the Red Kite are two obvious examples of the latter, whilst the otter – so plentiful today – was reported as having been locally extinct shortly before 1910. In 1594 Dean Monro recorded Oronsay as full of "fowmartis" and mentioned weasel bones, but Prof. Berry (1983) suggests that the latter may have been stoats, drawing attention to a small race of stoats living in Islay and Jura. Prof. Berry also mentions brown hares in Oronsay – "the last one was shot in 1927" – but it is possible that they were not native and had been introduced. The original Oronsay game-book still exists, having been preserved by the late Andrew S. MacNeill, and may well give details of other species that were extirpated. It was only in recent years that the feral goats were destroyed in Oronsay, although they continue to survive and thrive in Colonsay.

It may be that specific reference to particular birds and flowers will be made in later chapters, when the different areas of the island are described, since the characteristics of each locality are reflected in the wildlife. This chapter will be restricted to comments of a more general nature.

Birds

A total of 206 species of birds have been accepted as occurring on Colonsay and Oronsay. Of the historic records White-faced Storm-Petrel was the first record for Britain and Yellow-billed Cuckoo was the first record for Scotland. Since 2000 there have been ten species recorded for the first time: Bean Goose, Little Egret, Red Kite, Grey Phalarope and Red-backed Shrike are all European species. Four species are North American vagrant waders: American Golden Plover, Lesser Yellowlegs, Buff-breasted Sandpiper and Pectoral Sandpiper; there was also a vagrant from Eastern Europe, Black-headed Bunting. Ninety-nine species of birds have been recorded as breeding. Of these, five species bred historically, but no longer do so, namely: Moorhen, Coot, Nightjar, Corn Bunting and Yellowhammer. Since 2000, four new breeding species have been recorded: Shoveler, Hen Harrier, Sand Martin and House Martin.

Colonsay has only one bird which is actually named after it but it is unsurprisingly one of the most common, the bird known in English as the eider but properly called, in the Gaelic of this region, lacha-Cholasach ("Colonsay's Duck"). Oddly enough, an alternative name is lach-Lochlannach (Norse or Danish Duck), which is a clear reference to its Scandinavian origins – the word "eider" is itself derived from the Icelandic name. Pennant visited Colonsay during his "*Tour of the Hebrides*" and mentioned a number of the local birds. On July 7 1772 he records "Take boat and visit *Bird Island* [i.e. Eilean an Eoin, east side of Oransay], and some other rocks divided by narrow passages, filled by a most rapid tide. Saw several ***Eider*** ducks and some shieldrakes [shelduck]. The islanders neglect to gather the down of the former, which would bring in a little money."

He continues: "This is the bird called by ***the Dean*** of the isles, ***Colk***. From the circumstance of its depluming its breast, he fables that "at that time her flesh [moult] of feathers falleth off her wholly, and [she] sails to the main sea again, and never comes to land until the year end again, and then she comes with her new flesh of feathers; this flesh that she leaves yearly upon her nest has no pens [quills] in the feathers, but utter fine downs."''

The Dean's word "Colk", dating back to 1594, has a pleasing echo of "Colasach". The shelduck that Pennant mentions is still to be seen all around the shores, an extraordinarily beautiful bird. In springtime two or three broods of ducklings usually combine, as their mothers seem to operate a crèche system and will be seen with perhaps more than twenty fluffy little chicks following along. Sadly, not for long – the otter, the heron and the greater black-backed gull are ever present and the little tribe dwindles with the passing days. Pennant also mentions domesticated peacocks thriving at Oransay farm, and notes that "Barnacle [geese] appear here in vast flocks in September, and retire the latter end of April or beginning of May". Nowadays one would also note the Greenland white-fronted, greylag and Canada geese, and that all four species may be observed throughout the year. Both greylag and feral Canada geese are known to breed locally, and there are usually a few specimens of the other species detained by injury etc. Nonetheless, in wintertime, it is barnacle and Greenland white-fronted geese that form the largest flocks and they are unusual at other times.

David Jardine gives some details in "*The Birds of Colonsay and Oronsay*". He mentions up to 650 barnacle geese over-wintering, and perhaps 250 white-fronted geese, together with resident populations of about 200 greylag and up to 100 Canada geese. Seemingly the latter were first introduced by Malcolm Clark, the then game-keeper, in 1934 and we know that there were other non-native birds at about that time, including both black swans and flamingos in Loch Fada. The flamingos were to go down in local legend after the great freeze of 1947, when they were unfortunately caught in the ice – it is said that Lord Strathcona was urgently informed by telegram: "MY LORD YOUR PELICANS IS DEAD".

Pennant climbed Beinn Oronsay – "Lofty and craggy, inhabited by red billed choughs, and stares [starlings]". The chough is nowa-days a great rarity elsewhere, and its apparent abundance in Colonsay is a particular delight. It is a lively bird, always in company, often at play and very easily seen and heard, but it was not always like that. Writing in 1910, Murdoch McNeill says that

"The Chough (Cnàmhach) used to nest in various places, but it has not been much in evidence for a number of years." Since the late 1970s careful study of its habits encouraged local farmers to modify farming techniques and these efforts have been rewarded by the local resurgence of this nationally threatened species.

Early research suggested that a balanced insect population was important to chough breeding-success, and that decomposing cowpats provide an essential habitat for several species of dung-beetle which, in its, turn provided a vital food resource. It had been noted that chough are attracted to the insects to be found under rotting seaweed along the shore and in 1993 Andrew Abrahams, a Colonsay beekeeper, suggested that a species of mining bee (*Colletes succinctus*) might also be significant. This was confirmed by subsequent study – in appropriate sand dunes, mining-bee larvae are to be found at a density of up to 1000 per square metre and at a depth of about 5cm, providing a valuable food resource which is now known to be exploited in winter by chough (Clarke and Clarke, 1995).

Incredibly, despite their endangered and marginal condition, the chough is still under attack from man – in April 2002 one Matthew Gonshaw was successfully prosecuted at Thames Magistrate Court for crimes which included the theft of six chough eggs from Colonsay; he was sentenced to three months imprisonment. In fact, he was the first person to be imprisoned for a wildlife crime in Scotland.

Birds have always been vulnerable to man. As mentioned elsewhere, Symington Grieve discovered the skeleton of a great auk (*Pinguinus impennis*) in the Mesolithic middens that he excavated in Colonsay; this flightless seabird was easily captured and was an obvious food source until the species was eventually driven into extinction in the mid-nineteenth century. Less easily captured was the red kite (*Milvus milvus*), but it is said to have become extinct in Scotland after the last survivor was shot, reputedly in Colonsay, by somebody who wondered what it was. The red kite has since been re-introduced to Scotland.

On 23 October 1988, Colonsay's first recorded barn owl (*Tyto alba*) was discovered, but unfortunately it too was dead, having been mistaken for a pheasant! Rather more common is the sgarbh (also called sgart, green cormorant or shag), which was traditionally considered a great delicacy. Murdoch McNeill tells us that it used to be believed that after seven years a shag developed into a black-throated diver, and after a further seven years became a cormorant;

in maturity, at twenty one years, it became a great northern diver. Presumably the supposed succession reflected the relative population strengths of each of the species. Gulls eggs were also highly prized for the table, and never really fell from favour – until the late 1970s a jar of pickled gulls eggs could be found on the bar counter of the Colonsay Hotel.

Some birds have survived other threats. In the 1990s a number of un-neutered cats escaped into the wild and turned feral; their numbers exploded and they began to prey upon young rabbits. Within a very brief period they had ousted rabbits from some areas and taken possession of the burrows – no ground-nesting bird was safe, but the lapwing seemed to be the main victim and its numbers plunged. Thankfully, the cats have now diminished in number and the lapwing is recovering, as is another of their victims, the tern. In connection with the latter it is worth noting that the common and Arctic tern are endangered birds throughout most of Scotland – research by Dunstaffnage Marine Laboratory identified mink as the main culprit. These dreadful pests have fortunately – as yet – failed to reach Colonsay, and the island has therefore become an important sanctuary for terns and other threatened native species. On the other hand, nest-desertion following disturbance by humans (however unintentional) is another cause of decline, so one should not picnic, stay to read one's book or go bathing in the nesting season if terns are in the vicinity.

Another great survivor in Colonsay and Oronsay is the corncrake (*Crex crex*), whose Latin name so accurately reflects its grating call. Its home is in the sub-Sahara and it makes the lengthy journey northwards to its breeding ground each spring, normally reaching Colonsay in the third week of April. It is a very shy bird and unwilling to be flushed – which made it highly vulnerable to traditional harvesting methods. Nowadays, mowers work outwards from the middle of the field and sacrificial strips are left uncut to provide a refuge. Unfortunately, there are other dangers – there are feral cats and even some un-belled domestic cats living locally which take a toll, and almost every year one or two are killed by cars. Although it is unlikely to be seen, the corncrake can usually be heard beside the road to Kiloran Bay, or near the "S" bends at Machrins, or in the vicinity of the graveyard. Interestingly, the Gaelic version of the Old Testament was translated directly from the Hebrew and in *Exodus* ch.16 v.13 we find that it was the *gearra-gort* that providentially relieved the Israelites; the word is used for both quail and corncrake so one can decide for oneself.

Colonsay has many birds of prey, of which the most obvious is the buzzard. They will be seen at regular intervals almost everywhere, but particularly from the island road. They eat a lot of carrion, but will often be seen to fall upon a young rabbit or to take a starling – the actual kill is very sudden and impressive. Oddly enough, the buzzards seem to be no match for the ravens, who frequently attack them and put them to flight. In the area around Machrins one might notice a peregrine falcon, a merlin or a kestrel and in recent years the hen harrier has appeared. There is no evidence of breeding prior to 2005 and it is uncertain if the hen harrier will become a permanent resident as the absence of short-tailed field voles in Colonsay is said to make the island unsuitable for permanent occupancy.

The western cliffs of Colonsay host the largest breeding colony of seabirds in the southern Hebrides, particularly guillemots and kittiwakes, augmented by lesser but substantial numbers of razorbills and fulmars. The shags are another feature of the bird-cliffs, some of which nest low down, permitting a good view of both nests and sitting birds. All told, there are upwards of 25,000 breeding pairs on the cliffs, but their status cannot be taken for granted as they would be vulnerable to possible changes in food resources due to fishing or climate-change. Annual surveys monitor the situation and recently Seabird Protection Areas have been designated by the Scottish Government for important sites such as this; these are intended to protect the birds from "significant disturbance" and extend seaward for up to 2.5 miles.

Finally, one must mention the oyster-catcher, known locally as Gille-Bhrighde ("Brigid's Servant"). This bird provides a charming link with the pre-Christian era, when Brìd was an important member of the ancient pantheon, goddess of fertility and patroness of poetry and the arts. Brìd was incorporated amongst the Christian saints, and her straw dollies and other pagan emblems of fertility were adopted too. In one form, these developed into "St. Brigid's cross" which is woven from straw and is to this day in Ireland still dressed in bright ribbons upon her festival. The shape of her cross is picked out in black and white when the oyster-catcher takes flight, and it does not take much imagination to hear the salutation "Brìd! Brìd!" in its plaintive cry. It is a very common bird in Colonsay, and can still be seen at modern Eilean Treadhrach (north-east tip of Oronsay) which Blaeu's seventeenth-century map records as "Eilean Bhrideg". St. Brigid's Cross has been adopted for the logo of Colonsay's publishing company, House of Lochar.

Trees

Some of Colonsay's woodland is very old and pockets of native species are widespread. Birch, oak, aspen, hazel, rowan, willow, blackthorn, juniper and holly are all probably native to the island, and excellent examples will be noticed. Almost all these species have been exploited, with the exception of the undesirable aspen. According to legend in other islands, its leaves tremble in shame because its wood was used for the Crucifixion; in fact it is not even useful for firewood, let alone for joinery. Presumably the legend "explained" why it was reviled and extirpated in many areas, although here in Colonsay it thrives in gentle peace.

Birch wood is easily worked and can be used to make household utensils, and the bark is an important resource which can be used to make containers, also to produce glue and to flavour wine. Canoes can be made from birch bark, and the Tyrolean iceman carried arrows whose flights had been affixed by birch glue.

Oak has always been highly prized, and of course had important pre-Christian religious significance. The merits of oak are well known, but in the Colonsay context it should be noted that, like birch, it can be coppiced. This produces long, straight and strong poles which would be required for many purposes, including roofing, making sleds and for durable tools. The wood itself was used to make boats, and to produce charcoal for iron-working; the bark produces tannin for the curing of hides and also for dyeing. The coppicing at A' Choille Mhòr in Colonsay was first identified by John and Pamela Clarke in the 1980s and some of the trees may be very old. One may be sure that the resource was exploited by the religious communities of Colonsay and Oransay, and that therefore coppicing was abandoned at some date following the dissolution of the monasteries but outwith living memory; as yet, little authoritative information is available. I am therefore most grateful to Dr. Richard Gulliver for the following remarks:

1 Although the coppicing of oak has a long tradition in Scotland, the main period was the eighteenth century and early nineteenth century, and this was probably the heyday in Colonsay also.

2 In woods where coppicing was properly organised, the stools
were relatively evenly placed, whereas the stools at A' Choille Mhòr
are somewhat erratically distributed. This indicates to me that (i)
coppicing was not undertaken over a long period of time (ii)
coppicing was done on an "as and when" basis. Good coppice
management involves cutting blocks or compartments of a wood at
one time, and then leaving that block for e.g. 25 years in the case of
oak before returning to it again. (Often 25 years was the period used
for oak coppice in lowland Scotland in the eighteenth century.) The
adjacent block might be coppiced in the following year and so on, so
the cycle would run over many rotations. I do not see signs of this
level of management in A' Choille Mhòr, although the longer ago it
was abandoned, the poorer the evidence.

3 Several individual trees are multi-stemmed. This is usually an
indication of coppicing. However a felled broad leaved tree will
produce shoots from its base. If these are ungrazed, a multi-
stemmed tree will result.

4 During coppicing the new growth from the stool needs to be
protected from grazing. Similarly in a wood where timber production is important, the grazing must not be so intensive that
regeneration from seed is prevented. Grazing animals can be
excluded by temporary fences e.g. made of wattle, or semi permanent fences; turf dykes (sometimes stone faced); or all-stone dykes.
The absence of remains of stone dykes and apparent absence of
remains of turf dykes at either A' Choille Mhòr, or A' Choille Beag
suggests that woodland management was not the main, sole objective. These woods would probably be used for several purposes,
including winter shelter and spring grazing.

5 Overall therefore I suspect that coppicing on Colonsay was small
in scale and organisation. However it is intriguing that that A'
Choille Mhòr is sited adjacent to Port Olmsa and, for a period, it
was served by a well-made track to Colonsay House; i.e. bulky items
could be transported from this wood with less difficulty than many
other locations on Colonsay.

6 In passing, I am told that some scholars believe that there was no
monastery on Colonsay. Rather, some early records refer to
Oronsay and some to Colonsay (meaning Oronsay). Later people
interpreted these two locations as separate, whereas only one
monastery was originally intended.

Hazel nuts have already been mentioned (Chapter 1) as a protein-rich food source which was evidently exploited on an almost industrial scale by the Mesolithic inhabitants of Colonsay; "Before cereal cultivation, undoubtedly the most important plant food throughout north-western Europe were the nuts of this often many-stemmed, tall bush or small tree. The nuts are rich in oil, protein, starch and sugar, with vitamins B1, C and trace elements." (Dickson and Dickson, 2000). The tree itself coppices well and produces sturdy, pliable wands which are excellent for use in making creels, baskets, lattices and wattle. Of course it was also essential for the wattle-and-daub construction of walls. It should be remembered that wattle-and-daub was already of incredible antiquity even before St. Columba used it for his religious and domestic buildings, and that it was still used for housing as late as the eighteenth century. Dr. Gulliver points out that hazel also "self-coppices", as many plants produce young shoots from the base, year after year. In some years these will be grazed out e.g. in the Mesolithic by red deer; but in others they remain ungrazed. After several years one has a multi-stemmed tree with a few poles which resemble coppiced-by-man hazel. "Competition" between poles on the plant (self-thinning) ensures that only a small number of really large poles are present under natural circumstances.

Although we know that hazel was abundant in Colonsay in ancient times (in fact, some people used to believe that its Gaelic name "Calltuinn" may have named the island), it is less common today and, except at Scalasaig, produces very few nuts. On the other hand, willow thrives in modern times, and its woven wands ("wickerwork") were also used for wattle. Wattle was important as the base for pathways across soft ground and for fords, of which there would have been many in Colonsay, and very probably willow was more suitable for this purpose, being less likely to rot in damp conditions. Much of the willow or sally (*Salix*) of Colonsay is a scrub form, Sùileag or round-eared willow, and of little value, but grey sallow (Dubh Sheileach) is also common and was used for creel-making and also for tanning leather. Murdoch McNeill mentions that it was favoured by small boys for making whistles, and that the non-native Seileach Uisge or common osier (*Salix viminalis*) was used for making baskets.

Rowan (mountain ash; *Sorbus aucuparia*) produces excellent, straight-grained wood which can be readily worked and which also makes a good fire; it was thought by Murdoch McNeill to be perhaps the only locally native ash and its merits are no doubt reflected in the affection in which it is held. Hardly a house in Colonsay is without its rowan, although few people will admit that they have it as a deterrent to witches and bad luck; the berries alone are a sufficient justification, as they are very attractive to small birds.

On the other hand, the unrelated common ash (*Fraxinus excelsior*) may also be found in Colonsay – there are fine examples in a deep gully somewhat north of the cairn in A' Choille Mhòr. Although the trees have mostly fallen, they have living shoots. It seems that this gully is Glaic an Uinnsinn ("Ash Dell") but Murdoch McNeill points out that "Near the beginning of last century [c.1800] a path from Colonsay House was made through Coille-mhòr to a summer-house [An Tigh Còintich] at Cul-salach, and it is possible that the ash-trees were then planted".

Both hawthorn (non-native in Colonsay) and blackthorn were used for hedging purposes, and of course blackthorn produces sloes, the only stoned fruit that is native to the island. (Curiously enough, although blackthorn remains quite widespread in the island, in recent years it appears not to have borne fruit in quantity).

Turf banks (dykes) are a very old system of producing a stock-proof boundary. Their effectiveness could be increased by planting gorse or occasionally hawthorn on top. Alternatively dead branches of these shrubs could be utilised. In some parts of Scotland wattle was used to surmount the turf wall. Time has reduced their height, often they are now only 50cm or less; frequently they follow a slightly sinuous course across the landscape.

There were a variety of ways that hawthorns could be planted to make hedges in the eighteenth century, nineteenth century and into the twentieth century. Some were planted into level ground, some planted on a new low bank, e.g. about 30cm tall, and some planted on taller banks, on the ditch side. Some were planted in front of an existing stone wall, or on the ditch side of an existing bank which had a facing of stone courses. The standard system was for new hawthorn hedges to be cut-and-laid when they reached a suitable size. This hedge-laying is an art which is best developed in regions well supplied with hedges. After many years of neglect, the signs of previous periods of laying become lost, especially if the hawthorns are supplemented by new plants developing from seed. Any 'perched hedges' which topped the older, taller banks, would have been exposed and stunted, with a limited root volume. Little management would have been required. These older turf banks could be stone faced, or contain a good percentage of stone. (Source: Dr. Richard Gulliver, *pers. corr.*)

Dr. Gulliver suggests that the hawthorn hedges very close to Kiloran Farm and Colonsay House were probably nineteenth-century or early twentieth-century in origin. Some bounding the road have the remains of a stone wall and bank behind them. The wall frequently drops down to a ditch and is often the 'facing' of an earth bank. This can give rise to some interesting speculations as to the origins of the hawthorns. A stone-faced bank coming to the end of its life may have been planted with hawthorn on its road side, the wall providing some protection for the young hawthorn plants from stock grazing in the field. It is also possible that sometimes there may have been fruiting hawthorns in the vicinity for a long period, with progressively more hawthorn plants becoming spontaneously estab-lished on the road side of the wall. In this position they would be lightly grazed (e.g. by driven cattle) compared with the adjacent field, or effectively ungrazed. If the hedges were not laid, but simply 'topped', gaps in the bottom could have been filled by new seedlings. (*Thanks go to Angela Skrimshire and Netta Titterton for help with this section.*)

The taller turf banks are generally older, usually along the line of a boundary or march. In many places, sections of these centuries-old "dykes" or boundaries have survived – there are good examples beside Loch a' Raon a' Bhuilg, along the Balnahard march and along the northern march of Scalasaig approaching Loch Fada. In their day, all such dykes provided warmth and shelter to the live-stock and created a completely stock-proof barrier. It is curious to reflect just how much more expensive, unattractive and inefficient is the modern post-and-wire substitute which is now the fashion, erected with massive subsidy and inbuilt obsolescence.

Juniper had important medicinal properties as a diuretic and according to McNeill yielded an oil of medicinal value. He mentions also that "the green branches were burned for fumigating houses after infectious diseases", and that the berries were used for flavouring whisky. The same authority mentions that holly (*cuilionn*) was favoured for the making of walking-sticks, and that birdlime is produced from its bark, boiled and mixed with nut-oil. Birdlime, of course, was used from time immemorial to trap small birds as a food source.

Scotland has three native conifers, the towering Scots pine

(*Pinaceae* family), the prostrate juniper (*Cupressaceae* family), and the yew (*Taxoceae* family). Of these, probably only juniper is native to Colonsay, although the Scots pine may have been grown from seed native to mainland Scotland. Common ash may have been introduced by the McNeills c. 1800, and sycamore followed soon afterwards. The common *Rhodendendron ponticum* was an ill-judged introduction of c. 1850 which threatened to engulf the entire island and is now the subject of a major eradication scheme. It does not support wildlife and its flowers are poisonous to bees. Colonsay allegedly held the "last surviving colony of the Old British Black Bee", which was destroyed after the hard winter of 1947 when the *ponticum* flowered profusely and early. Fortunately this anecdotal information is not completely accurate – the bee in question (*Apis mellifera mellifera*) exists in a number of locations and even here in Colonsay has been nursed to recovery through the efforts of local bee-keeper Andrew Abrahams. Andrew has been working with Colonsay's black bees since the 1970s and now has 60 hives, each with about 50,000 inhabitants ("*Scotsman on Sunday*", 24 January 2010). Nonetheless, the incident underlines the need to totally eradicate *Rhodendendron ponticum*.

The Flora

There is an outstanding flora with significant local variations across the various habitats. The yellow iris or *Seileastair* will be encountered everywhere – being so common it is apt to be overlooked, but it is very beautiful. Almost as widespread is marsh marigold, whose luscious yellow flowers will be seen in many of the roadside ditches. The flowers of the machair (open dune-systems) are truly delightful and in certain areas the heath spotted orchids are like carpets. Honeysuckle is a particular feature of Colonsay and its heady scent can be almost overpowering.

There are six forms of *Hypericum* or St. John's wort that have been recorded in Colonsay. Tutsan ("*all healthy*") was once widespread in the grazings and, despite its name, is said to have induced madness in livestock if eaten. In some places, as many as four different types of St. John's Wort can be found within a radius of a couple of metres.

On the wetter ground one will notice bog-cotton, bog-myrtle, bog-asphodel and marsh lousewort, and closer inspection will reveal up to four species of insectivorous plants, including the attractive round-leaved sundew. This plant entraps tiny insects upon its delicate, sticky hairs then closes its leaves and digests them. Like all plants, the round-leaved sundew is now protected but Murdoch McNeill (1910) tells us that "some ladies mix the juice with milk so as to make an innocent and safe application to remove freckles and sunburns". (Since 1981 it has been illegal to intentionally uproot this or any wild plant, unless you are the landowner or have the landowner's permission.)

The bog-myrtle was not without its uses – in former days, children were given an infusion of the leaves as a cure for "worms". It was used in tanning, as a substitute for hops in making "heather ale", and the crushed leaves are even said to act as an insect-repellent.

Bracken (*Pteridium aquilinum*) will be noticed upon many of the hills – in the past this had a commercial value in some places, being burned to produce potash until over-exploitation depleted the resource and killed the trade. A nineteenth-century record relating to Jura (part of this parish at the time) suggested that this had happened there. Although it is unlikely that bracken was ever harvested commercially in Colonsay, it may have been used for bedding or thatching. At all events, it has been allowed to spread until it has now blanketed many hundreds of acres; some attempt to control it has been made in recent years, including spraying by helicopter. Unfortunately, the chemical is indiscriminate and destroys other, more desirable ferns.

In point of fact, bracken was no great scourge historically until seasonal, low-intensity grazing by cattle came to be replaced by intensive stocking with sheep. As Dr. Gulliver points out: "Any cattle that were over-wintered on the hill would trample the delicate [bracken] crosiers as they came through the ground; sheep being lighter and with smaller hooves do not have the same effect". The situation was exacerbated by the fact that sheep are a natural enemy of man – as sheep are introduced, human population will fall (and land will deteriorate), thus reducing the available labour force for activities which are quickly rendered marginal. Of course, the demand for potash had intensified with the success of the Industrial Revolution (c. 1760–1830) as it was required for the glass, soap and bleaching industries. It was quickly discovered that the available labour could produce larger quantities by burning kelp until, with the ending of the Napoleonic wars, the importation of guano was to put an end to kelping as well. Bracken did have other uses, for thatching, animal litter, fuel and compost material etc., and Dr.

Gulliver suggests that in Colonsay, due to a combination of the technical nature of the process, transportation difficulties, and local requirements for the basic resource, it was more probably used for such purposes than burned for potash. Walkers should note that its spores are reputedly carcinogenic, and that it should perhaps be avoided from mid-August until it has died down in November.

Common reed (*Phragmites australis*, a.k.a. *Phragmites communis*) grows in fine stands that may readily be enjoyed from the public road – for example, on the right-hand side of the road as one approaches the graveyard from Port Mòr, or close to An Dèabhaidh (where the road passes across Loch Fada). This was sometimes used for thatching in former times, and today it is valued for its highly decorative plumes. Rush was a more popular thatch, especially *Juncus articulatus* (jointed rush), which lasted much longer; it grows mainly by the sea – e.g. Port an Rafain ("Jointed Rush Harbour") in Balavetchy. Dr. Gulliver mentions that the most common thatching rush was probably a mixture of *Juncus articulatus* and a hybrid with sharp-flowered rush, *Juncus acutiflorus x articulatus*, the hybrid being somewhat more common locally. In 2009, two fragile stands of Bull-rush (*Typha latifolia*) appeared in new locations, beside the road at the Black Gate (junction of B8085 with B8086) and in Upper Kilchattan – unfortunately, they were both mutilated that year by persons unknown and it is questionable if they will survive. There is an established stand near Ardskenish farmhouse.

A plant of curiosity interest is a garden introduction, the familiar montbretia. This originated in South Africa and is likely to have been grown in the formal gardens of Colonsay House in the nine-teenth century. Everywhere that it was in cultivation, it was suddenly rendered unfashionable after 1879. This was the year in which a Frenchman, Victor Lemoine of Nancy, successfully crossed *Tritonia aurea* with *Montbretia pottsii* to produce *Crocosmia* x *crocosmi-iflora* (which was then known as *Montbretia crocosmiiflora)*. The new orange-coloured variety became all the rage, and the purer, flame red *pottsii* was rooted out and given away – but here in Colonsay it can still be seen in the gardens of the hotel and of the miller (Mill Cottage, formerly Torr an Tuirc). Keen-eyed visitors will note it in a number of other locations, and it also survives on the islands of Loch an Sgoltaire and Port Olmsa, the ghosts of former "rustic" pleasure gardens.

As one explores the island, one is struck by the very wide range of ferns, mosses, lichens and fungi that are encountered. Every rock is decorated by lichen, every hollow is enchanted by mosses and fungi, many of the trees play host to their own colonies of them all. These organisms are intolerant to pollution and are able to thrive because the island's modest rainfall comes largely from the Atlantic ocean. Elsewhere in Britain, throughout much of the country, the rain has been tainted by industrial activity and falls as dilute sulphuric acid. A total of 342 lichen taxa were recorded by the late Dr. Francis Rose in a pioneering study published in 1983, including two species which were new to the British list, and it was suggested that many more were yet to be identified.

Because Colonsay's climate is so very mild, the growing season can often extend into late Autumn – but whilst individual examples of herbaceous perennials can be found flowering at almost any time of year, May, June and July are of course the best months to enjoy the widest range of flowers.

Other Wildlife

There are no snakes in Colonsay, also no moles, squirrels, hedge-hogs, foxes, stoats, weasels, badgers, frogs or toads (although a toad was discovered in October 2000, having presumably arrived in a load of hay). Nor are there any deer, although this may not always have been the case. Such bones as have been found in archaeolog-ical research were believed to have been imported to the island, either as food or so that the bone itself could be processed for secondary use. The occasional carcass is washed ashore in Colonsay – presumably as a result of an ill-timed passage from Jura to Scarba – and there are obvious tool-uses for antlers and scapulae. On the other hand, Symington Grieve found "abundant evidence of the presence of the red deer (*Cervus elephas*) all through the deposits at Caisteal-nan-Gillean, Oronsay, and also in the lower strata of the Crystal Spring Cavern [Uamh Ùr]. The evidence obtained by my excavations inclines me to the opinion that red deer were numerous upon these islands during the period of the occupation of Caisteal-nan-Gillean, but afterwards gradually decreased in numbers until they were probably exterminated about the eighth or ninth century." Wild boar (*Sus scrofa*) finds are more readily persuasive that it was a native species, as there less obvious secondary uses other than as food, and there is some supportive place-name evidence.

On the positive side, Colonsay does have many species of creature that we all remember from our childhood, and which seem so much rarer now. There are, for example, plenty of dragon-flies on all the lochs, and there is a tiny shrew (*Sorex araneus*) to be found in leafy brakes. One can easily see common lizards basking on sun-baked rocks and walls, and may sometimes come across a family of slow-worms, the legless form of lizard that can be mistaken for a snake. Look out for the aptly-named hawkmoth, looking just like the eye of a fierce bird and presumably giving fright to predators. There are also "doodlebugs" (as this writer knew them as a child), those flying "stag beetles" like giant bumble-bees that are encountered on a summer's evening; I now know them really to be cockchafers, rather than stag beetles, which are not recorded in Colonsay. Apparently the cockchafer (*Melontha vulgaris*) can be a dreadful scourge in some places, developing in some years "countless myriads, the perfect insects stripping their trees of their entire foliage, and the larvae destroying, by devouring the roots, not only the grass of pastures, but crops of all kinds of farm and garden produce". In a report to the Académie des Sciences in 1868, it was calculated that the department of Seine-Infériure alone had suffered recent damage in excess of one million pounds sterling. There is a similar beetle in America, where it is called May-bug or Doodlebug: "such is the completeness with which the larvae do their work on the roots of grass, that turf may sometimes be peeled off in large sheets, like a carpet from a floor" (*Cassell's Natural History*, 1896). One can easily imagine how the name reached war-time Britain, but luckily enough this creature is, in Colonsay, utterly benign.

Rock pools are rich in spider crabs and sea anemones, limpets, winkles and dog-whelks; mussels abound, anyone with a rake can gather cockles and the more astute will have no trouble catching razor-shells (also known as sout-fish) on the sandbanks in a spring tide. Both sea and loch are frequented by otters (*Lutra lutra*) which, in early summer, can be seen together as the youngsters are taught to swim. The dog-otter absents himself from the rearing process, but the female will be seen close-inshore with one or two young – in principle, be alert near locations which are calm, where you are down-wind, and where fresh-water is entering the sea.

Some creatures are most easily seen from the sea, providing a good excuse for a boat trip. Although the otter (*Lutra lutra*) is actually no rarity, it can be somewhat elusive but it is often seen from boats, as are dolphin and minke whales. Common seals (*Phoca vitulina*) will be seen at Port Olmsa and Colonsay is the major breeding centre within the Firth of Lorne for the grey Atlantic seal, *Halichoerus grypus*. This noble creature abounds in the rocks and skerries all around the island, but the major colony is at Eilean nan Ròn off Oransay. In addition to locally nesting birds, one will often encounter gannets and (more rarely) shearwaters, puffins and even petrels.

Some of Colonsay's wildlife has a remarkable lifecycle and is subject to global influences; the corncrake (*Crex crex*) has its home in sub-Saharan Africa, and the Arctic tern actually travels from one end of the world to the other, 18,000 km. each way, spending part of its year (despite its common name) in Antarctica. In this context one must remember the European eel (*Anguilla anguilla*), still common in Colonsay but whose total population has fallen by almost 50% in recent years. This remarkable creature reproduces in the Sargasso sea and its *leptocephali* or larvae then migrate across the Atlantic to colonise fresh, brackish and coastal waters throughout Europe and parts of North and West Africa.

Almost 25,000 people depend upon the European eel for their living, and it appears that one problem affecting the species is the illegal harvesting and export of tiny "glass eels", initially to stock Asian farms and thence to supply Japanese tables. There is also the possibility that global warming is affecting ocean currents, and interfering with migration patterns. Despite these problems, one can still inspect the tiny elvers in Colonsay's isolated hilly lochans and marvel as to how they got there. As children, we were told that the larvae came down with the rain and, as adults, it still sounds fairly convincing.

Although Colonsay is host to a number of rare species, many of which are small and inconspicuous, these are properly the concern of specialists. There is a species of water-beetle said to have been unknown elsewhere when first discovered in A' Choille Mhòr in the 1980s, there are rare hybrid flora, there are interesting underwater plants in the lochs and around the coastline, there is even an unusual antipodean land-shrimp which arrived with an exotic specimen tree for Colonsay House. For the layman, the special charm of the island lies simply in the range and profusion of more familiar species and in the very varied habitats. As one explores each area of the island, one will be amazed by the diversity of the wildlife.

Chapter 4

SCALASAIG

Map: page ix

Scalasaig is an ideal starting place for an exploration of the island, since it is the usual point of arrival. All of the inhabited houses on Colonsay's east coast are centred on Scalasaig, which also hosts the harbour and pier, the hotel, the parish church, the medical centre, the fire station, the island's general store, post office and petrol pump, the village hall, the telephone exchange and even the official administrative offices. Scalasaig is the closest thing to a village that will be found in Colonsay, and had 38 inhabitants in 2010 (or 46 if you included Glassard).

Scalasaig is a Viking word, the -aig suffix meaning "inlet" or "creek" and signifying a landing place or harbour; it is usually taken to mean "Skalli's Harbour", Skalli meaning "Bald-headed", or otherwise "Hut Bay" (cf. Scalloway); perhaps it may mean "Harbour of the Great House", referring to its major feature, the "skaill" or "Hall" of Dùn Eibhinn. From an historical point of view, Scalasaig is important because it gives a commanding view of the vital Sound of Islay and because it has two good landing places, Scalasaig itself and Loch Staosnaig (slightly to the south). Its significance is indicated by the dramatic hill fort of Dùn Eibhinn and confirmed by the siting of the Parish Church upon a mediaeval foundation and beside ancient cist burials (discovered 1856). Although Scalasaig is not the smallest farm in Colonsay, extending to 649 Scots acres or 844 statute, it is disproportionately challenged since barely ten per cent is described as "arable and meadow" (66 Scots acres).

The arable land in Scalasaig lies along the foot of a glaciated valley and the moraine deposit extends up to a kilometre eastwards under the sea; where it emerges from tide-borne silts, a small area of clay supports a population of *Nephrops Norvegicus* (also called Langoustine or Dublin Bay Prawns). A narrow outcrop of limestone runs along the shoreline towards the Monument at Cnoc na Faire, with older phyllite sedimentary rock forming the lighthouse headland. Scalasaig farm is unique in Colonsay in that the arable land overlies ancient, igneous rocks, described as Augite Diorite, which were created deep within the Earth. Outcrops can be seen bordering the road along the Hotel Brae. Diorite is defined by *Geology.com* as "a coarse-grained, intrusive igneous rock that contains a mixture of feldspar, pyroxene, hornblende and sometimes quartz." Augite is defined as "a rock-forming silicate mineral of the pyroxene group. It is an important mineral in many basic igneous rocks." This rock may be examined in detail at the small roadside quarry north of Ben Odhran House, and some of it was used in construction of the harbour – dating from the early Palaeozoic period, it is probably more than 300 million years old. Running up from the northeast shore of Loch Staosnaig one can identify two Dolerite dykes, one of which re-appears in the harbour – these are said to be intrusions from the Tertiary period, embracing a period which ran from 65 to 2.6 million years ago. The northern part of the farm, running across to Loch Fada, consists of Kiloran Flags, described by the British Geological Survey as "Flaggy fine sandstones with thin interbedded phyllites and metasiltstones".

There are five listed buildings in this part of the island, also a range of monuments in the inventory of RCAHMS and numerous other places of interest, some of which are discussed below.

Buaile Riabhach Stones ("Brindled Fold") NR 388943 *(200 m. north of Scalasaig farmhouse, to the right of the old track)*
This D-shaped kerbed cairn may be late Bronze Age in origin (c. 100 BC) but it has not been excavated using modern techniques. From the impressive remains it is clear that this was a significant structure in antiquity although the original covering material has long been eroded. Sir John McNeill recalled (1881) that he remembered stones being removed from the remains, and that a dagger or sword was uncovered and subsequently lost.

Standing stone and cup-Marking NR 385942 *(50 m. west of Scalasaig farmhouse)*
This remarkable stone is lozenge shaped, slim but standing 2m high and almost as broad at its widest point. It stands to the west of Scalasaig farmhouse and may be clearly seen from the public road. In common with most such stones in Colonsay, it is aligned precisely on the east-west axis. Unlike the other stones, this one bears a number of cup-marks, circular depressions that are possibly associ-

ated with reverence for the sun. Elsewhere these can take a more developed form and are accepted as Bronze Age rock-art. It is said that cup-marks are never found *in situ* except on bedrock, so this standing stone must have been quarried and erected after the cup-marks had been made. Oddly enough, the marks have not been noticed by archaeologists but they can be seen quite clearly as the sun begins to decline – say by about 4.30 p.m. on a summer's day. (With binoculars, the cup-marks can even be seen from the public road).

Dùn Èibhinn ("Eyvind's fort") NR 382943 (*400 m. northwest of Scalasaig farmhouse*)

A magnificent Iron Age (c.600 BC – c. AD 400) fortress which dominates Scalasaig and which lies about 400m. to the north of the public road; like all such forts in Colonsay it is conspicuous by being very green, due to accumulated occupation detritus. Access can be achieved by passing close behind Scalasaig farmyard (not the house), keeping all buildings on the left-hand side and passing through a gate almost in the bed of a burn; from here the original track becomes fairly clear. Alternatively, if crops and animals permit, another track leads straight towards it from close beside the modern commemorative cairn alongside the public road.

The visitor is recommended to walk right around the base of the fortification before entering through the original entrance, a zigzag path at the north-eastern corner. In this way one can appreciate how impressive the structure will have been when the masonry was still in place, and the ease with which the entrance could have been defended. Note that the final approach is steep and somewhat awkward, before entering into a wider space within the thickness of the curtilage, contrived to give free play to any right-handed defender.

Dùn Èibhinn will have become a seat of the Dalriadic noblemen from Ireland 1,500 years ago and, in due course, was adopted by the Vikings. It became the centre to which the taxes and wealth of the Suderys ("Sudreyjar" or Southern Hebrides) were gathered for onward transmission. In the fullness of time, it was the home of Adomnàn ("Jarl Gilli"), one of the later Norse nobles, the fore-father of the mighty Somerled. After the overthrow of the Norse, Somerled's own descendants created the Lordship of the Isles and took over Dùn Èibhinn for themselves. During the rule of the Lords of the Isles, the ancient and "well-beloved" family of Clan MacPhee became their hereditary record keepers and for upwards of three centuries Dùn Èibhinn was their home. On 23rd August 1609, the Statutes of Iona were accepted by an assembly of chiefs which included "Donald McFie in Collonsaye, togidder with the maist pairt of thair haill speciall freindis, dependairis and tennentis…"

The numerous grassy mounds to be seen on the top of the monument are the remains of the mediaeval residence of the MacPhee chieftains. From that summit one can admire the commanding view of the Sound of Islay, and know that one stands where once stood the mighty Lords of the Isles themselves.

In ancient times, before the drainage was improved, the easiest route to Dùn Èibhinn was from Loch Staosnaig and across modern Achadh Tarsuinn ("Cross-lying Field"). A convenient route and easily defended.

The Hotel NR 389941
The Statutes of Iona in 1609 included provision for the establishment of an Inn in every island: "for releif of passingeris and straingeris, ordanit certane oistlairis to be set doun in the maist convenient placeis within every Ile … quilkis oistlairis sall haif furnitoure sufficient of meit and drink to be sauld for reasonable expensis."

As far as is known, the earliest reference to the Inn is in 1769 when a rental receipt mentioned "change houses". The document mentions "Balnahard, Scallasaig and others", and a careful examination of the architecture suggests that the present farmhouses at both Balnahard and Scalasaig conform to the original design of the existing hotel. The northern half of the Hotel appears on Wilson's estate map of 1804, as does the church and Scalasaig farmhouse, and these three late-Georgian buildings are probably the earliest post-mediaeval buildings in Colonsay apart from Colonsay house (1722). (Balnahard farmhouse had not yet been built when Wilson's map was surveyed.)

Formerly known as An Taigh-sheinse ("The Change-house"), the hotel is a listed building, category B. The main features of interest include the surviving original plan, the tongue-and-groove panelling in the dining room and downstairs corridor, and the skews. (These skews are stone-and-mortared caps which protect the roofing slates from high winds and are a feature of Colonsay's vernacular architecture.) The hotel was always at the hub of island life and at one time the entire population of the island was subjected to a mass-inoculation against smallpox, being induced to file through An t' Seomar Mòr ("The Big Room" or dining-room) where the procedure was administered. Rents were traditionally collected in the same room, the largest public room in the island, and each tenant was given a wee dram with his receipt.

Many tales are told of the sometime enterprising inn-keeper at Scalasaig, David Clark, a doyen of the trade. One such story concerns the present lounge, a sunroom built by David in the late 1930s. When all was ready, the room was furnished and they say he decided to further enhance the excellent view of the harbour by allowing a regular guest, G.K. Ward, to replace an appropriate window pane with magnifying glass. The idea seemed a great success, but there was a fatal flaw – the following morning dawned bright and sunny, and it was only by chance that an early-riser spotted the first wisps of smoke rising from the smouldering sofa…

Scalasaig Farmhouse *cf. the hotel*
Listed, Category B, the significant features comprise the elements of traditional design, although the original windows fell victim to a late twentieth-century fashion for pvc double-glazing. It is listed as "earlier nineteenth century", but the building is more probably late eighteenth century; as mentioned above, it appears on Wilson's 1804 map of the estate but without the steadings. Scalasaig farm was resumed by the Colonsay Estate in the 1990s, after which the farmhouse became a holiday let; the steadings date from the early nineteenth century and are currently semi-ruinous (2010).

Church of Scotland Parish Church
The church was built in 1802, at a cost of £444, 11s. 6d, supposedly to the design of Michael Carmichael, an architect who had carried out some minor work at Inveraray. In fact, the building is highly reminiscent of the much larger church at A' Chleit, in Kintyre, which was completed in 1790 on an estimate of £540. The first minister at A' Chleit was Rev. Alexander Stewart, who had moved there from Jura and Colonsay parish, so one can imagine that he will have able to give advice when it was sought from Colonsay. The design at A' Chleit is ascribed to Mr George Haswell of Inveraray, "chief wright to the Dukes of Argyll" who had designed a number of

churches in the area. Haswell had died in 1784 and we may suppose that Michael Carmichael was at least indirectly influenced by his work at A' Chleit. The piended or "hipped" slate roof would have been unusual in Colonsay at the time and is reflected in the design of the former parochial school (close at hand, now a private house). The most interesting surviving feature is the coombed panelled ceiling, but the interior was originally equipped with galleries accessed by external staircases (such staircases are a very distinctive Colonsay feature). The upper doors are now windows, and the place of the staircases has been filled by two porches. The church is a listed building, category B. The stone basin beside the porch is a font from the mediaeval chapel of Cille Chatan. The neighbouring house was the parochial school for both boys and girls, with master's house attached, and is mentioned briefly by John Buchan in "*Mr. Standfast*".

Smiddy Cottage *(50m west of the Hotel)*
Listed, Category B, as "House and shop" and also credited to Carmichael; the original entrance in the centre was moved to one side before the building was protected, although the double-glazing is a later feature. An unusual feature was a third, centrally placed chimney stack which was removed in the 1990s. The blacksmith's bellows survived in the adjoining smiddy (rebuilt 2003) and in front of that building are remnants of the trade. A stone with iron staple to secure cart shafts may still be seen, although a large flat circular stone with radiating grooves from a central socket has perhaps become grass-grown – it has certainly slipped from view. It was used to assemble the spokes and rim components of a wheel whilst a new rim was fitted. Until the nineteenth century, sleds would of course have been more common than carts.

The Monument
Erected by public subscription to the memory of Duncan McNeill (1793–1874), Lord Colonsay and inaugurated 9 August 1876. Almost 200 inhabitants of Colonsay had contributed "from a sixpence upwards" and almost 300 were present at 3 o'clock that day when Rev. Donald MacLean opened the proceedings in prayer. Speeches were made, including one in Gaelic by the new laird, Sir John McNeill GCB, which was acclaimed with "loud and prolonged cheering". Prof. Duncan MacKinnon, a Colonsay man and the

organiser of the whole affair, declaimed a Gaelic dedication, following which "substantial refreshments" followed at the hotel.

Duncan McNeill had been laird of Colonsay during a time of bitter adversity, in which the potato blight had been followed by smallpox, cholera and scarlatina; there had been heavy emigration to Canada, countered to some extent by more modest immigration from neighbouring islands. During his stewardship, the population of Colonsay had more than halved, from 979 in 1841 to 456 in 1871. Nonetheless, by his innovative and imaginative interpretation of the Drainage Acts, lawyer Duncan McNeill had been able to maximise the public relief available to his surviving tenantry. There seems no doubt that he was held in popular esteem and genuine affection.

Yet one may note that Sir John McNeill, Duncan's younger brother, had been the 1851 author of the "*Report to the Board of Supervision in Scotland*" which advocated assisted emigration instead of charitable support for the struggling highlander. From 1852, Sir John was secretary of the Highland and Island Emigration Society, and in December of that year presided at Campbeltown over the departure of the ill-fated "*Hercules*" for Australia. In 1883, Professor MacKinnon would serve as a member of the Napier Commission on Crofting, and Sir John's nephew, Malcolm McNeill, was to serve as Secretary to the Commission. It was a signal feature of all these proceedings that no evidence was ever taken in Colonsay by any of the powerful bodies which they represented.

The original monument carried glowing tributes in Latin (by Prof. Blackie), in English (by Alexander Nicolson) and in Gaelic (by Prof. Mackinnon), but it was struck by lightning seven weeks to the day after it was inaugurated and the inscribed undercroft was blown to smithereens. The monument was afterwards re-erected on a more modest undercroft, giving just the name and dates. Marks of the lightning bolt can still be seen, as can the substantial lightning conductor subsequently provided. Parts of the original structure can be identified elsewhere: forming steps in the hotel garden, as decorative pieces near the Mill Pond at Colonsay House, and re-used as quoin-stones at Ben Odhran House.

Additional places of interest
1. Field Walls. Scalasaig's magnificent "Galloway" dykes are worthy of particular note. Sections will be seen behind the war

memorial, on either side of the road as you approach "The Pantry" and in full glory traversing the hillside below Dùn Èibhinn. It seems that the original fermtoun was centred upon the scant remains at NR 38559 93889; in the vicinity there are traces of a number of buildings and vestiges of a former field system. An ancient trackway may yet be followed across Achadh Tarsuinn ("Cross-lying field") towards Dùn Èibhinn. Relatively soon after the McNeills had established themselves and built their own house, they built the farmhouse and the Inn at Scalasaig (both to the same plan). This will have been part of their initial improvements, probably in the late eighteenth century, in the wake of the '45. They will have been heavily influenced by both the architectural and agricultural revolutions being pioneered at Inveraray. A vital factor was the introduction of the modern plough which permitted heavier land to be taken into cultivation; this was the Scots plough or "swing" plough, invented by James Small of Berwickshire in 1763, and which remained in use into the twentieth century. In consequence of the changes, the position of the tacksman became untenable and entire communities came to be removed or "cleared"; the McNeill lairds carried out their initial clearances on their property in Jura and it was not until the 1790s that Colonsay was directly affected.

Initially in Scalasaig (and later at Balnahard) a conventional "farmhouse" with single tenancy was constructed, marking an end to the traditional run-rig system. The new system required stock-proof field boundaries, since the "abridgement of labour" put an end to the old reliance on summer shielings. New stone dykes were required, and specialist builders came up from the lowlands to build new and highly distinctive "Galloway" dykes, which seem to have been the earliest style in Colonsay. Hitherto, march boundaries and enclosures had consisted of low stony banks over-planted with thorn hedges (see Chapter 3 for more detail). Scalasaig's southerly dyke ran from the modern harbour in the direction of the Mòine Thomach ("Tussocky Bog"), but seems to have been diverted to join the current main road near the southeast corner of Achadh Tarsuinn. Another such dyke ran northwards behind the present War Memorial and thence up towards the hotel. There is another stretch of the northerly dyke which is highly impressive from a distance, but is actually rather less substantial and appears to have been built rather later, possibly around 1830. It encloses land which had not been enclosed by 1804, starting at the Glebe Wood and making its way towards the farmhouse, and it survives in a remarkably good state of preservation. The preference for vertical instead of horizontal courses was a feature of construction in Galloway and the Borders – the interstices allowed free passage of the wind to prevent drifting snow, and would provide painful footing to any sheep that tried to climb over, in view of their cloven-hooves. The most impressive section of the technically superior southern dyke may be seen beside the War Memorial.

2. "The Glebe Wood" NR 379940

This is the mature area of woodland which lies beyond the field opposite "The Black Gate" (i.e. the junction with the Oransay road); the name recalls the period when Colonsay's catechist (minister's assistant) looked after the religious needs of the island and had a smallholding hereabouts. He had 8 acres arable and 16 acres 2 roods pasture with which to sustain his family. Wilson's estate map of 1806 identifies his house (a few stones at NR 37887 93868 are perhaps its trace) and delineates the boundaries – in essence, Glebe Field, the whole of the Mòine Thomach and the strip of good land beside the road opposite The Quarry. This shows that the Mòine Thomach (a former lochan) had been drained at some date prior to 1806, a significant undertaking. The Glebe woodland was planted c. 1840, after a more suitable manse and replacement glebe had been provided on the present site, north of the harbour, which had been part of Glassard farm.

3. Bruthach a' Bheannain ("Corner Brae") NR 38876 94494

Within the bend of "The Old Road" at this point there is the well-preserved outline of a substantial circular building, some 6m in diameter with walls of about 1m thickness and with an entrance on the eastern side; although nothing is known of the building, Symington Grieve was told that this was a favoured site for the burial of infants who had died unbaptised. On the summit of Am Beannan, ("The Little Peak"), close to Cathair na Bantighearna ("Lady's Seat") which is at NR 39021 94404, one can see the outlines of a few reputed shieling-huts, for example at NR 39038 94433. During the growing season, cattle would be kept to the high-ground to protect the crops and such huts were used as summer dwellings by the herds; although this particular example seems to be both later and more substantial than most.

4. Dùnan a' Mhiodaire ("Little Fort of the Good Meadow")
NR 39193 94286
This "lost" dùn of Scalasaig was recorded by Symington Grieve in the nineteenth century but eluded generations of later archaeologists – it lies partway between the Brewery and the Hotel beside Caolachadh ("Narrow Field") and is accessible from either direction. In Viking times, the sea-level was rather higher than at present, so this dùn may well have been associated with the "vik" or "inlet" of Scalasaig. Piggott remarked (1946): "Dunan a' Mhiodaire. – I could find no one who knew the exact location of this, but suppose it refers to a rocky mass in the middle of what is still one of the best pastures in Scalasaig, between the village and the harbour, on the north side of the road." It seems strange that Piggott ignored the more likely location. A very similar dùn is sited immediately behind the fuel-pumps opposite the Post Office, at NR 394942.

5. House-sites. There are some relatively significant house sites running from about twenty yards north-east of the hotel at NR 38966 94203 and onwards in the same direction, perhaps 17th or eighteenth century. A little further down the hill was the site of pre-war "clay-pigeon" competitions, nowadays held at Machrins. In those days, the "clays" were blue balls made of glass and packed with feathers – providing a satisfactory illusion of authenticity when hit.

6. Wells. Three wells worthy of note include the excellent one opposite "Maggie Thomson's Cottage" [NR 38803 94105], which provided Scalasaig with its drinking water in high summer until as late as 1980 – the reservoir above Bruthach a' Bheannain was unable to cope with any period of more than five or six weeks without rain; less attractive was the well on the right at the top of the church brae, at NR 38931 94115. Both of these wells are already choked with vegetation and nearly lost. There is a surviving well in slightly better condition at the present glebe, between the new manse and Port a' Mhinistear ("Minister's Bay") at NR 39667 94497. This one is fully built, with a proper capping, and still shows faint traces of the lime which was regularly applied to all such wells – the last person to apply lime to this particular well was the late Ross Darroch, c. 1960. In November 2009, this too was fast-disappearing; another one lay a short distance to the north, but was effectively obliterated during the construction of the new manse.

7. Loch na Sgùid ("Loch of the Shelter"). There is a possible cup-mark at Loch na Sgùid. "Sgùid" apparently derives from an old German word which has carried into English as "shed" and it refers to a simple form of dwelling made by laying thatch across poles which have been positioned against some convenient vertical or overhanging rock face. Sgùidean are very common on Colonsay, but the one at Loch na Sgùid seems to testify to their antiquity through the apparent Bronze Age cup-mark which may be seen in the middle of the prostrate slab beside it at NR 38322 94764.

8. Tigh Dhonnchaidh an Oir ("House of Duncan of the Gold") is about 250 metres northeast of Loch na Sgùid at NR 38242 94949. It is tempting to think that this house may have been connected with Hector MacMillan, who was paid in gold to pilot a French ship in the mid-eighteenth century but absconded with the money instead, leaving his brother Ian to carry out the task. Perhaps Hector's son inherited the sobriquet?

LOCH STAOSNAIG WALK *This walk gives a glimpse of Colonsay through the ages; centred on Cnoc na Faire Mòr, it reveals something of the strategic importance of the island. Easy walking; allow 1.5–2 hours. Start at the War Memorial, close to the harbour.*

THE WAR MEMORIAL

The memorial commemorates nineteen persons, sixteen from the Great War and three from World War II – all of these persons had strong Colonsay connections. Their individual histories have been researched and published by Alan Davis in *"Colonsay's Fallen"* (House of Lochar, 2004). Note the impressive field wall passing behind the memorial.

From the War Memorial, walk south, keeping the Exhibition Gallery to your right.

THE HARBOUR

Built in the early nineteenth century at the supposed expense of the then Laird, John McNeill, almost certainly to the design of Thomas Telford (who also designed the slip at Feolin and the harbour at

Lagg, both in Jura, as well as the landing places at Keills and Carsaig). The manual labour involved was immense – on the north side of the harbour wall one can see a granite stone which was being prepared for use, but which had insufficient drill-holes and failed to split. The "feather-and-wedge" remains trapped fast in the rock – each such hole had to be cut by hand, with one man holding and turning the "bit" whilst two others addressed it with sledge-hammers. The harbour was a big improvement on the original and rather primitive landing place constructed at Port na Feamainn ("Seaweed Port"), built with the help of a small grant c. 1770 to permit the export of the flax crop. This was known as Laimrig nan Each ("Landing Place for the Horses") and lies to the south of the present slipway, being visible at low tide. The 1804 map shows a simple quay (no slipway, harbour wall or breakwater) where the existing "knuckle" is located, but this seems to have been added to the original drawing and may represent "work-in-progress".

In 1802, Telford was asked to report to the Lords of the Treasury concerning communications in the Highlands: "**COLONSAY QUAY** – An application for assistance in constructing a Quay in the Island of Colonsay, near the Isle of Jura, has lately been laid before us; and there is no reason to doubt of the utility of such a Work; but We would not consider ourselves authorized to grant any Aid towards making a Quay, except as it may form part of any Road to be made under our direction." Thus John McNeill may have paid the entire cost of the harbours at both Colonsay and Lagg, and 50% of the cost of the works at Keills. Unless, of course, he built a road to qualify for financial assistance. Careful study of the 1804 map shows no trace of any road or track from the harbour and no buildings in its vicinity. Perhaps the southern road was created in association with construction work at the harbour, and the one which is now in use was built soon afterwards, to meet the specifications of the Lords of the Treasury.

Unfortunately, Colonsay's harbour was never completed. Attempts to complete the work in the twentieth century were again abandoned with the outbreak of World War II and a further proposal in the early twenty-first century was rejected by plebiscite; this latter proposal was intended to create a non-drying basin of 2m depth. Nonetheless, the harbour was once a valuable asset to the island and at the centre of many activities; the MacAllisters built boats (and made coffins) at the Well House (two-storied building, outside stone staircase), nearby there was a sawpit and (in the north-west corner) there is the remnant of the weighbridge. A small crane was sited on the slip, but became redundant when the new pier was completed (1965); credit for the pier is attributed to the efforts of the then-hotelier and County Councillor, the late Arthur Jones. In the fullness of time it was sold to Caledonian MacBrayne for a nominal £1.00, allowing it to be improved by the addition of a linkspan. Since 2007, ownership of the pier, harbour, cattle pens and even the war memorial has passed to Caledonian Maritime Assets Ltd., a company wholly-owned by the government.

The limit of a remarkably high tideline is marked beside the door of the stone-built boatshed. Following the South African War, the island was provided with a Memorial, in the practical form of a Waiting Room for David MacBrayne's steamers; this building is now used as a gallery for local exhibitions. Set back a little from the harbour is Glen Cottage, built 1881 as the Telegraph Office. Note the well-preserved section of Galloway dyke through which the road passes, a very distinctive feature of Scalasaig farm; as mentioned elsewhere, the stones are laid in vertical courses, a technique introduced by the McNeills in the early eighteenth century. Further examples of Galloway dyking are to be seen at Balnahard and at Sgreadan, Upper Kilchattan.

Pass the cattle grid and go through the gate in the south-west corner of the paved area, which was constructed for light industrial purposes in association with the advent of mains electricity in 1985.

The house on your right as you pass through the gate was built after 1876 and has an attached "annexe", which was for many years the island store. It was operated by Donald McNeill and survived as a shop until the 1960s. The track winds up towards the Church, and was briefly the main route to and from the harbour; note that from this approach the buildings ahead and to the right form a modest but competent architectural composition. Soon after the church was built (1802), it seems that the hotel was extended and later, together with the Parish School, created a visual harmony that has now been lost to casual observation. (The school is now a private house and has been enlarged in recent years).

THE SCHOOL

Although the church was built in 1802, the school was evidently rather later; by 1876 it also served as the Post Office (the original "Mail Room" door and sign are now in the hotel). It must have been short-lived because it was closed when the Education Act of 1872 concentrated all education at the former SSPCK building in Kilchattan, and it clearly did not exist on 25 October 1824: "Butter recorded 20 pupils had attended Scallasaig School during the summer and 35 during the winter. The teacher, Malcolm McFadden, who was 36 years old, had 2 years' service with the SSPCK. His house was an old hut and there was no schoolhouse. The pupils met in an old cowshed, which did not have doors or windows. There was no other school on the island." The school became an annexe to the hotel between the wars and one resident built steps as a short-cut to the hotel brae… traces of Staidhear an Eirionnaich ("The Irishman's Steps") can still be seen.

THE CHURCH

A seventeenth-century map reveals that the Church is built upon the site of a pre-reformation foundation, and a neighbouring cist-grave confirms that this was a sacred site in the pre-Christian era. Curiously enough, although the present church was built as lately as 1802, it seems to have had a chequered history – by 1834 there was a need for repairs estimated at £32 but that need was perhaps ignored. A visitor in 1857 commented: "When built – perhaps sixty years back – it was rather a respectable place of worship for that time. It is now dingy and desolate-looking. Its largest windows are decaying, and have been injured also by the storms. They are now clumsily shut up by pieces of undressed wooden boards. The ground around the church is unenclosed. In this state, the building is found by cattle to be particularly convenient – "in cold a shelter, and in heat a shade." The apt reference to Isaiah 25:4 continues to be applicable – the redundant south doorway now houses an air-to-air heat pump which helps to protect the building by maintaining a constant temperature and humidity.

Continue past the church along the old track, leaving the modern road below you, on the right.

Note Garadh nan Craoibh ("Garden of Trees"), the mature mixed plantation of deciduous trees, planted c. 1850 by Lord Colonsay, which flourished in the lee of this rocky hillside. You are now crossing Na Drommanan ("The Little Ridges"), a glaciated area that shows traces of numerous small dwellings as well as extensive areas of lazy-bed. Many of the remaining boulders show the marks where they were drilled and split by wedge and feather technique to provide building stone. The track winds to the left, passing the "header tank" associated with the installation of a mains water supply in Colonsay (1986). There is a fine view of Dùn Eibhinn ahead, with Carn Cainnle ("Candle Cairn") behind it; the cairn is in line with mid-summer sunset when viewed from the dùn.

After passing through a rather boggy hollow, the track climbs again. This is a suitable point to break away to your left, climbing to the monument on Cnoc na Faire Mòr.

CNOC NA FAIRE ("OBSERVATION HILL")
Note: On a calm day, or with a light westerly, approach the summit quietly – there is a good view down into Loch Staosnaig and otters are frequently observed.

One of the few significant limestone features on the east side of Colonsay, Cnoc na Faire sustains a distinctive grass-grown summit. This is one of three look-out posts sited along this side of Colonsay which are all within easy sight of each other and of an associated hill on Islay, just behind the present lighthouse at Rubh' a' Mhàil ("Tribute Point"). Owing to dangerous waters both to the west of Islay and to the north of Jura, sailing craft wishing to travel between any southerly point (Man, Ireland etc.) and a northerly one (Skye, Inverness, Norway) would for preference pass through the Sound of Islay. Colonsay gained a vital strategic significance, since no craft could enter or leave that Sound without the risk of being sighted and intercepted from the island; small outposts at Rubh' a' Mhàil and at Eilean Fraoich ("Heather Island"), at either end of the Sound of Islay, secured the stranglehold. It was for this reason that Colonsay became a Viking headquarters, and the same strategic element was crucial in the eventual defeat of the Vikings, when their approaching fleet was attacked and destroyed at Rubh' a' Mhàil, by Somerled (Epiphany, 1165). An old name for Colonsay, Eileann Tarsuinn ("Blocking" or "Crosswise Island"), reflected a significance which persisted until the seventeenth century.

Return to the track, cross it to the left of the boggy hollow and continue westwards for 100 metres.

There are two upright stones here [NR 38666 93760], one of which (aligned east-west) is believed to be a small standing stone that was incorporated into a subsequent field boundary. The other stone is supposedly a fragment of that boundary.

Walk south, crossing the track once more and then abandoning it as you make your way down to the head of Loch Staosnaig ("Sea-loch of Stony Ridge Bay").

Amongst the short grass and heather to your right there are two prominent stone arrays which may be ancient burials [NR 38691 93621 and NR 38700 93528]. Looking south across the valley there is a small arable field, containing a Viking grave and the fascinating Mesolithic remains which were mentioned in Chapter 1. Dated to 8,700 years ago, postholes, fixed hearths, a midden pit, high quality flint tools and even apparent ornamental material suggest a sophisticated community. On the very summit of the hill behind the Mesolithic site [NR 387929] there is a kerb which marks the remains of an elaborate Bronze Age burial cairn, and in a corner of the bay, behind the fence, at NR 38810 93240 is Tobar Staosnaig ("Staosnaig Well"), an ancient well now sadly choked with vegetation but which would probably repay archaeological investigation.

LOCH STAOSNAIG

There is good holding ground and deep water in this sea anchorage; the Royal Yacht "*Britannia*" was a regular visitor for many years, which is why it is often locally called "Queen's Bay". Two markers at the head of the bay indicate the line of the 11,000 volt undersea cable from Islay, which was laid in 1985. The sandy bay provides safe bathing and is little frequented; a small, secluded recess on the south side of the bay will usually yield a handful of cowrie-shells.

From the shoreline at the bay, begin to make your way north-eastwards along the margin of the vegetation.

There is an interesting small dùn at the northern edge of the head of the bay [NR 38941 93455], into which a later hut intrudes slightly. It is bracken-crowned in summer, but courses of drystone masonry can be seen as you approach from the south-west (it is beside the third electricity pole on this line). Carry on past the fourth electricity pole and cross a low wall to enter a patchwork of small fields ("Na Leideagan") highlighted by a few gnarled whitethorns, the vestiges of once stockproof boundaries. On the rocks below a small cliff there is a Carraig ("Fishing-rock"), which can be identified by the bait-hole created in the living rock. Such bait-holes are pudding-bowl shaped and provide a mortar in which limpets, winkles and other bait were ground up before being cast upon the water to attract fish; they are always at a point where there is deep water and where the shore is steep-to. There are at least four at this location [NR 39120 93512], but access is difficult – the site is in line with the final mid-span before the electricity line turns away inland.

Continue along the path, which runs inland for a few metres and then to the right, close to the electricity turning-post, dominated by the bulk of Cnoc na Faire.

There is a sacred well beside the coll above you on the left, Tobar Na Gaoith Deas ("The Well of the South Wind") at NR 39208 93745; Symington Grieve recorded that it was "patronised by mariners and fishermen. They left votive offerings and small presents at the well and prayed for a south wind. I was told in all earnestness that their petitions were granted…" Continuing along behind the shoreline, ravens will often monitor your progress. Pass the scant stone remnants of Fang an Rudha Dhuibh ("Black Point Fank") at NR 39301 93646, about 8m x 2m; it is bracken-clad but identifiable by visible courses of masonry. After perhaps another 100 metres one approaches a small hollow beside the shore, where there is the outline of an eighteenth-century cottage at NR 39425 93680, set back in a sheltered but commanding position. John Clark (who farmed Scalasaig for many years) mentioned that this building served as a smiddy for sharpening the quarrymen's tools during the construction of the harbour. It is flanked on one side by a square-built byre, and on the other by a rather fine *sgùid* or "rock-shelter"; the house had a clear view towards Rubh' a' Mhàil across the tip of Eilean Mhàrtain ("Martin's Island"). Notice the rusty cables running up from the shore to the wreckage of the old "cable hut" – these were the submarine telephone cables, redundant since the advent of the radio-relay system in the 1960s. Closer examination will show that the cables run up a stone slip, made at the turn of the nineteenth century in association with the harbour construction. Seemingly stone was quarried here and transported to the building works by barge, although the actual facings for the harbour were quarried in Mull.

From here, there is the remnant of a wall, heavily robbed, the line of which leads directly from the ruined house to the harbour. A diversion out to the point will permit an inspection of the lighthouse.

THE LIGHTHOUSE

The modern lighthouse is solar-powered and replaces one which was fueled by gas. Elsewhere in the island has been preserved An Cruisgen ("The Cruisey", or "Oil-lamp"), Colonsay's original lighthouse, as designed by Stevenson; this has been gifted to the community by the Northern Lighthouse Board. Made of boiler-plate iron sheets, it was unfortunately cut up into sections and will require skilled restoration.

Return to the harbour, picking up a slight track that leads down to the gate at the light-industrial site; just before the gate, notice the Pot Barley Stone, carved into the living rock behind "The Pantry", in line with its eastern gable at NR 39386 93989.

POT-BARLEY STONE

This is a clach-chnotaidh ("Mortar Stone"), one of several such stones that once existed on the island; they were used communally to grind barley for the preparation of porrage and meal, perhaps also for brewing and distillation purposes. Fine-ground flour for bread was prepared by hand querns (one of which may be seen at the hotel entrance) or in a Muileann Dubh ("Black (i.e. "secret") Mill"), of which the best surviving example is at NR 376908.

Return to starting-point, perhaps visiting the Harbour Well, behind the Coast-guard Hut, at NR 39033 94077.

Chapter 5

RIASG BUIDHE TO BALAVETCHY
Map: page x

This area, on the east coast of Colonsay and north of Scalasaig, comprises two late mediaeval farms but has for many years been incorporated into the combined home-farm of Kiloran. It extends to c. 1400 statute acres, almost all of which is classified as "rough pasture". Riasg Buidhe ("Yellow Dirk-grass") is near the centre of a farm identifiable in late mediaeval records as one of "the twa Killoranes", which came to be known as Dùn Ghaillionn ("Homestead of the Blizzard"), whilst Balavetchy is still known by its original name ("Baile Mhaide" = "Pole Farm").

Nowadays the area is almost completely uninhabited, having just eight residents, all of whom live at Glassard ("Green Cape") in the south-eastern corner, closest to Scalasaig. In the 1841census the area had a total of 156 inhabitants, but even then only one household of three persons lived in Balavetchy. Of the rest, 64 lived at Riasg Buidhe itself, and 26 lived in four households at Glassard.

The topography of the area is heavily affected by glaciation – the contours have been sculpted to remove any cliffs or rocky outcrops and the exposed slopes have been denuded of any soil that might have existed. There is a small but very obvious area of limestone at Glassard, between the houses and the sea, backed by an extensive area of Kiloran flags. The limestone supports a healthy crop of grass, but the flagstone is more suitable for building use than for agriculture. The flagstone extends to the top of the hill and north-wards beyond Riasg Buidhe, but closer to Loch Fada is replaced by phyllites which continue beyond Riasg Buidhe as far as Rubha Carraig nan Darrach ("The Darrachs Fishing-Rock Point"). The phyllites are largely grass-covered, even to their summits, and also support the important ancient woodland at A' Choille Mhòr ("The Big Wood"). Beyond A' Choille Mhòr there is another area of marginal ground – Cnoc Mòr ("Big Hill") is an almost barren head-land, beyond which there is the aptly-named Coille Bheag ("Small Wood"), consisting of a sparse and struggling cover of pioneer species (mainly birch).

There are no listed buildings in this area, but there are five significant monuments.

Beinn nan Gudairean, NR 388948

There is an interesting and venerable brass plate on this summit, which identifies many of the places to be seen in clear visibility. The fact that it identifies the "Irish Free State" gives a clue to its age, since the term was abolished on 1st July 1937 with the adoption of Bunreacht na h'Éireann ("Constitution of Ireland"). The plate was erected in 1938 but, presumably, had been commissioned the previous year. The regular summer visitors of those days made many such contributions to the island, as was recalled by the late David Todd: "*The conclusion of the 1914/1918 War marked the end of an era which all wished quickly to forget. The release from fear and tensions showed in many forms and to those of us who returned to holiday at Colonsay it found expression in many daft days and in many daft ways…*"

David and Jane Todd, Sandy and Jean Cook, George K. Ward, James Tullo, Mrs. Tullis, Crawford Findlay, Mrs. "Nell" Logan and many others spent many happy summers based at the Scalasaig Inn under its benign host, the incomparable David Clark. They went in for amateur dramatics, ran regattas, went lobster-fishing, 'plash-netting, golfing and everything else. They put cups beside wells, made movies when such things were a complete rarity, and formed innumerable clubs, under the umbrella of the "Hon. Council of Colonsian Thiefs" – "*This Society was created in 1922. The Minutes presented mostly nonsense but the fun did help to while away the time in the long night journey round the Mull of Kintyre. The spelling of "thiefs" was intentional*". Most club crests were associated with "The Great Seal" – a three letter device made by adding two short side strokes to the Y of a Younger's beer-bottle label, so as to create a monogram meaning "*You're Looking Fresh*", the standard greeting. The brass plate was refurbished and its wooden nest was renewed about the turn of the century by the late Finlay MacFadyen. The designer was James Macaulay, a Glasgow based town planner (died 1971), who was also responsible for designing an indicator on Craigs Top at Greenock in the thirties (*David Squires, pers. corr.*)

The plate is of such interest that one can fail to notice that there is a small dùn on the very top of this, the second highest hill in Colonsay. It was originally about 14m in diameter and although very seriously eroded there is sufficient fallen material to show that it was significant. Its lofty position suggests that it may have been an observation post and in fact one can detect the foundations of just such a later use of the site; in the early part of WWII there was a Coastguard lookout station here, although it was subsequently transferred to Machrins. "*Gudairean*" is perhaps a corruption of "*dudaire*", "trumpeter", "war-horn blower".

Dùn Ghaillionn NR 402958 *(550 metres northwest of Riasg Buidhe)*
This is the site that was mentioned in Chapter 2 as having been the home of Iain a' Chuain ("John of the Ocean"). It is described by RCAHMS as being "severely ruined", presumably because a later rectangular building has been imposed upon the original structure. The interior of the dùn is only about 6m by 4m; the exterior of the wall can be seen along its southern face. The position of the dùn is exactly midway between the later farmhouse to the north-east and the latest of all, the shepherd's cottage at Bonaveh. It overlooks a former lochan and has commanding views, but one cannot but wonder if the more immediate attraction was the proximity to the neighbouring land at Cnoc na Bealaidh ("Broom Hill"). Both sites are within clear site of the hitherto unidentified Dùnan a' Chullaich at NR 382967 (the other half of "the twa Killoranes").

Hut-circle, Corr Dhùnan NR 38467 95180
About 400m north-west of Beinn an Gudairean there is a well-preserved hut circle of about 5.5m in diameter. The substantial wall is about 1.6m thick and survives to a height of 40cm. There is an entrance to the south, with a "stone-revetted forecourt". As so often in Colonsay, there is a small annexe attached to building, near the entrance but in this case its open side is somewhat exposed, facing to the west. *This site is hard to find – see note at the end of this chapter.*

Hut Circle NR 399962
Not far from the former avenue to Colonsay House, but not easy to reach because of boggy ground, a fence and a ditch. A gate at Ceann Loch leads from the avenue onto the hill. Described by RCAHMS as "situated on a terrace on the SE side of a low knoll" the hut-circle is about 7.5m in diameter internally, has its entrance on the south-east and has a small annexe attached to the west south-west exterior. Perhaps the annexe was for a dog or pig.

Chapel and Burial-ground, Riasg Buidhe NR 405954
RCAHMS recorded in 1975 that "there are no clearly identifiable remains of a chapel", but this is not strictly true. In summer, the site (NR 40562 95436) is heavily obscured by bracken but, even then, the wall-footings can be traced by persons familiar with the site. The casual visitor will easily identify the twin basins of a rock-cut pot-barley stone; the closest wall of the chapel is perhaps 1m to the south of this stone, which is very close to the north-east corner. A prominent gravestone within the chapel site is close to its south-west corner (facing north and hard against the south wall) and should help to establish its outline. The interior measurements recorded by the antiquary William Stevenson in 1880 were "about 18 feet by 12 feet" and these are verifiable.

Note that the important 9th-century cross now preserved beside Tobar Odhran at Colonsay House was originally sited at the east end of this chapel, and was evidently made for and at this location, since the stone is from the immediate vicinity. Latterly, it had been used to cover the wells upon which the community relied, some 100m east of the chapel, where water trickles from a vertical rock-face. Commander Stewart removed it for safe-keeping before 1880, although it seems to have been damaged in the process. (See below for further details).

Riasg Buidhe Settlement, NR 406955
Described by RCAHMS as a "nineteenth-century fishing settlement", Riasg Buidhe was clearly established on a site of ancient significance, as witnessed by the substantial stone-built chapel and high-status cross mentioned above. The surviving remains are typical of late eighteenth-century or early nineteenth-century clachans in Colonsay, as existed at Baleromin, Uragaig, Port Mòr, Scalasaig and – doubtless – elsewhere, save that Riasg Buidhe remained in occupation until after World War I and the buildings have not been demolished for re-use of the materials. The main "street" originates with a single cottage, onto which other buildings have been attached so as to amount to a total of eight dwellings. Although the men-folk were latterly involved in fishing, the community shared 63 Scots acres of pasture and may well have held one of the last-surviving run-rig tenancies in Scotland. (See below for further details).

Additional places of interest
The walk described later in this chapter includes a number of sites of interest.
They are listed here, together with a few others, loosely grouped by proximity and in a logical order.

1i: Glassard (Glas Àrd, "Green Cape") NR 39896 94814

The houses at Glassard were built in 1922-3, as part of a national programme to provide "homes for heroes" in the political aftermath of the Great War. They were used to re-house the former population of Riasg Buidhe, and with their completion Colonsay became the first community in Britain wherein every household had both running water and a fixed lavatory.

These houses are a reminder of one of Colonsay's unsung heroes, the remarkable Dr. Roger McNeill (1853–1924). The son of a Baptist family at Kilchattan, Roger McNeill attended the island's SSPCK school under the instruction of Neil McMillan and went on to enter Edinburgh University. He graduated in 1877 as Bachelor for Medicine and Master of Surgery, travelled the world as a ship's doctor and then became resident medical officer to the Infectious Hospitals of the London Metropolitan Asylums Board. During the 1880–1 smallpox epidemic, he served in the hospital ships *"Atlas"* and *"Endymion"* in Deptford and subsequently published a paper which gained him a First Class Honours degree and an Edinburgh University Gold Medal.

A student under Lister, Dr. McNeill never lost touch with his roots and returned to Scotland to take charge of the Gesto isolation hospital in Skye. He was an impassioned campaigner for public health and it was largely through his efforts that a code of preventative medicine was established; in due course he was appointed the first County Medical Officer for Argyll, the first such post to be established anywhere in Britain. He was an acknowledged international authority on the treatment and the prevention of tuberculosis.

Throughout his demanding career, he found time to work tirelessly on Colonsay's behalf; he campaigned for a resident doctor (first appointed in 1897), and exposed the "grossly unsanitary condition" of the island's housing stock. In 1914 he personally served as doctor to cover the early months of the war, and he still fought to educate and assist the islanders in the ongoing battle against "consumption", as tuberculosis was commonly known. In the closing months of his life he had the satisfaction of seeing the new houses built at Glassard, and he immediately arranged for the roofs of the vacated cottages at Riasg Buidhe to be burned to prevent their re-occupation.

At his death, Roger McNeill left Colonsay an Educational Bequest which is still extant, with scope which includes for the provision of nursing care for the elderly. The whole island turned out for his funeral at Kilchattan, and the Caledonian Medical Journal expressed the feelings of one and all: "'Slan leis, cha'n fhaic sinn a leithid a rithist" ("Farewell, we shall not see his like again").

The outline of the earlier nineteenth-century houses at Glassard can still be traced, from the period when it was a farm in its own right (167 Scots acres); a typical example (rear of modern No. 5) measures barely 12 square metres and housed a family of five. Interestingly, in July 1908 the botanist Murdoch McNeill noted a specimen of *Inula Helenium* growing in an "old disused garden, Glasaird"; it seems that this plant has survived, because it was rediscovered by Trevor Patrick in 2008, growing in the garden on the seaward side of No. 7, Glassard. Only one of the original Glassard houses survives, although it has gained an upper storey; known now as "High Tor", it is on the west side of the road, close to the cattle grid.

The *"County of Argyll Twenty-Sixth Annual Report"* was issued in 1920 and the author, Dr. Roger McNeill stated that "In the Island of Colonsay 7 dwelling houses for the working classes, old-age pensioners, and paupers are being erected by the proprietrix, Lady Strathcona... the four semi-detached houses are approaching completion and the remaining houses will be completed this summer." There seems to have been some delay, because it is known that the first tenancy was not awarded until 1922 as detailed below.

Glassard has grown in recent years but we seem to have identified all the early 1920s inhabitants, through the kind efforts of Mrs. Flora McNeill, Mr. Duncan "Sandy" McAllister, Ms. Melanie McKellar, Mr. Alastair Scouller, Mr. Donald "Gibbie" MacNeill and Mrs. Frances Patrick.

No. 1: Jimmy Reid.

No. 2: Duncan McAllister, uncle of Alexander Sandy McAllister and great-uncle of Duncan "Sandy"McAllister; Alexander and Hessie married in 1923 and took over the tenancy in that year.

No. 3: Coll McAllister and his wife Annabella (Bella) MacNeill.

This was the first house to be occupied, as Bella was expecting her eighth child, Donald, who was born in 1922 (d. Canada 2009). The tenancy was inherited by Katie "Coll" McAllister c. 1954 and the property is now the home of Alastair Scouller (who is Bella's great-great nephew).

No. 4: Alexander "Ceistear" ("Catechist") McAllister, father of Sandy & John. Alexander died 17th April 1927 and the tenancy passed to John. Note that Duncan, Coll and Alexander were brothers and another brother, Peter (the original Para Mòr of Glassard), was single and lived at No. 4 until his demise.

No. 5: Catriona "Alasdair", sister of Archibald McNeill, "The Bard".

No. 6: Sandy McPhee "Greusaiche" ("Cobbler"), followed by the Darrach brothers.

No. 7: Archibald McNeill, "The Bard", whose works include the fine song "*Oran na Glasaird*"; apparently his house was the last to be occupied. He was followed in the tenancy by Bella and Sarah MacNeill, aunts of Donald "Gibby" MacNeill.

No. 8: Mrs. Catherine McLeod with sons Donald and Iain MacLeod. Sandy McAllister did not remember her Christian name, but "she was a Darrach, Colonsay born and bred". Melanie McKellar identifies Mrs. McLeod as Catherine McFadyen, daughter of Neil McFadyen and Margaret Darrach. Neil had died at Riasg Buidhe in April 1901, and Margaret McFadyen died at Glassard September 1929, aged 97. Mrs. McLeod died at Glassard in 1956; her husband John was from Lewis and had been a shipwright in Greenock.

Note that Nos. 5 and 6 were originally built as a single unit "so planned that it may be occupied by one or more tenants according to the size of the family". This flexibility was based upon a common stair, but was altered at a later date to create two separate semi-detached houses.

1ii: The Mate's Seat NR 40248 95017

There was a direct path from the harbour to Riasg Buidhe, which can still be traced; reference to the Ordnance Survey 1st edition will help. The Mate's house stood midway between the two locations, and such provisions as he required would have to be carried on his back. In those days the common size of a sack of meal etc. was 10 stone (140 lbs.), so he was inclined to pause at this point – to smoke his pipe! Notice the adjoining rock, which provided a platform at the ideal height upon which to rest the sack.

1iii: The Mate's House NR 40443 95342
This is a building of particular interest since it is quite remote and has not been disturbed – it is an excellent example of a late-surviving mid-eighteenth-century home. The site is bracken-clad in summer but at other times of year one can clearly trace the main living area (c. 5m x 3 m) and the adjoining byre. We know little about "The Mate" beyond the fact that his name was Alexander Campbell and that he lived here in 1841, together with his wife Peggy (aged 50) and one servant, Barbara Blue (aged 20). At that time, he gave his age as 65 years and he was an "agricultural labourer". In the census of 1851, he was living alone and gave his age as 83 years, his place of birth as Islay and his condition as "pauper" (*i.e.* retired). His death is recorded on January 14th 1852. Records show a marriage on June 6 1828, between Alexander Campbell and Peggy McCannell; since no children were baptised to the union, it seems possible that this was the same couple.

1iv: Carn More NR 40119 95206
The name – "Big Cairn" – is sadly belied by the tiny and rather jumbled structure at the summit, but it seems that the original cairn was destroyed for some reason by a party of sailors in WWII. Duncan "Sandy" McAllister recalls that the children in Glassard decided to reinstate it on their own account, and the existing cairn is simply a tribute to their efforts. Some years ago, the hill was subjected to "muir-burn" to improve the grazing, and this revealed the outline of a very substantial structure, evidently of archaeological importance. Whether or not it will have been intact before it was destroyed by the Navy is unknown, but the surviving remains are sufficient to indicate an unrecorded burial site. It is noteworthy that this site mirrors the one at Milbuie (NR 387929), where there are the remains of a substantial kerb-cairn, 16m in diameter.

2i: A' Phàirc Dhubh ("The Black Park") NR 40164 96010
There were four houses with 27 inhabitants here in 1841, close beside the trackway that ran between Riasg Buidhe and the "old" road to Colonsay House (at that time, the only such road). Although the houses are difficult to identify, there is a hardy survival in one

garden, a lonely, stunted holly-bush. Not far away, at Laonery (now
the sheep fank) there was the house of the schoolmaster, Alexander
McNeill, with his five dependants. By 1851, another house had been
built, within the policies and beside the loch, home to Finlay
McMillan, "Wood Ranger", aged 48, born Colonsay – was this the
"Finlay of Colonsay, Stalker to Campbell of Islay" who was
photographed on 17 April 1846 by Robert Adamson? Almost
certainly, since he was a native of the island yet not resident here in
1841 – presumably living and working in Jura at that time. His
house has gone, but his image is preserved in the Scottish Portrait
Collection and at least the name of his house survives (Ceann Locha
or Kinloch).

2ii: Cnoc Bealaidh ("Broom Hill") NR 40064 95853

As mentioned above under Dùn Ghaillionn, this piece of ground is
worthy of attention. Sections of "lazy-bed" cultivation can readily
be seen, the small enclosure to the south (Goirtean nan Chaorach,
"Sheepfold") seems ideal for lambing and some traces on the
summit suggest more intensive agricultural use, perhaps for
winnowing or as a stackyard. Writing in 1909, Murdoch McNeill
referred to broom as having been "Recorded by Mr Miller. Within
living memory two plants existed: one on an uncultivated hillock in
Caolachadh, and one in Glaic-a-Chuill. Like the whin, it yields a
green dye". There are two places with each of those names, but it
seems likely that the reference was to the sites on the south-eastern
slope of Beinn a' Sgoltaire.

3i: Cnoc na Faire ("Look-out Hill") NR 40762 95984

There are three such hills, as mentioned in Chapter 4. This one
(with the three items which follow) is included in the recommended
walk. Cnoc na Faire is well-worthy of a visit in its own right, a fascinating spot with magnificent views and a very special aura. It is ideal
for picnics and sunbathing.

3ii: The Fever Village NR 4056396085

An interesting eighteenth-century farmstead, abandoned since early
in the nineteenth century allegedly due to smallpox. We are told
that "there is no treatment or cure" for this disease and that there is
a 30% mortality rate; the last known outbreak was in Somalia in
1977. Until the 1970s, local people consciously avoided this site.

3iii: Creag nan Teasaiche (Fever Rock) NR 40611 95981

Food was left here for the victims of the smallpox outbreak. Interestingly, it appears to be aligned east-west and it may well be the stump of a standing-stone. There are a number of cup-marks on the exposed upper surface, presumably dating to the Bronze Age. One might expect there to be burial sites in the vicinity, as yet unnoticed.

3iv: Port Olmsa ("Holm Port") and Carraigean ("Bait holes") NR 41020 96111

There is an extensive array of "bait holes" or mortars for ground-bait, all along the length of the natural quay at Port Olmsa. Note that this was the main landing-place for Colonsay before Scalasaig harbour was developed and it is linked with a curious tradition. A French ship – allegedly carrying Bonnie Prince Charlie – is said to have made a landfall here and to have engaged the services of two islanders as pilots. They were MacMillan brothers and were both paid in advance in gold, but one of them welched on the arrangement; the other gave faithful service and afterwards stayed with the ship and eventually settled in Dunkirk where he married and raised a family. Whilst there is every reason to doubt the personal involvement of Prince Charles, there is the possibility of a kernel of truth in the story. As mentioned in the Introduction to this book, Captain Thurot of the French navy made a sudden appearance in Islay, on February 16th 1760, where he obtained provisions by negotiation with three local lairds, including Godfrey Macneil; full payment was made, mostly in gold. He had apparently already spent some time in the area between Islay and Colonsay.

Famously, Thurot had spent many years as a smuggler and had an intimate knowledge of the British coastline. In 1759, he had been asked to lead an expedition to create a diversion in Scotland, whilst a major French force would proceed to reinstate Bonnie Prince Charles; his instructions were to capture or terrorise coastal population centres. All these details were eventually made public in *Chamber's Edinburgh Review*, so one can imagine how the reference to Prince Charles, to a Macneil and to a payment in gold could have created a local legend. Even more to the point, it is said that historian Nicholas MacLean-Bristol of Coll discovered an extraordinary document in the archives of the French Admiralty describing a contingency plan to seize Colonsay for a naval garrison. Details in the document are said to suggest some knowledge of both Port Olmsa and its hinterland. One wonders if there is any record of a MacMillan household in late eighteenth-century Dunkirk.

3v: A' Choille Mhòr NR 410965

The O.S. map depicts but does not identify A' Choille Mhòr ("The Big Wood"), lying just to the north of Port Olmsa. This is said to be a survival from the ancient Caledonian forest and provides a wonderful native habitat for wildlife of every form. The trees are of native species such as birch, alder, hawthorn, rowan, willow and aspen and they include magnificent sessile oaks ("sessile" meaning that the leaves are attached directly by their base, rather than by a stalk). Closer examination will reveal that many of these trees were at one time coppiced, being regularly cut to produce straight timbers ideal for roofing and other purposes. The coppicing ceased many years ago and had been forgotten until naturalists John and Pamela Clarke recognised the signs in the 1970s, thus explaining the placename Baile Mhaide ("Pole Farm"). The subject was discussed at greater length in Chapter 3.

In high summer A' Choille Mhòr is almost impassable without a guide, but between November and early June it is possible to walk through it. It is a perfect haven for delicate flowers and insects and bolder visitors who attempt it in summer are advised to keep close to the southern and eastern boundaries, where they should be able to follow a discernible path. To the east, there will be good views of a colony of Common Seals, and often a sighting of an otter family which has a holt on Eilean Olmsa. Down along the shore there are nesting terns – these birds are under great pressure and their breeding colonies are best avoided. Notice the lichens – there are 132 recorded species in the wood. Keep an eye open for orchids, including the fragile lesser twaeblade, for a wide variety of ferns, and for the beautiful hummocks of sphagnum moss. Sphagnum harbours a water supply of its own – if one gently presses one of these great mounds, one can see the whole thing wobble like an enormous waterbed. A' Choille Mhòr is a very special place and will repay careful study – butterflies include the purple hairstreak and there is even a unique subspecies of water-beetle.

3vi: Ancient structure in A' Choille Mhòr ("The Big Wood")
NR 4075 9641

An enigmatic structure, most easily discovered by careful reference to an Ordnance Survey map. A short but good track was evidently provided to link it to the old track leading from Port Olmsa to Kiloran, perhaps when this part of the island served as a pleasure ground for Colonsay House. It was first surveyed in 1974 and described as: "undoubtedly the remains of a small kerb cairn still in good condition. The site occurs on a wooded rock terrace and comprises a ring of four upright stone slabs approximately 6.0m in diameter, several fallen slabs, and two external stones (a false portal?) set at right angles to the perimeter of the kerb on the SE. The central area is filled with a disturbed scatter of stone slabs and rocks. Just off centre is a firmly embedded stone which may have been part of a cist." However, in 1981 J N G Ritchie stated that "Position and surviving remains suggest this is a round house".

N.B. The next four items can only be reached by going west from the outer edge of Cnoc Mór Carraig nan Darroch (not by walking south along the shore); access involves slippery, difficult rocks and is unsuitable for children or dogs.

4i: Carraig nan Darach (Fishing-rock of the Darroch family)
NR 41632 97204

This is rather a good example of a site for a "Fishing Rock", although the mortars are hard to reach and do not look as if they had much use. However, they do indicate habitation at this currently remote and uninhabited spot. A tiny house (3.6m x 2.4m) is at the top of the slope, at NR 41431 97321. Nearby, (NR 41436 97400) there is a remarkably well-preserved circular dwelling (unrecorded), complete with a small annexe, perhaps for a dog or a pig. The upright stone was perhaps to lead smoke through a central vent in the thatch.

4ii: Chain "grown-through" by rock NR c. 41659 97187

There was a great storm in 1880s which led more than 20 vessels to take shelter in the lee of Colonsay, close to and all along the eastern shoreline. Possibly this was the storm of November 1881, which overwhelmed the quarry at Easdale. During the night there was a wind shift and the ships were all put into danger – some went ashore, although none was seriously damaged. Many of them lost anchors and chain – one such vessel gave its name to "Roc *George*" at Glassard, where the ground tackle was discovered by David Johnston in 2007. Another was in difficulties here at Rubha Carraig nan Darach, where the living rock subsequently appears to have grown over and through the chain. An interesting curiosity, probably an accretion of barnacles; it is only visible at low tide and the exact location may be on the promontory about 50m south of the suggested co-ordinates.

4iii: "The Goat Cave" NR 41607 97145

This rather unpromising cave is a natural shelter for the feral goat population and is one of the places to which they resort *in extremis*. It was therefore regarded as a likely source for horn – the late Finlay MacFadyen used such material to make many beautiful shepherd's crooks. (There is another "Uamh nan Gobhar" at Balerominmor and a "Tigh Bhoc Góibhre" ("House of the Billy-goat") at Machrins).

4iv: Natural Arch NR 41645 97166

This is quite a small example but, if you happen to be hereabouts in any case, it might be worth noticing.

5i Former Home of Iain a' Chuain NR 402968

This little-visited and un-named dùn at Blàr na Bantighearna (Lady's Level) was the original home of John of the Ocean, as described in Chapter 2. Apparently the family lived here initially, but they had a cockerel which (because of their location) was the first to greet the dawn each morning. Unfortunately the laird, MacPhee, was living nearby in An Sabhal Bhàn (The White Barn) of the old Abbey, well within earshot. The insolence of this cockerel proved to be too much for his wife and, in consequence, the MacNeills were forced to relocate to Dùn Ghaillionn. More prosaically, with the dissolution of the monasteries MacPhee may have re-ordered the Abbey lands, taking Balavetchy for his own and dividing Kiloran into two new farms, of which Dùn Ghaillionn was awarded to the MacNeills. The other section, Dùnan a' Chullaich ("Homestead of the Boar") is at c. NR 382967 but its tenancy is not recorded.

Part of the original trackway to the old landing-place at Port Olmsa may be clearly seen beside the dùn and the area is rich in camomile. The surviving but heavily-robbed structure is about 12m x 8m internally, and the entrance can be recognised between two doorjambs on the south side.

5ii: Hut circle NR 40527 97111

This is a well-preserved and unrecorded site on the shoulder of A' Phàirc Gharbh. It consists of a double-chambered structure, comprising a hut circle of about 3.6m internal diameter and an associated D-shaped annex of 1.8m internal radius. The remains of a wall makes a connection with the footings of a detached rectangular building, c. 1.8m x 3m. The site is a lofty one and although there are interesting traces of occupation there is little sign of cultivation; possibly a shieling?

5iii: Glaic nan Cnàmh (The Dell of Bones) NR 40491 97229

The obvious biblical reference is slightly misleading as in fact the name seems to refer to an opening on the western side, near the top of the steep slope. Sheep or goats can easily enter it, but must be able to come out again backwards. They do not always achieve it.

5iv: ?? Natural souterrain in A' Phàirc Gharbh (The Rough field) NR c. 405971

Very possibly this place does not exist, but it used to be mentioned quite often in the "Bar Parliament". According to the tale, there is a small and unguarded opening in the ground high up at A' Phàirc Gharbh which is difficult to find but which drops into a bottle-shaped chamber from which it is very hard to escape. Various people described it – David McConnell maintained that the late Para Mòr had once had to go down into it with a rope, to rescue a sheep. In fact, just such a chamber does exist in Balavetchy, above the shoreline at Port Cheann a' Gharraidh, so perhaps this one really does exist as well.

5v: Sgùid Pioghaid (The Magpie Shelter) NR 36239 94981

Quite a good example of a Colonsay sgùid or shelter if you happen to be in the area. One of the few whose name is recorded and the only known reference to the Magpie locally (Murdoch McNeill).

6i: Modern burial sites

There are a number of isolated graves. Two stones from the monument in A' Choille Mhòr seem to mark a modern inhumation, there is a grave at Garradh nan Coineanan ("Rabbit Field") (NR 40787 97338) and another on Druim Buiteachan ("Witches' Ridge") at NR 40182 96576, aligned facing east. More remarkable are "The Sassenach Graves" at the foot of Cnoc Inebri ("Meadowslope Hill"), in a warm and sheltered spot (NR 40891 98149). Seemingly a location of choice – a resident of Balnahard was approaching the small ford at the foot of the Bealach when he met a stranger, who extended his hand in greeting. No sooner did their hands touch but the stranger vanished, and the luckless islander lost all power in his arm. Word got round and soon afterwards the stranger appeared again, this time to someone out shooting rabbits, who was too wary to approach him. Instead, he pointed his gun and asked him who he was and what was his business. He was told that he was the spirit of the poor sailor whose remains had come ashore recently, being washed halfway up the burn by the tide. When found, the remains had been but roughly buried, by placing them alongside the burn and tumbling the sandy bank down to cover them. Every time there was a flood, the remains were inundated and the sailor could get no peace. Once this was known, the remains were lifted and re-interred in their present, more acceptable location. The site of these graves is hard to find, but was identified by the late Dugie MacGillivray.

6ii: Viking Boat burial NR c. 40117 97765
The burial was discovered in 1881 and excavated by William Galloway, an architect who had been commissioned to carry out extensive restoration work at Oransay Priory (notably the east gable, the mullioned window and reconstruction of both the high altar and the western arcade of the cloisters). The discovery was attributed to his employer, Sir Malcolm McNeill and was the subject of a paper by Dr. Joseph Anderson (P.S.A.S. Vol xli, p.443).

The exact location of the site is not known, but the co-ordinates given above are for the spot that was pointed-out to the present writer in the 1970s. Note that another boat – MacLean's Birlinn – was also drawn up into the sand-dunes and allowed to moulder away; there might be some confusion between the two sites. Locations for both sites are given on a map published in "*The Book of Colonsay and Oronsay*" by Symington Grieve and re-used in the present book. Although there is nothing to see on site, the artefacts recovered from the excavation form an impressive display at the

National Museum in Melville Street, Edinburgh.

In brief: a Viking ship burial was discovered but it is unclear whether the vessel was buried in the upright position or upturned. The deceased was buried with his sword, spear, axe and shield. He also had the "elaborate" harness for his horse, as well as a set of scales and weights, plus three pierced (*i.e.* defaced) coins issued between 808 and 854 A.D. His horse was buried outside the perimeter of the ship, and there were stones at either end of the grave upon each of which a cross had been incised. Although this is usually described as "the only known" Viking ship-burial with Christian associations, one should remember that there was in fact another one, at Cill Mhoire (Our Lady's Chapel), in Oransay. An additional grave was discovered beside the main burial, and when first noticed was assumed to be that of a slave-girl or handmaiden; curiously enough, little mention is made of this second grave in modern reports.

Archaeologists choose to suggest that the grave is that of a merchant. One has to ask if this seems likely – it is evidently high-status, a merchant would be unlikely to have required both a ship and a horse, his crew would have been reluctant to destroy their means of transport and his armaments seem inappropriate. It seems more likely to this writer that he was a locally-resident significant leader or warlord, and that the coins and balance are open to inter-pretation. We know that at this period the Vikings had embraced Christianity, but in an imperfect manner – witness, for example, the human sacrifices associated with "the Conversion" in Iceland, or the belt-and-braces imagery on our own Dealbh an Leisg. There is also reason to suppose that Colonsay was influenced by develop-ments in Iceland at that time – the relics of St. Buo, the evangelist, were preserved in Oransay as "St. Buon Bardus" until the Reforma-tion, and there is an intriguing association between Balnahard and Aud the Deep-minded. It seems much more likely that this was the grave of an important person, who had been equipped with every advantage for the afterlife. The weapons, the horse and the atten-dant smack of pagan tradition, as does the coinage – specifically of no use in this world, but ideal to "pay the ferryman". From the nascent Christian tradition we can recognise the representations of the cross, and also the balance and weights. Nowadays we think of St. Peter as having the keys to heaven, but the Christian Vikings of Iceland recognised the Archangel Michael in that role, and for them his symbol was the balance in which he weighed the souls of the deceased.

6iii: Possible Bronze Age cemetery NR 39767 97686

Cist-graves have been found in this area. Martin Martin (1703) recorded the recent discovery of two, both containing human bones and "composed of five stones each". One might regret that they were merely mentioned as a curiosity by such an early writer, but two more were discovered by Liza Mulholland in 2007 and have not fared much better. They seem to have been examined on behalf of Historic Scotland in August 2008, and an additional five suspected cists were noted in the immediate vicinity. Unfortunately, no attempt at preservation has yet been made and even as late as April 2010 one of the graves (which had been half-heartedly "protected" by plastic bags filled with sand) was noted to be almost fully exposed to the elements.

6iv: Tigh Iain Darrach (John Darrach's House) NR 39672 97869

The site, which measures about 4m x 5m internally, can be clearly seen from the first passing place as the road ascends towards Uragaig, on a flat grassy knoll at the extreme south-western corner of Kiloran Bay. One of the most beautiful sites imaginable for a house, but also one of the most exposed. It is hard to suppose that John Darrach or his family had much comfort in the house; the current environmentalist campaign to "eat the view" would have rung hollow. We can trace a little of the history of this house – and wonder just how many people alive today could trace their recent ancestry to this spot.

In 1841, 55yr old John lived there with his wife Flory and their 15yr old daughter, Ann. John Darrach had married Flory McMillan in 1808; their daughter was baptised as "Shilis" on 9th April 1825 and was their only child.

By 1851, John gave his age as 72, Flory was 67 and their daughter was named as "July Ann", employed in General Service (presumably at Colonsay House). By 1861, "Julia" had married Angus Galbraith, and they were living in her parents' house together with Mary (4 yrs), Flora (2 yrs) and Donald (1 yr). By 1871, John and Mary had died, but Julia and Angus Galbraith had been blessed with three additional children, Lachlain, Ann and Julian (*sic*, a daughter).

The family does not appear anywhere in Scotland in the 1881 census, but that was the peak year of growth for Elderslie Township, Bruce County, Ontario and immigrants from Colonsay included families of Blue, Cameron, Darroch, Galbraith, McDougald, McNeill and Munn – most of whom came eventually to be buried in Rusk cemetery, which has as many Colonsay gravestones as are to be found in Kilchattan. It is extraordinary to know that as many as one million people now living in the New World should be able to trace their relatively recent ancestry to Colonsay, along one or other of their lines of descent. Most of them would have had their roots in some such habitation as Tigh Iain Darrach.

7i: **Supposed 16th-century House** NR 38573 95356

This important but unrecorded house was the home of Calum Caol Mac Mhuirrich ("Slender Malcolm Currie" – a Colonsay hero whose story is given in Chapter 9). The site has never been examined by an archaeologist and is difficult to interpret. In essence, it is based upon a circular dwelling of about 5m internal diameter, surviving at its greatest height to four courses of masonry. The entrance is from the south, and there are associated extramural buildings on either side of it. To the south-east side there is a circular structure of about 2 m original internal diameter, with a smaller structure beyond it. There is at least one substantial additional building to the south-west, attached to the main building and possible connected to it by a passageway.

This is the best-preserved building of its type in Colonsay, and the occupant is said to have been a retained member of the island's defence force, defined as "ane gentleman [*maintained*] in meit and claith, quilk dois no labour, but is haldin as ane of their maisters household men, and man be sustenit and furneisit in all the necessaries be the tennent, and he man be reddie to his maisters servis and advis". Although the house is in a slight hollow, it adjoins a concealed and strategically important lookout point, with commanding views from the Bealach of Balnahard and along the full the length of the vale of Kiloran and Loch Fada to the sea. *This site is hard to find – see note at the end of this chapter.*

7ii: **Tobar na Cailliche** (**Old Woman's Well**) NR 39040 95022

This much-loved well has an associated cup (awaiting a new chain,

April 2010), which was presented by David Todd and bears the YLF ("You're Looking Fresh") monogram based upon "The Great Seal" of Colonsay. The cup is inscribed "Drink your fill and Wish your will", which is a less robust message than that which was originally proposed: "Water by God, Cup by Todd". Passers-by often throw small coins into this well, which eventually will find their way to a charitable cause. Although the well is rather obvious, many people miss the associated house site, where the "Cailleach" lived – it is half-hidden in the heather on a small hillock 20 metres away, at NR 39029 95001

Walking Routes
Suggested Route 1:
The east coast, Riasg Buidhe to Port Ceann a' Ghàrraidh

It is entirely possible for a fit person to visit the sites described below in one connected – if demanding – walk; but for convenience, hints on other options are given at appropriate points in the text. Allow at least six hours for the full walk and, if alone, tell someone where you are going. You might wish to position a car at Kiloran Bay or arrange to be collected. Start from the highest point of the road from Scalasaig towards Kiloran. Just beyond it, turn right to follow a short track towards the northeast, leading to the coup (rubbish tip) at Glaic na h' Eala ("Swan's Dell"). Skirt the coup, keeping the fence on your right, and pick up a recognisable path, leading towards a roofless house.

Bonaveh ("Birch-foot") NR 39657 95431
This three-gabled two-storied house was built for the shepherd after the original farms hereabouts were combined to create a "sheep-walk". By 1878 the entire farm of Clunery, Dungallion and Glassard was in the control of Donald McNeill, for which he was paying a rental of £320. Donald McNeill, the then hotelier, was said to have had a special relationship with the laird, based upon a youthful indiscretion by "the Old Laird", but nonetheless he was paying the full rental – indeed, rather more than the £300 that was being paid for Balnahard at the time. He was a prosperous man – described in the 1881 census as a 43yr old Innkeeper, merchant and farmer of 1300 acres (of which fifteen were arable) and employing four men.

The existing house at Bonaveh was probably built in 1881 and it was occupied into the twentieth century – the census records of both 1891 and 1901 show that the shepherd was Donald Clark; his daughter, the late Mary Clark, often described the place as it was in her schooldays. Later occupants included the Buies, then the black-smith, Malcolm McIntyre, and finally Renee Hunter until about 1949. The roof was later removed, presumably to avoid paying property rates.

Incidentally, the site of an earlier shepherd's house was on the far side of Loch Turraman – this was the home of the grandfather of the late mother-in-law of Walter Williams, Dolly Ann Buie.

Continue along the path, which leads you to a ruined stone building, the precursor of the later house that you have just visited.

Home of a Direct Descendant of Malcolm MacPhee, d. 1623

This house was inhabited until at least 1871 by the "Ground Officer", Donald McPhee. Although he had been born in Jura, he is believed to have been a direct descendant of Malcolm IV d. 1623. Donald's father was Malcolm V, succeeded by Donald's elder brother John I, whose line survived in Canada until very recently. The identification is based upon the letter by "Dhushibh" which appeared in the "*Oban Times*" of March 25th 1935: "About the year 1840 John MacPhee and his young wife left Colonsay for Canada. He was the son of Malcolm, who was the son of Angus, son of Donald, son of Dugald, son of Donald, son of Malcolm, the Chief of the Clan who was killed at Eilean nan Ron in 1623." Malcolm "McFee" *a.k.a.* "McPhee" was born in Jura c. 1786 and his children were born at Brosdale, but he had moved to Riasg Buidhe by 1841, when the census shows him as living with his wife Ann (50yrs) and their children, Donald (20yrs), Cathrine and Peggy (15yrs), Mary (14yrs) and young Gilbert Clerk (9yrs); the emigrant, John MacPhee, had been their eldest son. Donald McPhee was next in seniority and remained in Scotland; in 1871 he was living in this house with his wife Mary and nine children, including three sons, John, Neil and Malcolm. The youngest, Malcolm, was 4yrs old at the time. In later life Malcolm was the proprietor of the Port-sonachan Hotel and is believed to have been "Dhushibh", the author of the letter to the "*Oban Times*". The story does not end here – see Chapter 9.

Carry on down towards the sea, picking up the very obvious route across the bare rock surface. Cross Abhainn a' Bhead ("The Mate's Stream").

Riasg Buidhe ("Yellow Dirk-grass") NR406 955

When you reach the ruins of Riasg Buidhe, note a sycamore tree well over to your right, on a low rocky cliff. When you have explored the old village, you might choose to follow the sheep track that starts beside the sycamore and go southwest, following the line of the coast at an elevation of about 20m. You may see otters in the little bay, and possibly will see some of the wild goats of Colonsay, said to have been introduced by a stray vessel of the Spanish Armada. After about 2km of fairly rough going you will find yourself back at Glassard. The gate off the hill is on a line between the fourth and fifth building on your left, otherwise just follow the obvious route to rejoin the main road at the foot of Spion Kop (NR 39875 94922).

The history of Riasg Buidhe is obscure; although the name is commonly translated as "yellow dirk-grass" there are other and more intriguing possibilities. We know that the old earth-goddess Brìd was held to be the mother of the daoine-sidh (the fairies for whom are named Clan MacPhee; the female form is ban sidh ("banshee")), and that she was known under many names, one of which was "Bui, "the Pale Yellow One", goddess of Winter Sun". Although a derivation from the original Bui is not suggested, in the same way that "Brìd" became Christianised and preserved ("Brigid"), the name of Bui also survived; one such survival was as a boy's name, "Buo". In "*The Saints of Ireland*" by Mary Ryan D'Arcy, we learn that the Feast Day of St. Buo is February 5, and she quotes from an Icelandic writer, Angrim Jonas:

"*In the ninth century, a northman, Helgo, received an Irish exile Ernulph with his religious family and gave him welcome and permission to build a church dedicated to Colmcille in a village called Esinberg. He states that a holy Irishman by the name of Buo while yet a young man became a distinguished missionary in that same province.*"

There were close connections between Colonsay and Iceland at that time. More to the point, we know that in the mediaeval period, one of the attractions of Oransay Priory was that it housed the relics of "St. Buon Bardus" (*i.e.* "the learned and pious Buo"). As further confirmation of St. Buo's significance in the area, we find that 17th missionaries reported to Rome that they had administered the Sacraments to numerous persons centred on this parish called "Giollabuidhe" ("Devotee of St. Buo", modern Buie or Bowey). The name survived locally until very recently and it is, perhaps, possible that Riasg Buidhe was at one time little more than a hermitage dedicated to St. Buo.

This is, of course, mere speculation, but on the south of the village is the rocky knoll which held An Caibeal ("The Chapel") and graveyard. A number of post-mediaeval gravestones can still be identified, although the chapel can only barely be discerned even in winter (see details above). It stood at the landward end of the knoll, 5.4m x 3.6m; close beside, on the north side, there is a rock-cut basin and at the east end of the chapel stood the small stone image of Dealbh na Leisg ("The Image of Sloth"), mentioned in Chapter 2, the origin of which is approximately contemporaneous with the life of St. Buo.

This eighth-century cross was carved from a slab of local stone, and originally was 1.3m high. The obverse bears a very fine representation of a monkish figure, and it is not too fanciful to notice the whorls that continue the artistic and religious tradition of pre-Christian Argyll. The lower part of the cross carries an image reminiscent of the Christian pisces symbol, and this was further reinforced by a "fishtail" at the foot of the shaft.

The reverse seems to be associated with a more virile tradition, possibly a symbol of fertility or potency. It has been described in various ways – writing in 1880, William Stevenson contented himself by remarking that the stone "is dressed only in front, undressed on the back", a masterly example of ambiguity. Symington Grieve went so far as to say that it was "carved only in front", but entertainingly records that King Edward VII "created some amusement by remarking it was a very good likeness of the chief engineer upon the royal yacht". The Royal Commission does at least admit to there being a reverse side, saying "the top of the head is carved in the round, the division being marked by a moulded collar *(sic)* which begins below the ears and continues onto the back, where it splits to enclose a lozenge-shaped hollow".

In truth, this is a piece of local stone carved with great skill and artistry which may be held to incorporate elements of an earlier tradition within its Christian imagery, a fine example of "belt and braces". Being local stone it suggests a high degree of contemporary Colonsay skills, and by association with Riasg Buidhe it suggests some importance for the area at that time. The small but excellent natural harbour and the close proximity of the lookout hill of Cnoc na Faire may provide the explanation.

[The Riasg Buidhe cross was removed to Tobar Odhran ("St. Oran's well") at Colonsay House in the nineteenth century and may be seen there today. Unfortunately it was broken at the time and only 1.05m survives. It is without doubt Colonsay's most important work of art and stands comparison with even the best of the mediaeval work in Oransay.]

Unfortunately, there follows a gap of over one thousand years in our knowledge of Riasg Buidhe. The present "street" of houses appears on the 1855 Admiralty chart; the buildings probably date from between about 1810 and 1815 and seem to have replaced an earlier farmstead, which is depicted on Wilson's 1804 map. The new buildings were still associated with a small runrig or joint-stock farm, in contrast to a crofting township, but without any middleman or tacksman. The records do show that a Ground Officer was appointed instead. The farm in question was very small, 63 Scots acres, all in pasture – which seems strange, since there is what appears to be a winnowing-yard some 50 metres immediately to the east of the row of houses. Possibly it is a remnant of the earlier farm. At all events, the 64 inhabitants of Riasg Buidhe (1841 census) will have been obliged to supplement their living by working for the estate until, in the late nineteenth century, a short-lived herring fishery was created and they were provided with skiffs. According to tradition, McAllisters who had formerly operated a ferry at Portnahaven in Islay were brought to Riasg Buidhe to give instruction. In fact, Coll McAllister, an existing fisherman, moved into the village from Dùn Gallion at about that time, so the tradition may be merely a hint as to some family connection with Portnahaven. The Colonsay boats landed their catch at a fishing-station in Loch Gruinart in Islay, but a great storm in the 1880s silted up the approaches. To add to the problem, steam trawlers from the east coast made such inroads into the stocks that the whole enterprise had to be abandoned; the ruins of the fishing-station may still be seen in Islay.

The villagers of Riasg Buidhe struggled on, catching lobsters and winkles along the Colonsay shore and salting herring, mackerel and saithe for winter and for bait. On the uninhabited Jura shore they made rudimentary improvements to the natural harbour at Corpach and used it as a base to extend their territory, bivouacking in the caves and returning at weekends to sell the catch. In those days, before WWI, it was possible to send lobsters up to Oban on the steamer to be at Billingsgate Market before the following dawn, a procedure which would be impossible today.

Riasg Buidhe was only one of a number of such communities, with counterparts at Uragaig, Port Mòr, Baile Raomainn Mòr etc., and it is remembered with affection for the strength of its identity and the diversity and talents of its inhabitants. By coincidence, it survived longer than its contemporaries and eventually the inhabitants were re-housed as a community, thus further preserving its traditions. Many modern inhabitants of Colonsay have family connections with Riasg Buidhe and hold it dear to their hearts.

As you stand at the head of the main group of houses looking east, the house to your right was known as the "An Caibeal" ("The Chapel"); about 4m behind its southern end one or more graves can be seen, possibly associated with the nineteenth-century famine years. The most obvious grave appears to be within a circular enclosure of 4m internal diameter; it is possible that this enclosure has been created on top of a pre-existing hut-circle. The larch close at hand seems to be of the same age as the stand which was planted within the estate policies, at Ceann Loch. Graves to the east of the chapel are marked in some cases by headstones and in others by recumbent flags – they are all aligned to face east. The knocking-stone or "pot-barley" stone beside the chapel will have been for communal use – the oblong cavity would be for shucking the barley and the mortar would be for grinding it.

The eight houses in the row are of varying date, but the most westerly one is of particular interest as it still contains the wooden crucks of a much earlier form of construction. The use of crucks pre-dated load-bearing walls, and they carried the thrust of the roof right down to the ground. It would be interesting to have this timber dated, although such crucks were the property of the tenant and could easily have been re-used in any particular period of construction. Notice that the houses have chimneys as a later addition – originally the fire was in the centre of the building and smoke exited through the thatch or through a smokehole. The chimneys were encouraged by an improving laird, John McNeill (1767–1846), who provided a grant of £10 or £12, but the inhabitants were not keen. In fact John Loder (1935) remarked that "the inhabitants took as reluctantly to their chimneys as the tenants of modern cottages are said to take to the baths with which they are now provided." However, during the 1840s, cholera became a major scourge in the over-populated slums of Britain, forcing urgent improvements to sanitation. The opportunity was seized by young Henry Doulton in 1846, who persuaded his father to diversify. Their new range of glazed pipes was displayed at the Great Exhibition of 1851 and took the market by storm. It is possible that the glazed pipe used in the chimney of the end house is an early Doulton pipe.

Mrs. Flora MacNeill has kindly identified the households of the early twentieth century. Closest to the chapel, An Caibeal was the home of Jimmy Reid and his sister, whilst the large two-storied house was that of Peter Campbell and two MacLugash sisters; in front of it was Tigh Alasdair Og, the empty home of "Duncan Balnahard's father". The other houses were in "the street", numbered from the western end:

1 The Bard's House, Gillesbuig McNeill and sister and mother
2 Mrs. MacFadyen, *a.k.a.* Mairead Darroch
3 Neil Darroch and his sister
4 Capt. Hugh Campbell and g/m Anne McCalder
5 Coll McAllister and wife and family
6 Gilleasbuig Alasdair and sister, Catriona
7 Alasdair Cholla (McAllister), father and grandfather of below
8 Maggie and Peter McAllister's parents and family

Slightly conflicting information was gleaned from Barbara "Colla" Satchel's articles in "*Gairm*" magazine (see "*The Corncrake*" archives), and the forthcoming publication of the 1911 census (April 2011) will be of interest.

From here, if you wish to cut short the trip, you have the option to return to the road, or to make your way along the coast to Glassard. Otherwise, you can easily identify the green summit of Cnoc na Faire, about 500 metres northeast of Riasg Buidhe; this can be reached with reasonable ease and provides fine views; in very wet weather you might find it easier closer to the sea. As you draw nearer, you can identify the ruins of "The Fever Village" about 200 metres to the west. Unless you intend to curtail your walk, it is probably best to visit the ruins before you climb onto the summit of Cnoc na Faire.

Na Tobhtachan ("The Ruins"), now known as "The Fever Village" NR 40563 96085

There is a poignant story about the "Fever Village", which consists of ruined farmhouses and a neighbouring house, Coll McAllister's.

According to the tale, sometime about 1855, children from these houses found a "cist" or chest washed up one day on the shore at Port Olmsa; they opened it up and discovered "plaidean" or woven fabrics which they took home to their parents. Unwittingly, they brought tragedy into their homes, for this chest was flotsam from a craft which had been stricken with smallpox and the families were both struck down. As it happened, a daughter of Sir John McNeill, the diplomatist, had been born in Persia and had been inoculated against the disease – selflessly young Ferooza McNeill (1834-71) left the comfort of Colonsay House and came to stay with the affected households. Every day, food and other necessities were left for her to collect at Creag na Teasaiche ("Fever Rock"); Ferooza stayed to nurse the victims until the end and then, unable to bury them, she burned the houses over their remains.

Although based on fact, the story is perhaps a conflation. Very possibly such a smallpox outbreak did lead to the abandonment of the main farmhouse, perhaps before Ferooza was even born, and Creag na Teasaiche got its name at that time. Rather later, in the 1850s, the family of Coll McAllister was living in the better-preserved house 100 metres to the south-west of the farm, when that household was struck by cholera. They survived and then removed to a better house in Riasg Buidhe – perhaps, during their sickness, Creag na Teasaiche was used again and retained its old name, despite the fact that "fever" is associated with smallpox rather than cholera. The fact that Ferooza had been inoculated against smallpox will have been known, but was not strictly relevant. Her father was a qualified doctor and she may well have been able to take charge of the situation. There certainly seems to be no doubt that Coll's family was afflicted by cholera; fortunately nobody died, but it is remembered that he burned the house himself. Study of the two buildings shows that Coll's house is very much less ruinous than the farmhouse, supporting the view that the two events were separated in time by perhaps a generation or more. There were originally two buildings at the farmhouse, one of which may have been quarried to build Coll's house.

Do not linger at the ruins of the older building, although the virus is said to be far from robust, but make your way back towards Cnoc na Faire, bearing a little towards the south so as to identify and visit Creag na Teasaiche.

Creag na Teasaiche ("Fever Rock") NR 40611 95981
This stands on the flank of Cnoc na Faire, about 100 metres south of the ruined farmhouse. As it happens, it has clearly had a much older significance, since the entire surface is covered with cupmark decorations so typical of the Bronze Age in Argyll. It appears to be aligned east-west and it will be found that it can be used as a sundial by use of a twig. Very possibly it was originally a standing stone which became broken in antiquity and, if so, the upper portion may yet be discovered in association with a grave. These cup-marks are hitherto unrecorded.

From here, make your way through the short heather and grass to the summit of the hill.

Cnoc na Faire ("Observation Hill") NR 40762 95984
This is the second Cnoc na Faire ("Observation Hill") in the chain which was mentioned in Chapter 4. In many ways, this is a more impressive site, surrounded as it is by natural defensive ramparts. From here there is direct line-of-sight to both Beinn nan Gùdairean *(the meaning is obscure, perhaps "Trumpeter Hill" as in Tocsin)* and Cnoc an t'Samhlaidh ("Relay Hill"), both of which are believed to have been part of the mediaeval communications system. In the distance there is a fine view of Corrievreckan, reputedly the second greatest whirlpool in the world. To the south, one can see far into the Sound of Islay and, near at hand, note the former harbour of Riasg Buidhe, Port a' Bhata (Boat Harbour). Looking north, one has an excellent view of A' Choille Mhòr ("The Big Wood") and to the north-east, there is a commanding view of Eilean Olmsa ("Holm Island") and the small anchorage that it protects. Until Scalasaig harbour was built in 1806, Port Olmsa was the main landing place for Colonsay and one must assume it was the point of departure for the early emigrants. In September 1791, no less than 28 men, 28 women and 86 children from Colonsay were "deprived of their farms by their landlords" and transported to Wilmington, North Carolina on board the *"General Washington"*, possessed of nothing but the clothes in which they stood. They were surplus people, almost certainly cleared from ancient holdings in Balavetchy and Kiloran.

Decision time: *if it is decided to curtail the walk, one should have little diffi-culty in regaining the ruins and, with a map, following a line of low hills around* *towards the west in order to join the estate trackway at the north-east end of Loch Fada. On the way, note the small dùn beside Cnoc Bealaidh – this is Dùn Ghaillionn, mentioned in Chapter 2 as the home of Iain a' Chuain ("John of the Ocean").*

Instead, but more adventurously, there is the option to continue. Descend towards Eilean Olmsa and approach A' Choille Mhór from the sea. Head at first towards the east, so as to lose height in following the shallow (but slippery) gullies; as you enter the bracken and heather be careful to identify a suitable "target" – ideally the distinctive rocks just beyond the inlet of Port Olmsa, which are covered in bright yellow lichen.

Port Olmsa ("Holm Port") NR 41020 96111

Approach quietly as you may be rewarded by good sightings of otters, seals or feral goats. As has been mentioned, this used to be the main landing-place for Colonsay and some background information is given above at 3iv. The natural slipway is easily identifiable beside the sheltered, sandy inlet – an excellent place for swimming and picnics. Common seals may be seen, perhaps hauled-out on Eilean Olmsa at low-tide. An otter spends time on the island as well – sometimes on the rocky shore, and at other times to be seen making its way along the prominent cleft leading up from the sea. There will usually be a group of shags at the nearest islet, and often a nest to be seen on the corner of Eilean Olmsa. It is locally said that the "sgart" will only nest on a north-facing cliff – this is one of the few such sites, and there is another at Slocht nan Sgarbh ("Cormorant's Gully"). Incidentally, the sgart was at one time considered to be something of a delicacy in Colonsay; apparently it would be skinned rather than plucked, and had to be boiled before roasting, so as to modify the flavour. The traditional landing-place can easily be identified and one can see numerous bait-holes or carraigean which extend all along the "slip" and for some distance beyond, suggesting that this deserted spot was formerly well-frequented. Otter spraint will often be observed hereabouts.

A natural path leads along the southern side of the inlet, inland from the edge which is at a height of about 10 metres, passing an attractive well and rivulet before reaching a natural stairway down to the sands. Be careful at the top of the descent, there is a partially concealed but very dangerous drop to your right; and at bottom, the inter-tidal rocks are very slippery – it is safest to go on your hunkers. As you cross the sand, notice the extraordinary sycamore ahead of you – typically this species exhibits a faintly "layered" effect below its crown, but it is highly developed in this instance. Just beyond the tree there is the outline of the only obvious dwelling in the vicinity, and also the remnants of a small jetty that was constructed as a hobby by the 2nd Baron Strathcona, who had a special affection for this place.

Depending upon the time of year, the next stage may be a challenge – you will be making your way northwards, but it is not recommended that you follow the shoreline as it would cause disturbance to the common seals (pupping in spring) and to a myriad of wildlife – otters, oyster-catchers, a tern colony, the ravens etc. So, you must choose between going through the woodland or skirting its southern edge and then going behind it, across Beinn nam Fitheach ("Raven's Peak"). From late June until mid-October the woodland route is definitely not recommended *unless you have a guide, but you will have no difficulty getting across Beinn nam Fitheach so the more testing woodland route will be described instead. Whichever is to be your choice, turn inland from Port Olmsa and go through the gate at the corner of the enclosed woodland, being careful to re-secure it. Distances have been given as actual average paces, which may be a help to some readers. If you really do get lost, consider retracing your steps or heading east, downhill, until you reach the fence-line closest to the sea.*

A' Choille Mhór ("The Big Wood")

Walk away from the sea, keeping the fence on your left, noticing the aspen on the cliff beyond and the shaded dell of Tobar nan Craoibhe Chrithich ("Aspen Well"). The going is tussocky but fairly easy and after about 100 paces you will be passing a south-facing bank which, in springtime, hosts a riot of early primroses and the first Peacock butterflies. The next 100 paces will be tricky in high summer due to the towering bracken, but it is possible to persevere, wending your way through young birch thickets but still following the fence line. By this stage, you will begin to notice the predominance of oak trees on the bank beside you; after a further 100 paces you must duck under a few boughs and climb a slight incline, leading up to your right at an angle away from the fence. (At the halfway point, where the fence turns away, there is an incongruous garden escape, a Japanese Azalea which is quite noticeable when in flower). You are now in amongst the oaks, still climbing a slight incline – after another 60 paces, quite suddenly, you will find yourself at a junction between two overgrown trackways. Apparently, these tracks were paved by one of the McNeill lairds, who used to keep a goat-cart for his amusement. Turn right at this point and visit the cairn at NR 4075 9641, described at 3vi (*above*). Just before you reach the cairn, there is a birch tree sporting a quite spectacular gall. Such galls are the result of insect intervention, whether feeding or egg-laying, which create increased but localised hormone production in the host. The most commonly noticed effect is the creation of "witches' brooms", which will be widely seen in Colonsay's birch trees.

If the bracken is high, turn back from this point, regain the fenceline and make your way out of the wood, either returning towards the policies of Colonsay House via the gate at NR 40304 96790 or crossing behind the woodland via Beinn nam Fiteach to regain the described walk at Lochan Clach ("Stony Loch") NR 4085 9690. Otherwise, if the bracken permits, continue beyond the cairn, descending into a dell, after which you will continue in the same direction until you reach the fence-line closest to the sea.

Pause in the middle of this first dell and look around you (50 paces). You will be able to identify examples of coppiced oak – the young trees have been cut back and new shoots have grown up from the stump. In some cases these have been restricted to a pair, perhaps for roof couples; and in one case no less than eight shoots were kept, perhaps intended as ribs for a boat? Once you are familiar with the pattern, you will be able to identify numerous other examples. Continue along the "path", with a muddy hollow to your right. After 170 paces or so, you will notice an oak sapling within a tree guard – such guards were fitted in the 1990s, so one can begin to appreciate the age of some of the larger trees. By 2010, this sapling was 5ft high and with the girth of a pencil. In light of this, the intriguing questions concern the coppicing – when was it done? When was it abandoned? Surely long ago, since there is no memory of the practice locally and the woodlands became a pleasure-ground in the mid-nineteenth century.

The trees are festooned with honeysuckle – in some cases of surprising maturity, more than 4cm in circumference (there is a good example at this spot). As you continue, the damp patch on your right evolves into a small burn and after 100 paces you re-enter an oak glade. In another 30 paces you reach the fence-line, beyond which there are glimpses of the sea and the associated wildlife. You may have noticed marker posts and bird-boxes which, like the tree-guards, are relics of a burst of interest engendered in this woodland when it first was recognised as a Site of Special Scientific Interest; sadly, the enthusiasm was short-lived.

Turn left and follow the line of the fence … 25 paces to a corner post, then 195 paces to the next corner, where you cross a reasonable burn, thick-grown with hemlock water-dropwort in summer. Cross about 20 paces in from the fence, then follow the inviting gully straight ahead, minding your head at the top, where there is a low branch. Pause after another 50 paces, to get your bearings. Coppicing will be very evident hereabouts, Now, identify the fence, about 15m to your right, and proceed, leaving it at an angle of about forty-five degrees. In 30 paces, cross a damp gully, noting the attractive ferns and mounds of sphagnum moss. Tutsan will be found growing 20 metres to your right, but ignoring that diversion press on for another 30 paces…

Suddenly, you find yourself in an enchanted glade at NR 41198 96622, where there is a magical undulating carpet of sphagnum moss and a host of delicate flowers. There are clumps of hazel, a lone whitethorn bush and in the left-hand corner a long-abandoned pathway leading back towards the south-west – it passes the only silver birch in the wood, the leaves of which are very distinctive when viewed from sea in early spring. Further along that pathway, one would reach magnificent fallen trees at Glaic an Uinnsinn ("Ash Tree Dell"), perhaps the oldest ash in the island – at the head of the dell (NR 41052 96635) is one of the few demonstrable relics of the Victorian pleasure-garden, a simple footbridge.

But our own path leads between the whitethorn (*northern corner*) and a truly splendid specimen of a mature oak with massive spreading boughs. Curiously enough, this is very close to the edge of the oak-growing section – leaving that great tree behind and to the right, strike inland and slightly uphill. You must rely upon your sense of direction here. After 75 paces, pass midway between a final pair of oaks, and in another 40 paces negotiate a plashy incipient burn. Carry on for another 35 paces to cross another muddy burn and, ahead of you, you might notice a tree with a rather distinctive "hobbit-hole" at its base (NR 41241 96747). Follow the same line for just another 60 paces (*heading towards the vertical face of Cnoc Mór Carraig nan Darrach if it is visible through the leaves*). At this point you are in exclusively birch woodland and there should be an attractive tiny lochan or mere in the gully ahead of you, covered in splendid bright-green weed. At its head (*to your left*) you pass across an old wall and will see the northern fence-line ahead of you. There is a slightly precarious stile at NR 41250 96817 (with a "sinn fhein" or home-made gap for your dog close at hand).

Cross the fence and turn left, following the fence-line. It is boggy and tussocky; near the summit there is a nice clump of great hairy woodrush, and on the left, under a low cliff, a rude rock-shelter or sgùid so typical of Colonsay. Passing over the summit, there is a slight drop to a field-gate through which you should pass – beware the barbed wire which can easily snag you at this point. The rocky summit straight ahead of you is Corr Dhùnan, beside Loch nan Clach, the point you would have reached had you chosen the alternative route across Beinn nam Fitheach. It has a great display of stonecrop.

Corr Dhùnan ("Peaked Mound") NR 41114 96984

This is the remnant of an eighteenth-century homestead, running from Slochd nan Sgarbh ("Shags' Pool") up to Lochan Clach ("Stony Lochan"). Along the side of the burn, one can see the slabbed boundary wall; at the top of the brae, the remnants of simple buildings can be traced and also cultivation rigs or "lazy beds" – note that these have been hand-dug, since a plough would have left a slight turn at the end of each rig. The dwelling might have been at the top of the lazy-beds, behind the rock outcrop at NR 41080 96991. Very possibly, this will have been home to one of the families exiled aboard the "*General Washington*" in 1791. It is an ideal picnic spot and gives an excellent view of the sea, so keep an eye open for cetaceae, particularly where a slight current can be detected rounding the island towards the north-east.

If desired, it is fairly easy to make one's way towards Kiloran Bay by heading north now, from Loch nan Clach ("Stony Loch") to Lochan Gainmhich ("Sandy Loch") and onwards into the dunes. The suggested and more attractive route is to descend to the seaward side of Cnoc Mór Carraig nan Darrach ("Big Hill above the Darrochs' Fishing-rock"), which is the impressive almost bare rocky eminence at NR 414972. There is an inviting natural path that can be seen from the top of Corr Dhùnan. It leads around the base of the hill, about 100m to the north of a corner post in the fence-line, which is beside an obvious patch of green. The path is safe and easily followed, with great views. After passing the bulk of the hill, you should head slightly inland again, after which Dùnan nan Nighean should soon be identifiable.

As you approach *Dùnan nan Nighean* by this route, you will be at the head of a slight slope – just before the summit there is a well-

preserved hut circle at NR 41436 97400, of about 3.6m interior
diameter. Note the sheltered entrance, which is slightly angled to
reduce draughts, and the smaller structure beside it on the outside,
perhaps for some domesticated animal. The large stone was perhaps
the fireback, to lead the smoke upwards to a central vent. Even in its
original state, the wall would not have been much higher – such a
building provided shelter and warmth, but very little creature
comfort.

Dùnan nan Nighean ("Home of the Maidens") NR 41572 97595

Having identified your objective, be sure to climb the final section
by the south-eastern approach in order to get the best effect. Dùnan
nan Nighean is wonderfully atmospheric – the lintel stone is *in situ*,
and one enters the "fort" by a narrow, stone passageway. Inside,
one has the perfect trysting place, secluded and with outstanding
views. This largely mediaeval structure is said to have been a mater-
nity refuge for the McPhee womenfolk, although a 1949 excavation
revealed pottery of possibly Iron Age date. However, not everything
at Dùnan nan Nighean is quite as it seems – it displays more than a
touch of artifice.

Reference has been made to a former pleasure-ground at
Balavetchy which seems to have been created hereabouts in the
early nineteenth century and of which tiny traces still exist. Ian a'
Chuain's original home was beside Blàr na Baintighearna ("Her
Ladyship's Meadow"). That name is a clue, as is the once-paved
track to Port Olmsa along which the McNeill lairds could travel in a
goatcart. On the east side of Eilean Olmsa there is a clump of *montbretia* and traces of a summer house. In A' Choille Mhòr itself are
survivals of woodland walks, still identifiable in winter, also the
silver birch and perhaps even the "Ash Dell" are hints of artifice.
Here at Dùnan nan Nighean it is easy to see the neat staircase and
the once-beautiful *parterre* by which one approaches – these are
further traces of the pleasure ground, and completely enchanting.

It has been suggested that in its original form Dùnan nan
Nighean was a passage grave. Evidence for this includes its size (too
small for normal occupation), the septal stones that may be seen
athwart the passage entrance, and its orientation. At dawn on mid-
summer's day, observation shows that the rising sun casts its first
rays directly along the passage; this may be proof of nothing, but the

experience is magnificent and easily repays the modest inconvenience of an early start.

It is possible to strike inland now, heading for the sand dunes at the back of Kiloran Bay. Otherwise, if intending to complete the walk, look northwards from the summit of the dùnan and identify the gate about 150 metres away, just beyond a bright-green boggy hollow. This leads into A' Choille Bheag, which is your next objective.

A' Choille Bheag ("The Small Wood")

This woodland was badly damaged by fire in the 1960s and by subsequent over-grazing, but in recent years it has been made stock-proof and is protected for natural regeneration. As you pass through the gate, bear down slightly towards your right and pass through a slight hollow before reaching a small but open plateau.

The Stone Circle

This structure at NR 41720 97717 has no name and has never been noticed or recorded in any other publication. The circle is 70 feet in diameter, and is almost perfect – it is particularly impressive if a large party is present; people can be positioned to highlight the line of the boundary which may be otherwise obscured by vegetation. A few comments can be made – the fact that the site has no name suggests that it is not a Victorian folly. One can see that there is very little bracken growth within the circle, although it does abound in bluebells; and there is little sign of birch regeneration within the circle. It has been suggested that the bluebells indicate very ancient woodland and that the absence of bracken may indicate a high concentration of carbon, as if there had been fires upon the site over a prolonged period. In winter, one can see another structure some 10 metres towards the southeast, which appears to be a ramp; is it possible that the reasonably prominent but broken stone on that side of the circle lined-up with some sort of marker on the ramp to assist in celestial observations or predictions? The obvious point of interest would be the summit of Beinn an Oir, the highest of the Paps of Jura, and one can imagine that in antiquity the fires of mid-summer (Christianised as St. John's Eve) would have been focused on that point. It is a curious site and awaits proper investigation.

Continue now towards the northeast and Port Ceann a' Ghàrraidh ("Port at the End of the Boundary"), noticing the remarkable birdlife – there are plenty of small songbirds here, which thrive upon the sheltered but more open habitat. Because there is no live-stock, the arachnids have come into their own – it is almost like walking through the Palace of the Sleeping Beauty. The webs have formed a forest of their own, with threads of every size running between every twig and almost every leaf and blade – look closely, and see the spiders themselves. Some are absolutely tiny, others would look good in a horror film – walking will be slow here, because it is difficult to pick a route which will not damage these intricate creations.

Approach Port Ceann a' Ghàrraidh quietly as you may see an otter in the sea below, or feral goats on the opposite shore. This is a peaceful spot (NR 41950 97972), ideal for a pause; you may well see a Golden Eagle above the hillside to your north.

From Port Ceann a' Ghàrraidh, turn to the southwest, aiming to pass to the north of Dùn Dubh ("Dark Mound"). As you cross the burn, look out for bog bean and royal fern, and perhaps lesser twae-blade orchids on the other side; as you ascend, following the slope towards a wooded glade, there are some fine specimens of aspen. As you walked through A' Choille Bheag you may have noticed slight traces of old pathways, and now you will find that you are walking up a narrowing, climbing glen at NR 41669 97908, unmarked on the map but actually called Asgaill Dùin Duibh ("The Oxter of the Dark Hill"), which must have been a highpoint of the old pleasure ground. This glen is moist, well-sheltered but not too dark – it contains a wonderful selection of mosses, lichens, fungi, and ferns and supports a rich colony of plants and insects; it is an absolute jewel.

At the top of An Asgail, keep to the right to avoid a morass; there is a strong fence post and rough stile (NR 41483 97905) over which you can climb and beside it there is a place where a dog can squeeze under the fence. There is a sheep path to your left which will lead you downwards and onto the green grass of the machair.

As you pass behind Dùn Dubh, glance to the right where you will see a distant stand of sycamore on the flank of Cnoc Inebri ("Meadow-slope Hill"), beside the romantic ruin of a tiny house, which is yet another part of the pleasure garden; and as you approach Lochan na Gainmhich you will pass beside the substantial ruin of Tigh Cóinnteach ("The House in the Moss") at NR 41142 97751. This is also known as Faing nan Each ("The Horse-fank") and is where ponies were kept, at the very centre of the Victorian pleasure-ground, so ghillies could bring picnics to the desired location or provide transport for more delicate members of the house-party.

Continuing, the route winds around to your right, behind sandy dunes which are covered in – quite literally – millions of tiny snail shells. Fraser Darling described such situations: "Full advantage is taken of the lime-rich conditions [of the machair], and snails abound in such quantities that there may even be inter-specific competition. *Helis aspersa*, *Hellicella itala* and *Cochlicella acuta* are found, and several slugs (*Agriolimax* and *Arion* spp.)" This area is rich in flowers – centauri, scarlet pimpernel, mountain thyme, storksbill, soft cranesbill, mouse-eared chickweed, lousewort, etc.

As you come over the crest of the slope, tiny Lochan Gainmhich will be on your left- at this point you will be able to identify two prominent mounds which border the damper ground, e.g. NR 40830 97736. When rabbits were first introduced to Colonsay in the early eighteenth century, special warrens were built to house them, here and at Ardkenish Glen. Timbers and stones had to be laid down to create a matrix that was covered with sand and turf; apparently such care was necessary at the time whereas now it would be unthinkable. It does seem strange to be told that, within just 300 years, a species which was prized and carefully preserved could be reappraised as vermin.

From this point, turn left across the dunes to regain the main road at An Crosan and head for home.

Suggested Route 2:
Visiting the house of Calum Caol MacMhuirrich (1 hour, medium difficulty)
Start from Loch Turraman and walk up the "old road" so as to visit Tobar na Cailliche (Old Woman's Well) [NR 39040 95022] and her house-site 20 metres further on at NR 39029 95001 (see 7ii above). Continue up the track for another 80 metres or so, then turn to your right to ascent the steep slope – you will see a communications mast to your left, but you should be heading more to the right, following the remains of the path used by the Coastguards in WWII.

There was a look-out post on this hill in the early years of the war, until it was replaced by the one at Machrins. As you approach the top of the slope you will quickly identify the O.S. "trig-point" on the summit of **Beinn Gudairean** (see note under RCAHMS sites, above).

After inspecting the dùn and brass direction-plate, identify the isolated farmhouse in the distance at Gortain, at the back (west) of Upper Kilchattan. Walk towards it for 400 metres, to find the **Hut-circle at Corr Dhùnan, NR 38467 95180** (see note under RCAHMS sites, above). This will not be easy in the heather, but the stones which flank its doorway will help; in the vicinity you may notice traces of an ancient field-system.

Leaving the hut, climb the slight slope to the north and identify Kiloran farm – in particular, notice the white gable of the old farm-house and the length of straight road running towards it. Make that your leading point and you will quickly reach the ruins of Calum's house, having passed a small sgùid or rock-shelter on the way (see 7i above).

On leaving the ruins of Malcolm's house, head to the north-east on rising ground and you will soon be able to identify the coup (fence, recycling containers etc.) beyond Loch Turraman. Make this your final objective; you will find probably yourself drawn a little too far to the left, towards the sheep-fank, but can correct this from time to time. You will have very little difficulty if you maintain your heading.

Chapter 6

BALNAHARD
Map: page xi

Balnahard (Baile na h'Airde = farm at the cape) lies at the north end of Colonsay and is effectively separated from the rest of the island by a rampart of forbidding hills. Behind those ramparts lies some richly fertile land; its strongly defensive capabilities have proved important, because there are significant archaeological remains from every period in Colonsay's history. The farm comprised 850 Scots Acres, including 117 described as "arable and meadow" according to David Wilson's 1804 survey. Nowadays about 60 statute acres of arable land is cropped for silage. Balnahard, like Balavetchy, is completely uninhabited, but this was traditionally the home of the Mac Mhaolain family (*anglice* "MacMillan", or more commonly in Colonsay, "Bell").

We know from the Statistical Account of Scotland that in 1794 the total population of Colonsay was 718, even after the exodus of 1791 aboard "*The General Washington*", when the writer acknowledged that "a considerable proportion of the inhabitants crossed the Atlantic". Since there were fifteen farms at the time, two or three of which had already been "cleared", Balnahard may have had a population of about 60 souls, working the land on the "runrig" system under an hereditary tacksman.

In 1806, ownership of the island passed to John McNeill, a gifted and "improving" agriculturalist who had worked the island as factor on behalf of the existing laird. He had already created a home farm by the dispossessions of 1791, but he now adopted a more progressive approach and offered financial inducements to persuade the tacksmen of Balnahard and also "Kerramore and Ballevourich" (part of modern Kilchattan and Kiloran) to emigrate. He chartered an excellent ship, "*The Spencer*", and arranged for them and their subtenants to settle in Prince Edward Island, with sufficient funds for each family to be established in 100 acres of freehold land. These emigrants reached their destination on 22 September 1806, a total of 64 males and 51 females having survived the journey. The youngest was Gilbert McLean, just 3 months old, and the oldest was

Duncan Bell, at 78 years; at least one third of the party had Bell or MacMillan connections.

Of course, those people who remained in Colonsay will have had an imprecise account of what had taken place, which led to a traditional tale as recounted by the late Andrew MacNeill (in 1997). Incidentally, one should know that Andrew was not speaking naturally or using his normal vocabulary in this instance – it was quite clear that he was passing on the account as he had received it, and it is also clear that the story was originally given in Gaelic and had been translated into English *viva voce*:

"Did you ever here how the Bells came to be cleared from Balnahard? Well, it was like this… there was some sort of a dispute that they had, something to do with how the land was to be worked that year and they couldn't come to any agreement. Eventually they decided to put it to the laird, so a couple of them went down to see him in Kiloran and they explained the whole matter and asked him to make a decision. "Well", said the laird, "I am very busy just now, but I will think the matter over and do you come back in such-and-such a time (it might have been the same time and place next week or in two weeks) and I will let you have my decision." So, they went away home and came back again as was arranged to see what he had decided. "Well", he said, "I have thought about it carefully and this is what you'll do. Go you back up to your houses and pack up your traps, because there is a boat coming tomorrow to pick you up and you are all going over to Canada. And that is what they had to do. They say that they did not even come back down from Balnahard, but sailed away from the beach there and up to Oban where they joined the ship."

In fact, there was no reason to go up to Oban and they will have sailed directly from Colonsay to the New World; but the traditional story indicates that runrig was still in operation, which was at the heart of the matter. Runrig meant that individuals worked narrow strips of land which adjoined those of their neighbours and which were re-allocated from time to time in the interests of parity. Of course, this required close co-operation amongst the joint tenants of the (unfenced) land and provided no incentive for improvement of the soil. The minister, whose statistics were quoted above, confirmed that change was in the air when he had remarked in 1794 that:

"The system of converting arable into pasture, is making rapid progress in Colonsay. The best part of the island is under black cattle; these are in great request among the graziers, and thought to be a very fine breed. The art of abridging labour, and keeping a few good cattle, has not yet established itself in this distant corner. Those innocent animals, the sheep, are totally banished, although … nature seems to have destined the heath-covered hills for their use."

The new, "improving" laird had taken the hint and was determined to "abridge" labour completely, by clearing the land and renting it at high rent as a sheep-walk for lowland graziers. As is now known, sheep, "those innocent animals", are a deadly enemy to man – where there are sheep, there will be depopulation. Worse still, because of selective grazing and through the damage caused to natural drainage, the quality of the land is quickly and irredeemably degraded. Balnahard is a good example of this process – since 1806 the farm has never thrived, despite generations of capital investment. Families came and families went, but for two solid centuries it has been operated only by absentee farmers or as an adjunct to some greater interest elsewhere.

In some cases, the tenancies lasted for generations, but in others it was quite fleeting. In Kilmartin graveyard one can see the following inscription:

In memory of / Euphemia MacAlphin / spouse to Alexander MacTavish / late tenant Drimfin, North Knapdale / who departed this life / 18 July 1842, aged 59 years / erected by her son / Archd. MacTavish, Taxman / Balnahard, Colonsay / also his sister Euphemia / died August 1858, aged 34 years / also the above named Archd. MacTavish / late tenant, Daltote / who died at Saltcoats / 7th April 1908, aged 87 years / his second son Alexander MacTavish / who died at Glasgow / 5th March 1930, aged 79 years / Until the day break.

Thus we see that Archibald MacTavish was born c. 1821 and was in Balnahard c. 1842; his second son was born in c. 1851. Yet, so insubstantial was their presence that the name MacTavish does not appear anywhere in the 1841 Colonsay census. In point of fact, there were 32 residents at Balnahard in 1841, labourers for the absentee farmer; and by 1901 there were only three (by which time the "farmer" was Prof. Donald Mackinnon, Chair of Celtic Studies at Edinburgh University).

At present (2010), the freehold of Balnahard Farmhouse and steadings is owned by David Hobhouse, whose family have held the agricultural tenancy for over seventy years.

There are no listed buildings in Balnahard, but there are significant monuments listed by RCAHMS:

Cairn, Cnoc Beag, Beinn Bheag ("The Small Hill") NR407984

This is on the "old" route to Balnahard, just below the summit at Bealach na h'Airde ("Cape Pass"), about 10m in diameter and about 1m high. There are "several massive kerbstones visible round the perimeter" and the large broken slab at the centre may mark the site of a ruined cist grave.

Cup-markings, Uamh na Mine ("Meal Cave") NR404985

"On the southeast face of an isolated boulder situated in the mouth of Uamh na Mine ("The Meal Cave") … there are two cup-marks, measuring 60mm in diameter by 40mm in depth." Actually, they are outside Uamh Shìorruidh ("Endless Cave"), and the "boulder" is in fact a piece of fallen rock. The author discovered that there are very many more cup-marks up above, where the rock originated. In addition, David Jardine has found other examples, on a rocky knoll up on top of the cliffs.

Standing Stone, Clach a' Pheanais ("Penance Stone") NR421999

Aligned east-west, this stone is not far from a Bronze Age cist grave, discovered by David Hobhouse. Doubtless this was a revered pre-Christian site that was "sanctified" by the neighbouring chapel. The stone is 1.25m high and 1.2m wide. It is only 0.3m thick and it stands at an angle.

Standing Stone, Cnoc a'Charraigh ("Standing-stone Hill") NR426994

Prominently positioned but in an area which is nowadays of limited agricultural value, this stone is 1.4m high and about 0.5m by 0.4m in girth. A neighbouring prostrate slab is enigmatic – it has been assumed to cover a cist-grave, or perhaps to be a fallen standing-stone. A presumably natural mark on the surface of the slab resembles a sword-blade in quite remarkable detail. Digital photography of the underside (via a convenient rabbit burrow) reveals nothing of interest.

Fort, Dùn Meadhonach ("Middle Fort") NR414999
In a magnificent location, this fort is one of a chain which runs along the western coast of Colonsay. The summit is about 55m x 24m and it stands upon a rocky knoll at an elevation of about 30m. There are the remains of an annexe at a lower level on the northeast side. The entrance can still be traced as a stairway leading up from the south. The fort was presumably associated with the safe harbour at Port Sgibinis ("Ship Point Harbour"), from which there is easy access. It is at the centre of a fascinating tradition, which will be mentioned as part of the described walking route.

Dùn NR421995
"This dun occupies the summit of a small knoll... it measures about 14m by 8m within a wall of which several stretches of the outer face are still visible". Beyond noting the entrance on the east, and that the interior is divided symmetrically by a spine of rock, it attracted no particular comment when surveyed for the RCAHMS.

Dùn, Port an Obain ("Port of the Pools") NR409996
On a grassy knoll, overlooking the ferrying place for crossing to the Ross of Mull; 8m x 6m within a low surviving wall. Well worth a visit. Interesting traces of other buildings are close at hand, possibly mediaeval.

Hut-circle NR413998
400m north-northwest of the farmhouse, on a south-facing slope and of 5m internal diameter.

Hut-circle, Beinn Bheag ("Little Peak") NR405986
Not far above Tobar Chaluim Chille, this impressive hut-circle on the flank of Beinn Bheag is up to 6.8m in diameter within a wall which is 1.8m thick. The entrance is on the south-southeast, and the building has at some point been reduced in size by interior walls, creating a sub-rectangular space – perhaps it was adapted in connection with the nearby shielings (NR406986)

Chapel and Burial-ground, Cill Chaitrìona NR421998
The chapel is thought to be dedicated to St. Catherine of Alexandria (whose carved representation may be seen in Oransay) and stands about 7.1m by 3.5m within very thick walls (1.5m) and to a

height of about 1m. Four funeral cairns can be easily identified, also an associated house of about 5.5m internal diameter. A mortar or font lies outside, near the south-west corner of the building, and there is an echo of an altar within. The structures are within a recognizable garth, in the western corner of which may be seen a rude but attractive cross, well-polished by the cattle. It bears a very close resemblance to the Cross of St. Catan, which was recently discovered near Port Mór (see Chapter 9). Another cross, more ornamented, was recovered from the site in a damaged condition c. 1880 and is now preserved in the National Museum. This latter cross has a simple cruciform inter-laced design carved upon it in relief enclosing four cross-head holes which pierce the stone.

Tobar Chaluim Chille ("St. Columba's Well") NR404986

This well is easily accessible from the caves and associated cup-marks at Uamh Shìorruidh, and is very convenient for the hut-circle at Beinn Bheag (NR 405986). It is built in traditional style, with a solid lintel and a corbelled chamber. Like most ancient wells, it has a tradition of healing and good-luck; supplicants left small offerings of cloth or ribbon until the late nineteenth century although nowadays a small coin is more usual.

Shieling, Beinn Bheag ("Small Peak") NR406986

This is a substantial structure and in an unusual location if it is indeed a simple shieling, but local tradition had it as a hiding-place for cattle in times of peril. Certainly it is a place that casual marauders would be unlikely to visit, and it is quite invisible, even from the top of neighbouring Carnan Eoin ("Bird Hill"). In essence, a surrounding dyke forms a roughly circular enclosure of c. 56m diameter, within which there are the remains of four substantial buildings. Outwith the dyke is a smaller building, on the eastern side, which might command a view of Bealach na h'Airde. To the west, and at a lower level, there is an additional enclosure and faint remains which might be associated with more conventional booleying.

Shieling, Càrnan Eòin ("Hill of the Bird") NR410985

Although many people climb Colonsay's highest hill, very few visit this site which is about 100m to the east of the summit. There are "vestiges of at least five roughly circular structures" in a slight hollow. Each consists of a single chamber about 2m of internal diameter and with walls from between 1m and 2m in thickness. There are traces of external annexes on two of the buildings.

Additional places of interest

The walk described later in this chapter includes a number of sites of interest. They are listed here, together with a few others, loosely grouped by proximity and in a logical order.

Leab' Fhalaich Mhic a' Phi ("MacPhee's Hiding Bed") NR 40618 98385

This is one of seven such lairs which allegedly mark the route of the last MacPhee clan chieftain, who was hunted down and executed in 1623.

Port Easdail ("Horse Dale Harbour") NR404984

This is at the centre of an area of plutonic activity and an area of particular geological interest. Most of the island consists of low-grade meta-sedimentary rocks, enlivened by fascinating dykes and erratics, but the Lewisian gneiss of Balnahard and the syenite and breccia etc. of Port Easdail provide a contrast. The exact relationship between the contrasting geological formations is not as yet fully determined.

The Whale NR404995

A chance outline on the raised beach at Sgibinis inspired artist Julian Meredith to create a "sculpture" of a whale, 183m in length. It is best seen from the air, otherwise from the summit of Beinn Bheag or Carnan Eoin.

Georgina's Stone NR403993

The pillar-stone on Meall na Suiridhe was erected by David Hobhouse as a gift to his sister, Georgina, to mark the occasion of an important birthday (May 2003).

Clach na Gruagach ("The Gruagach's Stone") c. NR 4155 9975

An interesting example of a libation stone. At every milking, some of the first milk from each cow was poured into the basin "for luck". There was a practical purpose of course, as it would reveal signs of mastitis etc., and such a practice was widespread. Identifiable sites are now quite few and this particular example is of particular interest insofar as the stone has been especially selected and erected in position. The natural basin has also been artificially enhanced by leveling and by the addition of a drainage channel.

Carraig Nighean Maol-Choinnich ("Bald Kenneth's Daughters Rock") NR 41834 00259

A large, rounded boulder, weighing perhaps 30 tonnes, which appears to be balanced perfectly upon a point no larger than an egg.

S.S. "WASA" – shipwreck on beach, Tràigh Bàn, Balnahard

The scraps of wreckage still to be seen along the shoreline belong to the wooden Steam Ship "*WASA*" of Liverpool (1919) which caught fire and was taken under tow before she grounded in Balnahard Bay and was subsequently wrecked. She was in ballast at the time. The wreckage was later dynamited by salvors trying to extract copper fittings and scrap, and the bulk of the wreck is about 200 metres offshore. It is now a favoured place for fishing.

Lewisian Gneiss outcrop, Tràigh Bàn, Balnahard

Just beyond the very north end of the bay, there is an exposure of Lewisian gneiss, one of the oldest rocks on earth and one which is relatively unusual in the Inner Hebrides. It is described as an igneous rock, folded and highly metamorphosed, about 2,000 million years old.

Sgùid nam Ban Truagh ("Shelter of the Miserable Women"), near Tràigh Bàn, Balnahard

Set back about 100 metres from the shore, on the south side of the bay, under Cnoc Corr ("Steep Hill""). This is probably the best preserved of all the sgùidean or "rock-shelters" in Colonsay, and clearly was in occupation within historic times, presumably in the opening years of the nineteenth century. The outlines of the accommodation arrangements can be clearly seen, and the cultivation rigs or "lazy beds" of the last inhabitants survive. When the inhabitants of Balnahard were cleared to make way for a lowland grazier, there may well have been one or two folk who were simply too old or frail to make the journey. It seems that this sgùid was occupied by just such people, who were allowed to remain on in their home until nature took its course.

Port Araraibhne ("Port of the Small Cornfields"?) NR 424986

This is rather a good natural landing-place and unsurprisingly one can see the remains of a circular dwelling (hitherto unrecorded) at the head of the beach. Slight traces of cultivation and other dwellings can be found in the immediate vicinity.

Shieling at Maol Buidhe ("Yellow" or "Favoured Hill") NR 419981

This is a previously unrecorded site. Clearly it served as a shieling and one can discern small structures beside the houses which may have served as cleits, to store butter and cheese etc. Closer examination of the various buildings shows that the original structures were circular. They are sited beside the ancient trackway from Port Ceann a' Gharraidh leading up to Balnahard – famously the route by which a MacLeod raider from Mull, Iain Mhic Iomhair, was pursued to his death as he attempted to swim out to his ship. It seems possible that this site would reward archaeological investigation.

Walking Route

Balnahard is somewhat remote and a worthwhile visit will entail a round trip of about 16 km. Vehicular access is not normally permitted, although exceptions are usually made for registered disabled persons with access to a suitable vehicle. It is a splendid walk, but there is no shade – on a sunny day, parents should take particular care to protect young children. Allow at least 6 hours, rather more if you decide to make your way back overland, along the east coast.

Leave the public road at An Crosan ("The Small (religious) Cross"), where the track crosses Abhainn a' Mhuilinn ("The Mill Burn") and leads north across the sand-dunes. Cars may be left inside the gate. The walk to be described totals about 16km, but at all times you will be reasonably close to the farm track and should be able to turn back if desired.

As you breast the first hillock (300 metres), you will notice a deep hollow to your left – this is perhaps the site of the important Viking ship-burial, the subject of an impressive display in the Royal Museum, Edinburgh. In addition to his boat, the male occupant of the grave was buried with his horse and its rich harness, also a sword, spear, axe, shield and arrows. A bronze scales, balance beam and lead weights were also buried, together with some coins. The coins were issued by Eanred I (808-41) and Wigmund, Archbishop of York (831-54); taken with the scales, many people have thought that they suggest the burial site of a trader. On the other hand, Barbara E. Crawford (author of "*Scandinavian Scotland*"), points out that the grave goods as a whole might be just right for a Viking chieftain, "who had based himself on this favoured island of the Inner Hebrides from where he carried out his raiding and 'trading' activities".

Interestingly, two stone slabs which protected the grave bore crudely incised crosses; these are quite extraordinary, making this the only Viking ship burial ever to be discovered with overt Christian associations. The incongruity is further heightened by the close proximity to Iona, and by the presence of other human remains, which the Victorian excavators suggested could indicate a sacrificial hand-maiden! At all events, the mixed messages inherent to this burial are reminiscent of Dealbh na Leisg, and were discussed in Chapter 5. Note that an alternative site is marked upon the map in this volume, as remembered by Symington Grieve, who assisted in the excavation.

Whilst crossing the sand-dunes, keep an eye open for chough; here and elsewhere the grazing is managed for its benefit, since its diet includes both burrowing-bees and dung-beetles. It is jet-black apart from its orange beak and feet, and can be easily identified by its distinctive call and by its very playful and sociable aerobatics. As you near the far end of the dune-system, notice the extraordinarily large "lazy beds" on your right; presumably an ill-judged attempt at cultivation damaged the maram-grass and the wind exaggerated the profile of the rigs. Perhaps originally known as Muran Bèarnaiche (meaning "Mutilated Maram"), the name lost its significance and the ridges eventually became "Barney's Sandhills". These days, the protection of the marram grass is a high priority throughout the Hebrides, but there is an even-worse example of ancient damage near Seal Cottage in Oransay, where the sandy soil has actually engulfed the field wall.

Cross the burn (for the story of the Sassenach Graves, see Chapter 5). Turn towards the sea instead of following the track up into the hills, but note the

*spot… if anyone is unwilling to scramble across some rocks or to climb a difficult
1m high rock, they will need to return to this point shortly and follow the track
instead.*

Almost as soon as you leave the track, close in below the rocks, there
is an unusual structure (NR 40623 98324). It consists of two
conjoined stone chambers, each with an internal diameter of c. 1m
by 4.5m. They are of drystane construction, surviving to a height of
perhaps 0.4 m; it seems that they are not kilns, because natural
shell-sand obviates the need for lime, and they are in the wrong
locality for kelp-burning. Continue towards the sea.

Leab' Fhalaich Mhic a' Phi ("MacPhee's Hiding Bed") NR
40618 98385

Looking upwards to your right, you will be able to identify this
recess within the rocks, one of seven such hidden lairs. According to
tradition, when Somerled's grandson – Angus Og – wished to gain
prestige for his name, he married a daughter of O'Kane, an Irish
chieftain with an ancient and highly-respected pedigree. As her
dowry, the bride brought along the younger sons of many of the
most prestigious families within her father's dominion, such as
MacAllister, MacPhee etc. Angus gained immediate prestige from
this entourage, and awarded important positions to each of the
young men – thus MacPhee became the governor of Colonsay, an
hereditary post which remained in his family for more than three
hundred years. The last MacPhee chieftain was Malcolm, who
unfortunately surrendered himself to the Earl of Argyll on 21
December 1615, promising to do service to the Crown but in
circumstances that created grave suspicion. He was therefore sent to
Edinburgh and detained there until granted a pardon on 13 January
1618. In the meantime his superior, Colla Ciotach MacDonald, had
taken personal control in Colonsay so MacPhee returned to find
that his own position and authority had been much-reduced. We do
not know what happened next, but MacPhee seems to have spent
some time in hiding in various locations before he was tracked down
by MacDonald and executed in February 1623, together with four
henchmen. Colla Ciotach MacDonald must have had some justification (or powerful friends) because he was successful in defending
himself against a charge of "fellone and crewall Slauchter".

Port Easdail ("Horse Dale Harbour") NR404984

As you approach the sea, you will find yourself at a small circular bay, almost enclosed by protecting rocks. The geology of this area is apparently of some interest, being the centre of a "plutonic intrusive mass". It has been said that this is in effect the floor of the interior of a tiny volcano. The very striking lamprophyre dyke running from the south-southwest cuts through the breccia (defined as "a rock of angular stones etc. cemented by finer material" O.E.D.). The outer islet and the inner edge of the promontory to the south consist of syenite, which continues around to the north side of the bay – syenite is a fairly rare coarse-grained igneous rock. The breccia may seemingly be divided into two phases – an outer marginal phase "very basic and full of boulders" and "an interior acid phase free from boulders" (Craig, Wright, Bailey, 1911). These are deep waters, but any geologist in your party will be in clover.

Assuming that the tide permits, follow the right-hand or northern margin of the bay, which will involve a slight scramble over rocks between patches of sand. After about 100 metres enter a large recessed corrie, sheltered by high cliffs.

Uamh Shìorruidh ("Endless Cave") and Cup-mark
NR 40399 98557

There are a few caves here – if you have a torch, do inspect Uamh Shìorruidh. It is "T" shaped and you will be able to turn to the right when half-way along. This was inhabited in the late Neolithic period (about 5000 yrs. ago) and faint traces of midden material and a low wall have been identified near the entrance to this side-passage. Storm tides can reach this point, so little organic material will have survived and in any case there are signs of unauthorized "excavation" by vandals.

Leaving the cave, turn left to identify the two cup marks on the face of a large slab of fallen rock – the only ones to have been officially noted by RCAHMS. Beyond them, the remains of a stone stairway lead up to Uamh na Bantighearna ("Lady's Cave"), which contains a neat stone bench. This will have been a part of a Victorian pleasure-ground – the Lady of the household could enjoy picnics and the delightful view without exposing herself to the direct rays of the sun; the bench and the stairway will have been a part of the conceit.

Facing away from the cave, identify steps which have been cut into the rock. There are two at a low level, there is then a substantial hurdle because a piece of rock has fallen away, but the steps can be seen to continue. This may be impassable for some people, or for your dog if you cannot lift it – in which case you must go back along the shore to rejoin the track, or to take a short-cut past Leab' Fhalaich Mhic a' Phi. If you do go back, follow the track upwards until it is almost level, except for three slight humps. Just before the second one, marked by a rocky bluff close to the left-hand side and by a prominent roadside way-marker, scramble down the steep, slippery slope to your left. About 15m from the road, facing towards Kiloran Bay, is an ancient Holy Well, where you will rejoin the main route. But, if you can surmount this obstacle in front of Uamh na Bantighearna, do so and follow the path onwards for about 4m, then turn right and pause. Note that this is a vertiginous spot and children must be controlled.

Cup-marks NR 40391 98575

The cup-marks already noted were on a rock which had fallen from above – here you can see many more such cup-marks, associated with the Bronze Age. Another array was identified in Chapter 5 and there are further examples here, on the cliff-top, which were discovered by David Jardine.

Continue along the easy and obvious path, steadily climbing and perhaps noticing that steps have been made wherever needed; these are fairly shallow, saucer-like depressions; we do not know when they were made, but they do lead directly to a very ancient well. Follow the path until you reach the rough moorland at NR 40377 98614, then turn right for about 100 m.

Tobar Chaluim Chille ("St. Columba's Well") NR 40477 98622

This well is held in great affection locally and many people still choose to leave some tiny token on the sill; in the past, it was often a coin or a button, perhaps a piece of cloth. A silver cup was presented by a lady visitor c. 1906 but has been removed for safe-keeping to the Post Office (where it may readily be seen). The present, bronze, cup was obtained in distant Bhaktapur in 1987 and the legend reads: "TU GLUAIS FAICILLEACH LE CUPAN LAN" ("Go warily with a full cup"). Although such an excellent well will have been adopted by St. Columba, it has a longer history. It provided fresh water for the Neolithic and Bronze Age inhabitants of the caves which lie close below (north side of Port Easdail), and also to the inhabitants of the hut circle on the upper side of the track (NR 405986). In more recent times it will have served the extensive shieling community on Beinn Bheag (NR 406986).

Join the track, just above the well, turn left and continue northwards and down-wards through Bealach Gaoithe ("Windy Pass") for 1 km.

Port Sgibinis ("Ship Point Harbour")

Sgibinis was one of Colonsay's Viking harbours and it is possible to identify a natural slipway beside a small stack in the north corner of the bay. The bay is backed by a fine raised beach, and many people feel that some of the visible hollows were perhaps "roosts" where boats could be safely over-wintered. The raised beach was modified in 2002, when a visiting artist, Julian Meredith, created the representation of a whale, 183 metres long; you are invited to add a stone or two of your own. Another startling construction of considerable merit is the consumption wall which borders the track as it climbs the hill – this wall is created entirely from circular boulders and in its heyday must have been a remarkable sight. (Please do not be tempted to take stones from this wall to enhance the whale).

Follow the track alongside the wall of rounded stones.

Assemblage of Cairns NR 40706 99403

At the top of the raised beach, there is a remarkable collection of rough cairns, of indeterminate origin. Closer examination suggests that a majority of the heaps are in fact simply cairns, but there are others which appear to consist of circular walls with open interiors, a little like simple huts. In connection with similar cairns in Oransay, John Gray (who was the farmer there in the 1990s) raised the interesting suggestion that they conceivably reflected a period of plague or disease – could it be that afflicted individuals were sent to live on a raised beach until the pestilence had passed? Food could be provided for them by some agreed system, and the raised beach would make it easy for the survivors to bury those who succumbed.

At the top of the hill, the track turns sharply to the right and you have a view of Balnahard Farmhouse. Cross the grid and turn left at this point, across the field, towards a large heap of stones.

Mound of Stones NR 40879 99495

One might like to pause at this point and perhaps speculate about this considerable mound. It seems unlikely to have arisen from field-clearance, otherwise many other fields would have similar mounds. On close examination, it does appear to have an underlying struc-tured form – could it be the site of an early farm? The heavier land (the arable fields of today) would have been difficult to work before the introduction of the modern plough in the eighteenth century and it is perhaps possible that the farm operated in two halves… the northern half would have had most of the best land, running down to Balnahard Bay and beyond. The southern half would have been based at this spot, with the land above Port Sgibinis and perhaps running north to Na Dùintean ("The Forts"), opposite the modern farmhouse; it would also have had the benefit of the ferry, which was based here at Port an Obain. Notice also another mound, 100m to the north – this is less obscured by stone, and shows clear construction detail.

Continue towards the field gate to your north, crossing lazy beds. Beyond the gate, turn left.

Unrecorded hut-circle NR 40966 99688

The hut may have been connected with the operation of the ferry (see below).

The wall at this point recalls the sad fate of a ship-wrecked sailor, who managed to make his way to the shore and up the shingle to this point. Having seen the house, he perhaps paused for a rest – his body was discovered next day, on the landward side of the wall. This was Birger Oest-Larsen of the Danish Merchant Navy, found 6th January 1942 and interred at Kilchattan. He had been mate on S.S. "*Crusader*", which was torpedoed on November 14th 1941, far out in the Atlantic. In the interim he had survived more than 54 days in a lifeboat which had travelled more than 1,200 miles; when found, his remains were still warm.

Dùn at Port An Obain ("Port of the Pools") NR409996

This was in former times the ferry point for Iona and the Ross of Mull. With a standing lugsail, tacking was an awkward manoeuvre and so ferry routes were planned to be short and to run across the prevailing wind, allowing the ferryman to make his crossing and return with minimum difficulty. Thus there were three ferry routes to Colonsay and Oransay from Islay and Jura, and this one to Uisken in Mull. In antiquity the monks seem to have used a much longer one as well, from Port na Luinge in Oransay to Iona.

From the top of the dùn, one can trace the route to be rowed through the rocks out to the "sailing point"; the topography is very similar to that at Uisken. Notice also that Balnahard farmhouse has been built in the exact location which affords a view of sea conditions – it was originally built as an Inn (to the same plan as the one in Scalasaig), at a time when the ferry was probably still in occasional use. Faint traces of buildings can be seen at the foot of the dùn, including one which has a massively thick wall on the seaward side, possibly to protect an over-wintering boat.

Descending towards the north, one approaches the burn and brackish pools for which this place is named, passing one or two wee bothies. Cross the burn and ascend the obvious glen and its continuation – which has a tiny and mostly subterranean burn of its own. It has been said that valleys, canyons etc. are not created by the scouring action of a water-course, but by the way in which the water leaches material from the subsoil. By this theory, through time, the water-course creates a tunnel for itself and it is only when this collapses that the incipient valley is created. Perhaps this is an example of the process – certainly, during heavy rain, the roaring of the invisible burn is highly impressive.

Continuing on the same line, one will encounter quite a good example of a sgùid or rock-shelter (NR 41239 99932), as has been described elsewhere; pause for a breather, then continue the ascent, choosing the right-hand of the two gullies on offer. You pass through an apparently ancient wall-like structure, keeping higher ground to your right and eventually the path levels-off beside a slight gap on the seaward side (and the ruins of yet another small bothy). Look ahead and upwards, to your right, to identify an impressive rocky outcrop fringed by recognisable masonry.

Dùn Meadhonach ("Middle Fort") *or perhaps*
Dùn Loisgte ("Burnt Fort"), Home of "The Richest Woman in the World" NR 414999
This fort is nowadays officially known as Dùn Meadhonach ("Middle Fort"), and it is one of Na Dùintean, which referred to a supposed line of three, of which the third (and most northerly) was

Dùn Crom ("Crooked Mound"). At some point an insignificant hillock to the south became mistaken for Dùn Loisgte, hence the whole line was moved along and the names became confused. Regardless of the name, this is a fascinating place.

About 1880, the historian Symington Grieve recorded a story that at one time Dùn Loisgte had been the home of the richest woman in the world, a lady whom he identified as Aud, the daughter of Ketil Flatneb, and the wife of Olaf the White, King of Dublin from c. 853 AD. According to the story, after she had been widowed by the death in battle of her Viking husband, Aud retired to live at this spot in Colonsay. Possibly a powerful relation was established at Dùn Eibhinn, Scalasaig, but her own retinue allegedly lived in Dùn Meadhonach, the large hilltop adjoining Dùn Loisgte. About a year later, according to local tradition, she removed to Iceland, where she married "the king". The attraction of the story is enhanced by the fact that Aud was in fact an identifiable historical character, whose career is well documented in the Norse sagas. Usually known as "Aud the Deep-Minded", she is noted for having been a Christian and, of course, was a near-contemporary of St. Buo; she is likely to have been living when the ship-burial took place at Kiloran Bay (with its Christian crosses), and when *An Dealbh Leisg* was commissioned. Her husband was indeed a king in Ireland, and seemingly died soon after 870 AD (when he captured Dumbarton Rock), although it is suggested by some that Aud was sent back to the Hebrides before his death. The sagas state that Aud then lived for a year "in the Hebrides" before making her way via Caithness, Orkney and Shetland to Iceland, which was newly settled. There was, of course, no "King of Iceland", but there were powerful and established landholders and Aud gained her sobriquet ("Deep-Minded") by the skilful way in which she arranged highly advantageous marriages amongst them for each of her grand-daughters. Accepting, as one must, that the sagas were not readily available in post-mediaeval Colonsay one can only assume that it was through genuine tradition that Archibald Buie of Uragaig could have been familiar with such a story.

It is entirely possible to ascend the dùn by scrambling up its nearest or southwestern flank, and to descend towards the south-eastern (or farmhouse) side – but you must decide for yourself if it is safe to do so in light of local conditions. This is one of nine major fortresses in Colonsay, dating originally from the Iron Age (c. 600

BC – c. AD 400). In addition to the remains of a curtain wall and an annexe at a lower level, the footings of three buildings of a later era can be seen in the northwest corner of the upper level. The archaeology was described at the start of this chapter – from the summit one can appreciate the magnificent views and strategic significance of the site. Whether or not you ascend the dùn, leave it behind as you cross a small series of lazy-beds. You will be going east and can see Balnahard farmhouse ahead of you and below. Do not continue towards it, but bear thirty degrees to your left and descend into a small corrie; continue ahead, bearing slightly to the left around a bluff and then following a sheep-path through a small area of bracken. Straight ahead of you, beyond a grassy track, you should see a distinctive, free-standing and substantial isolated stone rising from a narrow base. This little hollow (prob. Blàr an Ime "Butter Green") was where the cows were milked.

Clach na Gruagach ("The Gruagach's Stone") NR c. 4155 9975

It was once customary to give the first milk from each cow as a propitiation to the wee folk, to ensure good luck. On a practical basis, it also ensured that any indication of impurity could be seen before it contaminated the rest of the churn. The libation was carefully poured into the small basin that can be seen, chiselled into the upper surface of the Gruagach stone, and it could be examined as it trickled away. This is a particularly fine example of such a stone and, just by examining its footings, one can see that it was erected with great care. It is possible that it is a survival of some earlier tradition – it looks like an altar, and bears a marked resemblance to Altair Fear Mhitchel ("Fr. Mitchel's Altar"), at Lower Kilchattan.

The gruagach ("long-haired person") was apparently dressed in the clothes of a gentlewoman of a byegone period, was mindful of the cattle and kept them away from danger. Evidently she found it amusing to release the cattle in the byre at night, making people get out of bed to tie them up, when she could be heard "laughing and tittering in corners" (Grieve). She had long flaxen hair and sometimes would be seen walking alongside of people, but she was never known to speak. Elsewhere, as in Skye, the gruagach seems to have been a young man, but highly effeminate.

The Balnahard stone, also known as An Sgonn ("The Lump"), stands about 1.5m high. They say that at one time the Gruagach was captured and bound to the stone, so tightly that the weals made by the rope can yet be seen, spiraling down the pillar.

Section of "Galloway" Drystane Dyke
Close beside the Gruagach Stone there is a magnificent stretch of Galloway dyke. This form of dyking was discussed in Chapter 4, so it is sufficient to note that the section here is very possibly the finest surviving example in Colonsay and well worthy of close attention.

Leave this area by heading northwards up the grassy glen, passing a disused sump and following the line of a small ditch. It will be found that the ditch originates at a rather fine well (NR 41670 99846) – until recently this provided the water supply to the farmhouse, hence the ditch and sump. The name is uncertain, probably either Tobar Leob Amaid ("Well of the Clumsy Clot"?) – or perhaps Tobar Leab a' Muidhe ("Churn Rest Well"?) After the well, bear to the left and pass over the crest of a ridge; there is higher ground to your left (Dùn Crom) and you will be roughly following the line of a wall, some metres to your right. Just possibly, you might wish to divert onto the northern flank of Dùn Crom to inspect two curious stones, reminiscent of large fish (NR 41674 00087). Otherwise, after crossing the ridge, continue along much the same line as you descend, with a view to crossing through one of the gaps in the wall and skirting the hillside on your right. There are nice views down to Port na Cuilce ("Reed Harbour") and out across the sea towards the Torran Rocks. As you come around the shoulder of the hillside, you will notice a very distinctive boulder lying at its foot.

Carraig Nighean Maol-Choinnich ("Bald Kenneth's Daughters Rock") NR 41834 00259
This carraig or "pinnacle" stone is a remarkable natural curiosity, an enormous boulder weighing some 30 tonnes or more and measuring about 2 metres in height and 3 metres in circumference, perfectly balanced on a point little bigger than an egg. Old placenames are always open to interpretation and this one is no exception. "Maol" can mean "the brow of a rock", whilst "coinnich" is defined as "meet, face, oppose, encounter"; very probably we should simply call it "The Equipoise" in translation.

DECISION POINT: you may wish to continue to the north point of the island – just cross the burn below Carraig Nighean Maol-

Choinnich, ascend the slope on the other side and follow your nose. If not, you can reduce your walk by about one mile by simply following the burn upwards to level ground, then continuing in an arc, around to your right, to Cill Catrìona ("Chapel of St. Catherine"), where we will rejoin you shortly.

*

If you decide to visit the north point, try not to follow the coastline on your left unless you are happy to extend your walk somewhat – there are one or two dead-ends which will force you to make diversions. These are well worthwhile for the views, but if you are short of time bear rather more to your right until you pick up the well-defined glen leading down towards Bealach Lamalum ("Lamb's Holm Pass"). This area of Colonsay's northern cape is like a tiny *"Lost World"* of Conan Doyle, reached in this case through a single narrow defile and then quite suddenly opening out onto a secret plateau. As you leave the defile, there are the faint outlines of a couple of rectangular huts on your right (NR 42386 00798), and on an extremity of the rocks in Poll Bàn ("Fair Pool") there is a carraig ("Fishing Rock") (NR 42198 00807). Elsewhere on the plateau (amongst the low rocks on the eastern side) two more bothies can be found (NR 42387 00950), and one can recognize the remnants of a carefully constructed pathway leading up onto Lamalum itself.

This is a great place to pause and savour the moment, then pass onwards to the far end of the western sandy beach (another Port an Obain), and turn to your left, passing through a couple of stony hollows before ascending the short, flower-covered turf that constitutes the very tip of Colonsay. At the top of the slope (NR 42214 01047) you will be looking down upon Eilean Dubh ("Dark Isle"), subject to an almost ceaseless rolling swell; the surge of the tide is quite un-nerving, yet at high tide people have been known to take the inside passage with impunity.

In early summer this area is populated by breeding seabirds, so you should not linger – but there is time to glance to the right and indentify a very unusual "natural arch", which is in fact rectangular in shape. This is Uinneag Iorcail – usually translated as "The Window of Hercules", an attractive notion that we may as well accept. As you descend again, study the vertical rockface on the other side of the gully – the thriving plant clinging to the fissures at the top is Scots lovage (*Ligusticum scoticum*).

Retrace your steps, up through Bealach Lamalum again and follow that line until you reach a sheep-fence and views across the sand-dunes towards the east. Follow the fence to your right across open machair and in due course descend to reach Cill Catrìona, as mentioned above.

*

Cill Chaitrìona ("St. Catherine's Chapel") NR421998

The central structure is a chapel dedicated to St. Catherine of Alexandria, said to have been at the heart of a nunnery endowed in the mid-fourteenth century by Amie, the wife of John the Good, Lord of the Isles. (Note however that Symington Grieve was given a traditional dedication to St. Cairine, an ascetic; which by corruption became "Cille-a-Trina" (Chapel of the Holy Trinity)). To the north-east can be seen a circular building 5.5m in diameter; it was a substantial structure and, if rabbits have been active, it is sometimes possible to see two or three courses of the original masonry. There are a number of funeral cairns near to the chapel and, in the western corner of the enclosure-dyke, there is a very fine cruciform slab. This cross is heavily polished by use as a scratching-post, but it is unlikely that the arms of the cross-head were ever much more than vestigial. Just beyond the northern extremity of the site is a standing stone known as *Clach a' Pheanais* ("Penitence Stone"), believed by over-imaginative Victorians to have been used by the nuns in flagellation ceremonies. It is Bronze Age in origin and, with a neighbouring cist grave (see below), will have identified the site as significant; all the Christian sites in Colonsay are to be found in close proximity to pagan burial grounds. The conical hill just beyond the fence was also significant – it was known as Cnoc 'ic 'Ille Mhinniche ("Hill of the Son of the Servant of ??) and on its summit there is a small libation stone, that served the same purpose as the Gruagach's Stone.

The outline of an altar can be seen within the chapel, and a stone basin may be seen nearby. At one time the site was noted for its healing-stones, but these have largely disappeared. One of them, "the priest's foot" is beside the loggia of Colonsay House – such stones were believed to cure afflictions in the part of the body that they resembled.

Leave the chapel and walk towards the prominent modern barn, so as to regain the main track. At the southeastern corner of the barn a small wooden enclosure marks the site of an exposed Bronze Age cist grave; the grave was examined by archaeologists when it was first discovered by David Hobhouse, but contained no identifiable remains (NR 42248 99859).

At this point, turn left to enter a protected Site of Special Scientific Interest, following the slope down to the magnificent Tràigh Bàn "White Strand" of Balnahard Bay. Later you will probably return to this point and follow the farm track towards your original starting-point.

This area has been fenced and is carefully managed for the benefit of the native flora, and also for the good of the chough population, which favours such terrain at certain seasons. The flora is typical of a good Hebridean machair and in summer can be quite breathtaking. Botanists will find some species of outstanding interest, but most of us will be content with upwards of one hundred readily identifiable plants. Look out for ladies' bedstraw, fairy flax, marsh bedstraw, scarlet pimpernel, harebell, eyebright, the speedwells, birdsfoot trefoil, wild thyme, burnet rose, carline thistle, dune gentian, field gentian, hawkbit, mountain everlasting, rue-leaved saxifrage, violets and a host of others. Some specimens may be difficult to identify, particularly if stressed, and it is nowadays often a good idea to supplement notes with a digital photograph for subsequent reference. All the flowers are, of course, protected by law.

Machair is the natural coastal grassland which is so typical of Scotland and which originally inspired the game of golf. In his day, Professor Mackinnon and his guests played it here in Balnahard, but without a formal course. Instead, the participants used a bow and arrow – whoever had "the honour" fired the arrow, which became the "pin" for that particular hole.

The bay itself is very beautiful and makes an ideal picnic spot; there is a perfect lagoon for safe bathing at the northern end, and just a little further on, at Croisebrig ("Cross Slope"), there is an outcrop of Lewisian gneiss, one of the oldest rocks in Europe and something of a rarity in the inner Hebrides. A colony of nesting kittiwakes may be noticed at the margin of the fenceline at Leac Bhuidhe ("Yellow Flagstone"), whilst a large colony of shags is normally in attendance on Sgeir nic Fhionnlaidh ("Finlay's Daughter's Skerry").

From the bay, it is possible to make your way back by way of the east coast, the normal route for which has been indicated on the map. There are no particular hazards, but that route can be quite testing on a warm summer's day. Most people will leave that option for another time; they should return to the track beside the big barn and follow it down the glen.

After a kilometre or so, you will pass Balnahard farmhouse, which was built to the same plan as Scalasaig farmhouse and Scalasaig hotel in the mid- or late eighteenth century. A rental record of that period suggests that Balnahard was also an Inn, and as mentioned elsewhere it seems likely that it was sited to gain maximum shelter whilst still affording the ferryman a view of the sea.

Balnahard Farmhouse and steadings:
Balnahard farmhouse is most famously associated with Prof. Donald Mackinnon (1839–1914), a Colonsay native whose remarkable career brought great honour to the island. A crofter's son, he attended a pre-Education Act school of the humblest kind, which he later commemorated in the famous essay "*An t' Sean Sgoil*". In 1857 he embarked on study for the ministry, but instead became a teacher and in 1863 enrolled at Edinburgh University where he graduated in 1869 with First Class Honours, gaining employment as Clerk to the Church of Scotland Educational Scheme. After the Education (Scotland) Act of 1872, Donald Mackinnon became Clerk and Treasurer to the Edinburgh School Board. He was a man of extraordinary probity and erudition and this was recognised in 1882, when he was appointed to the newly-created Celtic Chair at Edinburgh University, a position which he held for over thirty years. In March 1883, he was appointed to the Napier Commission ("*Royal Commission of Enquiry into the Conditions of the Crofters and Cottars in the Highlands and Islands of Scotland*"). By 1895, Donald Mackinnon had taken the tenancy of Balnahard, which he retained until his death there on Christmas Day, 1914.

Another lengthy association with Balnahard began in the late 1940s when Lady Konradin Hobhouse adopted the tenancy, on her own behalf and that of her heirs. She was a remarkable lady, and people still recall the astonishment of her factotum when a number of crates arrived, which proved to contain the components of a light aircraft, something along the lines of the "Flying Flea". Lady Hobhouse gave instructions that the machine was to be assembled in readiness for her arrival, but was on no account to be flown until she could be there in person. The factotum managed to overcome any such temptation and, in fact, contrived to get the entire project quietly shelved.

Passing the farm steadings, note the octagonal building which is known locally as a "mill-round", more commonly called a "horse-gang". One or more horses were yoked to a beam which, when turned, operated a geared mechanism and transmitted rotary power by an underground rod into the adjoining barn. Part of the drive mechanism is leaning against a corner of the building. No less than four such facilities were provided in Colonsay, strategically spaced at Balnahard, Kiloran, Machrins and Oronsay.

Continue along the track, and in due course pass Tobar Chaluim Chille again. In all likelihood you will have seen enough for one day, but bear in mind that there is an interesting hut circle above you on the shoulder of Beinn Bheag, and there are very interesting shieling remains close to the summit. As the track begins to descend towards the dunes, there is a fine Bronze Age kerbed cairn on the grassy slope to your left, 10 m in diameter and 1 m in height. Energetic folk will make a further diversion here, to climb to the summit of Carnan Eoin ("Hill of the Bird"), Colonsay's highest peak at 143 metres. The views are excellent and include the artistic representation of the whale, 183 metres long, which was created at Sgibinis beach in 2002. There are additional hut-circles to the east of the summit.

As you descend Am Bealach you will pass a rather good specimen of an aspen tree, in the gully beside the track. The aspen (*Populus tremula*) is regarded as a pioneer species and is one of the remnants of the ancient Caledonian forest, but it is dioecious (*i.e.* each specimen is either male or female) and it is believed that the relatively sparse distribution of the species impedes pollination. As a result, seed production is thought to be rare in Scotland and reproduction is largely vegetative. On the other hand, aspen roots can remain alive for many years after the death of the actual tree – thus young trees can suddenly appear in unexpected locations.

Walk back across the dunes to regain your starting point.

Chapter 7

COLONSAY HOUSE AND GARDENS

Visitors are always welcome to enjoy the Woodland Gardens of Colonsay House, which comprise the bulk of the policies. The formal gardens, to the rear of the house, are open to the public on a regular basis throughout the summer months and by prior application at other times. Details are available locally and through Scotland's Gardens scheme. The main house is a private family residence and as such is not open to the public, although it is possible to rent holiday accommodation in the Garden Wing.

Kiloran Abbey

Until the reformation, the site of Colonsay House was occupied by the Abbey of Kiloran ("*Cille Odhran*" = St. Odhran's Chapel), first mentioned by Pope Innocent III in 1203 and said to have been a daughter-house of Holyrood. Grieve states that the foundation was c. 1180, at the instigation of Reginald, Lord of the Isles, and that Black Monks, "canons regular of the Order of St. Augustine" were brought from Holyrood for the purpose. There is no firm evidence of this connection, and it is possible that a reference to a relic of the True Cross (i.e. the Holy Rood) has been misunderstood; such a relic might have been possessed by the abbey and would have assured the wealth and prosperity of the community. Although the abbey itself has totally disappeared, interesting traces survive, of which the most obvious is *Abhainn a' Mhuillin* ("Mill Burn"). The monks, who doubtless stocked Loch Fada with trout, diverted the drainage of that loch and created a mill lade almost one kilometre in length, which still flows beside the site of their house. The millpond remains extant, as does the mill race, to be noticed later.

More romantically, an interesting plant is to be seen at the corner of the roadside just north of Colonsay House, *Senecio fluviatilis* (Broad-leaved Ragwort); it seems to have been first noted about two hundred years ago, and there are those who wonder if it could have escaped from a remnant of the monastery garden and survived at this location. Further and incontrovertible proof of the sanctity of the Abbey itself exists in the many graves which surround the modern house; both Kiloran and Oronsay were highly favoured and funeral parties came to the island from far and wide. Coffins were not normally used and the remains were usually wrapped in closely-woven fabric before interment, although in 1846 "a stone coffin and human remains were found". Inhumations start little more than 45cm below the surface and because of the competition for space are very closely packed.

On an historical note, we know that some part of the Abbey was in use until the early seventeenth century, for Alasdair MacCholla Ciotach was born in *An Sabhal Bàn* ("The White Barn") c. 1620. In 1630, Andrew Knox, the "*pseudoepiscipus*" and titular Bishop of the Isles, was appointed to the benefice. Very probably An Sabhal Bàn was destroyed during one or other of the Covenanter assaults upon the island between 1639 and 1647, but in 1695 Martin Martin reported that "*Kilouran* is the principal Church in this Isle, and the Village in which this Church is, hath its Name from it." That church is now lost, and it is said that the ruins of the abbey proper were destroyed for the construction of the present dwelling. Grieve mentions that "there is carved stone lying in the flower garden and resting against the wall of the mansion-house, which is said to have come from the ruins of the ancient abbey. It is 11 inches in height and 1 foot 1 inch in breadth". This seems to be the fragment of an Early Christian cross to be seen on the loggia, bearing "in low relief part of a cable-moulding... the arm contains interlaced knots with pointed terminals" (RCAHMS).

Colonsay House

Colonsay was traditionally part of the lands of Clan Donald, and as late as 22 October 1687 King James VII of Scotland reconfirmed possession of the island to Sarah MacDonald, the Catholic grand-daughter of Coll Ciotach MacDonald. Unfortunately the Scots king was ousted soon afterwards by the Dutchman, William of Orange, who landed in England on 5 November 1688; within a few years he had annexed Scotland and even changed its name to "North Britain". The Duke of Argyll took advantage of the political confusion to invest various properties in Argyll, including that of Sarah MacDonald, and to re-allocate them amongst his "kindly folk". Despite his personal vicissitudes, Argyll's family retained control of Colonsay and in 1701 they granted permanent possession to Donald McNeill of Crear in exchange for his former properties in Knapdale.

McNeill was a significant scion of an extended family which had made itself useful to the Campbells throughout the seventeenth century, and thereby to the Protestant faction of the English Court. For example, in 1615 Hector McNeill of Taynish had been an active informer during the "rising" of Sir James MacDonald. He had sent his reports directly to Lord Binning, Secretary of State:

"Two speciall men that held of Argyle befoir ar newlie rebellit with thame, Mcduphe of Collinson, and his haill name, and Donnald Gigaich Makean who held Jura of Argyle…"

It was the fulfilment of an ambition when, within three generations, the McNeills gained formal rights to these very lands. They had harried Sarah MacDonald during her tenure of Colonsay, then gained *de facto* control under Argyll, and in 1701 managed to "regularise" the position. By 1730, similar tactics had gained them a title to the north part of Jura. In 1737 the clan chief emigrated to South Carolina together with many of his McNeill following, and the leadership fell briefly to McNeill of Colonsay until the collapse of the clan system after the '45.

In the early years the McNeills might have been supposed to have lived in the existing buildings at Kiloran, but instead they were driven to maintain themselves in the small island fort in Loch Sgoltaire because of local hostility. Donald died c. 1701 and was succeeded by his son Malcolm c. 1707, by which time the Act of Union had signalled a period of political and economic stability. By a strange twist of fate, Malcolm married Barbara Campbell of Dunstaffnage, grand-daughter of Colkitto's old friend. A more infamous connection was with her great-aunt, Janet, known by her own clan as "The Black Bitch of Dunstaffnage":

"this wicked woman was in the practice of seizing in the night all the followers of the Family of McDonald who was and is still the chief of the inhabitants upon that Island [i.e. Islay]. By this womans orders the people would be bound hand and foot and carried away in boats and Birlines in the night time and before day and left on Desart Rocks and Islands in the seas there to perish… There was another wicked woman at Dunstaffnage [Barbara's mother?] that had the same practice of persecuting the remains of Coll MacDonalds and his son Alexanders men…"

Malcolm McNeill

In due course, Malcolm swept away the old village of Kiloran and built his house, presumably at the time of his marriage and very possibly with the help of Barbara's dowry. The original house (date-stone 1722) is the square building at the centre of the present complex, consisting of two main storeys and an attic, with a cellar under the southeast quarter. The dormers and the porch are later additions, and one wonders if the chimney stacks might have been somewhat lower in the original phase.

The McNeill family was very active in military and commercial affairs and tended to leave the management of their estate to junior branches, as tacksmen. Thus in the latter half of the eighteenth century, the estate was managed by Alexander McNeill, tacksman of Oransay, who married Mary McDougall, daughter of Alexander McDougall of Dunollie. Theirs was a significant union which allied the commercial interests of two powerful local families and their nine children included John (1767–1846) whose education was centred upon the very latest agricultural developments. It was John, "The Old Laird", who eventually purchased the estate from his cousin and instituted the sweeping agricultural reforms which brought lustre to his name, but from which the island has never recovered.

John McNeill

John McNeill re-organised the farms, commenced the drainage, manured the land, built the houses, ran the mill, exploited the kelp and dramatically improved social and economic conditions on the island. He also uncorked the *genie* of emigration – at first he transported some of the tenants to America, later encouraged more to remove to Canada, and then was almost overtaken by a tidal Exodus. Finding himself without sufficient labour, he had to spend his latter years in trying to attract inward migration, mostly from Jura and the Ross of Mull.

The present appearance of Colonsay House is largely due to the efforts of John McNeill, who purchased the estate in 1806. His architect is unknown, but the work is clearly highly fashionable, with the offices and additions designed to give the appearance of symmetry. This palladian style was a tribute to the work of Andrea Palladio (1508-80) in Vicenza and Venice, introduced to England in the seventeenth century by Inigo Jones and popularised in the eighteenth century by Lord Burlington and others. It is known that the architect of Colonsay Parish Church in 1802 was Michael Carmichael, who had worked at Inveraray and who had been considered for the construction of the Highland Church there, as designed by Robert Mylne. The McNeill account must have been a large one, because in addition to all the work in Colonsay, it was John McNeill's son Duncan (1793–1874) who built the mansion-house at Ardlussa in Jura.

In summary, John McNeill added matching single-storied bow-fronted rooms on either side of the main house, which face southeast across the garden. These extensions are effectively screened by the two pavilions and curved corridors which he added to either side of the main façade, which faces to the northwest. No doubt, in warmer climes these corridors would have been colonnades. He also added extensive additional accommodation to the eastern end of the house, including a courtyard and staff accommodation, constructed the front porch and drew everything together by judiciously balanced fenestration.

Donald Smith, 1st Baron Strathcona

The last of the McNeill lairds was Major-General Sir John Carstairs McNeill V.C., G.C.V.O., K.C.B., K.C.M.G., (1831–1904). He became equerry to Queen Victoria in 1890 but had spent much of his time at Osborne, in the questionable and expensive company of Edward, Prince of Wales. Following a catastrophic blunder in the Sudan, Wales intervened to prohibit Parliament from censuring Sir John's conduct, but nothing could save him from the folly of his extravagance. In order to purchase and maintain Colonsay, Sir John had secured a number of advances from a powerful acquaintance, Donald Smith of the Hudson Bay Company, possibly at the suggestion of Wales. The first such loan was obtained in April 1886, but Sir John had originally encountered Donald Smith in course of the Red River Expedition of 1869, where he had served under Wolseley. In his letters, Sir John addressed him as "Dear Uncle Donald", as indeed did Wales himself; this and other debts were still outstanding at his death. Doubtless Sir John's position as equerry to the Queen will have been helpful; Donald Smith was raised to the peerage in 1897, and in 1900 was granted the privilege of a Special Remainder, whereby his title was allowed to be passed on through his daughter. In settling Sir John's estate, his heirs agreed to sell

Colonsay to his creditor for £44,000 in total, the equivalent of £4.4 million in 2010 (based upon Gross Domestic Product deflator – see www.measuringworth.com/ukcompare).

Lord Strathcona and Mount Royal, G.C.M.G., G.C.V.O., D.C.L., L.L.D., D.L., High Commissioner for Canada, had been born in 1820 as Donald Alexander Smith, at Forres, Morayshire (d. 1914). His extraordinary career with the Hudson's Bay Company had earned him the respect of all the world, and an immense fortune. He is probably best remembered now for the construction of the Canadian Pacific Railway, but he was a statesman of great sagacity and a major philanthropist. His charitable donations are known to have exceeded $7,500,000 in Canada and £1,000,000 in Britain, in the values of his day. These are extraordinary sums in today's currency (2010) – he personally gifted the equivalent of more than $340 million in Canada, and more than £93 million in Britain (based upon the relative value of earned income).

Lord Strathcona was clearly in a position to have his new property put into good order and it was he who added the second storey to the east wing of Colonsay House. The additional storey does not affect the front elevation, but it has completed the transformation of the garden façade from lingering Palladian to French Château. These three main phases of building, together with the Loggia, have created the house in its present form.

Colonsay House Gardens

A map of the gardens may be obtained from the ticket-office.

The early years

The policies surrounding Colonsay House are first mentioned by Thomas Pennant, who noted in 1772 that trees thereabouts "grow very vigorously", and suggested that ash and maple might do well. His suggestion was evidently noted, because in 1810 Dr. Walker commented favourably on an ash plantation, then about thirty years old. The traditional coppicing of A' Choille Mhór formed an attractive backdrop to the woodland paths, analogous to walks in the policy woods, but wilder; and it is clear that "The Old Laird" created an extensive pleasure ground at Balavetchy (see Chapter 5).

The gardens that we see today were also pioneered by John McNeill, since it is recorded by Loder that "The woods around

Colonsay House were planted early in the nineteenth century. The trees were only induced to grow by building protective walls, behind which strips of sea-buckthorn and alder provided further shelter". Within this sheltered area, John McNeill laid out the pattern of the formal gardens, and from photographic evidence we know that the planting was established and mature by the 1880s. The earliest identifiable gardener is commemorated by a gravestone at Oransay Priory, with an engraved image of an eight-tined hay-rake lying on its back and crossed by a vertical garden spade, inscribed: "1765 / ANDr PIRIE AND / HIS SPOSE PEGGY / McNEAR 1808".

Known descendants of Andrew Pirie now live in Canada, as do those of John Oliver, who was appointed as steward for "The Old Laird" in the opening years of the century and whose subsequent emigration was quite eventful. It is fortuitous that we happen to know something of his career and hopefully it makes for a justified digression.

John George Oliver was born in Hawick, Roxburghshire in 1777, and married Helen Smith in Kilmarnock, Ayrshire on 19 September 1808. He was evidently a highly qualified man, since he was brought to Colonsay and into the service of John McNeill, a leading agriculturalist. He clearly got on well with his employer, for his son was christened as "John McNeill Oliver", the first recorded example in Colonsay of a double forename. The son, born 1809, was baptised in Colonsay on January 10th 1810, and a memo survives from that period:

"Labourers 180 days complete, cleaning out whins and willows etc. in the west field, containing about ten acres of land. Ploughing the same field 51 days with one strong plough. Harrowing with the iron break-harrow 20 days. Oat-seed sown 12 bolls." (Signed) John Oliver."

The Olivers did not linger long in Colonsay, and in 1812 the family set out for Nova Scotia. They sailed from Glasgow, aboard the English brig *"Bacchus"*, bound initially for Pictou. They set sail on August 24, with a crew of 10 and 19 passengers. The other passengers came from Inverness and Nairn, and the Muster Roll survives, giving details of the family as follows: John Oliver, 32 years, "Calasa, Argyle Shire... contracted to be carried" to Pictou, "to follow his Employment as a Labourer", together with his wife Helen, 25yrs, "going with her husband", and children John, 3yrs, and Helen 5yrs, "going with the parents".

John Oliver declared himself to be a common labourer, since as a skilled man his emigration would have been forbidden. Unhappily, his timing was worse than he supposed and coincided with the outbreak of the second American War of Independence. On November 27 or 28, when *"Bacchus"* was in the gulf of Canso and barely forty miles from Pictou, she was captured as a prize by the schooner *"Revenge"* of Salem, Massachusetts. Together with her passengers and crew, *"Bacchus"* was taken to Boston and held in the custody of the U.S. Marshall.

The family is recorded in the register of "British Prisoners, Massachusetts Maritime", a ledger which had been opened in August 1812. Prisoners No. 87 through 92 are given as John Oliver, Helen Oliver and their children John (McNeill), Helen, James and William. We see that the family had increased by two in the course of the journey, possibly an example of Colonsay's known propensity for multiple births. In due course, John Oliver and his family were delivered to the British Agent at Boston, December 11, 1812, to make their way as best they could to their intended destination.

Possibly the British Agent was able to help in some way, because an immediate application was made for a grant of land. John Oliver made his application for a grant of land in Nova Scotia on December 12, 1812 (the day after his release in Boston), and on January 11, 1813 was granted 350 acres on the French River at New Annan.

Back in Colonsay, John Oliver was succeeded by John Addison, who specifically came to Colonsay "to create the gardens" in 1811; he married Susan Young and their daughter Ann Addison married Donald Ross McPhail from Mull. John Addison retained a lifelong connection with the island, since he had another daughter, Fanny, born around 1857, who married Malcolm McNeill of Balerominmor Farm (520 acres) at St. Mary's Parish Church in Edinburgh on June 4th 1890. Fanny was about 32yrs and Malcolm was about 53yrs at the time – their daughter, Hester Young McNeill, was born at the farm on 17 July 1891 and the census shows that the "father-in-law" John Addison (86yrs) and another of Fanny's sisters (Susan, 42yrs) were living with them at the time.

At a later date, some gardeners can be identified by the census. In 1841, the head gardener was William Russell, but in 1851 there is nobody so designated. The vacancy was soon filled, for on November 14, 1851 the marriage was recorded between "Angus

Currie, gardener, Killoran and Jessie Mc(Rulcha?), Killoran". In 1861 Alexander McLeod of Kirkcudbright is recorded as "Gardener master". Alexander McLeod must have come to Colonsay before 1857 and remained at least until 1867, since he is to be found in 1881 at Sudbury House Lodge, Harrow on the Hill, Middlesex, together with his wife Mary and their children, all of whom had been born in Colonsay: James, 24, Ellen 21, Mary 17 and Christine 14.

In 1871 we find Malcolm McNeill in post for the first time, assisted by Dugald McNeill and John Blue, all natives of Colonsay. Malcolm McNeill was to hold the position for over 30 years and in 1891 was briefly joined by his gifted 17 year old son, Murdoch.

Murdoch McNeill went on to train at Kew Gardens and between 1903 and 1908 used his leisure moments to study the botany of his native island. Fortunately he was also a Gaelic scholar and he carefully recorded the local names and uses of all the plants, which he published in 1910 as *"Colonsay, Its Plants, Climate, Geology, etc."* Murdoch McNeill records that "the earliest planted trees now to be seen in the island (1910) are a few old specimens of Ash and Elm, survivors of a semicircular line of trees which marked the boundary of the original mansion-house garden. These, together with a clump on the southern slope of Beinn a' Sgoltaire, are believed to have been planted more than a century and a half ago – possibly soon after the first part of the mansion-house had been built, in 1722". A possible remnant of this early phase may be seen in the shape of a "dry" ditch running away to your right as you approach Colonsay House by the (modern) front avenue; this seems to have been a "sunk fence", a common landscaping feature of the time. The rather dangerous sloping bend on the adjoining public road preserves the memory in its name, "Bruthach na Ha-ha", a name that was recorded by Mr. Walter Williams of Uragaig; when the road was built, the ha-ha became its eastern boundary and may yet be traced for some 50 metres or so.

Murdoch McNeill goes on to confirm that the first extensive planting of trees began from about 1820, and that in the early years "many places had to be planted over and over again." The modern visitor should therefore be aware that the sheltered micro-climate within the gardens is not a fortuitous circumstance, but was created by generations of dedicated labour and investment.

The Woodland Garden

It is convenient to approach the Woodland Garden from the first sharp corner in the main road from Scalasaig, at a point about one kilometre north of the crossing through Loch Fada. Turn right and follow the track to Pondside Cottage, where a gate gives access to the policies.

On the left, notice the attractive rock garden, which includes some fine azaleas. Through the hedge on the right, one can see the Mill Pond, a survival from the mediaeval abbey; when abreast of the east end of the pond, turn towards the Pond, noticing some large granite blocks. These blocks are remnants of the original Monument at Scalasaig, described in Chapter Four. As you walk along the mill dam, a mound on the left marks the site of the old mill, which remained in use until c. 1865; just beyond it, one can see the old mill race, chiselled through the rock some 500 years ago. At the far end of the dam, one passes over a lock gate which channels Abhain a' Mhuillin and can then turn right, towards the west end of the Mill Pond.

In "*Summer in the Hebrides*" by Francis Murray, one can read in full "*Miss Hester M'Neill's Song – composed by her when her father's mill was pulled down at Killoran*". The family moved to Balerulin and Hester was moved to write some poignant verses, of which this was the Chorus:

Mo chridhe trom is duilich leam
'Smuladach a tha mi,
Cilloran a cuir cùl rium
A' diùltadh a bhi blàth rium...

My heart is sorry and heavy,
Mournful that I am;
Killoran turns its back on me
Refusing to be warm...

Look out for candelabra primulas in this vicinity, also the exuberant skunk cabbage and gunnera; from late May there will be damselflies and dragonflies over the water. At the western end of the pond, turn left, away from the bridge, and just follow the pathways that take your fancy. You will be rewarded by some remarkable species rhododendrons and all the other pleasures of a woodland walk; alert botanists will probably notice some interesting native flora, specimens of which thrive in this sheltered environment.

In the fullness of time, you will emerge onto a rough track, the original road from Scalasaig to Colonsay House; the exact point will depend upon how thoroughly you have explored the 32 acres which were available to you. Having reached the track, turn right if you wish to walk towards Scalasaig, whereby you will regain the main road within 2 kilometres. On the other hand, turn left if you wish to return to Pondside Cottage, and just follow the avenue. In due course you will enjoy a very pleasant view of the garden façade of Colonsay House on your right and the track will descend towards a bridge across Abhainn a' Mhuilinn. Turn left, beside the burn, and then choose which of the paths to follow – all will enable you to regain your starting point.

The Woodland Garden is extremely sheltered and very rewarding at any season of the year. Even in deepest winter there will be shrubs in flower and it always makes a pleasurable retreat on days of storm or rain. In recent years, determined efforts have been made to eradicate the invasive *Rhodendendron ponticum* and as the work progresses all sorts of long-hidden nooks and arbours are being revealed.

The Formal Garden

As is clear from old maps and photographs, the basic structure of the ten-acre formal garden was established and mature by the latter half of the nineteenth century, after which and until the end of the Great War the programme was largely one of care and maintenance. Throughout the bulk of this period the garden was under the care of Malcolm McNeill, but his son Murdoch returned to Colonsay after completing his formal training at Kew and elsewhere. In 1926 the island was inherited by Donald, third Lord Strathcona, who decided to concentrate his attentions upon Colonsay and therefore disposed of a conflicting interest, an estate at Glencoe. Husbanding his resources and his talents, and encouraged by his father-in-law, Gerald de Vere Loder, 1st Baron Wakehurst, he embarked upon an ambitious expansion of the exotic species.

Donald Howard, third Lord Strathcona, commenced operations in 1928 and provided Murdoch with a taskforce of up to twelve labourers. A certain amount of reclamation and preparatory work was apparently required, suggesting that standards had been allowed to slip; and of course a good deal of labour was devoted to the upkeep of the kitchen garden and greenhouses, mowing of lawns and general maintenance. Nonetheless, a steady programme of introductions was maintained until 1959, interrupted only by World War II. Many new species and hybrids of rhododendron were introduced, together with exotic shrubs and trees from New Zealand and South America, and they have thriven to the extent that many have now become prolific self-seeders. Curiously enough, (as mentioned in Chapter 3) an unusual land-shrimp (*Arcitalitrus dorrieni*) was discovered in leaf-litter at the manse some years ago and was identified as having originated in the Antipodes. It was eventually ascertained that one of the shrubs from New Zealand had been transplanted with a massive root-ball, from which the harmless land-shrimp had colonised the estate woodland. Subsequently it had been carried elsewhere on carts, before the introduction of motor-cars in 1947; an interesting study (Moore and Spicer) suggested a rate of dispersal of 25m per annum and a maximum density of 680 per square metre.

An unusual example of installation art has been created in the walled garden based upon a redundant lens, rescued from the Stevenson lighthouse at Rubh a' Mhaill in Islay. It is quite striking to see such a lens at close quarters and it is an attractive feature which adds considerable impact to its surroundings. The work was carried out by Mr. David Sutherland in the late 1980s.

On an historical note, it is interesting to know that the lighthouse feature is on the supposed site of An Sabhal Bàn ("The White Barn"), which had been the tithe-barn of Kiloran Abbey. This former barn is said to have been adopted as the residence of the McPhee chieftain in the late sixteenth century and subsequently became the home of Colla "Ciotach" McDonald. Thus it was here that young Alasdair MacCholla was born, in memorable circumstances. Weapons on the wall rattled in their scabbards and pistols cocked of their own volition. "This is a portent!" exclaimed the midwife. "Yes it is!" cried Colkitto, "Get a bucket! Drown the child at once!"

Tobar Odhran

Tobar Odhran ("St. Odhran's Well") lies in the northeast corner of the formal garden, close to the avenue. The well itself is, of course, very ancient and will have served the abbey community in its day. In ancient times it was blessed by St. Odhran, whose curious history bears repetition. Apparently the island was afflicted by a serious drought and the resident clerics prayed fervently for it to be lifted. In a confused traditional account, St. Odhran agreed to sacrifice himself and was buried alive, only to be unearthed a few days later when the drought was still unbroken. At this unearthing, he is said to have said "things which were unorthodox" (interpreted by some as an account of the hereafter), whereupon St. Cattan, his brother, is said to have quickly interposed with the command (in Gaelic!) "Sand! Sand for the eyes of Odhran!"

In the late nineteenth century Archibald McNeill of Garvard and his brother Malcolm McNeill of Balerominmore stated that the exact words (in translation) were "Earth upon Oran's eye before he says the next word" and these words were carved upon Oran's headstone. According to Symington Grieve, who recorded the tradition in some detail, this stone was said to have survived until Colonsay House was being built, "when it was thrown away".

The tale could conceivably be based upon fact. The dedication of a new graveyard by human sacrifice is not unheard of in early tradition, but it is in any case conceivable that an ascetic cleric, fasting and praying fervently, could enter a catatonic state which would be taken for death. Another priest would be summoned, the arrangements for interment be made and the final consolations of religion be administered. The entire community was suffering from the drought and had lost its leader – very possibly in such circumstances, the veil perhaps slipping from the face of the supposed "deceased", his incoherent mumblings could have caused great distress. Since only Our Lord could return from the dead any such incident would have been long-remembered.

The eighth-century statue standing beside the well is Dealbh na Leisg, originally sited at Riasg Buidhe and described elsewhere (Chapter 5). The curious stone resting on a quern is an unusual survival, thought to be the lower axle or turning-point for the wheel of a muileann dubh or "Black Mill". The masonry of the well is bordered by the 3.9m long jawbone of a Blue Whale, *Balaenoptera musculus*, stranded in Sloc Grudaig, Sgibinis in July 1916 and measured by Murdoch McNeill as 78ft (23.4m) in length overall.

Elsewhere in the gardens there are preserved a number of healing-stones from Cill Chaitrìona, Balnahard, which were believed to have the power to cure physical ailments. The most easily identified are known as "The Priest's Feet" and may be noticed with other curiosities in the vicinity of the Loggia.

Plate 1: Galloway Dyke, above Glebe Wood at Scalasaig

Plate 2: Pot-barley stone, beside chapel at Riasg Buidhe

Plate 3: Cup-marks on Creag na Teasaiche (Fever Stone), Cnoc na Faire

Plate 4: Bait holes at landing place, Port Olmsa

Plate 5: Coppiced oak in A' Choille Mhòr

Plate 6: Dunan nan Nighean, Balavetchy

Plate 7: Glaic nan Cnàmh (Dell of Bones)

Plate 8: Ferry point, from dùn at Port an Obain, Balnahard

Plate 9: A typical sguid or rock-shelter, Balnahard

Plate 10: Clach nan Gruagach (Gruagach stone), Balnahard

Plate 11: Section of Galloway dyke, Balnahard

Plate 12: Cill Chaitrìona (St. Catherine's Chapel), Balnahard

Plate 13: Crois Chille Chaitriona
(Cross at St. Catherine's Chapel)

Plate 14: Parts of the original
Monument, in decorative use
at Kiloran Gardens

Plate 15: Bronze-age graves,
"excavated" August 2008 by
Historic Scotland, then aban-
doned to the elements.
*Picture shows situation in
December 2010.*

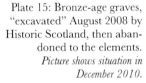

Plate 16: Slochd Dubh Mhic a' Phi (Macfie's Dark Gully)

Plate 17: Corn-kiln, showing flue vent, Port an Tigh Mhòir

Plate 18: Port na Fliuchan

Plate 19: Eilean Dubh Iain Mhitchel (Fr. Mitchell's Retreat), Loch a' Sgoltaire

Plate 20: Altair Fear Mhitchel (Fr. Mitchell's Mass-rock)

Plate 21: Boyhood home of Prof. Donald Mackinnon

Plate 22: Interior of byre-end of same, showing daub

Plate 23: Ballan Stillach (Pillary)
showing cross, Machrins

Plate 24: Brangas – alleged Viking stone of punishment

Plate 25: Colonsay's first motor car, an Austin which came in 1947

Plate 26: Kelper's hut, Ardskenish – note finishing detail to left of doorway

Plate 27: Port a' Chrochaire – where Colkitto kept his birlinn

Plate 28: Dùn na Mara (Sea Fort), looking out through entrance passage

Plate 29: Teampull a' Ghlinne – showing apparently three phases of masonry

Plate 30: Port na h-Iùbhraich (Port of the Barge), where St Columba landed

Plate 31: Luba nan Eisearan (Oyster Pool), early twentieth-century oyster-beds, Garvard

Plate 32: The Prostrate Cross, An Fhaoghail (The Strand)

Plate 33: Rubble base at site of Crois an Tearmaid (Sanctuary Cross)

Plate 34: A' Cloich Thuill (The Pierced Stone) *a.k.a.* The Elephant's Trunk, Oransay

Plate 35: Looking south from Carn Cul ri Eireann, Beinn Orasa, Oransay
Plate 36 (left): Priory Cross by Mael-Sechlainn O Cuinn, erected by Prior Colin c. 1500
Plate 37 (right): Memorial stone: I W Colburn, Architect, 1924–92

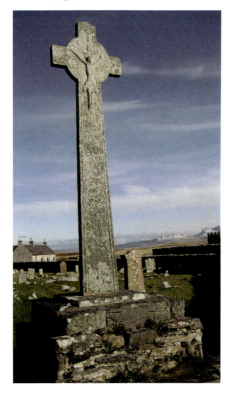

Plate 38: Tigh Cearc (Hen House) *a.k.a.* the Kelpmakers' House

Plate 39: Athach Cealp (Kelping Kiln)

Plate 40: Caisteal nan Gillean – important Mesolithic site

Plate 41: "Coco" – a faithful friend and great hill-walker

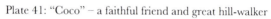

Chapter 8

KILORAN BAY, URAGAIG
AND LOCH AN SGOLTAIRE
Map: page xii

This area of about 600 acres comprises part of a former farm, one of the "twa Killoderans", which disappeared during the early-nineteenth-century agricultural reforms of "The Old Laird". To the east, the marginal land from the other original Kiloran had been used to create a number of small farms, Dungallion (145 acres), Riasg Buidh (63 acres), Glassard (167 acres), and Clunery (128 acres); none of them was a great success, as was seen in Chapter 5.

Meanwhile, here on the west side, the better land from the remaining "Killoderan" was attached to the former farm of Balavetchy, helping to create a valuable home farm for the proprietor. At a slightly later date (c. 1820?) the marginal land from this western farm of "Killoderan", Dùnan a' Chullaich ("Boar Homestead") at NR 38253 96638, was used to create two new crofting townships, known as Northmuir and Uragaig. Northmuir (named for Beinn a' Tuath, "North Hill") lay to the south and west of Loch an Sgoltaire, but the land was very poor indeed and that township was completely cleared again in the 1850s. By contrast, Uragaig contained some small tracts of fertile land and was much more sheltered, so it was never entirely deserted. When they were originally established there were eight crofts in Northmuir, averaging two acres of arable, and seven crofts in Uragaig, averaging four acres arable. At the turn of the present century just one working croft still survived although through inducements offered by the Crofting Commission this number has now increased to three, all in Uragaig. Land has been purchased and at least two more crofts are to be established here through the work of Colonsay Community Development Company.

The figures from the official census give definition to the poignant tale of earlier decline. In 1841 there were 24 houses and 138 residents between the two townships, with an average age of 22 years; by 1901 there were 6 houses and 25 inhabitants, with an average age of 42 years. The families still remaining in 1901 were

MacMillan, Buie, McLugash and McPhee; all had long associations with the area and the family of 90 year-old Anne MacMillan had been there for sixty years or more. As late as 1881, the 37 inhabitants were still exclusively Gaelic speakers, but by 1901 only 11 of the 25 inhabitants could not speak English as well. In 2010, there were six residential houses and ten inhabitants within the area, also seven "holiday homes".

The geology of the area includes the narrow band of limestone which surrounds the extensive sand-dunes behind Kiloran Bay and the rather more extensive area of "Kiloran flags" which comprise Uragaig and the area surrounding Loch an Sgoltaire. The area of flags tends to be ill-drained, barely productive ground, but Cailleach Uragaig and the cliffs to the south consist of "Staosnaig Phyllites" and, as such, support a rich herbage.

There are seven sites of historic interest listed by the Royal Commission, as mentioned below; a few additional sites of interest are listed thereafter.

Bronze Age Cemetery at Kiloran Bay – see Chapter 5 NR 39767 97686

Bronze Age Cemetery and Chapel Site, Cill a' Rubha ("St. Maelrubha's Chapel) NR 39310 98163
Three cists were discovered here in 1882 and their capstones may still be seen on the rocky knoll 120m north of Creagan. Two of them contained inhumations and the third contained pottery fragments, suggesting perhaps that it had contained one or more cremations. One of the skeletons, that of a male of about 50 years of age, was removed and is on display in the Museum of the Royal College of Surgeons at Edinburgh. It is believed that, with the advent of Christianity, St. Maelrubha visited the island and sanctified the site. There are no visible remains of his "cell", but the site is defined each springtime by a swathe of bluebells, possibly outlining the ancient garth which may have been a hedged enclosure.

Cup-markings, Uamh na Mine – see Chapter 6 NR 404985

Fort, Dùn Tealtaig (? "Culdee Dùn") NR 389983
A minor promontory structure defined by RCAHM as a fort despite the fact that the limited habitable area would seem very small in

proportion to the length of the "defence" earthwork. Within the earthwork there are signs of four banks or structures, of which the most westerly is taken to be a habitation. The other works may indicate small cultivation plots, as may the three slight terraces to the north of the (later) quarry which interrupts the curtain enclosure.

Fort, Dùn Uragaig ("Fort at Raised-beach Inlet")
NR 381982

This magnificently-sited promontory fort is within plain view of Dùn Meadhonach in Balnahard (see Chapter 6) and barely one kilometre north of the much slighter remains at Meall Lamalum ("Lambs' Holm Headland"). Taking full advantage of the elevated character of the ancient marine platform, the fort is sited some 30m above the rock-girt shore, utterly impregnable save across one narrow, sunken causeway. The defensive wall was some 2m thick and survives to a height of up to three courses. The entrance path is well-defined and one can still enter through the original central gateway. One can recognise the footings of seven distinct buildings, each of about 4m internal diameter. No archaeological study has been made and the site is something of an enigma. Symington Grieve noted that the landward entrance to a sea-cave, Sloch Dubh ("Black Pit" NR 38155 98183), is within the outer fortification, perhaps providing a possible avenue of communication in calm weather.

Viking Ship Burial, Kiloran Bay – see Chapter 5 NR 40117 97765

Fortification, Loch an Sgoltaire ("Cleavage Loch")
NR 386972

The fort stands upon an island in the loch and the main fortification was constructed in May 1615 during the "rising" of that year, to protect a pre-existing structure from artillery attack. From the shore, one can see the roof of a nineteenth-century summer-house, which has been built within a square-shaped courtyard and replaces the original house of refuge. The courtyard or "inner enceinte" is about 15m square and is protected by substantial walls of about 2m thickness. A drum-bastion at each corner varies from 4m to 5.5m in diameter. There is a pentangular outer "fortification" and the island perimeter has a neat perimeter wall, but these could possibly have been nineteenth-century enhancements when the cottage-orné was built; the surviving ornamentation is very slight – but an elegant tea-service which was especially created for it is said to be preserved at Colonsay House. There was also rather an attractive pleasure-garden, and various flowers and plants can still be identified, such as the early form of Montbretia and a non-native hop-plant. According to local legend, in the darker days of WWII, the laird buried the family valuables on the island – including the "last spike" of the Canadian Pacific Railway, which was driven by Donald Smith on 7th November 1885. Apparently he bent the spike, which had to be replaced, and so was able to keep the original one.

Additional places of interest

Uamh Ur ("The New Cave") NR 39594 97930
This was also (briefly) known as "Crystal Spring Cavern", a name favoured by Symington Grieve who investigated it quite thoroughly soon after it was discovered, July 1879. His researches over the following three years were published in Proceedings of the Society of Antiquaries of Scotland. There were plentiful signs of human occupation and the collection of detritus included the bones of deer, pig and horse. The cave contains a shallow well of pure water, and a rocky surface nearby which allegedly shows signs of use as a whet-stone; the innermost chamber has some stalactites and stalagmites. The main cave runs about 20 metres into the cliff, and the full width of the side chambers extends to some 55m. Access details are given below; please do not visit this cave without a spare torch and do ensure that somebody is aware of your intention.

Sloch Dubh Mhic a' Phi ("McPhee's Hidden Gully") NR 39431 98167
This cave is on the croft of Mr. Walter Williams and the most convenient access is via his private steadings if permission can be obtained. The cave consists of a lengthy passageway, giving access to a very secluded tiny beach. There is an opening in the roof at the midpoint – this is the unguarded entrance to a lengthy drop, so do not go rambling about on the field above. Symington Grieve records that at one time a "hoard of money and trinkets" was found above the landward entrance. The traditional story about the cave is best given by Murdoch McNeill:

"A clansman of the Laird of Lochbuie (Mull) who visited Colonsay was gleaning after the reapers in the Glen of Ardskenish; and MacPhee, the chief of the island, who was under a geas or taboo not to let pass a sword-stroke, coming round to see the shearers, when passing the Mull man cut off his hand. On finding this out, the McLeans came over to avenge the deed. When he heard of their arrival, MacPhee, accompanied by his servant and his famous black dog, left his residence at Kiloran and escaped to the hills. As they were retiring over Beinn-a-Sgoltaire they heard the wails of MacPhee's wife – herself a daughter of Lochbuie – who was being maltreated by the McLeans because she would not tell them where her husband was hiding. MacPhee exclaimed to his servant: "Good were your promises to her the day she gave you these trews," pointing to those that his servant had on, "that you would see no harm come to her." "Unlucky is the time you remind me of it," answered his henchman; "if I and the black dog were with you we would defy them; but I will now return, and I shall be slain, and you shall be caught also." MacPhee, retiring to the cave in question, which is open at both ends, set his black dog at the one end while he took his stand at the other, and both so well defended their respective posts that it was only by opening a hole through the roof that the McLeans were able to get at them. This cave ever since has been known as Slochd-dubh-Mhic-a-Phì."

Dùnan a' Chullaich ("Boar Homestead") NR 38253 96638

This is an important but unrecorded farmstead; its location had been "lost" for generations until it was rediscovered in the 1990s by Dr. Richard Gulliver in the course of his study of Colonsay flora. It is the western of the "twa Killoderans" which were first mentioned in a lease of 1541 – after the Dissolution of the Monasteries, it seems likely that the original Abbey lands of Kiloran were divided into two parts, separated by east Loch Fada.

The site has never been examined by archaeologists and is rather complex. In essence, there is a flat grassy circle some 25m in diameter on the top of a well-drained knoll, possibly originally approached from the western side. There are numerous small but inter-connected buildings within the main complex, represented by wall-footings of up to 60cm in height. The main complex appears to have an entrance on the north side and has the superficial appearance of a small courtyard with three chambers to one side and another in an opposing corner. Running away to the southeast there is a bank which connects to another isolated small building. There is an oblong chamber associated with the bank, and a similar one to the west of the isolated building. In addition to all this, there is a rounded chamber within stout walls (possibly 3m square overall) between the apparent "courtyard" doorway and the main approach. Bordering the main circle of occupation on its western side there is a short but substantial stone-and-earth embankment. On the southeast face of the outer approach to the knoll one can see an extensive scatter of stone and there are one or two examples of isolated stones which appear to have been set into the ground, possibly to help gather domesticated animals.

To reach the site, walk up the track towards the southern dam at Loch an Sgoltaire until it levels off beside the prominent concrete header tanks (known locally as "The Alamo" for obvious reasons). Leave the track at this point by walking straight ahead, under the power lines and then walk up the southern side of the burn ahead of you for another 50 metres or so… Dùnan a' Chullaich is on the crest of the rise.

Na Tobhtaichean ("The Ruins") *or* Na Toiteanan ("The Burnings") NR 38239 97039

There are three substantial ruined croft-houses in a line across the slope of Beinn a' Tuath – the map reference is to the middle one. There are also some much less substantial ruins in the same area – these are the only traces that survive of a community that ceased to exist at some point in the 1850s. The late Para Mòr MacAllister was a gifted historian and raconteur, with an extraordinary memory for detail, and he had heard a story in his youth that the people of this area had been "cleared to Australia, to make a sheepwalk". This would have seemed likely enough, since Sir John McNeill, brother to the then laird, was Secretary to the Highland & Islands Emigration Society. On the other hand, careful study of the records of that Society has not produced any Colonsay names, and the laird, Duncan, 1st Lord Colonsay, had no reputation for clearances. Unfortunately, there is no other known tradition about these people, or what became of them although it seems likely that – apart from natural "wastage" – many were relocated elsewhere within the island during the post-famine population collapse. Nonetheless, there is likely to be some truth in the tradition and an Australian dimension may yet emerge. The census return of 1841 shows thirteen households in North Moor, whereas by 1851 there are only nine in "Benatuath"; the census of 1861 does not mention the area.

The two walks suggested below both use the car-park at Kiloran Bay as a starting point. The first one duplicates (in part) a very short section of the much longer Balnahard walk (Chapter 6), insofar as it includes the caves near Port Easdail.

Kiloran Bay Walk (1 hour)

The bay is more than a mile in breadth and presents an outstanding picture – to north and south it is bordered by striking hills, to the west it looks out across the turquoise waters of the Firth of Lorn towards the remote and beautiful peninsula of the Ross of Mull and to the east it is bounded by the magnificent sun-kissed golden sands of Tràigh Bàn ("White Strand"). Note that the bay is formed by a limestone syncline (Chapter 1) whose strata can be traced running back down towards the head of the bay and curving round to contain the magnificent dune system. These dunes are therefore remarkably rich in calcium, being more than 80% pure, and until recently the sand was used as a free and apparently inexhaustible source of fertiliser. Nowadays any exploitation is strictly controlled in order to protect this unique habitat.

The dunes at Kiloran compare very favourably with those at Balnahard and any botanist unable to walk to the north end of Colonsay may wish to thoroughly explore the southern and eastern margins of this system. Persons whose mobility is restricted will find that there remains a wealth of interesting species of flora within one hundred metres of the car-park, which is also an excellent place for bird-watching. Unfortunately cattle no longer graze this area and rank vegetation has already ousted some of the more fragile species – early casualties include both tway-blade and lesser butterfly orchids which used to thrive hereabouts.

As one descends from the car-park to the sandy beach, notice the block of pink granite at the foot of the slope (sometimes buried by sand); this is an erratic boulder from somewhere about Loch Rannoch in the Scottish Highlands – or perhaps Ben Cruachan – and was deposited here by glacial action some 10,000 years ago. On reaching the strand one should cross the burn, Abhainn a' Mhuilinn, probably by paddling. If it is in spate, it is perhaps best to walk upstream for a couple of hundred metres and cross there; if so, notice the flat, blue rock exposed beside the sandpit, and upon which one can easily see pin-sharp striations in the surface that were caused by glacial friction thousands of years ago.

It is always very pleasant to walk along the margins of Kiloran

Bay and a worthwhile objective will be found in the caves which lie at the north end, just beyond Port Easdail. If one walks one way along the margin of the sea, and perhaps goes back the other way along the top of the dunes, one will have a chance to enjoy the full variety of flora, birdlife, the tang of the air and the roar of the surf. The surf here is immensely powerful and, although the bay is believed to be totally safe, one should be ever-watchful for the unexpected rogue wave.

At the northern end of the sand, one passes over a small ridge and down into Port Easdail ("Horse" *or perhaps* "Waterfall Dale Harbour"). This little bay was caused by igneous activity many millions of years ago, as is evidenced by the way in which an outcrop of rare syenite is encircled by igneous material. This latter material is described as "plutonic", having supposedly been solidified at a great depth underground – in effect, this was at the bottom of a volcano. Beyond the igneous material can be seen bands of breccia, where limestone has cemented individual rocks into a common mass.

Continue across the little bay, hugging the shore line and being alert to tidal conditions; the vestige of a rocky path can be followed for about 80 metres beyond the limit of the bay, whereupon one enters a tiny recess, sandy floored and facing south, at the back of which is the small fissure known as Uamh na Mine ("Meal" *or perhaps* "Pounded Cave"). On one's left there is the unmistakable entrance to Uamh Shìorruidh ("Endless Cave", *pron.* "eerie"), which can be explored quite safely. This cave was seemingly inhabited from the late Neolithic period and a deposit of midden material survives within the inner section. To the right of the main entrance there is a mighty slab of fallen rock; on the southeast face there are two Bronze-age cup-marks, both about 60mm by 40mm in depth.

Further into the recess, there is a "natural" staircase running up to a higher cave, Uamh na Baintighearna ("The Lady's Cave"). In fact the access has been slightly contrived and this upper cave has been made to resemble a rustic bower … it is a tiny remnant of the nineteenth-century pleasure ground of Balavetchy and provided a quiet retreat from which one could enjoy the view whilst protecting one's complexion from the glare of the sun. Immediately opposite the mouth of Uamh na Baintighearna there is a genuine flight of steps, which has been carved into the rock. The bottom one is damaged, but it is possible to scramble up with care, and to find oneself upon a path leading to St. Columba's well (see Chapter 6). More significantly, on either side of the path there are a large number of cup-marks – clearly the ones already examined really belong up here and have been dislocated in some ancient rock fall.

Upon regaining Port Easdail, one may return to the car-park either by following the shore line or by striking inland for 150 metres to pick up the track from Balnahard to the main road.

Uragaig and Loch an Sgoltaire Walk (30 minutes to 3 or 4 hours, by choice)

The following walk is absolutely wonderful and falls into ideal segments which will suit everybody. The first section can be anything up to one kilometre, very easy to undertake and full of interest. More adventurous walkers extend it to four kilometres and see the bird cliffs. Others might like to go the full seven kilometres, but they will certainly need a map and should be confident of their ability in difficult and remote terrain.

From the car-park, follow the road uphill. As it levels off, there is a passing place on the left – just beyond this point one can look down onto a small bracken-clad plateau – just across the stile one can see the remains of Tigh Iain Darroch ("John Darroch's House") at NR 39672 97869 – see Chapter 5. The late Ena Williams remarked that John's daughter married a Galbraith and they moved first into the further house at Uragaig Bheag, then emigrated to Canada, but they were not long there when the husband was killed whilst felling a tree. Apparently families who went were given £10 by the Estate to help them on their way.

As you walk on, you will note that this area is warm, sheltered and rich in native flora. There will be groves of silver birch, hazel and mountain ash, also clumps of gorse and goat-willow, all of which are a haven for birdlife. The roadside plants include primrose, dog-rose and the distinctive burnet-rose which is such a feature of Colonsay; enjoy the orchids as well – it would be hard to miss early purple, northern marsh or heath spotted varieties, but there are others. The limestone seems to enhance the devil's bit scabious, but every sort of favourite will be seen – violets, wood sorrel, wood hyacinth (bluebell), harebell, primrose, mountain thyme, St. John's wort – the list is endless. Possibly the most memorable plant is the heady-scented woodbine, hanging in cascades from the roadside rocks and trees.

After 150 metres there is a junction to the left and anybody wishing to explore An Uamh Ùr ("The New Cave") should strike off to the right at this point, staying parallel to a rocky outcropping which winds downwards towards the sea. After about 100 metres the route leads into an enormous bramble thicket, and one must be prepared to tunnel through it and then slither across a treacherous jumble of moss-covered boulders before reaching the mouth of the cave. One is rewarded by the chance to explore an interesting series of chambers, extending some 75 metres or more into the cliff – two torches are essential, in case one of them fails. If alone, make sure that somebody knows where you intend to go.

The turning to the left would lead to Uragaig Bheag; on 16 June 2000, the late Ena Williams mentioned (*pers. comm.*) that there had been three houses at Uragaig Bheag until the Scarlet Fever outbreak of 1874. The ruins of two of them still stand, behind the Estate holiday cottages, which were built to replace them. One of these was home to the McEachern family, which was stricken by the disease; the survivors are said to have abandoned the croft and moved to Bowmore, Islay only to succumb there to a second epidemic just a few years later. Disregarding the turning, continue along the metalled road until a cottage can be glimpsed ahead; **there is a bench at this point and it may be taken as marking the end of the very easiest section of the route.**

The track continues up a short but steep brae, then levels out upon the even surface of an ancient marine platform, now standing some 50 metres above sea level. This is Uragaig ("Stony Landing-place") proper and is bounded on the landward side by cliffs that were created by the action of prehistoric waves. As the track winds its way through the croft lands one will notice a change in the birds and the flora. One will usually see rock doves hereabouts, also ravens, chough and the occasional bird of prey; in recent years a young golden eagle has been seen quartering the ground but this may be just an immature bird with no territory of its own. Occasionally, a sea eagle has been noticed, presumably from Mull. Beside the track one will see hare's tail, cotton-grass, grass of Parnassus, butter-wort, louse-wort, tormentil and other plants typical of sour, brackish land. The drainage in this area is poor because of a clay pan which lies just below the shallow soil, doubtless a legacy of the prehistoric action of the sea against the cliffs.

After a kilometre or so, the track descents towards a fertile spit of land that lies between Port nam Fliuchan ("Tide-foam Landing-place") and Port an Tighe Mhóir ("Big-house Landing-place"). Eventually it terminates at a private house, at one time the home of Sam MacPhee, who achieved local fame as cashier for a Scottish bank, and therefore signatory of its banknotes. On the way the track passes a much older building, restored in recent years but formerly known as "Crumble Cottage" – this is where the late Frank Nicholson witnessed some sort of atmospheric or other phenomenon of a curious nature. Frank was in no way impressionable or fey, and was in fact rather surprised by the incident; but he was adamant about the facts. He was kind enough to record the details, subject to the proviso that the incident remained embargoed during his own lifetime:

"This event occurred fifteen years ago but the impression left on me was vivid and I recall every detail.

Donald McArthur, Clive Cottle and myself were restoring an old steading known as Crumble Cottage at Uragaig, (a) quarter of a mile over flat, grassy ground from Dùn Tealtaig.

At that precise time we were digging a drainage trench and the other two set off to take a trailer load of spoil to be dumped over the cliff near to Pigeon Cave.

I continued digging and suddenly became aware of the murmur of a number of voices. Looking up, I saw clearly in the strong sunlight a large group of people about fifty paces away from me. They were standing chatting as though at a garden party, the women seemed to be dressed in a style of the late (19)20's with short-skirted waistless frocks and cloche hats, the men in flannels and blazers, some with straw boaters on their heads.

Convinced that I was hallucinating I turned away, checked my breathing, pulse and as far as I could judge, my temperature, all normal considering that I was working fairly hard on a warm, sunny day.

I could still hear and see this vision when I turned again to face them. They totally ignored my presence and the fact that by this time my companions were returning with the tractor and trailer. When they rejoined me I waited for them to comment on the scene but obviously they saw nothing unusual. We got on with the work and after a few minutes I asked them if I looked and behaved normally but didn't say why I asked. They assured me that my appearance and behaviour was no odder than usual.

By now the group of people was fading, becoming insubstantial and then disappeared and the clear sound of the voices ceased.

When we stopped work for the day about two hours later I drove straight to the surgery of Dr. Hall-Gardiner and told him the story. At my request he gave me a medical check-up and found nothing wrong but was naturally somewhat sceptical… F.S. Nicholson, 19/10/95"

Perhaps make a slight deviation now, after passing the cottage. To visit Port an Tighe Mhòir or Dùn Tealtaig ("Hut-bay Fort") one will need to approach the private house and turn right, leaving three gates as found. Dùn Tealtaig is easily approached from the south-west and will be found to occupy a dramatic and commanding position. The original "fortification", which is undated, consists of a low rubble and earth bank which survives on the east and south approach to the promontory. The more obvious structures nearer the summit are thought to consist of a building (the most southerly structure, NR 38901 98405) and a few small garden plots. Although classified as a "fort" by RCAHMS, it has been suggested that Dùn Tealtaig may instead have been a Culdee establishment. The Céile Dé ("Companion of God") chose to live an ascetic life of prayer and self-sacrifice; the movement was associated with the Iona tradition and was active from the mid-eighth century. The eighteenth-century Scottish poet Thomas Campbell celebrated such men from Ireland:

> *Peace to their shades. The pure Culdees*
> *Were Albyn's earliest priests of God,*
> *Ere yet an island of her seas,*
> *By foot of Saxon monk was trod.*

The meaning of "Tealtaig" is obscure. Symington Grieve maintained that the correct local name was "Dùn Ceilte", which he translated as "Fort of the Hiding-place". The present writer sees no "hiding-place" in the vicinity and wonders if the place-name could give independent support to the "Céile Dé" theory.

Port an Tighe Mhòir is associated with the McLugash family and it is interesting to examine the slight ruins of the eponymous big house and, hard against the nearby cliff, the well-preserved remains of a corn-drying kiln (by far the best example in Colonsay). To do this, descend by the well-constructed zig-zag path and cross the head of the beach. The remains of the house are currently (January 2010) buried in impenetrable briars, but the kiln is easily found (NR

39034 98249) and worthy of inspection. It consists of a central chamber, beautifully made, measuring 1.5m internal diameter on the visible floor surface. This inner well rises 0.6m with a slight outward batter, then is stepped-out by an additional foot to become c. 2.1m in diameter and rising, at its highest surviving point, by another 0.6m or so. The approach to this chamber is from the southwest side by means of a well-constructed flight of steps. The entrance to the flue is on the northern side, with an opening about 0.45m wide and about 0.3m high – the top of the flue at the point of entry is about 0.3m below the existing surface of the floor of the kiln chamber. The wall of the structure on the northern side is about 1.8m thick and this seems to have been true for its entire length except where it accommodates itself to the natural rock face. The flue provided the draught for the kiln and there is an eyebolt set into the rock-face about 2.4m above it; possibly this supported a pulley mechanism to regulate the airflow.

Returning to our main route, turn left through a field gate just before the private house and, keeping the garden fence on your right, follow it past a right angled corner, then continue up the hill, leaving the house behind you on your right and keeping to the edge of the arable ground. Turn left at the top of the slope, to follow the upper edge of the arable ground and pass over the heather ridge, whereupon you will get sight of the sea. Identify the junction of two fences, and the gate at NR 38901 98405.

The route is now approaching the bird cliffs of Cailleach Uragaig ("The Old Woman of Uragaig"), and will follow them along towards the west. It will be easy to choose a path, but do remember that the grass can be slippery and that in some places there is an overhang; there is a grassy track beside the fence line and a good stile at the far end. If you choose to walk on the seaward side of the fence, remember that the cliff is heavily indented, so it is best to observe the birds opposite you rather than try to see the ones beneath you. There are huge numbers of birds to be seen, and the different species tend to have their favourite corners. The guillemots are first, then there is an area favoured by fulmars, after which one encounters the kittiwakes; the shag is rather less choosy and will be found hither and yon. One or two of the cliffs are inaccessible to grazing animals and one can see flourishing displays of roseroot, scurvy-grass and sheep-sorrel.

As a guide to relative proportions, the following table is based upon the seabird population of Colonsay and Oronsay as entered in the Seabird Colony Register of the Nature Conservancy Council in the 1980s:

Fulmar 1,738	Shags 236
Black-headed gull 126	Common gull 134
Lesser black-backed gull 54	Herring gull 1,866
Greater blackbacked gull 76	Kittiwake 11,292
Common tern 80	Arctic tern 1,448
Guillemot 13,541	Razorbill 1,450
Black guillemot 397	

By 2000, Colonsay was recognised as the principle seabird centre in the Southern Inner Hebrides, with a total of over 50,000 birds, and the census of that year revealed:

Fulmar 2,600	Guillemots 26,000
Razorbills 2,700	Kittiwakes 13,000

For further details see *The Birds of Colonsay and Oronsay* by David Jardine.

The cliff path leads out to a small promontory, almost separated from the main peninsula by a striking natural arch and accessed by the resultant natural bridge. The defensive possibilities of the site were clearly valued because, as one crosses the "bridge", one notices that one is approaching a substantial defensive wall. This is Dùn Uragaig ("Raised-beach Fort") and the most obvious entrance is through the original gateway.

As one enters the fort proper one can readily identify three buildings on either side of the entrance, hard against the curtain-wall, plus at least one platform which may have been the base for a hut or garner. This is a protected ancient monument of uncertain date, and about which no history survives. In a half-remembered tradition it is said to have been a "Danish" stronghold, suggesting perhaps something other than mainstream Norse. It will be noticed that it has a commanding view towards the Ross of Mull and in particular of the approach from the Sound of Iona. Perhaps coincidentally, this is the closest point in Colonsay to Iona itself, but one can only speculate as to the purpose of an impregnable fortification at such a spot. One can readily understand the need for a simple look-out post, but this structure could clearly have held a garrison of upwards of a hundred men and their followers, and it would surely have required at least half that number to defend the wall.

It is rather pleasant to rest awhile at this spot, speculating upon its possible history. In early summer the area is carpeted with flowers – seapinks, squill and campion, highlighted by varieties of moss and lichen. From the edge of the cliff one has an excellent view of the surface of the sea some 40 metres below, where tidal currents provide a rich food source for the myriad sea-birds. Close at hand there will be fulmars, gliding so effortlessly in the updraught of the breakers, and in the background there will be kittiwakes, charmingly billing and cooing. With binoculars, one can study the rafts of birds floating on the sea itself – common guillemots, bridled guillemots, black guillemots, and razorbills can all be seen, and now and again one may spot the distinctive bill of a puffin. Puffins do not breed in Colonsay, but are regular visitors to such areas as this, where strong tides must round a headland. Here and there, one will see cormorants and shags in flight, taking full advantage of the benefits of "ground effect" to minimise their energy requirements. In former days the shag or "scart" was a delicacy in Colonsay; apparently the bird was skinned rather than plucked, then boiled for a while, after which most of the fishiness would have dissipated and it could be roasted. It was a popular dish, but its eggs were only eaten in dire necessity – they are said to taste truly dreadful. Incidentally, whilst scanning the waves keep an eye open for basking shark, which have become rather more common in recent years – this the second largest fish in the world, and can be up to 10 metres in length. It feeds on plankton and tends to drift, mouth wide-open, very slowly on the surface.

This could be taken as the end of the first serious segment of the route, *and some readers may choose to turn back. For others, leaving Dùn Uragaig, follow a line leading directly away from the access stile, going southeast across the heather towards the head of Port nam Fliuchan. The scenery is outstanding but one should pay careful attention whilst descending the tricky route onto the raised beach; if in doubt, strike inland and descend to join an old cart-track. Either way, you should find yourself on a remarkable raised beach, surrounded by low cliffs and numerous small caves.*

It was Professor Watson who identified the Norse origin of the name "Uragaig", from "urð" = "heap of stones" and "vik" = "inlet". The Gaelic name of the beach itself is Port nam Fliuchan, where "fliuchan" means "wetness" and refers to the massive banks of tide-foam that can develop here after an Atlantic storm, sometimes up to four metres in height and lying in great drifts right up the beach. One or two of the caves show sign of habitation – these, and others, were in use on an occasional basis up until the end of the nineteenth century. When disease struck a household, Lord Colonsay insisted that the home should be vacated and then disinfected with quick-lime, which he supplied for the purpose; at such times, or when a cottage required major renovations, it was often found convenient to resort to one or other of the caves. One of them, Uamh Bhòid-heach ("The Bonnie Cave") was thought to be particularly fine and, writing as late as 1882, the antiquarian William Stevenson noted that "there is an old man living in Greenock who was born in ... the Bonnie Cave".

Looking southeast across the shingle of the raised beach, one can identify (at NR 38403 97994) a path running upwards towards the southwest, following the natural run of the land. At one time this was an important route, in daily use, and as one follows it there will be vestiges of the work that made it suitable for use by the small garrons or ponies of the day. Starting upwards, follow this path for about 200 metres, when it will cross the bed of a small burn (NR 38341 97852).

At this point, the second major segment of the route has been completed. To cut short the walk and regain the car-park at Kiloran Bay, turn left along the line of the small burn and continue up onto the open heathland, keeping the inland cliffs on your right-hand side. After about 200 metres, a large agricultural barn will become visible and it will be possible to choose a suitable route to regain the public road at that point. The heathland underfoot is quite safe but a bit boggy; it would be easy to turn an ankle, particularly in dry weather, so it is important to pick one's steps. Do be prepared for frequent stops – the flora is quite outstanding and additional species hereabouts include marsh ragwort, marsh lousewort, bog asphodel, cotton grass and species of insectivorous sundew.

However, those intrepid souls who intend to make the full circuit will continue to follow the faint traces of the old path, crossing the burn by a slight ford. In late spring, the small gully to the right will have a breathtakingly beautiful display of roseroot, unassailed by ruminants. Follow the path upwards and onwards, taking the left "fork" in about 50 metres to pass below a prominent rocky outcrop. After another 100 metres or so there will be an inland cliff on the left and a rather tricky fence-topped wall to be seen ahead of you. Although the line of the path lies straight through, it has been blocked by the fence so it may be easiest to do a dog-leg to the right and cross the fence nearer to the sea. Having done so, and if it is late springtime, approach the seaward end of the fence and admire the profusion of salt-tolerant plants such as thrift, sea-campion and roseroot growing in a sheltered but sheep-free gully. Then go back along the fence-line and turn right at the inland cliff, to follow the original line of the path.

In about 50 metres, you will reach a small coll at NR 38236 97613 and the remains of a tiny homestead, possibly eighteenth century. This is an important landmark (especially if you have to retrace your steps due to high bracken or other difficulty); leave the cottage on your left and from this point the track continues in the same direction for another 100 metres, passing across a hollow slope, then it turns slightly to the right and starts to climb. It works its way slowly towards the top of the higher ground on your left-hand side and after another 150 metres you will notice two white lichen-covered slabs (at NR 38073 97457). The track now zig-zags, so as to gain height gradually. (In essence, it is leading you towards the letter "B" of "Beinn a' Tuath" on the O.S. 1:25000 sheet, ref. NR 381971). The pathway will originally have been used to collect peats from the hill, carried in creels by the small ponies of that time.

On reaching the plateau of higher ground (NR 38033 97377) look straight ahead, inland, and identify Beinn a' Tuath with its rather modest cairn. Heading towards it, it is possible to bear slightly to the left and follow a gully down towards Loch an Sgoltaire ("Loch in the Cleft"), but a slight diversion to the actual summit is recommended and will give an excellent view of the whole of the former "Northmuir". Looking towards Iona, there is a good view of the Torran Rocks and, looking inland, one can see Loch Turraman and the neighbouring fank – said by some to represent the very centre-point of the islands! Closer at hand, it is easy to imagine the difficulty with which 48 people struggled to make a living from this hillside, and as one descends towards the southern end of the loch one can expect to encounter the ruins of one of the more substantial cottages (NR 38239 97039).

There is a good view of Loch an Sgoltaire, which is 60 metres above sea level and which, at the northern end, is about 24 metres deep. Its waters originally debouched at both ends but the northern outlet was dammed in the 1860s, to create a lade for the new mill at Balerulin. In the 1920s Lord Strathcona created an additional dam at the southern end and installed filtration equipment, work which was undertaken by mainland contractors McDougall of Oban. This provided a gravity supply to Kiloran and all of Kilchattan, until in the 1980s it was superceded by the public supply which now serves the entire community. A modern and highly sophisticated water treatment system has recently been installed, ensuring that Colonsay's water quality is in line with the highest of EEC standards.

Although it is not particularly rich in aquatic vegetation, Loch an Sgoltaire hosts a native population of slow-growing brown trout, which attain a length of about 24cm in their third year. The tiny islands are a favoured breeding ground for feral Canada geese, first introduced in 1934, and other species hereabouts include the tufted duck. In times of storm, vast numbers of seabirds sometimes congregate on this loch, affecting water potability in ways that could only be countered with the aid of the new computerised monitoring system.

One can easily see that there is a building on the largest island in the loch, although from the shore details are not precise. In fact, what one can see is a Victorian bower or summer house, built within the curtilage of a fortification. In 1615 Sir James MacDonald made a desperate attempt to attract the attention of his monarch and to bypass the machinations of Argyll; to do this, he made a dramatic escape from confinement at Edinburgh and made his way to the west, where he raised a token rebellion. His gambit proved to be ill-judged, but during the course of the action he relied heavily upon his lieutenant, Coll MacDonald of Colonsay. On Sunday 18 June 1815, Coll landed at Colonsay with a force of 300 men and devoted the next fifteen days to improving the defences of the little fort upon the island in Loch an Sgoltaire.

One imagines that the pre-existing building will have been little more than a cabin, depending upon its isolation for its security in much the same way as a crannog. Knowing that something more substantial would be required if government artillery was involved, Coll surrounded the cabin with a sturdy wall, about 2m high and 2m in breadth, enclosing an area of 15m x 14m, with a strong drum-bastions at each corner. The whole thing was surrounded by an outer pentangular curtain wall which followed the natural features of the island, again incorporating drum-bastions at the corner. Incidentally, aerial photography shows that there is no truth in the legend of a secret stepping-stone pathway to the island. The loch is very deep and extremely cold – the only access to the island is by boat.

Coll's fortification was never used in anger, but it was to provide an invaluable retreat from time to time. The island is known as Eilean Dubh Iain Mhitchel ("John Mitchell's Hiding-island") and is said to be named for a catholic priest who once based himself there. It is known that Alasdair MacCholla brought priests with him from Ireland in 1644 when he empowered Montrose, and it is likely that there will have been a priest in Colonsay throughout the period of Sarah MacDonald's tenure until late 1688. Throughout that period the island was subjected to harassment and one can imagine that Fr. Mitchell would have valued the security and comfort of the small house, screened within its protective walls. (Sadly, it has not yet proved possible to identify Fr. Mitchell in the clerical records – apart from Franciscan missionaries in the 1620s, only one other post-reformation priest is known by name. Apparently a Fr. David Galwey (1579–1634) was a Jesuit missionary in the Inner and Lower Hebrides who laboured in Islay, Oronsay, Colonsay, and Arran; but his exact dates are somewhat uncertain; one source says he died in Cork on December 23rd 1649.)

A hint of Fr. Mitchell's difficulties can be seen in the process by which the McNeill interest supplanted that of MacDonald in Colonsay. In the McNeill family records it is stated that "Donald of Crear resigned his castle of Sween in Knapdale and took Colonsay at the point of the sword". He registered arms in the Lyon Office in 1670, and "Donald changed Crear, Drumdrishaig and lands in Knapdale with Archibald Earl of Argyle for Colonsay and Oronsay in 1672." From legal records it is confirmed that there were regular attacks upon Sarah MacDonald's possession throughout this period and there is a tradition that when the McNeills finally got control they themselves had to live in Eilean Dubh Iain Mhitchel for their own protection.

During the nineteenth century, the ruins of the original cabin were cleared and an attractive bower was built within the curtain wall, another part of that substantial pleasure-ground which has already been discussed. Interestingly enough, a Catholic altar-stone has deliberately been set into the threshold of the entrance gate, where every visitor must step upon it. The consecration crosses are clearly to be seen and one cannot but reflect that this act of calculated blasphemy has in fact helped preserve the memory of Fr. Mitchell's service to the island. At the same time, of course, it brought no luck to the McNeills…

Whether or not one climbed to the top of Beinn a' Tuath, it should be easy to find the ruined cottage on its south-eastern flank at NR 38239 97039. From here it would be, of course, quite possible to make one's way back to the main road by going around the south end of the loch and following the water treatment plant access track.

Instead, and to complete the suggested walk, pick up the rough path leading north-eastwards from the cottage and along the contour line towards another such ruin. You will pass over a rare piece of fine turf – if you stamp upon it, it rings hollow. You will pass the second ruin shortly afterwards and can then pick and choose from amongst the various tracks, descending gently to the lochside, where it will be found that there is fairly easy walking along the nearest (western) side. At the northern end of the loch, negotiate a fence and cross the dam. From this point, follow a rough but well-defined track down the hill, looking out for a large agricultural barn ahead and to the right, between two modern houses. As the track descends to level ground and turns to the right (almost in line with the hydro-electric poles to your left), you may be able to identify a rough path running up to your right towards a stile in the fence-line at NR 39030 97862 (perhaps 30 metres away from you); if so, you can use it to follow a convenient path along the border between the fields and the foot of the ancient sea-cliffs. Otherwise, you can just make your way towards the big barn, thus regaining the original track. By either route, there is an easy stroll back to the car-park at Kiloran Bay.

Chapter 9

UPPER AND LOWER KILCHATTAN
Map: page xiii

Kilchattan encompasses most of the present-day croft-land in Colonsay, about 800 acres in total extent and including about 155 acres of "arable and meadow". It seems that most of the crofts were created from two of Colonsay's original "tacks" or farms, which were vacated when the MacMillan and Currie families relinquished their interest in the early nineteenth century. These families emigrated, and "the Old Laird" used the vacated land to create model holdings for former runrig tenants. His estate map of 1804 survives and indicates some twenty holdings, which were drawn with mathematical precision so as to provide each tenant with about seven acres in all. Although the original number is uncertain, when the Crofting Act of 1888 gave occupants security of tenure the common grazing was divided into nineteen shares, seven on the south hill and twelve on the north. The modern road intersects ten of these holdings rather neatly, with four acres of arable on the western side and three acres of "meadow" running down towards the loch.

The division between "Upper" and "Lower" Kilchattan runs along the ditch on the north side of the track to Gortin, which was formerly an important watercourse. This used to carry flood water from an extensive lochan which separated Gortin from the rest of the crofts; this lochan was drained in the late nineteenth century and a new watercourse was created leading down towards Port Mór.

It seems that some of the crofts existed even prior to 1804, at Baile Iochdrach ("Lower Homestead"), which is the land running from the graveyard out towards to the promontory. Professor Mackinnon made mention of this: "Before… the old Laird… purchased the estate from his cousin (in 1805), there was a substantial tenantry in Machrins, Balnahard, Kilchattan, and elsewhere, who lived in rude comfort on their holdings. Those in the lower end of Kilchattan, near the sea, were the least affected by the changes which then took place."

The new crofts were, of course, deliberately designed to be unviable as independent units, so that the tenantry would be obliged to seek such additional work as was available to them. The only such work was provided by the landlord, who thus secured a reliable and inexpensive labour force to gather his kelp, plough his land and harvest his crops. The womenfolk were available for domestic duties and the processes of linen and wool production. The result was that the era of "The Old Laird", 1805–46, was one in which he could enforce rapid and genuine improvements in Colonsay, accompanied by spectacular financial rewards for himself and his family.

The returns which accrued to the proprietor were truly phenomenal, especially when one remembers that income tax (where payable) did not exceed ten-per-cent. For example, in 1811 a visitor reported that Colonsay and Oronsay produced about 150 tonnes of kelp each year, worth up to £3,000 to the proprietor. As a yardstick, in 1810 the minister was paid £86. 16s. 9d for the year, which might be said to equal £58,274.29 in today's money if the minister's salary had increased over time in line with average earnings. (Note that the status of a Minister in those days would have been at least comparable to that of a doctor, with commensurate salary; a doctor today receives about £100,000 p.a. and a Minister receives about £25,000). The calculation uses data found on www.measuringworth.com and has no particular bias. Based upon exactly the same formula, we see that the Laird was paid the equivalent of slightly more than £2,000,000 for his kelp in that one year, and we know that prices and quantities were sometimes higher in other years. The beauty of the situation lay in the fact that his employees earned 1s 6d. per day, which by this formula equates to £50.33 today, and had to return their earnings to him as rent for their tiny holdings. In fact, the employer did not even have to pay the wages in the first place: "Vouchers indicating the number of days and hours worked were issued, but could only be cashed at stated intervals. In the intervals, these vouchers circulated as freely as money. Thus a local paper currency was put into use".

Lord Teignmouth, who visited in 1836, confirmed that John McNeill had created the crofting district of Kilchattan, having "transplanted hither his tenants from less favoured situations." He goes on to give a useful description:

"The farms (crofts) are small, but separate. The tenants are encouraged to improve their allotments, by five years' leases, and by exemption of rent during the first part of the time. They build their own houses: some of these belonging to crofters were superior to any which I had yet seen, except those built by the proprietors in Isla. They were of stone, neatly constructed without mortar, and well thatched; containing two, and sometimes three, good dwelling apartments, a store-house or barn, a byre, and perhaps another apartment built *in a run*. The dwelling-apartment and kitchen were furnished with fire-places … the interior indicated comfort.

"The most marked difference appeared in these cottages, which were furnished with chimnies, the use of which Mr Macneil encourages, by allowing £10 and £12 to the tenants, who build their cottages with such appendage. In those the white-wash on the walls was unsoiled, the floor was clean and carefully swept, and the furniture kept in the same manner: those, on the other hand, in which the fire was laid in the usual fashion, were filled with smoke, and the inmates, despairing of contending with the soot, abandoned their dwelling to filth and disorder. Yet the people, even when they have their chimney, will not make use of it, placing their fire on the floor on the usual pretext that the *wee things* may be able to get round it.

"The cottages in Colonsay are overrun with poultry, which are suffered to perch on the beds and looms; on the beds may be occasionally seen a nest, in which a new-laid egg had been duly deposited… The population of Colonsay is 1000, and is insufficient for the labour required; it has been too much thinned by emigrations to America, about ten and three years ago [i.e. c. 1823]… Mr Macneil is lord paramount and magistrate of the Island."

Note that Lord Teignmouth was writing in 1836; readers are referred to the petition that was mentioned in the Introduction to this book – presented to Parliament in April 1837, it seemed to describe a very different place.

However, good examples of such cottages as have been described can still be seen; the original Homefield ("Holm-feld", Norse) is on the better land described by Professor Mackinnon, behind the graveyard, and is one of the superior dwellings, built *"in a run"* and with an integral chimney. That dwelling was 4.8m by 9.6m on the interior. The building to its west, on Baile Iochdracht ("The Lower Part of the Township") is of some interest as having been the childhood home of Donald Mackinnon, and it preserves some interesting architectural features. There is a massive fireplace at the western end, also window etc., with walls pointed in mortar but the owner, Donald "Gibbie" MacNeill, draws attention to the contrast at the eastern end. It seems that this, the lower end, was reserved for the livestock, with ventilation rather than a window and with the walls pointed in a clay daub. Elsewhere, the disused cottage beside the entrance to the Gortin track is rather more basic, and can readily be imagined with a rush thatch and a central smokehole. Yet the cottage closest to the school veers in the other direction, having no less than three chimneys, at least one of which is purely for "show". The cottage of Cnoc nam Ban also sports three chimneys, but the ruins behind Cnoc na Fad and "Alister Annie's" have none. A later croft-house stood just behind the present house at Cnoc na Fad and had chimneys in the gable-ends; it was demolished and the stone was used for road-mending (Donald "Gibbie" MacNeill, *pers. comm.*). A very good example of an early cottage has been preserved at the heart of a modern dwelling, at Druim Haugh.

In reference to Baile Iochdrach, Donald Mackinnon commented that "The soil was of the best, and the holdings were less contracted than elsewhere. There the tenants were decently comfortable and able to stand the shock of the potato failure." The same could have been said of Gortin; elsewhere the new crofts created in 1806 were simply too small – there were at least six crofts in Sgreadan even as late as 1841, although these were later combined to make one "farm"; families in those days were large and quickly outgrew the capacity of the available holdings. With relatively good housing and education, many of the inhabitants became ambitious and were receptive to the opportunities in the New World, as described by those who had already made the break. On the other hand, conflicting reports left some of those behind in an agony of indecision, as this extract from a letter illustrates:

Killechatan, Aprile 7, 1822

A Charaid Ghradhaich,
Tha mi ga mheas 'na mhor throcair bho'n Tighearna gu bheil an cothrom so air a bhuileachadh orm gu scriobhadh a t'ionnsuich mar a dhiarr thu orm anns an litir a scriobh thu di 'mionnsuidh,

ni thug mor thoilinntin dhomh le chluinntinn gu robh thu fein agus do theaghlach maille ri do Chairdean nar Slainte – mar an ceudna, tha mi ro thaitneach do'd Litir do bhri gu bheil mi tuigsin gu bheil thu a ginnseadh na firinn mu thimchiol an aite, oir tha moran do Leitirichean a tighinn an so bho chuid do na chaich a-nunn, nach 'eil idir a' ginnseadh na firinn – oir tha cuid a tha ga mholladh gu h-anabarrach agus cuid eile a tha ga dhiteadh air an doigh cheadna, air chor is gu bheil iad a [mearachd?] araon. …

My Dr. Sr. your friend & Most humble Servt
Malcolm Mun

Beloved cousin,

I consider it a great mercy from the Lord that this opportunity has been granted me to write to you as you asked me to in the letter you wrote to me, which gave me great pleasure to hear that you and your family together with your cousins (friends) are in good health – also, I am very glad to have your letter because I understand that you are telling the truth about the place, for there are many letters coming here from some of those that went across, that do not tell the truth at all – for there are some that are praising it a great deal and others that are condemning it in the same way, to the extent that they are both [in error?] …

(Transliteration by Alastair M. Scouller, Colonsay, 27 August 1997)

Malcolm Munn never did summon up the courage to emigrate; for him and others like him the lure of 100 acres freehold in Canada was simply not enough to embolden them. In the years that followed there was to be grinding poverty in Colonsay, ceaseless labour and the dreadful losses attendant upon a series of calamities – smallpox, scarlatina, cholera, consumption and the potato blight. As conditions deteriorated throughout the Highlands, the government began to act.

In 1851 Sir John McNeill, third son of Colonsay's "Old Laird" and brother of the current laird, conducted an investigation for the government as Chairman of the Board of Supervision for the Relief of the Poor; conspicuously, no evidence was taken in Colonsay. Sir John McNeill was also a lynch-pin of the Scottish Australian Emigration Society, which sent thousands of people overseas in deplorable conditions – the disastrous voyage of the "*Hercules*" was under his especial supervision. Later, his nephew Malcolm was to serve the Board of Supervision in the same capacity, and was even seconded as the Secretary to the Royal Commission on the Crofters and Cottars in the Highlands 1883-4 (popularly known as the Napier Commission). Donald Mackinnon, son of a Colonsay crofter, was appointed as a Commissioner to the same board, and the pair of them heard (without comment) the evidence of eyewitnesses to the enormities which had occurred. By then, Sir John McNeill G.C.B., P.C., had become laird of Colonsay himself and was married to Emma, daughter of the 7th Duke of Argyll. It is worth re-iterating that, in these and other enquiries, no evidence was ever taken in Colonsay and the McNeill lairds remained exempt from any outside scrutiny.

In "*Gloomy Memories*", Donald McLeod made detailed reference to appalling crimes against the peasantry in Barra and cites the statement of Rev. J. L. Buchanan: "It was a most unlucky day to the Highlands that Sir John McNeill was commissioned to investigate their condition; and the one-sided Report which he has laid before the Legislature of our country shows how incompetent he was for the undertaking. Our analysis of the annexed document, which he obtained from the Parochial Board of Barra, and which by the way was considered by the pro-clearings and expatriating Press the cream of his trashy Report, will show every unprejudiced reader how little confidence may be placed in Sir John's evidence."

McLeod himself describes an official visit to Skye, in 1850, when the Commissioners asked members of the Parochial Board to show them cases of extreme poverty. "So at daylight they started, and they were in the first instance directed to a poor widow's abode. "Is this one of the worst cases you have to show?" enquired Sir John; being answered in the affirmative, then says he, "Mr. Smyth, we must see what is within"; in they go, the widow with her three fatherless children were in bed. "*Holo*", cries Sir John, "have you any food in the house?" "Very little indeed sir", was the reply. Sir John, by this time was searching and opening boxes, where nothing but rags and emptiness was to be found; at last he uncovered a pot where there was about three pounds of cold pottage; Smyth discovered a small bowl or basin of milk. Sir John bawls out with an authoritative tone, holding out the cold pottage in one hand and the basin of milk in the other, "Do you presume, gentlemen, to call this an extreme case of poverty, where so much meat was left after being satisfied at supper?" Some of the party ventured to mutter out, "that is all the poor woman has." "Hush", says Sir John, "she was cunning enough to hide the rest". Sir John's dog made a bolt at the pottage and devoured the most of it; the party left; did not go far when the dog got sick. "That d-n cold pottage has poisoned my valuable dog," says Sir John; the servant was ordered back to the inn to physic the dog. The whole investigation of the day was conducted in a similar manner; only the dog was taken care of, and not allowed among the pots of the perishing people."

It is only fair to give balance. Sir John's daughter (*"Memoir of the Right Hon. Sir John McNeill, G.C.B."*, 1910) stated of the Report "Its conclusions are as true today as they were in 1851. It is still the "final word" on the Crofter Question" and she quotes as follows: "The habit of depending upon the proprietor, on the destitution funds, on someone who is to think and provide for them, is one of the most serious impediments to a permanent amelioration of their condition, and one of the advantages of emigration to the Colonies has been the effect of new circumstances counteracting this disposition." This follows just a few pages after her quotations from Lady McNeill's diary *"Journal of our **dolce far niente** Life at Ardlussa"*, a far cry from the life of the peasantry.

Here in Colonsay, in 1841 there were a total of 260 people living in 46 houses in Kilchattan, but without any security of tenure. By 1891 there were 97 people in 23 houses, of which at least twelve enjoyed the limited security granted by the Crofting Act of 1886. Even with such security, the lives and occupations of the crofters were still tightly circumscribed – for example, in 1906 Archibald Campbell obtained a lease of Peter McNeill's former croft. The agreement was bound by fifteen major conditions of the Estate, running to three pages of closely printed text. In addition, the landlord inserted special clauses: "The subjects do not constitute a crofter's holding within the meaning of the Act", and the landlord "reserves power to resume any part of the subjects let without notice…"

Sub-tenancies were forbidden, and immediate vacant possession could be required in the event of insolvency; three clauses made provision for way-going crops, terms of rental and the like. Buildings, roads, ditches and fences were to be properly maintained, and the tenant was bound to cultivate and manure the arable land according to a "five or six shift rotation" and "no part of the meadow, outfield, or unenclosed land shall be broken up for tillage without the Landlord's consent in writing."

"The Tenant shall not dispose of or remove from the farm any of the straw, hay, or turnips grown thereon, but shall consume and convert into dung the whole thereof, and lay it out on the farm…"
"The Tenant shall not, without written authority, cut or allow to be cut any bent or any peats" and where permission for peat-cutting was given strict guidelines were to be observed. All mineral rights and kelp-cutting were strictly reserved, but the tenants "shall have liberty to take and gather shell-sand, and so much as may not be required by the Proprietor for other purposes, of the drift sea-ware found on the shore of their respective farms, for the purpose of manuring or top-dressing the arable lands or enclosed meadows, but not for any other purpose…"

"All game, rabbits, wild-fowl, and salmon and other fishings are reserved to the Proprietor" and "the tenant shall have no claim against the Proprietor for damage done to his crops by ground game…" The Proprietor reserved the right to resume land for plantations, roads, adjustments of march dykes etc., subject to an adjustment in rental to compensate for any loss of arable land. Tenants were also bound to pay their share of the Blacksmith's wage, and to "take all their grindable corn to the mill of Kiloran" and to "pay the accustomed multures and dues" etc.

Of course, that was long ago and things were expected to change under the 1976 Crofting Act, by which crofters obtained the right to buy-out their tenancy, but even then the transition was a painful one until it was finally settled by the Scottish Land Court in September 1991. The Landlord had accepted a tenant's right to buy, but sought to "maintain control of all road access to the land", as reported by "*The Scotsman*". The landlord apparently opposed unlimited rights of access – "Can the court see the whole future? Could the court for instance envisage the possibility that the croft might become a favoured nuclear waste dump for the Western Isles, and that there would be lorries line astern up this road forever and a day, putting nuclear waste in a large hole in the middle of the croft?" Apparently not, since the court took the view that any such development would in any case "become a matter for the planning authorities" and it found in favour of the tenant.

There are eight sites of historic interest listed by the Royal Commission, as mentioned below; a few additional sites of interest are listed thereafter.

Cists, Lower Kilchattan NR 366948 and NR 362948

A number of cist-graves were discovered around Druimhaugh (1856) and Drumclach (1870), but the records are very imprecise. One of the two cists discovered in 1870 had a decorated stone near its capstone, 0.75m in length by 0.1m broad and 0.05m thick. It had "seven diamond or lozenge-shaped forms produced by a series of rectilinear lines or grooves crossing each other at an angle of 45°." The stone itself was lost, but a cast is preserved in the National Museum of Antiquities. By chance, the first Ordnance Survey was being prepared at that time so it is likely that these cists, which are indicated, were accurately placed.

Standing Stones, Drumclach NR 367949

These impressive stones are a prominent feature and it is believed that they mark cremation sites. Excavation between the stones was said to have uncovered a souterrain, which was not explored, but RCAHMS suggest that this was very probably the top of a cist-grave. The southerly stone is 3.1m high, and the one closer to the road is 2.6m high. They have become known as "Fingal's Limpet Hammers" because they resemble giant versions of the stone tools so commonly discovered in Oronsay's Mesolithic remains which might possibly have served such a purpose.

Fort, Meall Lamalum ("Lambs-holm Headland")
NR 368969

The scant remains at this site might easily be overlooked, but there are the distinct remains of two walls which may well be the vestiges of an ancient promontory fort. The outer wall is more noticeable at the northern edge, where it survives as a rubble bank, about 1m in height. The inner, or main wall is much more obvious, especially when viewed from a height. It has two entrances, one at the middle and the other near the northern extremity, behind which there is the outline of a small hut. The faint outline of three further huts can be identified on the northeast edge of the main plateau.

Dùn Meadhonach ("Middle Homestead"), Drumclach NR 365947

This distinctive dùn can be identified from the roadside *e.g.* from the graveyard, it lies slightly to the west of the houses and set back against the high ground. It stands on a distinct knoll, 12m in height, and has a clearly flattened summit; it looks quite green, due to occupation detritus. The entrance was at the northeast end, and access from any other point would be quite difficult. During the mediaeval period, this was said to be the seat of the chief of the MacMhuirich ("Currie") family. "His house was called "Tigh an tom dreis" (Bramble-knoll House), and according to highland custom he himself was known as "Fear an tom dreis." *Proceedings of the Society of Antiquaries of Scotland vol 34* (1899 –1900): "*Notes on some cup marked stones and rocks near Kenmore, and their folklore*" by Rev J.B. Mackenzie (former Minister at Colonsay).

Hut-circle and Field-system, Druim nam Faoileann ("Seagull Ridge") NR 359960

This is an oval building, 4.5m by 5.5m within a low bank and on the very edge of a small series of lazybeds; the latter seem to be rather later, and to have perhaps taken advantage of pre-existing fertility. There are no other ancient remains nearby and the location is a little unusual.

Hut-circle, Tòrr an Tuirc ("Mound of the Boar") NR 381960

Seldom visited but quite distinct, this hut-circle is close to the summit of Tòrr an Tuirc itself, which is about 150m north-west of the cottage. It measures about 8m in internal diameter and its wall stands to about 0.25m high and up to 2.5m thick. As so often in Colonsay, there is a small annexe, about 2m by 1.5m, attached in this case to the western side of the hut-circle but with no visible sign of an entrance. The entrance to the hut itself is believed to be to the east.

Cill Mhoire ("Our Lady's Chapel"), Upper Kilchattan NR 37743 95792

The site is badly obscured by an extensive growth of bracken, lying about 90m northeast of the Baptist Chapel and (to judge by Blau's map) not far from the lochside in mediaeval times. The chapel measures c. 7m by 4m internally, and is orientated; the entrance is not obvious and the remains are comparable to those of Cill Chaitriona, Balnahard. The interior contains the base of an altar and at least one apparent grave-marker. In winter, one can trace part of the outline of a surrounding garth and certain stones which are locally believed to be grave-markers. RCAHMS suggest that these are "merely natural surface boulders", but it seems strange that these should happen to appear in this location with no others in the vicinity. The site was one that was used for the burial of stillborn and un-baptised children in pre-Victorian times, and was also the place of interment for the MacLeans killed at Glaic a' Mhuirt (see below). Each township or farm had its own chapel at one time, and this one will have served "Upper Kilchattan", formerly called "Bollevery", "Ballevoir", "Ballemoir" etc. in old rental documents.

Cill Chatain, Lower Kilchattan NR 36295 95020

The dedication is to St. Catan, *floruit* c. 600, Ferial Day February 2nd, a cousin of St. Odhran (*see Chapter 7*) and the site is close to the cist-graves of an ancient cemetery. Unfortunately, although the walls still stand to a height of 2.3m at maximum, the western end of the building has been lost. It originally stood 8.3m by 4.5m and was orientated (as were all the graves, although the practice has been abandoned in the "new" graveyard nearby). There is a window in the east wall, and another at the eastern end of the south wall; there may have been another to match it at the western end, with an entrance through the west wall – this would maximise the light, but no supporting evidence survives. There are two aumbries, one either side of the eastern window. The holy water font survives and is preserved at Scalasaig Parish Church. The construction bears close examination as it is based upon locally-available stones, most of which have been beach-rolled in prehistoric times. This is, of course, the oldest building in Kilchattan and one can notice marked but very gradual variations in the masonry of the township as one moves further from the sea.

Kilchattan is the only surviving secular or non-monastic stone-built church of pre-reformation Colonsay, since Teampul na Ghlinne is known to have belonged to Oransay Priory. RCHAHMS state "This church can be identified as that which served the medieval parish of Colonsay, known as Kilchattan in the post-Reformation period", and they go on to say "The church of Colonsay was confirmed to Iona Abbey by a papal bull of 1203, but in the later Middle Ages the parsonage may have been attached to Oronsay Priory." Also: "The Parish church is mentioned by Monro in 1549 ("*It hath ane paroch kirke*"), but it is not known how long the building remained in use for worship."

This is an interesting question. The original dedication was as a monkish "cell", and the building is situate in "Templefield", a Gaelic-Norse name which, by reference to "temple" reflects early usage (the other local names for places of worship were "eaglais" and "caibeal"). Perhaps this building replaced its predecessor in the fifteenth century. In 1549 Monro also visited Oransay "*quherin ther is ane monastery of chanons*" but the Reformation Parliament followed soon afterwards (1560) and we know that by 1625 even the Priory of Oronsay was in a ruinous condition. Nonetheless, the Parish of Kilchattan was mentioned as late as 1632 when "John, bishop of the Isles, granted to Coll M'Gillespick V'Donald of Colonsay a lease of the teinds of the parsonage and vicarage of the parish of Kilchattan in Colonsay, and of the whole lands of that island"(*Origines Parochiae Scotia* 1854).

A number of place-names (e.g. "Mass-hollow" and "Field of the Servant of the Holy-man") commemorate the importance of the foundation, but there is no locally-remembered tradition of Kilchattan having served as the "parish church" of Colonsay. On the other hand, we have strong traditional and circumstantial evidence to suggest that early seventeenth-century worship was centred at Pairc na h'Eaglais, Balerominmòr, and that subsequently weddings – the last surviving public sacrament of the Old Faith – were held in the open air. As far as one can tell, the Reformation was but ill-received in Colonsay and it was not until the early eighteenth century that some half-hearted attempts were made to introduce Presbyterianism to the island. From contemporary accounts, there were no usable buildings at that time and a very basic structure had to be erected (at Machrins) before the church at Scalasaig was finally constructed in 1802. In view of all the circumstances, it seems most unlikely that Kilchattan was ever used for post-Reformation worship.

Additional Places of Interest

Curious stones: NR 38370 95886 and 37580 95847

The first of these is the stone opposite Tòrr an Tuirc cottage, which seems to be a marker of some sort, possibly for a grave.

The second reference is to an upright stone some 100 metres behind the boundary between the Baptist chapel and the school which stands almost 1.5m high and has clearly been erected for some purpose. It is not orientated; could it have been a scratching post for cattle?

Miogaras NR 375961

Several long stretches of drystane wall are noted by RCAHMS.

Here also is the abandoned croft (lying about 300 metres behind Kilchattan School). It is possibly associated with some of the cultivation ridges to be seen running up the south-facing but peaty hillside nearby. The meaning of the name is obscure… possibly some form of "mi-chorraiche" as in "gently sloped" lies at the root. It is not marked on Wilson's 1804 survey, nor upon the 1855 Hydrographer's Chart, but it does appear as Meog Airidh ("Whey Shieling") on the Ordnance Survey 1st Edition map. On May 11th 1851 an unbaptised child of 6 months died there (at "Migras"), surnamed McLean.

In the census of that year, the inhabitants were William Buie, a farmer of eight acres arable, 31 years, born Jura and his wife Mary, 27yrs, born "Kilmichel" (Kilmichael Glassary). They had two young children in the household, also Sarah Buie 72yrs, William's mother, a retired cook and a niece, Sarah McFarlane, 11 years. The only other family was that of John McConnell, a farm labourer of 39 years, born in Colonsay, and his Edinburgh-born wife Rosy, with their four young children and a very young "visitor", Margaret McPhee, 9 months old and born in Colonsay.

From the 1841 census, we can speculate that Effie and Peggy Bowie, 20 years, were twin sisters of William Buie and that it was at Colonsay House that his mother had served as a cook. The same census shows the McCannall family, and 75 year old Angus Bowie as head of the family in the croft (died in 1850), together with four sons and a female servant, 15 year old Ann McInnis. By coincidence, a baptism on May 31st 1852 is of "Archibald, son to Mary McInis, said to be fathered by Archd. McLean, a seaman out of Campbeltown, 5 years old."

Black Mill and Still, Mullairidh c. NR 37045 96880 and c. NR 36907 96330

There are faint traces of a mill beside the un-named burn, draining from Mullairidh ("Sheiling Bluff") and, close at hand, the remains of a reputed still, supposedly the last one to remain in use following the "Old Laird's" onslaught on illicit distillation in the 1830s. There is a meadow in front of the still or kiln, with a small hut set into its surrounding wall. Possibly a dog, or even a young man, was employed to keep a guard over the ripening crop, in the absence of stock-proof fencing.

There was also a curious spring in the north-eastern wall of the natural basin upstream, where water weeped out through a tiny hole; the opening had to be kept clear with a twig and it was called something along the lines of "the pin-hole well". (Donald "Gibbie" MacNeill, *pers. comm.*)

Uamh a' Phìobaire (The Piper's Cave) c. NR 36907 96924

It will be seen that the entrance to this cave has been blocked by a wall (no longer intact) following an unfortunate incident many years ago. Apparently the cave, which must have subsequently collapsed, was at one time extremely long, leading steadily downwards, and people wondered how far it might extend. One day a piper volunteered to explore it and so made his way into its depths, accompanied by his dog. His companions followed him across the surface above, tracing his route by the faint strains of *MacCrimmon's Lament*. It was only when they had reached the higher ground at An Dubh Chàrn that they lost the sound and went back to the cave-mouth to await his return. Unhappily, he never returned, nor was heard of ever again, but a couple of days later his dog was discovered, in a pitiful condition, beside the tiny crevice below An Binnean Crom at Balerominmòr. The poor creature was alive, but devoid of its hair, which had been entirely singed from its body.

S.S. "*Arandora Star*" Memorial c. NR 36907 96924

In July 1940, SS "*Arandora Star*" was sunk by submarine action at a position 100 miles west of Bloody Foreland in Donegal; more than 800 souls were lost, including German and Italian internees and British naval and military personnel. Some of those who were lost were brought by tide and current to Colonsay where they were laid to rest. These events caused a deep impression locally, and the islanders have maintained an interest in the tragedy and a concern for all those who were affected by it.

Every year, all such victims of conflict are included in the Remembrance Day service but a special monument was erected at this spot, where a young Donald "Gibbie" MacNeill and his father recovered the remains of such a person. In a special bond arising from this tragedy, all inhabitants of Colonsay have been granted Honorary Citizenship of Borgo Val di Taro, the hometown of

Giuseppe Delgrosso. The memorial and neighbouring cairn are a tribute to all those who died, and especially to the very many whose remains were never recovered. Visitors are invited to add a stone to the cairn.

Leab' Fhalaich Mhic a' Phi ("MacPhee's Hiding Bed")
c. NR 36940 95931 and c. 36801 94934

The history of these hiding-places has been mentioned elsewhere (see Chapter 6). Suffice now to identify these locations – the one at NR 36940 95931 is on the Dubh Chàrn ("Dark Cairn") and at first sight is in an unlikely location. However, if one remembers that the vegetation would have been very different in the early seventeenth century, one can easily identify places of possible concealment amongst the whins and shrub that will have covered such an area.

The second location is on the face of the low cliff at Druimhaugh and it is easy enough to see that one could lie un-noticed on the ledge; there will have been sympathetic households hereabouts, as this was MacMhuirrich land and the clansfolk were ancient allies of Clan MacPhee.

Ouachitite Dyke NR 36883 94812

This is a remarkable geological curiosity and worthy of examination. There is an exposure close beside Leab' Fhalaich Mhic a' Phi at Druimhaugh, and a rather more obvious one at the position given, which is beside the old pathway to Scalasaig. Do not take samples or damage the site – the fact that the rock is believed to be slightly radioactive may help to protect it.

On July 8 1773, Thomas Pennant visited Colonsay and noted: "I met with no very remarkable fossils. Black talc the *mica Lamallata martia is nigra* of Cronsted, *sect. 95*, is found here, both in large detached flakes, and immersed in indurated clay." This is the first published reference to the dyke, and happens to provide a helpful clue in identifying the route that he followed from Oronsay to Kiloran.

In *"The Geology of Colonsay etc."* 1911 it is confirmed that "The Kilchattan dyke has long been known in the island, and our attention was first drawn to it by Mr. Archibald Campbell. (It) is not a typical monchiquite, as it contains no olivine and … it is also exceptionally rich in biotite; these features mark it as belonging to the ouachitites as defined by J. F. Williams [*"The Igneous Rocks of*

Arkansas" 1890]. … The fine dark matrix of the rock is full of minute scales of black mica, and there are also rounded white spots or "ocelli" and vesicles filled with calcite and analcite. The most striking peculiarity of the rock, however, is the presence of large black phenocrysts of biotite, augite and hornblende, which make it a typical "lamprophyre"".

Uaigh an Fhomhair ("Giant's Grave") NR 37101 94799
A.S. Henshall (1972) describes the monument:

> "Overgrown with heather, it stands no more than 2' high, in a hollow on a moorland hillside, and consists of a passage of large, earthfast, stone blocks leading into an irregularly shaped chamber which is partially walled with coursed slabs or small stones.
>
> "Stones are piled against the outside of the structure and extend about 5' from the internal wall-faces. This might represent the remains of a cairn, but there is no sign of cairn material beyond this unless a low curved bank of stones running from the NE to the W of the structure and some 16' from it might be regarded as the rim of a robbed cairn. It seems more likely, however, to be the remains of a wall of a small enclosure; there is another close to the E side of the structure. Only 16' SE of the chamber, a rock outcrop rises so steeply that a cairn cannot be extended farther on this side. There is an upright stone 1'9" high 24' to the W of the passage."

This is a curious structure which was excavated and de-bunked by Stephen Mithen in recent years, although even then it was not totally explained. Prof. Mithen has confirmed that this is not a passage-grave and that it appears to be a dwelling of some sort – in view of the location, it was perhaps a shieling or a shepherd's hut. Prof. Mithen did discover old bottle remains, confirming that this has been a picnic site in Edwardian times.

Cuidh Chatan (St. Catan's Heel") c. NR 3621 9475
A detailed account was published in 1881 (P.S.A.S.): "About 200 yards south from Port-Mór, and 50 yards off the road on the left hand going south, is a small cavity in a rock about 12 by 6 inches, partly natural and partly artificially made. This cavity is called the heel or

shoe of Chattan (Cruidhe Chattain). Formerly, persons desirous of leaving the island, and wishing to have a favourable wind, consulted one of the oldest Macvourichs (Currie), who, after cleaning out this hole, and making use of the necessary ceremonies, pronounced a favourable wind to those desiring it. Only persons named Macvourioh could procure the favourable wind. The old church of Kilchattan is in sight a quarter of a mile south of this place."

In 1923 Symington Grieve reported that "the basin is oval in shape", 11.75 inches long by 11.75 inches deep. "The cuidh generally contains water, as it is exposed to the weather and rain gathers in it... The first impression one gets when looking at Cuidh Chatain is that it has been used for making pot barley at some early time. However, a closer examination makes that doubtful, as the hole is too deep, not quite perpendicular in the rock, too narrow at the mouth, and not so situated that the wooden hammer for husking the barley could be worked with the most advantage." Unfortunately, the present writer has been unable to identify the site with certainty.

Tobar Chatain ("St. Catan's Well") NR 36286 94864
"The Holy Well, Tobar Chattan, is situated on the croft of Mr. Angus McNeill, Druim Clach, in the face of the bank opposite Kilchattan Church to the east". This reference by Symington Grieve was not really sufficient to identify which of the various springs was meant, and the site could no longer be identified, even by the late Donald "Garvard" MacNeill, who kindly devoted time and effort to assist the writer in a search. It was therefore an extraordinary coup when it was rediscovered, on 5 September 2007.

Keith Rutherford was intending to build a house on the site and engaged Clare Ellis, an archaeologist, to carry out a survey. "A controlled topsoil strip was undertaken ... within the probably nineteenth-century backfill of a spring was recovered a roughly tooled cruciform slab, 1.09 x 0.28m, which may have originally served as a marker stone of the holy well of "Tobar Chattan"". So when was the well destroyed, and by whom? A new house was built at Homefield in 1898, and at the same time an existing old style "in-a-row" line of cottages on the opposite side of the road was removed. It seems possible that, in exchange for the useable building stone, crofter Neil Campbell of Homefield and his son, Archie, agreed to dispose of any remaining rubble by the simple expedient of dumping it on the marshy ground surrounding the ancient well.

Altair Fear Mhitchell ("Fr. Mitchell's Altar")

c. NR 36384 94751

The following description is from 1881, P.S.A.S. "About 300 yards and due east from Port-Mor, and in at the bottom of the hills, is a piece of isolated rock about 8 feet high and 4 feet diameter. At one side is a raised- bench reaching to about 4 feet from the top. On the top of this rock is a small round hole of about 4 inches diameter and depth. This rock is the altar of the Man Mitchell *(Altair fear Mitchell)*." This is the same Fr. Mitchell as was mentioned in connection with Loch an Sgoltaire (*see Chapter 8*); it has been said that the socket was to support his crucifix.

A ramble through Kilchattan, starting at the Mill and going south to Port Mór

In 2010 there were 33 residents in fifteen inhabited houses, and by then the twenty original crofts were represented by six active crofting units. There were a total of 33 dwellings, including holiday homes and second homes, and planning consent had been granted for up to ten additional houses. Because it has been such a heavily populated part of the island in recent centuries, there are many thousands of people worldwide who can trace some part of their ancestry to this area and therefore a walk through the district will be of interest.

The mill was created about 1865 to replace the mediaeval one at Kiloran, but it had a short life and after it was abandoned in the 1920s "it was used as a bothy by tradesmen, mostly from Oban, until the school kids, mostly the Glassard boys on their way home, smashed all the windows, which were never replaced. Hence the whole building fell into disrepair" (Donald "Gibbie" MacNeill, *pers. comm.*). The roofs were later stripped in order to avoid liability for rates. In the 1990s the mechanism was removed and the building was converted to use as a self-catering holiday home. The overshot wheel was fed by a new lade from Loch an Sgoltaire, known as Abhuinn nan Toitichean ("Burn of the Ruined Houses") because it passed through the abandoned township of Northmuir.

The road passes through Balerulin, a probable corruption a Baille Mhaolin, ("MacMillan Homestead") and three modern houses can be seen on the right. The third of these is the school-teacher's house, although for many years the teacher lived in the school itself. The field is known as Pàirc Stroyan because it was at one time a particularly well-favoured meadow, where the then farmer (Stroyan) kept his best calves.

The next house on the right is known as Torr an Tuirc ("Mound of the Boar"), which is actually the name of a small mediaeval homestead lying 150 metres to the north-west. This was the miller's cottage – in 1901 the miller was 25 year-old John McNeill who lived there with his widowed mother and his five siblings. When the family was first moved here, from the old mill, young Hester McNeill registered her regrets in a sad song which was quoted in Chapter 8.

Next, one reaches the dangerous bend known as A' Chachla Mhór ("The Big Gate") and one can glimpse the old stone piers on the right, overgrown by brambles; from this point, the road formerly passed through that gateway and continued on a much higher route, which can still be traced for the first 500 metres. It seems to have been interrupted by the holding known as Sgreadan, but the line of continuation is indicated by that of the original houses, although some of these only survive as byres or mere foundation outlines.

Just beyond A' Chachla Mhór, and also on the right hand side, there is a gorse-sheltered hollow known as Glaic a' Mhuirt ("Murder Hollow") at NR 38233 95874, where eight MacLeans were despatched by a single man, Calum Caol MacMhuirich ("Slim Malcolm Currie"). The incident probably took place in the early sixteenth century. The MacLeans had visited Colonsay on a raiding party which had been overcome and put to flight after a pitched battle, in which the Bells of Balnahard had arrived just in time to win the day. Calum was returning to his home at Iodhlann Chorrach ("Steep Stackyard") on the other side of Loch Fada (see Chapter 5) when he noticed something glinting in the setting sun. Making his way to this spot, he discovered the MacLean stragglers in an exhausted sleep, with the sun reflected by the metal of their swords. Silently, he cut their throats one by one, so ensuring the immortality of his memory.

Continuing along the road, you will notice a "hedge" of alder, running off towards the loch. This was planted as a windbreak, from local seed, by John and Pamela Clarke in the 1980s. Although the trees have succeeded one can readily appreciate that they have had to struggle.

The next building is the Baptist Manse, a very curious structure.

Lord Strathcona (1995) mentions that the Baptist Manse was built in the 1930s to the design of (Arthur Forman) Balfour Paul. This was confirmed by Donald "Gibbie"MacNeill, (*pers. comm.* 1st Jan. 2009) who mentioned that Cnoc nam Fad was built for the crofter, Murdoch Buie, when he retired from Balnahard – and that the architect's surname was "Paul". Donald said Paul also built "Keeper's Cottage, beside the kennels", as well as the house now known as Gart a' Gobhain for Donald (?) Munn. Donald went on to say that the oddest house Paul built was the Baptist Manse – the roof caused great trouble during construction and the plans had to be constantly revised. Cnoc nam Fad was built in the early 1930s, when Donald was only five years old, and he remembers that the present shop at Scalasaig (Creag Odhran) was built a good deal later than the rest, but was possibly a Paul design.

This information is interesting, because it connects with an entry in "*Argyll & Bute*" by F. A. Walker (2000), a volume in the respected series "*The Buildings of Scotland*". In this work, reference is made to the building of "estate workers houses c. 1935" by Basil Spence. The connection seems to have arisen because Balfour Paul, or "Baffy" (1875–1938) – son of the Lyon King of Arms – had in 1931 given office-space in his practice to a former assistant, William Kininmonth, and William had thereupon formed a partnership with a friend of his own, Basil Spence; both Kininmonth and Spence had been working in Lutyen's practice in London. In 1934 "Baffy" invited Kininmonth and Spence to merge their practice with his own and thus some of the work that was commissioned from Balfour Paul's practice was apparently undertaken by Basil Urwin Spence.

It is noteworthy that all of the Colonsay buildings in question have unusual roof and mullion details, also more than a hint of "Arts and Crafts" design, the taste for which survived rather late in Scotland; but the Baptist Manse is sufficiently individualistic to beg further consideration. All of the architects in "Baffy's" practice had worked on religious buildings and one wonders if it is coincidental that the Manse reminds one of popular representations of the Ark of the Covenant. Although there is no resident minister, the Baptist Manse is in use throughout the year by visiting ministers. Various groups and individuals are encouraged to make faith-based visits to the island, and members of the congregation are very active in community work locally.

About 250 metres of bog now intervene, and then the ruins of a mediaeval chapel dedicated to Our Lady ("Cille Mhoire") may be seen lying close to the road on the right-hand side at NR 37743 95792. Access is convenient via the gate next to the entrance to the Baptist Chapel. The mediaeval building, which is orientated, will have served one of the original farms that were swept away by the reforms of John McNeill. The eight MacLeans who fell victim to Calum Caol MacMhuirrich were all buried here, and it is said that at one time the bodies of stillborn and unbaptised infants were laid to rest in this quiet spot.

Just beyond Cille Mhoire is the Baptist Church, which was built in 1879. The Church was founded by the missionary zeal of Rev. Dugald Sinclair, who made his first visit to Colonsay in 1812 and whose message was well-received. The laird, John McNeill, was hostile to the mission but Sinclair was a determined man who eventually so far won him over that two of the laird's own daughters were converted. One of these girls was baptised in Loch an Sgoltaire by Rev. Grant of Tobermory, probably in the 1820s. Although Colonsay was not directly affected by the Disruption, it is true to say that the unhealthy relationship between the laird and the established minister had been as damaging in Colonsay as elsewhere. When committed missionaries visited the island, their message was sown in fertile ground.

Kilchattan Primary School is the only school in the island at present and it appears to have been built to the design of Thomas Telford, who is believed to have been responsible for the harbour as well. The building seems to be adapted from his "Plan and Elevation of a Manse of one Story", published as Plate 59 of "*A Biographical Atlas to the Life of Thomas Telford by Himself*" 1838. It eventually replaced two earlier establishments, the Parochial School at Scalasaig and that of the Scottish Society for the Propagation of Christian Knowledge – An t' Seann Sgoil ("The Old School") – which was sited at Port Mór. In former days the SSPCK school served Kilchattan and the parochial school served children on the other side of Loch Fada, whilst outlying children were taught by peripatetic teachers who would go and stay for a period in such *bailtean* or fermtouns as Balnahard, Ardskenish and Balerominmór. In this, they were not unlike the tailors, tinkers, pedlars and other itinerant service providers of the age. Everything changed with the Education Act of 1872, when compulsory education for all children was introduced and resources were concentrated in the one building. Kilchattan Primary School had twelve pupils in 2004, but by 2010 the roll had fallen to seven; its past-pupils include many successful individuals in challenging positions all over the world.

Some 300 metres behind the school are the faint remains of Miogras, a long-abandoned croft that was the original Colonsay home of the Mackinnon family. Subsequently it was occupied by the Buie family, many of whose descendants have prospered in Canada. Closer to the road is Sgreadan, now known as "School Cottage", and formerly the home of the MacPhee family; it was one of their daughters, Jane, who died in labour in 1895 without medical assistance. Her husband, Giles Butt, was the butler at Colonsay House and Dr. Roger McNeill protested so vehemently on behalf of the island that a resident doctor has been stationed in Colonsay ever since. Sgreadan was a large and prosperous holding, technically a "farm" of 60 acres, and is distinguished by a substantial drystane dyke of which the remains are still impressive. As in examples at Scalasaig and Balnahard, it will be noticed that the construction consists of vertical rather than horizontal courses of undressed stone, with smaller stones to fill the interstices, creating what is known as a Galloway dyke. The gaps in the wall are said to prevent the formation of snowdrifts, and the deceptively precarious appearance is said to discourage sheep from climbing upon it.

Home of a direct descendant of Malcolm MacPhee, d. 1623

Some readers may recall (Chapter 5) that a direct descendant of Malcolm MacPhee was living above Riasg Buidhe in 1871. This was Donald McPhee, and he held the position of "Ground Officer", one of the few positions of rank that existed at the time. In the census of 1881, Donald and his wife Mary had moved to Sgreadan, where he is described as a "Farmer" on 60 acres. No other inhabitant of Kilchattan has the status of a farmer in the census, most are recorded as "crofters" with four acres although two have eight acre crofts. Significantly, nobody else has walled fields, and in fact Donald's house even sports an additional chimney, "just for show". In 1891, Donald is still there, at 71 years, with his wife Mary (61) and four unmarried children, Hugh (38), Neil (27), Jessie, (22) and Sarah (19). A good photograph of that period exists in the collection of the RCAHMS, showing the occupants in front of the house; there is a copy at the hotel. By 1901, the farmer was Neil McPhee, living there with his widowed mother, his sister Sarah and the five children of their late sister, Jane Butt. It might be interesting to trace the male descendants of Donald or his near-relations; in theory, their DNA signature should be sufficient to identify the chiefly line of descent in this very ancient family.

The next building alongside the road was one of the typical crofthouses which were described as being built "in a run", and was converted to a modern bungalow whilst retaining much of its original character. At the time of writing it has been empty for some years and awaits additional renovation. As one gains the top of the hill, the seemingly empty field on the right contains traces of a number of cottages (NR 37372 95595), one of which is close to Tobar Cheiti Thorcuil ("The Well of Katy, Torquil's daughter"). The name is surprisingly modern, and commemorates the demise of Katy McNeill at that spot sometime after 1861.

Across the loch one can see Creag Mhór ("Big Cliff"). On the near side of the loch, the surface of which has been dramatically lowered in recent years, one can see the remains of stone piers used in the early nineteenth century for the steeping of flax. This was an essential part of the process leading to the production of finished linen, fine specimens of which still survive in Colonsay. These stone piers were at that time at least a metre below the surface, and have only been exposed in recent years by excessive drainage work. Some years ago, the loch was declared to be a Site of Special Scientific Interest, not least to protect the *Najus flexilis* (slender naiad) which is scarce in Britain, but the protection seems to have lapsed. The waters used to conceal the remains of an impressive wood, which was inundated some 4,300 years ago in some sort of climate change, contemporaneous with the arrival of the first farmers. Sadly, the remains of these trees are nowadays only too visible and will have crumbled away within a very few years.

Walking onwards, one passes A' Mhaoil Dhubh ("The Black Mount"), which is the highest of the crofts. The summit to the south, beyond the loch, is Carn Mór ("Great Cairn") which bears the imprint of an ogre's foot; stepping across the valley, "Loosecruibitan" (the ogre) left a matching footprint on a boulder at Mhaoil Dhubh.

Loch Fada ("Long Loch") is the collective name for what was once a single sheet of water but now consists of three adjoining lochs, known (east to west) as Locha an Pairce Duibh ("Loch beside the Dark Field"), Locha Gortain Artair ("Loch at Arthur's (?) Field)" and Locha 'n Iar ("West Loch"). At the western extremity of Locha 'n Iar one can see the outline of two crannogs or artificial islands, which were probably used in former days to protect vital seedcorn from grazing animals and casual depredation. Unfortunately, these are now exposed above the surface of the water, so any archaeological remains will soon be destroyed. Nearby, no longer hidden below the surface of the water, there are two more of the flax piers – there were ten in all, to serve twenty crofts.

Close to the road is a rough and somewhat incongruous building – this is a former generator shed, constructed by Army volunteers in the early 1970s. Before the advent of mains electricity in 1984, a rudimentary but ruinously expensive domestic supply was provided by the short-lived Colonsay Community Electricity Association, with generator stations dotted at strategic intervals across the island.

Approaching the point where the track leads off to Gortin, one is leaving Upper Kilchattan and the marshy field to the left recalls that fact in its name, Lèana na Cachaileth ("Gate Meadow"). When that meadow was created, by the partial draining of Loch Fada in the early 1900s, a perfect example of a stone axe was discovered by crofter Archie MacConnell; a dug-out canoe was also discovered but unfortunately it was drawn onto dry ground and allowed to disintegrate. Gortin, up to the right, was a fine croft which was worked by the Martin family for more than 150 years; they were weavers as well, and for generations were pillars of the Baptist faith. Gortin has the reputation of having more hours of sunshine than any other house in the island. Beside the road, Mr. Iain McGilvaray is in possession of a croft which has remained in the one family for even longer – in 1841 his forefather, Malcolm Black, was still working that croft at 70 years of age, a widower with seven of a family to support.

The road now rises slightly as Drumclach ("Stone Ridge") is approached on the left, an enormous shingle bank or raised-beach thrown up in antiquity and separating Loch Fada from the ocean. This ground is warm and supports good grazing, so has been attractive since pastoral life began in Colonsay, as is witnessed by the impressive monoliths erected by Bronze Age farmers more than 3,000 years ago. These stones stand about 3 metres high and mark cremation sites; unusually in Colonsay, they are not orientated.

Curiously enough, at the spring tide closest to modern Easter, at about midnight, the full moon is directly in line with the stones. Nearby, a souterrain was discovered many years ago but it was not examined and may not be contemporaneous. Perhaps inevitably, the name of "Fingal's Limpet Hammers" has been adopted, although it is doubtful that the name pre-dates James MacPhearson and his "*Fingal, an Ancient Epic Poem*", published in 1762. The large, level platform in the same field is called An Iodhlann Mhór ("The Big Stackyard") and being in such a breezy position was used by the crofters for winnowing their corn; some commentators have suggested that in Viking days it may have served as a "thyng" or council-place (*pers. comm.* Barbara Crawford, author of "*Scandinavian Scotland*").

Access to the summit of Carn Mór and a challenging walk to Scalasaig via Dùn Eibhinn is gained by following the track towards and behind Seaview, then climbing the grassy valley of Bruthach na Diollaid ("Saddle Brae"). A map and compass will be useful if the complete walk is to be undertaken.

The road now descends sharply towards Port Mór, passing through exposed sections of the raised beach at the 30 metre and 15 metre contours. On the right is the graveyard and the ruins of a late-four-teenth-century Catholic chapel, dedicated to St. Catan (*Cille Chatain* = Kilchattan). Until the late nineteenth century, the graveyard had no surrounding wall and inhumations were protected from distur-bance by substantial cairns; such cairns would be removed in due course and reused to protect a later grave. For this reason there are few early inscribed gravestones, one of the earliest being that of Donald McNeill, who died in March 1795 at the age of seven years. His father was the schoolmaster and, from the records, we know that his father had been employed in Colonsay by the SSPCK since 1781, when there were 66 boys and 5 girls on his roll.

The gravestones are a valuable resource for family and social historians, so all legible inscriptions have been transcribed and are available locally. Only one supposed centenarian is known, Mrs. Mary Martin (neé Docherty) who died 2 April, 1910. Some of the unmarked graves could tell a poignant story, particularly in relation to the years of famine and disease around 1850 – for example, the parochial Register of Deaths for 1851 details one such family:

"Jun 12 Peggy McMillan, dr. to the late Jas. McMillan, Kilchattan 34 [yrs];
Jun 30 Dolly, widow of the late Jas, McMillan, Kilchattan 74;
Jul 7 Jas. McMillan [jnr.], Kilchattan, the 3rd. out of one house 42".

The old church is carefully orientated and parts of the wall survive to their full height of about 2.3 metres; the building would have been gabled and the splayed ingoing of the eastern window survives, together with two aumbries. Traces of the original plaster can still be seen, although details of the coursed rubble construction are fully exposed. The church is on the site of an earlier foundation, which had itself adopted a hallowed place of the pre-Christian era, as is confirmed by the cist graves which have been discovered here-abouts. A headstone within the church reads "EMV 1789" and probably is that of a Currie (McMhuirich). Perhaps the "E" was for Eachunn (Hector) or – less likely – Effie (Euphemia, originally Aphrica).

The next house is Homefield, built in 1898 by Neil Campbell to replace the earlier dwelling, still standing at the back of the field. The family has a fascinating history – for example, Barbara Camp-bell of Homefield married Neil Munn on 6th June 1852 and by the following year the young couple had gone to Canada with Neil's parents, Alexander Munn and Flora McPhail and his eight siblings. They were preceded by two of Alexander's brothers, Rodric and Charles, who had settled in Prince Edward Island and Erin Town-ship, Guelph. Alexander and his family went first to Limehouse, Esquesing but in 1855 Barbara and Neill, together with his brother Donald, moved on as Pioneers into Bruce County. "Their journey took several days; five miles from their destination, one of the horses broke its leg while fording the Saugeen north of Paisley. The horse had to be destroyed; belongings had to be carried on their backs, and Mrs. Munn, her year old baby Alexander on her back, had to walk the rest of the way to Lot 11, Con. 6. Here they erected a log shanty and in it were born, eventually, two boys and two girls." Unfortunately Neil was crippled in 1862 whilst felling a tree; there-after, Neil took up the trade of a tailor and Barbara devoted herself to his care until he died fourteen years later.

Homefield and the land running out behind it form Baile Iochdrach, the original and best croftland in Colonsay which was mentioned above as having pre-dated the reforms of "The Old Laird". Professor Donald Mackinnon's family had moved to Baile Iochdrach after their early years in Miogaras and his final resting-place is in the old churchyard. He learned to play shinty in the glen beside the old house, Glaic na Aifrionn, ("The Mass Dell") and his most famous essay, a classic in the Gaelic language, is also set in this area. Entitled *"Seann Sgoil"*, it is a description of the school he attended in the 1840's and the education that was afforded in such a typical Highland school, before the Education Act of 1872.

At the foot of the hill the road passes close to Port Mór ("Big Port"), the only refuge along the west coast; one can see the slight remnants of a harbour in the northwest corner. Until the 1880s there was a row of fishermen's houses where the bookshop stands today – in fact, the footings of the end gable can still be seen in front of the bookshop. In 1881, these cottages were all flooded by the sea in a tremendous gale, the same gale that destroyed the slate work-ings at Easdale and drove more than twenty vessels ashore in Colonsay in the one night, fortunately without loss. Port Mór was also the scene of a dramatic rescue in December 1848, when the barque *"Clydesdale"*, inbound for Glasgow from Charleston, was driven ashore with shredded sails. Five men managed to save them-selves by clinging to the wreckage, and twelve more were saved by islanders who launched their fragile craft in the face of mountainous seas. Despite every effort, six members of a crew of twenty three were drowned.

On the south side of Port Mór there is a tiny sandy bay whose name preserves the memory of Donald Mackinnon's school – Port an Tigh Sgoil ("Schoolhouse Bay"), for it was here that the children were taught to swim. The school itself lay just to the landward side of the cattle-grid (NR 36090 94498) and its outline can still be traced, intersected as it is by a more recent drystane dyke. The late Donald MacNeill once came across initials carved into nearby rocks, presumably by the children. It is a fitting place to conclude this ramble through Kilchattan, a building that once housed all the hopes and ambitions of this then-vibrant community.

Lachlan Mackinnon's authoritative translation of a part of the text describes the school itself in 1845: "A large dark building with low walls of unhewn stone, bespattered on the outside with clay, and on the inside blackened with soot. There was an opening on both sides of the house but with no door to either of them. In the winter a bundle of heather supported by a shinty stick was the sole protection against the western gale. This bundle was used up little by little for kindling the fire, and then a bundle of straw took its place until a thieving cow or horse came the way. The earth floor was dank and cold, save only in the centre where burned two fires to which each pupil contributed his peat. The windows were half-closed with turfs, and in the roof were two holes through which eddied the smoke that did not find a way through door or window…"

Other walks in Kilchattan:

1 The Bird-cliffs: follow the track to Gortin Cottage, pass to the left of Gortin crofthouse, respecting the privacy of the occupants, and follow a slight stony bank up to the boundary gate. Follow the same line of direction across Leana Mhór ("Big Meadow"), so as to pass to the left of an interesting lochan, Rioma Dhubh-Charna ("Black Cairn Marsh"). Donald "Gibbie" MacNeill remarks that it only became a lochan in recent times, since crofters ceased to drain the area. Turn right along its western side, picking up an old peat-cutters' track. Look out for Canada geese, grey heron, mallard and an otter, also water lilies and yellow iris. This track will lead you part-way towards Aoineadh an t' Sruth ("Sea-ledge of the Stream"). Without children or pets, you will find that it is relatively easy to walk out along the steep southern bank of the Aoineadh until you are above the sea, in a perfect position to admire the cliffs and birds. Afterwards, retrace your steps to the head of the gully, then head northwards to see Meall Lamalum and descend to Port Bàn, from which there is a fine view of Aoineadh nam Muc (*a.k.a.* "Pig's Paradise", *lit.* "Whale Terrace"). One could return via Mullairidh (difficult) or simply return to Gortin along a more direct line.

2 An Rubha ("The Point"): A fairly easy walk along the north side of Port Mór, keeping between the fenceline and the sea; there are bait-holes to be seen about 50 metres after leaving the track. On reaching the Point, one might turn back but it is not too difficult to work one's way around into the very attractive bay to its north (two gates near the corner of the field are an option), and then onwards to Druim nam Faoileann ("Seagull Ridge"). If you decide to continue northwards, there is easy going along the top of Binnein Riabhach ("Brindled Hill"). The alternative route, below the cliffs, involves a very steep descent at one point, a scramble across huge boulders and a vertiginous pathway; fine if you are fit, but unsuited to young children etc. This route can be pursued all the way to Uragaig, and is known as Dreis Nic Ceothain – as Murdoch McNeill remarked in connection with one section: "Dreis-*nic-Ceothain* is named after a young woman who had the hardihood to walk across that dangerous ledge". Loder gives the meaning as "Ewan's Daughter's Cliff Path", but perhaps she was an Ó Catháin, a family that thrived in Colonsay until the disasters of 1647.

Chapter 10

MACHRINS AND ARDSKENISH

Map: page xiv

For many visitors to Colonsay, Machrins and Ardskenish will be central to their stay. Here one can enjoy safe bathing, easy walking and a very wide variety of birds and flowers in outstanding scenery. The eighteen hole golf-course on the links extends for 4775 yards across the natural turf of the machair, and another area plays host to Sports Day and lively games of cricket and football. The area is mercifully free of fence-blight and one will often encounter sheep and cattle ambling along the verges of the single-track roadway.

In the mediaeval period there were four *bailtean* or fermtouns on this land, two for Ardskenish ("the two Erskynnis") and two for Machrins, Machaire Bheag ("Little Machair") and Machaire a' Clibhe ("Cliffside Machair"), a reference to the inland cliffs beside the present road. Machrins is an anglicised plural of a Gaelic word which is already in the plural, "machairean", referring to the undulating, flower-studded links turf so typical of the finest Hebridean coastlines. During the nineteenth century a process of rationalisation began, whereby the land was amalgamated and rented to a lowland grazier, together with a big new farmhouse and steadings. The distinctive octagonal building is similar to others that exist on other Colonsay farms and is known as a "mill-round". These mill-rounds enabled the farmers to become independent of the miller at Kiloran and therefore brought an end to his trade.

The modern farm of Machrins is one of the largest, running to a total of 2,020 acres and including 1,880 acres of rough pasture; the arable consists of about 60 acres in pasture with the balance in silage. In 1841, at least seventy seven people lived on this farm, in sixteen households. Forty one people lived at "Machrins Clova" i.e. Machaire a' Clibhe (close to the modern steadings) in ten households, there were sixteen more in three households at "Auchadaruch" ("Oak Field") above Milbuie, and the rest lived at Ardskenish. By the census of 1861, most of the population had gone and the (absent) farmer of 1600 acres was a Mr Johnstone, four of whose relations were all living in the new farmhouse, the entire family having been born in Johnstone itself, in Renfrewshire. In 2010, there were but two inhabitants in just two remaining households.

As one approaches Machrins from Scalasaig, the long straight section of road is bordered by free-flowering gorse, some of which is almost always in bloom. Over to the right, soon after passing the turning to Oransay, there is a fine coppice of blackthorn, a magnificent spectacle during its very few hours of perfection It flowers about 20th April, but the delicate blossoms are quickly affected by wind and sun and you have to be lucky to see them at their best. In early June, the roadside ditches are profuse with yellow iris and overhead there will be ravens tussling with a buzzard and very often a peregrine falcon, sparrow hawk or kestrel. At the end of "the Machrins straight" one reaches the first field, which is called Sgùid Bhrìdeig ("St. Brigid's Shelter") in reference to the rocky overhang in the cliff which borders the southern edge of the field.

This was an area of great significance in ancient times, and St. Brigid is the Christian successor to a much earlier earth-goddess figure. St. Brigid is the patroness of music, poetry and art, and in her more ancient form was also the spirit of fertility and plenty; until recently (very recently indeed), the last sheaf at harvest was reserved for her, and the finishing touch to a thatch was knotted in her honour. In Ireland, her distinctive straw-fashioned cross is still "dressed" in gay ribbons on her patronal-day, something which in Colonsay is remembered in the name of the oyster-catcher, Gille Bhride ("Servant of St. Brigid"). The bird's call often sounds like "A' Bhrìd, A' Bhrìd", and the jagged pattern of her cross can be seen in a bright flash as the bird takes to flight.

Pennant mentions four stone chapels in Colonsay in 1773, and one of them was hereabouts, at Sgùid Bhrìdeig; gravestones have been unearthed by the plough in living memory. Approaching Machrins farmhouse, the outline of a ruined cottage can be seen to the left of the road, a house which was left unoccupied after the sudden departure of the latest incumbent, a German spy! According to the story, the cottage was occupied in the Great War by a lady living alone, by the name of Kallenburg. She was fond of nocturnal rambles, but people became suspicious and one night she was followed out to Dùn Gallain, where she was seen to be shining a light out to sea. Worse still, her signals were acknowledged, presumably by one of the Kaiser's fleet. The mainland authorities were alerted and she was quickly apprehended and taken away. The late Dugie MacGilvaray remembered hearing that "she had a map, sewn into her hat".

Strangely enough, although there is no evidence to support the story of her being apprehended, an antiquarian bookseller reported a manuscript document which undoubtedly was created by this lady. The document consists of lengthy extracts from the work of a late eighteenth-century author of great renown, her grandfather, set out upon paper which has been decorated with seaweed. The author in question, Jean Paul Richter (1763–1825), was highly acclaimed – for example, his *Quintus Fixlein* (1796) was translated by Carlyle in 1827. Indeed "for a few years Jean Paul was the object of extravagant idolatry on the part of the women of Germany". The seaweed has been compressed into the paper itself by a special technique known as "Nature Printing" which imparts not just the outline of the weed but the actual pigments of its colour tones. The work, produced in Colonsay by Ms. Emma Richter-Kallenburg, is dedicated to one Maud Ranken, presumably her companion or a close friend, and is dated 1900.

Nothing more was ever heard of Miss Kallenburg, but the story had a curious echo in World War II, when a merchant seaman from Colonsay found himself ashore one evening in the neutral port of Cobh, in Cork. A German submarine had been allowed to make a brief but vital entry to the harbour on humanitarian grounds and the Colonsay man fell into conversation with one of her crew. As they parted, the German sailor suddenly called him back – "Hey! You might like to have this, my friend". The Colbhasach was astonished to be handed a copy of the current edition of "*The Oban Times*".

The road winds on for another kilometre or so, bordering the arable fields to the left, and then running out onto the open machair of the golf course. Many people choose to park on the convenient concrete pads that will be noticed, known locally as "the RAF huts". In fact, they were built as a base for a Canadian signals unit in World War II and assisted in guiding aircraft homewards from their Atlantic patrols, back towards the big sea-plane bases at Oban and Loch Linnhe. The following remarkable story was current at the time, suggesting that the Signals Unit confirmed an instance of "second-sight".

Apparently, a man living in Ardskenish in the early nineteenth century, known as "Hugh of the Glen", was accepted in his lifetime as having the gift of second-sight, and some of his predictions were fulfilled long after his death. It was remembered that he had shown great signs of distress on one occasion whilst walking in this area, covering his ears and complaining of a dreadful noise. His companions quizzed him, and he could not understand that they could hear nothing – he described it as a deafening, discordant noise such as he had never heard before. All this was half-forgotten when the Canadian camp was erected, together with a substantial generator to power the signals unit and everything else. People suddenly remembered Hugh's prophecy, but whether it was really the generator that he had heard is unknown. The Canadians were very fond of dance music, and rigged up loudspeakers around their huts – the late Peter MacAllister was of the opinion that Glen Miller's music might have been a little too modern for poor Hugh.

There are no listed buildings in Machrins or Ardskenish, but there are nine significant monuments listed by RCAHMS:

Cist-graves – near NR 359934
A cist with inhumation was discovered "in a bunker" of the golf course in 1920 and in the following year "quite a number of cists" were found, but they were not examined and the exact location is not known.

Standing Stone, Càrn Glas ("Grey Cairn") NR 354920
In 1976, RCAHMS described a prostrate slab as a possible fallen standing stone (1.3m x 0.5m x 0.2m). Loder provides a photograph – the exact location seems to be NR 35460 92069 – the stone appears to have stood within a circular setting, about 1.8m in diameter. Another standing stone marked on the 1900 O.S. map at NR 3720 9324 has "disappeared".

Fort, Dùn Gallain ("Fort of the Strangers") NR 348931
This is a very prominent site, commanding the whole of the Machrins area and protecting an ideal Viking harbour, the approach to which is via a straight, clear channel just below the northern flank of the fort. The actual fort occupies the very summit of the hill, about 30m x 20m within a surrounding wall up to 3m thick. To the east of this is a noticeable natural gully, the defensive capability of which has been enhanced by an outer curtain wall.

This outer wall must have been impressive in its day, and the rest of the site is protected by steep cliffs.

Dùnan nan Nighean ("Maidens' Homestead"), Ardskenish
NR34705 91182
This easily-recognised dùn is on the western shore of Tràigh nam Barc ("Boat Strand") some 320m south-east of the farmhouse. The structure is about 15m x 5m internally and is surrounded by the vestiges of its facing wall. The entrance is described as having been protected by an outwork about 1m thick. On the landward side the natural lie of the rock has been modified, so as to create the appearance of something very like a slipway for a boat – the masonry is quite apparent.

Dùnan gach Gaoithe ("Windy House") NR 357938
This prominent site is on the rocky knoll beside Tobar Fuar ("Cold Well") in the north-east corner of Machrins Bay ("Tràigh an Tobair Fhuair"), and serves as the 2nd tee for the golf course. The summit is about 12.5m in diameter; there is but little trace of the original dwelling, although one can easily identify supporting masonry, particularly on the eastern side. The original entrance was presumably from the north-east, as is the case today.

Dùnan Leathan ("Broad Homestead") NR 381934
This is an oval-shaped structure 17m x 13.5m internally, on the summit of a rocky knoll to the west of the road leading to Milbuie and overlooking both Mòine Thomach ("Tufty Peatland") and the approach from the anchorage at Loch Staosnaig. The outline is very clear, but little of the structure survives. In a sheltered gully there are a few native oaks, the remnants of a woodland that was once quite extensive. The neighbouring land is poor and one might guess that this served as an outlier or annexe to Dùn Eibhinn.

Cnoc nan Gall (Hillock of the Stranger") NR c. 358932
"In 1902 a number of iron clench-nails, a human tooth and a horse tooth were found in the sand-dunes at Cnoc nan Gall" RCAHMS. The items, which are preserved in Glasgow Art Gallery and Museum, were supposed to have formed part of a Viking burial. Furthermore "In 1891 excavation of a mound in the sand-dunes (c. NR 3593) revealed a burial accompanied by, among other objects,

a sword, shield fragments, a spearhead, an amber bead, a bronze pin, a penannular brooch and fragments of horse harness" RCAHMS.

Viking Burial and Settlement NR 357933

This site was excavated in 1973. The settlement consisted of four houses which had been built of wood or turf, outlined by upright slabs of stone "dug into the sand". Two hearths survived in good condition, and finds included a saddle quern and the bones of cattle, sheep, pig and roe-deer. Carbon-dating put the period of occupation around 800 AD, plus or minus 80 years, and the archaeologists concluded that the plan-form of the buildings suggested that they were of native origin. About 14 m to the east south-east of the settlement there was a long-cist burial, the occupant of which had been buried on his side, facing to the south-east and with slightly bent knees and hips. Interestingly, a small dog had been laid in the grave with its head resting on its master's knees – the archaeologist described it as an old dog, somewhat arthritic, very like a modern Corgi (*pers. comm.*,J.N.Graham Ritchie). The grave was radio-carbon dated to between 710 and 850 AD and small finds (fragments of knife, decorated bronze etc.) suggested that it was a Viking burial.

Ballan Stiallach ("Pillory Stone") NR 367932

This is a cross-marked stone beside the old track to Ardskenish, 100m south of the old Machrins farmhouse. On the east face there is the outline of "the lower half of a simple cross standing on a horizontal band". Unless, of course it is the lower half of a cross of Lorraine; in the sepulchral cave Uamh an Rìgh ("Cave of the King") in Loch Tarbert, Jura there are numerous crosses on the wall and ceiling, presumably associated with funeral parties on their way to Kiloran or Oransay – all of these have the distinctive double-bar associated with the Crusaders' Cross. The Ballan Stiallach is close to the site of Tigh na Suidheachan, a simple preaching-house with benches made of turves and which remained in use until 1802. Penitents were pilloried in a jougs or set of irons attached to the cross; seemingly the stone was broken to remove the jougs, which were thrown into the bog at the eastern end of the modern runway, Lochan Mòine Nic Còiseam, ("Bog-loch of Còiseam's daughter"). Incidentally, it seems that Còiseam MacCoinnich (Constantine I) ruled 862–77 as "King of the Picts" and therefore the name was at one time quite popular.

Additional places of interest

The walk described later in this chapter includes a number of sites of interest. A few other places are mentioned here, some of which might easily be overlooked.

Brangas, Plague-site and curious Well, above Coire nan Caorach ("Sheep Corry") NR 36585 94259

Brangas ("Branks") is a distinctive hog-backed stone said to have been associated with pagan penitential practices. Symington Grieve measured it at 5 ft 10 in long, 2 ft 1 in broad and 1 ft 6 in thick. It rests upon two stone pillars, between which there is a hole about 1ft square and 2ft deep, which never seems to silt up or disappear. The person to be punished was said to have been laid upon it and chained down, although its location alone suggests that it can hardly have had very frequent use. It is nonetheless curious to note that this stone does have a name and retained some sort of traditional significance until the early twentieth century. It is at the back of Meall a' Chàise, variously translated as "Plague Hill", "Steep Bluff" or "Lump of Cheese". Donald "Gibbie" MacNeill was told that there had been a plague in the island and that the infected persons were isolated in small huts, faint traces of which are said to survive. About 50m from brangas, to the southeast, there used to be a well "remarkable in having a slab of stone as a door which pulled up, working in a groove between stones, much on the same principle as a guillotine" (S. Grieve). Sadly, the present writer has not been able to discover it – Symington Grieve saw it but even by the 1930s it had become overgrown by the bog. Nearby, on Beinn nan Caorach, there are said to be two ruins, one of which was a "Temple of the pagan Norsemen"; although Symington Grieve did not see these ruins, he had been told about them by a "reliable source." Loder seems to have identified one of them, "near the top of Cnoc Tigh Moine ("Peat House Hill"). Could this have been at NR 37230 94145? *See note below under "Huts and Habitation Sites".*

Leab' Fhalaich Mhic a' Phi ("MacPhee's Hiding-place")

There are three of these. One is easily reached from the junction between the aerodrome road and the main road – it is a small ledge close beside the old footpath to Port Mòr (about 6m up from NR

36237 93960). The next one is out at Dùn Ghallain, and should be approached with great care – the grass is slippery and a fall would be fatal. The ledge is approached from the northern end of the outer wall of the fort, where one can climb down onto a sloping grassy terrace. The point of descent is from NR 34890 93166 and the hiding place itself is at NR 34883 93212, where it is about 3m above the slippery, dangerous slope. It consists of a platform about 2.4m x 1.8m, well-sheltered by a rock overhang and providing excellent views of Lower Kilchattan. The third one is on the western flank of the aptly-named Carn Spiris ("Pointed Cairn") c. NR 35953 92522, quite near the summit and affording excellent concealment if there were to have been (say) a decent juniper thereabouts. Like most of these ledges or "beds", it is easily seen today, but in former times there were few sheep in Colonsay and the vegetation would have been much more vigorous.

Cille Chiaráin (Kilkerran), Cnoc nan Gall ("Hill of the Stranger") c. NR 35740 93264

St. Ciarán was reputed to be able to travel swiftly across long distances over land and sea, "without recourse to boat or ferry"; thus he seems to be a very appropriate patron for Colonsay Aerodrome. The exact site of his foundation is no longer known, but was presumably very close to the cist-grave described above, which may have been placed in hallowed ground. The dedication is to St. Ciarán of Clonmacnoise c. 516-48 AD, whose feast day is Sept. 9th. St. Ciarán was a contemporary and tutor of St. Columba, and was one of "The Apostles of Ireland". His accepted dates closely echo those of St. Odhran, and the length of their earthly careers seem providentially to echo that of Our Lord. Nonetheless, St. Ciarán was a very real historical figure, famed in Scotland where he was also acclaimed as "The Apostle of Kintyre". Indeed, he gave his name to Kilkerran (the old name for Campbeltown), where he is still held in great affection. In Ireland, he is of outstanding importance as, in his 28th year, he was the founder of the important Abbey of Clonmacnoise, one of the most celebrated of Irish religious houses. Hearing of his death at the early age of 33 yrs or so, St. Columba penned a hymn in tribute, of which only a corrupted fragment survives:

Quantum Christe O Apostolum mundo misisti hominem
Lucerna huius insul lucens lucerna mirabilis

A great apostle sent by God
Hath blessed this isle with light ;
His beams, diffused through all the land,
Dispelled the gloom of night.

St. Ciarán was the son of a carpenter, chariot-maker to the King of Tara, and it is as Mac an t'Saoir ("Son of the Sawyer") that he is the champion of all McIntyres. He was noted for his piety, for his knowledge and for his charity – indeed, so great was his generosity that he was expelled from one religious house for fear that he would reduce it to beggary. We do not know if he ever visited Colonsay – it is certainly not impossible. If so, it would probably have been c. 545 AD when he assisted St. Columba on an exploratory expedition. The saint's memory is also preserved in the name of Eilean Cill Chiaráin, the small tidal island at the mouth of Port Lobh. As a child, he kept a pet fox which used to carry his satchel, and when he left home to join a monastery, a family cow followed him faithfully. For years, the cow provided milk to the community, and after death it provided the cover for *Lebor na h'Uidre* (*The Book of the Dun Cow*), one of Ireland's oldest surviving manuscripts.

Cille Choinnich (Kilkenneth) NR 35547 91918

No identifiable trace of this chapel can be seen – any slight remains have possibly been covered by the wind-blown sands, although some people think that it may have been sited on the opposite side of the burn. Nonetheless, the firm tradition of its suggested location is confirmed by the fact that human remains were said to have been found at that spot.

St. Choinnich, the son of a celebrated bard, was a close friend of St. Columba and accompanied him on his famous trip along the Great Glen to meet King Brude of the Picts – in fact, it was St. Choinnich who miraculously stayed the king's sword when he raised it in anger against them. St. Coinnich's dates are given as 521-99 AD and his feast day is October 11th. He is said to have been born at Glengiven in Derry, he was ordained in Wales and travelled as far as Rome. He subsequently continued his studies in Ireland, and then went as a missionary into Scotland in 565 AD.

Adomnàn gives an interesting story, the bones of which see St. Columba and his companions out at sea and running into danger, whilst St. Choinnich was settled quietly at his own place. Suddenly,

St. Choinnich leaped up from the table and rushed to his church to pray for their safety. Despite the distance, St. Columba saw his haste and said "Now I know, O Choinnich, that God has heard thy prayer; now hath thy swift running to the church with a single shoe greatly profited us." In the "*Life*", various details have been added, placing St. Choinnich at Aghaboe etc., but one can see how easily this could be a true account of St. Choinnich and his chapel providing a true course to a safe landfall for a boat coming into Traigh nam Barc ("Boat Strand") from the open sea. St. Choinnich is also commemorated in both Iona and Tiree.

Cille Bhrìde (Kilbride)

In the early period of Celtic Christianity, the three most revered saints in Scotland were St. Columba, St. Choinnich and St. Bhrìde (or Bridget) and it was not until the twelfth century that St. Bhrìde (c. 451–525 AD) came to be overtaken by the popular devotion to Mary, Mother of the Saviour. The very earliest site of this chapel must have been very close to Sgùid Brìdeig ("Bridget's Shelter") NR 37553 93251, and was perhaps near the pre-Christian standing stone (now missing) which is marked on the 1st Edition Ordnance Survey at NR 3720 9324; in certain conditions, however, it is possible to trace the faint outline of a building about 100m to the east of the sgùid, at NR 37628 93279. This latter structure, if it ever existed, seems to be about 5m x 6.3m, within walls 0.75m thick. At all events, by the mediaeval period, a stone chapel had been built in the corner of the field closest to the sharp bed on the modern road (c. 25m west of NR 37232 93423) but the surviving ruins were swept away by the Lowland tenant farmer, William Stroyan of Wigtown, in 1881: "On the farm of Machrins on the west coast, almost due south from Kilchattan, half a mile east from the farm house, and in the middle of a park in which oats grew this year, is what looks like a rubbish heap, overgrown with weeds, and which is this winter to be cleared away. This rubbish heap is the remains of Kilbride (*Kil-a-Bhride*). It was unknown to the farmer, but known and described by many of the old natives. The form of the building and foundations are easily made out amongst the weeds. It stands east and west, and measures about 27 feet by 18 feet." (William Stevenson "*Notes on the Antiquities of Colonsay and Oransay*" S.A.C.)

The religious significance of the area – and its central location – were such that a post-Reformation chapel was built here by the

Colonsay catechist in the closing years of the eighteenth century. "An old man, Mr Gilbert M'Neill, farmer, Lower Kilchattan, while working as a farm servant on Machrins during the time a former proprietor had it in his own occupation, assisted to remove the foundations. This old building went under the name of the Preaching House *(Tigh Sermonachaidh)* or House of Sermons, and was also called House of Seats *(Tigh na Suidheachan)*, from its being seated with turf benches. It is said to have been long and narrow, and to have served as the parish church till the present one was built, and the minister is said to have lived at Ardskinish." (William Stevenson *"Notes on the Antiquities of Colonsay and Oransay"* S.A.C.)

St. Bridget was an Abbess in Kildare, and came to be the Christian personification of Brìd, the goddess of fertility, beauty and good fortune in a much older tradition. Through St. Bridget, old traditions ranging from corn-dollies to the barely-restrained fertility rites of Mayday where able to be carried into the Christian era and, to this day, St. Bridget's feast day is May 1st.

Martin Martin, in c. 1695, describes the Colonsay devotion to St. Brigid at Candlemass: "Another ancient custom observed on the second of February, which the papists there yet retain, is this – the mistress and servants of each family take a sheaf of oats, and dress it up in women's apparel, put it in a large basket, and lay a wooden club by it, and this they call *Brüds-bed*; and then the mistress and servants cry three times, *Brüd* is come, *Brüd* is welcome. This they do just before going to bed, and when they rise in the morning they look among the ashes, expecting to see the impression of *Brüd's* club there; which if they do, they reckon it a true presage of a good crop, and prosperous year, and the contrary they take as an ill omen."

Of course, there are many records of superstition and curious events in Colonsay – one of them was published in *"The Secret Commonwealth"* by Robert Kirk, an Episcopalian minister, in c. 1690. It seems to refer to an historical event, a raid upon Colonsay by Colin Campbell of Islay and about 100 men, on the 17th and 18th June 1639. The "straw crosses" seem to be examples of Crosóg Bríde, which it is thought may originally derive from the pagan sunwheel.

"A woman, seemingly an exception from the general rule [that men have the Second Sight], and singularly wise in these matters of foresight, lived in Colonsay, an Isle of the Hebrides. [This incident of which I tell was] in the time of the Marquis of Montrose [and] his wars with the Estates of Scotland, [and the woman] being notorious among many, was examined by some that violently seized the Isle. [They demanded to know] if she saw them coming or not; she said [that] she saw them coming many hours before they came in view of the isle, but earnestly looking, she sometimes took them for enemies [and] sometimes for friends. Moreover they looked [to her Second sight] as if they went from the Isle, [and] not as men approaching it, which made her not put the inhabitants on their guard.

"The matter [that is, reason] was that the barge wherein the enemy sailed was [that is, had been] taken a little before from the inhabitants of that same isle, and the men [invading] had their backs towards the isle when they were plying the[ir] oars [to row] towards it. Thus this old Scout and Delphian Oracle was at last deceived and did deceive [her fellow islanders unwittingly]. Being asked who gave her such sights and warnings she said that as soon as she set three crosses [made] of straw upon the palm of her hand, a great ugly Beast sprang out of the Earth near her; and flew into the air. If what she inquired had success according to her wish, the Beast would descend calmly and lick up the crosses; if it would not succeed, the Beast would furiously thrust her and the crosses over the ground, and so vanish [back] to his place."

Unrecorded Dùn, Ardskenish Glen NR 36394 92436

This farmstead has not been noticed or recorded hitherto – although one could predict its existence, it is only in recent years that it has been exposed by muirburn. The dùn itself consists of a slightly enhanced natural chamber upon a rocky knoll, modified to create a hut-site. The associated masonry is most easily recognised on the southern side, to the right of the entranceway. Additional lily-gilding has been noted elsewhere on the site, which stretches towards the small lochan. Beyond the lochan there is a distinctive and well-constructed cairn of unknown purpose. About 100 metres to the north-east of the cairn are a number of enigmatic structures e.g. at NR 36480 92635 there is a distinctive circular feature of 8m internal diameter, the outer wall of which stands to about 0.9m. About 30 metres to its north-west is a similar structure (NR 36470 92672) conjoined to the boundary of a small enclosed garth or field.

A' Choille nan Fearnan ("Alder wood"), Milbuie Brae
NR 380932
This woodland was planted in early spring, 1991, by John and Pamela Clarke on foot of a Forestry Commission grant to the Estate. Fifty per cent of the trees are alder, remainder are a mixture of birch, oak, hazel, rowan, grey sallow and aspen. Most of the stock came from west coast of Scotland sources, but a significant proportion had been grown from local seed – the oak came from seed gathered in A' Choille Mhòr. Pedie MacNeill cut swathes through the heather to provide sheltered beds for the young trees. Some of the alder was planted below the electricity wires, in the hopes that it would grow tall enough to be coppiced from time to time, thus leading to multi-stemmed regrowth and denser cover for wildlife.

Huts and Habitation Sites
Above the roadman's quarry, on the northern face of Cnoc an Ardrigh ("Hill of the High King"! – more probably "High Slope" or "Shieling" Hill) there are at least two sgùidean and a circular hut (internal diameter 2.7m). The sgùid at NR 37896 93603 is "D"-shaped, 1.8m x 2.7m internally.

A more substantial dwelling is at the roadside (NR 37404 93460), about 3.6m in internal diameter within walls 0.9m thick and standing to about 0.75m. It was approached from the south-west and there seems to be an enclosed area to the side, possibly a lairage.

A little further west along the roadside is Tigh Bhoc Góibhre ("Billy-goat's House"), a rather neat shelter about 1.2m x 1.8m with a height of about 1.2m.

High in a glen above Loch Raonabuilg is a substantial platform 5.4m x 7.5m at NR 37230 94145, which seems to have been superceded by a later structure built within it, perhaps 3.6m x 2.4m. The structures are orientated and one wonders if these could be both the "Temple" and the "Peat House" referred to by Symington Grieve and Loder. Close at hand is a simple sgùid with a simply outstanding view to the south-west – an ideal picnic location at NR 37284 94046

A more accessible habitation site was at NR 36198 94089, which adjoins the ancient track from Machrins to Port Mór and where one can identify field enclosures etc.

A partial sgùid at NR 36428 93540 (very close to the modern

road) remained in use until the nineteenth century, when it was still thatched and inhabited – an inattentive cow grazed its way out onto the roof and caused a great sensation when its four legs came bursting through into the dwelling beneath.

Miscellany

To the east of the quarry, a concrete slab is beside the road at NR 37545 93442. This was the former Coastguards' Hut, 2.7m x 4.2m based upon a foundation fully 4.5m x 6.0m; about 150m to the north-east one can see a former telegraph pole, which was used in breeches-buoy practice until that apparatus was overtaken by SAR helicopters in the 1990s. Running behind the pole there is an excellent example of a head-dyke – this one surrounded the then Glebe and at NR 37581 93567 still stands fully 1.2m high, and up to 1.5m thick at the base. This massive construction of earth and stones would have been topped by a stock-proof thorn hedge. The road used to follow a different route and can be traced from the old Coastguards' Hut up towards Milbuie via NR 37725 93433, where its bed is very obvious – was this Bealach an t' Sìthein ("The Fairy Pass") of Murdoch McNeill (p.30)? The last person to travel this route in earnest was the late Dugie MacGilvaray who took a tractor along it in the 1960s. A remarkable "hidey-hole" at NR 37340 93212 is about the right size to conceal items of value or even an individual; it is presumably natural but just possibly would be worth examination. Two stones at NR 36587 93595 are about 6.0m apart and one of them looks like a possible fallen and broken standing stone (they are not orientated); as you walk up towards Loch Raonabuilg ("Bag-shaped Loch") you can identify the site of a black-mill and, rather unusually, the fashion in which the stream was diverted into zigzag channels, to regulate the flow of water to the mill. The burn itself has its source in a spring at NR 37414 93981.

Suggested Walks

From the RAF Huts one has an excellent view towards the ocean and also across the machair and the beautiful sandy bay. This is a good base for anyone who has a walking difficulty or who favours very easy going, but it also provides the starting point for slightly more ambitious walks outlined below.

Machrins and/or Ardskenish Walk

This walk includes some spectacular views, some interesting historic sites and a wide variety of habitats. There will be the chance to see a range of birds, flora and mammals – seals are probable and an otter is quite possible. The walking is easy but wellington boots are advisable; allow 4–5 hours to enjoy the full walk, but it is easily divided into two separate sections, when you should allow about 2 hours for each.

Start where the road passes the concrete pads beside the 1st tee of the golf course if you are undertaking either the combined walk or just the Machrins section; if you are only going to Ardskenish, start at the airstrip, walk round its western end, head for the 7th Green beside the ford and pick up the text at "Ardskenish Walk", below.

THE LIFTING-STONE

Somewhere beside the 18th green, you will notice a large stone lying on the short grass – this is A' Clach Thogalaich ("The Lifting-stone"). It was said to have been brought up from the shore in a creel and used as a challenge to the young men of the island, who would be taken to have reached manhood when they could lift it onto the back of a cart. It was damaged during WWII when some service personnel knocked off a corner to improve the grip; it is awkward rather than heavy, but be careful: an *Ileach* ("Native of Islay") suffered a fatal strain when lifting it in the nineteenth century and it was buried for years to avoid any repetition.

To the west of the 18th green, you will see a well-worn path running up the hill, which will lead you up to the Lookout Station.

THE LOOKOUT STATION

On the summit is the former Coastal Lookout Station, theoretically maintained for use by ornithologists and artists and which (when in good order) makes an excellent belvedere. Unfortunately it has deteriorated in recent years and, in 2010, the shell remains sound but does require total renovation. Straight ahead is the peninsula and raised beach of Rudha Aird Gheal Nis (pron. "rooard-alan-ish", meaning "Tip of the White-pointed Cape") and, in the distance (a little to the north), Stephenson's mighty lighthouse of Dubh Heartach ("Black Pinnacle-rocks"). To the right, the road at

Bealach nan Sac ("Pass of the Loads") runs behind Garbh Chladach ("Rocky Shore"), a swirl of rocks and islets which provide a quiet haven for the grey Atlantic seal in the pleasant days of summer but which presents a scene of awesome ferocity in winter gales. In the distance can be seen the Ross of Mull and a scattering of the Treshnish Isles, whilst on the horizon the white "golfball" of the CAA radar system serves to identify Tiree. To the left are Tràigh an Tobair Fhuair ("Strand of the Cold Well"), the promontory of Dùn Ghallain ("Fort of the Stranger" i.e. the Viking) and, in the distance, the distinctive sands of Ardskenish strand.

Descend the fairly easy slope towards Traigh an Tobair Fhuair and bear left, towards the head of the bay.

TRÀIGH AN TOBAIR FHUAIR
The concrete foundations hereabouts are associated with the wartime signalling unit, mentioned above. The large and incongruous iron structure is a stone-crusher, sad memento of a plan to make concrete blocks locally and thus avoid the cost of freight. The bay itself was the scene of ancient conflict when the islanders tried to resist powerful invaders – *"Latha Cath na Sguab, air Tràigh an Tobair Fhuair ri taobh tuath Dhùn Ghallain"*, "the day of the battle fought with staves, on the strand of the cold well, to the north side of the strangers' fort". Human bones have been discovered in the sand and it is held that digging for bait is unlucky, being apt to bring on a storm. At the north-east corner of the bay, notice the 2nd tee of the golf course – it is on top of Dùnan Gach Gaoithe ("Windy House"), an ancient homestead and a listed monument. The small concrete bunker is the trapper's redoubt for clay-pigeon shooting.

Continue southwards along the shoreline, passing the eponymous Tobar Fuar ("Cold Well") in the bend of a small stream; the burn has changed its course and original well has become choked – its site is now visible as a strip of concrete.

MACHAIR
The land on the left is the natural machair for which this farm is named (plural = machairean), sandy soil stabilised by muran ("maram") grasses and host to a wide range of distinctive flora. This is the also the natural habitat of golf – the Colonsay course is said to be 200 years old and is the un-gilded work of the Original Architect.

Enjoy the lapwings, ringed-plovers, redshanks, oyster catchers, pipits and wheatears; there is normally a pair of shelduck too, and even a few terns, although their numbers have plummeted in recent years. The golf course itself is a popular haunt of both ravens and chough. Out in the bay, look for seals on Eilean Dubh ("Dark Island").

After crossing the main bay, step up onto the grass again, heading for a point slightly inland of the prominent cairn on Dùn Ghallain.

VIKINGS

As you leave the main bay, you come at once into a much smaller, creek-like bay in an area where both redshanks and peewits abound. This is a typical Viking harbour, Port na Beiste ("Otter Port") – note the perfect if unobtrusive entrance through dangerous-looking rocks and the ample space to over-winter both craft and crews. Colonsay and Oronsay were major Viking strongholds, with the greatest known concentration of ship burials and other significant remains; they had a major settlement at Machrins and archaeological investigations have revealed extensive activity – including breadmaking facilities on an almost industrial scale. In recent years a visitor came across a fine-toothed comb, carved from bone and in almost perfect condition, just lying on the grass where a rabbit had been digging; another person found a beautiful bronze pin, delicately engraved. These and other treasures from Colonsay and Oronsay may be seen in the National Museum and other major collections.

Keep going – by now you should be able to see the (red) flag at the 13th hole, to the east of Dùn Ghallain, and have little difficulty finding a convenient path across a rushy plain. At the 13th hole, bear to the right and up towards the summit of Dùn Ghallain.

DÙN GHALLAIN

In late summer, look out for grass of Parnassus as you approach the 13th hole; the axle and rusting chassis on the right (NR 35144 93258) as you pass the green is all that remains of Colonsay's first motor-car, a Morris Seven introduced to the island in 1947 by the then doctor. As you approach the summit, note the substantial fosse and the quality of the stonework where it survives in its original courses – this was a commanding vantage point and was perhaps genuinely adapted by the Vikings themselves, as the name suggests.

It is distinguished from other forts – mostly attributed to the Iron Age – by the fact of its splendid isolation. All other forts in Colonsay and Oransay have line-of-sight communication with at least one or two others, but Dùn Ghallain stands alone. On the summit, one can readily trace the outline of a number of small structures and it is possible that these are signs of mediaeval re-occupation; certainly there is a tradition locally to that effect, for this is said to have been the dwelling-place of Shomhairle Liath.

Shomhairle Liath ("Grey Samuel") was a factor and (in Loder's perfect phrase) "an elderly voluptuary". He lived at Dùn Gallain and made very free with his tenantry and more particularly, with their womenfolk; one night the menfolk came upon him in his sleep, whereupon he was "seized, blinded and emasculated" but otherwise unharmed. He thereafter lived in a remote shieling south of Milbuie until his death, supposedly when the roof fell in on him. He was never buried, and the ruins of his house may yet be seen in a gully to the east of Carn Airigh Shomhairle ("Samuel's Shieling Cairn").

From Dùn Gallain, there is an excellent view of Ardskenish to the south and, looking to the north, one can see the safe passage through the outlying rocks to the Viking harbour. Close at hand is a hidden cave, Leab' Fhalaich Mhic a' Phi ("McPhee's Hiding-place"), one of the seven recorded hiding places of Malcolm MacPhee before his capture and execution in 1623.

Make your way to the head of Port Lobh, which is the bay to the south of Dùn Ghallain. It has a good sandy bottom and is a pleasant place to swim, but for safety and warmer water wait for an incoming tide.

ATH NAN CORP

A clump of gorse beside the burn, close to the 7th Green of the golf course, marks Ath nan Corp ("Corpse Ford") at NR 35985 93724. In the early 1640s Angus MacCholla, blinded with rage by Argyll's injustice, is said to have encountered a woman and child at this ford as he went to challenge the then factor, Donald Ballach McEwan. Hearing that the child was a Campbell, Angus is said to have beheaded him on the spot; although in all fairness, it should be remembered that this story is almost certainly just black propaganda coined by the Covenanters.

If you are only walking the Machrins section, turn back towards the north and follow the track around the western end of the aerodrome and identify Cnoc nan Gall, which has historic remains as described above. Then make your way back across the links to regain your starting point.

Ardskenish Walk

If you are walking the Ardskenish section, cross the burn and continue south, passing the 8th Green and following a track which passes through a gap in the drystane dyke. A Mesolithic shell-mound at Druim Sligeach ("Shelly Ridge"), just before you reach the dyke, has been the subject of geophysical prospection by University of Glasgow. This is part of an attempt to develop non-destructive means to interpret such sites. After 150 metres or so you will reach a very muddy section which is relieved by a short length of plank bridging. As you regain the track, you might like to explore some 80 metres to the north-west (to your right) where a green enclosure, ridged by lazy beds, encompasses an unrecorded scatter of cairns, possibly an abandoned burial ground. Returning to the track, continue southwards along an open heath until you see the open view from Bealach Gaoithe ("Windy Pass").

BEALACH GAOITHE

There is always a breeze where this rocky little pass opens out into views of silver sands, and it can be very welcome in summer. On the left is a rocky overhang and the outline of a levelled floor – this is another sgùid, the very distinctive form of Colonsay dwelling which can be traced back to the Bronze Age; light poles were leaned against the cliff and thatched with heather to provide a primitive shelter. The word is from a Germanic root, giving "shed" in English; appropriately enough, there is an eponymous example at Loch Sgùid, beside which there is a possible unrecorded Bronze Age cupmark.

To the right of the track is a grassy slope where pyramid bugle may be found. Ahead lies a beautiful strand, protected by a broad expanse of rock and aptly named Plaide Mhór (literally "Great Blanket"; *cf.* French "plage"). Look for grey Atlantic seals, also golden eye, tufted duck and Colonsay's own special bird, the eider duck.

Follow the track as it leads down into the dunes and off to the left, meandering along in the general direction of Beinn Orasa. Look out for violets, milkwort, speedwells, scurvy grass, soft cranesbill, storksbill – perhaps pause for a while in some sheltered hollow. Remember that you are heading towards Beinn Orasa as there are one or two opportunities to go off on a false trail. Eventually, the track passes under an overhead power-line at which point (NR 35171 91693) you should abandon it and head straight towards Beinn Orasa, passing through a patch of muran grass and then emerging on open pasture, Rioma nan Sadharcan ("Lapwing Marsh").

In a paper published in 1929, Symington Grieve made specific reference to this part of Ardskenish, in remarkable terms. "An old man at Kilchattan on Colonsay, told us that until recently several men were living who could remember the point [of Ardskenish] as an island; and he mentioned two, who are still alive, who he believed would recollect it, and he could remember himself when the neck of sand, dry at high-water, was not above 20 feet in breadth, and now at the narrowest point at high tide it will be the third of a mile; and from the accumulation of sand blown from the beach the land at some points, according to the Ordnance Survey map, is nearly 40 feet above the sea-level." Since the dune system appears to be based upon firm bedrock, one can only assume that what Grieve had recorded was the faint folk-memory of some devastating sandblow in the distant past.

TRAIGH NAM BARC

The bay ahead of you is Traigh nam Barc ("Boat's Strand") and on the far side you will see An Dùnan ("Little Fort"), a small Dùn or mound near the point. St. Columba is said to have landed thereabouts, at Port na h-Iùbhraich ("Port of the Skiff" or coracle) and then established his first foundation in the very shadow of his cousin's fortress of Dùn Cholla, on the site now occupied by the mediaeval Teampull na Ghlinne ("Temple in the Glen"). From here he is said to have negotiated for a "forward position" in Iona, on the border with Pictland, but he never lost his links with Colonsay or his especial love for Oransay, which was known then as Hinba and became his personal spiritual home. Adomnàn, St. Columba's biographer, describes it well, identifying it by its "bag-shaped arm of the sea" and by the fact that it lay on the direct sea-route to Ireland from Iona. The "bag-shape" refers, of course, to An Fhaoghail ("The Ford"), the tidal strand which at high tides separates Oransay from its sister, Colonsay. (There will be further references to St. Columba in Chapter 12).

Whilst thinking of St. Columba it is pleasant to recall some of his miracles as recounted by his hagiographer. As mentioned above, Adomnàn describes St. Kenneth sitting quietly at his chapel, when he becomes aware that St. Columba is in danger at sea. Going outside, St. Kenneth prays fervently and by apparent telepathy guides St. Columba and his craft towards safety. Anyone who stands where St. Kenneth's chapel stood, at the head of Traigh nam Barc, can see how the geography could accord with this ancient tradition. It takes little imagination to picture the joyful scene as the saintly friends embraced one another in relief.

Bear off to the right, following a fence-line and approaching a low drystane dyke, beyond which lies a well protected inlet and sandy bay, Port Cheann a' Gharraidh.("Dyke-end Harbour"). One can appreciate that this was a safe and sheltered refuge for boats in bygone days, although now it used only by the birds. Look for redshank, dunlin, greylag geese, shelduck, heron, teal and, if fortunate, grey plovers. In winter flocks of up to 300 Barnacle Geese make an impressive sight. Note that fresh water is usually running from an overflow at the brick-built well-house to your right, useful on a hot day. Continue along the shore to the next small bay.

DÙNAN NAN NIGHEAN NR 34705 91182

This small dùn ("Home of the Maidens", or more likely "Boathaven Homestead") is at the entrance to the natural harbour of Port Cheann a' Gharraidh; note the natural slipway beside it, which has been artificially improved in ancient days, as can be seen from some of the rough masonry still in position.

Continue along the shore, pass through a gap in the dyke and bear right to a low summit.

Possible variation: To prolong the walk by perhaps an hour or so, continue along the shore, keeping an eye open for a well-preserved kelpers' kiln at NR 34159 90876. The small but rather neatly constructed building above the raised beach at NR 34073 90873 is 2.4m x 3.6m within and may well have provided shelter for the kelpers, who had to tend the fire for 72 hours or more at a stretch. The individual lichen-covered stones on the raised beach, undisturbed for generations, are worthy of study – there seem to be lichens of every possible hue, and the patterns are amazing. Passing beyond Port na Luinge ("Longship's Port") you soon reach the end of the peninsula. Birdwatchers should note that the small offshore islet of Sgeir nan Sgarbh ("Cormorant Skerry") is an apparent waypoint for birds and the careful observer may be well-rewarded; look for puffins in particular. Return along the spine of the peninsula, to avoid difficult terrain along the west side. You will notice a significant number of cairns in something of a group; it is possible that these were erected at the time of a plague (NR 34263 91078).

From the low summit, note the small lochan with perhaps reed bunting and curlew in the vicinity, then turn back towards the north, passing through the remains of a small clachan and to the left of the more modern house. The clachan is of interest, being the best-preserved and most easily examined example in Colonsay. The most southerly building is "D"- ended to the east, and about 2.4m x 5.4m internally. The buildings in the main group have very substantial walls and are mostly rectangular in shape – in some cases they may be two houses "in a run", but in at least one case there seems to have been provision for a byre within the dwelling.

ARDSKENISH FARM

Ardskenish was formerly a farm in its own right and it is interesting to see the post-mediaeval remnants of the substantial clachan, so closely juxtaposed against the late-eighteenth-century cottages which, in turn, became the byre to the modern house. The substantial ruin close to the house was probably that of the tacksman's home (NR 34454 91436), a rare survival, and just beyond it lie the circular remains of a much older dwelling (NR 34451 91451), perhaps from the early seventeenth century. The census records of 1841 show that 20 people lived at Ardskenish, in three houses, and in 1851 there were 16 people in just two houses; over the next thirty years, numbers remained stable at 10 persons in two houses and then the new house was built, which in 1891 had six inhabitants including one "Frances Hotham, Boarder, Ret.Lieut RN". Perhaps he was connected with the family, or just loved the island – he is buried at Kilchattan, having died on 13th February 1900, at only 49 yrs of age. The 1890 Electoral roll records Francis Hotham as "Tenant of house" whereas Archibald McNeill, John McNeill, Malcolm McNeill, and Roger McNeill are all recorded as Electors, whose place of abode was Ardskenish and whose qualification to vote was as "Joint tenant of farm". The 1901 census shows two houses at Ardskenish, both unoccupied so that marks its end as a working, inhabited farm. Of course, the house remained in use from time to time and it is said that two Mackinnon ladies were living at Ardskenish during the war when, one dark and stormy night, they heard a loud noise like an explosion. The next morning, their factotum (Jimmy "the butler") went outside and discovered that the roof had been struck by an aircraft ; it was such an unlikely event that a number of people went down to Ardskenish to see for themselves when they heard about it – no word was ever heard as to the airplane involved. After the war, the house became a guest-house once again, operated by Barbara and Sid Satchell, and subsequently it became a second-home. When that last resident family left Ardskenish, the father was sufficiently moved to compose the following poem, as if written by his young son, Callum – suitably "orphaned" for added poignancy. It is given here in full by kind permission of his family.

Continuing north, the field wall is on your right. Pass through a gap and enter the dunes once more; ignoring the track, bear left as if towards the south-west corner of Mull, passing through the muran grass to reach the strand of Plaide Mhór.

This is a good spot for otters – if you do not see the creature itself, keep an eye open for its spraint and also for its track across the sand, where its tendency to drag its tail makes for a distinctive mark. When you reach the shoreline, there will be cowrie shells a short distance to your left. Seals abound and, as you look towards the Ross of Mull, you will probably identify the measured, menacing movement of the sea, breaking on Bogha Samhach ("Silent Reef"). Along the shoreline, the keen ornithologist may be rewarded by sightings of purple sandpiper, godwit, or grey plover.

From here it is an easy journey back towards Àth nan Corp, either along the shore or through the dunes to Bealach Gaoithe where you rejoin the track. After Àth nan Corp, follow the track around the western end of the aerodrome and identify Cnoc nan Gall, which has historic remains as described above. Then make your way back across the links to regain your starting point.

Exodus *by Sid Satchell*

Steadily shouldered, easing with the rump,
held the cart to even progress
over sea-air salted
firm low grass.
A blanket to the ground,
pillowing every lump.
A house now standing empty
by itself there all alone
a tribute to the builder
with its solid slates and stone.
To the east the nearest neighbour
by track three miles away
in the west across an ocean
the mass of U.S.A.
Sad thoughts filled head face forward
a widow with the driver sat,
the boy, eyes in pools at brimming
and forgotten legs,
hanging down the tail-board at the back.
Afloat yet fixed those eyes in staring,
long lengths the blinks between,
unconscious to discomfort
unfelt compelling ease.
Receded curvature returning
with each plodded climb,
disinterring bitter sadness
then a burial on decline.
No strokes of brush with colours oiled,
and gold could ever frame,
the endless mental pictures
as to the gallery of his mind they came.
The farmhouse joined by drystone walls
to facing sheds for stock,
in strength against Atlantic's tearing
winded rage
and held in outflung arms

with silk smooth breasted rock.
Slanting to a setting sun,
matched dappled white, a rippled sea,
flowered Parnassus grass
pureness and beauty in silent rivalry.
Heralding falling years came geese
black and white, and grey,
wings in arc and clamour stilled,
controlled graceful slipping from the sky
to where in peaceful grazing
with the sheep,
the crisp short grasses by.
The great bay's south point needled,
as a compass set,
from where heated engulfed waters
eastwards stream,
long journey with its warming help
unseen.
Snubbed nosed northern headland,
folds deep-set sea shell sands,
hard packed glistening left by falling
tides,
singing shorewards on each drying wind
it rides
to undulate in rows of Marram planted dunes.
Coast hugging sea duck
at making tides appear,
arrowed ranks in swiftly ordered flight,
regroup to corrugating rafts
as they alight.
The Eider on her plucked down nest
low in the heathered moor,
fears not the hooves of beasts that graze,
but man, who takes his greedy toll,
cheating the Raven of his natural cull.
Rush ringed pools with mosses padded,
float proud mothers heading
dark small balls of wool at feeding.

Broken winged Mallard protecting feigns,
Sea-gulls' green-brown mottled eggs
on high cliff's edge retains.
Held out necks to burrows peering,
Shelducks at their homestead
seeking.
Drumming Snipe, the Curlew's wail,
steep rock creeks hold flocks
of Teal.
Light blue Squills, and Orchids, why a shy
one sweetly scented.
Louse, Milk and Butter worts, coloured starlets
surrounding Stonecrop-patterned boulders
jutting from the peaty loam.
Autumn flowering Gentians
on slopes that face the east,
miss golden rays and flaming reds
in modest shrinking from a bedding sun.
Iris clumped, a first in early spring,
sulphur yellow cheery waving flags
the changing season's message bring.
Pictures in their endless line
were passing without pause,
soon to be forgotten in future's unused
years of time.
Lighted window from a distant space,
relieving pressure in father's hand,
darkened fears retreat, and pleasured speed
returns to flagging pace.
No lighthouse beam held greater might
than an oil lamp burning
on the darkest night.
From seeded soil, crops are mown,
a table set, the harvest home.
Shorter days, shorter hours,
in-calf cows in winter byres.
Snow-flaked ground treads
crunching sound,

a bite with intake air.
With silent cock, lethargic hens,
brought coaxing to the open pen.
Sheltered beasts with steaming rise
lowering feed to a dung heap's mounting size,
by their instinct only, fear steps in,
contentment without means to think;
a browsing life, a certain end,
they have no god, they make no sin.
Flooded waters pressures gain,
rounded drops roll down
as on a window pane.
A foal from open country wild
to be broken in a city's stable yard.
At last, from unturned head a sigh,
recalled as to a duty voicing.
"Is all well there at the back?"
Will kindness be there for the dog?
What happened to the cat?
Repeated question, with intake breath
as if the fear it drives,
the wandered mind brought back replied,
"Yes, Mother, it's sun that's in my eyes."

Chapter 11

BALEROMINDUBH AND BALEROMINMÒR

Map: page xv

Up until the late sixteenth century, Colonsay farms were somewhat closer in concept to extended communities, with insubstantial dwellings in almost casual groupings to exploit specific resources or opportunities. Those early farms had been quite large and inefficient and in due course most of them were subdivided into two or three parts, each with a modest hamlet at its heart. Thus the former Baile Rumaich (= "boggy farm", from *rumaich* = "marsh, quagmire, puddle, slough") was divided into two parts, which later were distinguished as the "dark" portion (Baleromindubh) and the "large" portion of the farm (Balerominmòr). The bog in question is a very extensive one, lying at the heart of the original farm and very nearly isolating it from the neighbouring communities.

The existing farmhouses are apparently both of nineteenth-century construction, but that at Baleromindubh is the earlier one. It is possible to date it with reasonable accuracy, since it is known to have been built by the Old Laird as a dower house for his mother. This lady was a daughter of Alexander McDougall of Dunollie and, according to a traditional account, the house was deliberately built with a commanding view up the Firth of Lorn and towards her ancestral lands. Mary McDougall was born 1741 and widowed before 1788. "Mrs. McNeill, the Laird's mother, moved from Oronsay to Baleromin Dubh, a new house near the port of Scalasaig, which her son had built for her" when he himself moved to Colonsay House; this must have been in or soon after 1806.

In the census of 1841, five households are recorded as living at "Baleraomin Du"; three are the homes of agricultural labourers, one is the home of a mason and the other is that of Hugh McCalman "Minister of the Gospel"; Hugh was the Assistant Minister for the Church of Scotland and had married in the parish in 1836; presumably he lived in the main house. Interestingly, Dr. Liddell has discovered a letter from Rev Hugh MacCalman of "Balerominmore" to the Procurator Fiscal in 1841 concerning the church's intervention in the matter of an illegitimate birth (Alex

MacMillan and Flora Blue).

It is unclear from the census who was actually farming the land even in 1851, although the main house seems to have been occupied by the MacLugash family. The earliest recorded "farmer" in Baleromindubh arrived after that date, being 25 yr. old John Campbell, from Knapdale, who is recorded as farming 350 acres there in 1861. By 1871 he had 435 acres and had married a girl from Greenock, although by 1881 he has dropped back to 320 acres – the differences probably relate to "Scots" or "statute" acreage. It is interesting to notice that the garden ground at Baleromindubh is surrounded by sycamore trees, a non-native that was first introduced to Colonsay by the Old Laird, at some date prior to 1811.

Meanwhile, a Colonsay man, Angus MacNeill, is recorded as farming 700 acres at Balerominmòr in 1861. It is not certain where Angus will have lived – in addition to a wee clachan, there was an isolated house on the slopes of Dùn Cholla, of which the footings still survive. Angus MacNeill had been a cattle herd at Ardskenish in 1841 and clearly was re-located when that farm was engrossed by Machrins. Angus has disappeared from Balerominmòr by 1871, but in 1881 another Colonsay man appears, Malcolm McNeill, who is recorded there as farming 520 acres; by that date we may assume that he is resident in the newly-constructed farmhouse (which is marked on the O.S. map).

It seems possible that Malcolm had some special connection with the laird – see Chapter 5. In 1886, the laird, John McNeill, had written to Donald Smith to say that "A farm on Colonsay was about to become vacant and McNeill (i.e., the laird) wanted to borrow money to buy stock for it" (Donna MacDonald, 1996). He borrowed £2,500 at 4% and the same again the following year, incurring debts from which he never recovered; was this to provide stock for Malcolm – and, if so, why? It will be recalled (Chapter 7) that soon afterwards (June 1890) Malcolm married Fanny, the daughter of the former Estate gardener John Addison, and that the wedding took place in Edinburgh.

In 1841, the total population of Baleromindubh and Balerominmòr had amounted to 74, but this fell away quickly when the farms were modernised. In 1901 there were only 11 inhabitants and in 2010 both farms were completely uninhabited with the exception of two people engaged in aquaculture. The farmland has been resumed by Colonsay Estate, and the farmhouses are now used as holiday accommodation.

Records from the early seventeenth century include a number of events connected with Baileraomainn. One of them concerns Malcolm MacDuffie, last chieftain of his family, who was pardoned of rebellion on 14th March 1620 and made his way home to Colonsay. Unfortunately for him, he then committed some crime which obliged Colla Ciotach MacDonald, his landlord and former companion-in-arms, to act against him. Malcolm tried to evade capture, but was eventually pursued to a hiding-place at the extremity of Eilean nan Ron ("Seal Island"), off Oronsay. From here he was brought back to Colonsay and bound to the standing stone at Balerominmòr, where he was executed together with four followers, including two of his sons. The executions took place in February 1623; in June of that year Colla Ciotach was arraigned for this "fellone and crewall Slauchter", and was punished for non-attendance at the court. In due course Colla Ciotach seems to have fully justified his actions and the penalties were rescinded. No record of Malcolm's crime survives, but his execution was clearly judicial, having been conducted solemnly and in public view; the fact that there was a cross carved upon the standing stone reinforces the condign nature of the punishment.

In the following year, August 1624, Fathers Cornelius Ward and Paul O'Neill visited Colonsay in the course of their missionary activity based at Bonamargy in Antrim. They sailed across from Oransay and will almost certainly have used the harbour at Balerominmòr, which was where the island birlinn had its haven. Although they only stayed a couple of days they gave spiritual comfort to the islanders, baptised five persons and converted nineteen newcomers to the faith. As it happened, the laird (Colla Ciotach MacDonald) was away at the time and they reported to their superiors that they could not obtain food or shelter in his absence. Since he was known to be a staunch Catholic and a good friend to the missionaries, this gives a puzzling insight into local conditions at the time; perhaps the recent execution of Malcolm and his companions made islanders ultra-cautious. "*Imo ea nocte qua ex insula egressum meditabamur, littus sub dio nobis domus erat; caena conchae marinae, quas ipsi in littore colligebamus.*" "They spent their last night there on the beach in the open, and their only meal consisted of shellfish which they collected on the shore". Since they will have taken what shelter they could from their boat, we can confidently assume that they spent that uncomfortable night in the small bay at Balerominmòr, Port a' Chrochaire ("Port of the Hanged Man").

Some years later, in the Civil War, Colla Ciotach's son Alasdair MacCholla was appointed as the commander of the Royalist forces raised in Ireland by the Earl of Antrim; thus it was that a Colonsay man empowered Montrose and secured a string of famous victories against the king's enemies. In preparation for these events, Alasdair was in Colonsay in November 1643 when a Parliamentary ship, the 180 ton "*Paul*" of London, was forced by storms to take shelter in Colonsay. The records suggest that she probably sheltered in Loch Staosnaig, just below Baleromindubh, where she lay from Wednesday 22nd November until Sunday 26th.

"On Sunday afternoon, Alistar MacDonnald, son to Coile Mac Gillespicke, accompanied with fifty men came into the ship, and the master, thinking it was the Tutor of Caldor and his company let them all in purposing to make them welcome.

"But as soon as they came in Alistar laid [hold of] the master and told him he must arrest him in the king's name and presently hurled him down to his boat and caused likewise lay hands on the Master's Mate and one more of the company.

"Some of Alistar's men lifted the door of the overlap under which some of the crew were at meat; six of his Hagbutters shot down and deadly hurt one in the head and one in the arm. The Master gunner would have blown up the overlap, but not having things ready, he only let fall some powder and fired it, which so terrified Alistar and his company that they took to their boats, leaving one of their men and one of the crew slain above the hatches. Before they left they cut the cable with their swords thinking the ship would be driven ashore; but the crew put out another anchor, and it blew so hard that none could come off the land that night"

At dawn, the crew set sail again and eventually arrived at Oban bay, below Dunollie Castle. It is not known what happened to Robert Paul, the ship's master, and the other captives. One wonders if they might have settled in the island – on the north side of Loch Staosnaig there is a place still known as Cùil Fail ("Paul's Nook"). Alasdair MacCholla had a brief but glittering career, was knighted after the victory at Kilsyth and became the Governor of Cahir in

Co. Tipperary; but he was murdered on 13th November 1647 after the battle of Knocknanuss, the single biggest battle of the Civil War.

Later records are somewhat less turbulent. When Martin Martin visited Colonsay in 1703, he mentioned a crucifix which had formerly stood on the high altar at Oronsay "in which several precious stones were fixed; the most valuable of these is now in the custody of Mac Duffie, in black Raimused village (i.e. Baleromindubh), and it is used as a catholicon for diseases." This information is doubly interesting, since it reveals that a MacDuffie was still a tacksman in Colonsay at the time. In 1656, Presbytery had considered the cases of various fornicators in Colonsay and in addition to public penance in Islay had ordained that the miscreants should produce testimonials of "sober carriage". The testimonials were to be obtained from "Johne Campbell baillie of Colonsay and Donald McDuffie", the latter being presumably a tacksman and very possibly an earlier custodian of the catholicon. It seems reasonable to suppose that Donald McDuffie had held the tack of Baleromin and this was therefore the latter-day residence of this ancient family.

Martin Martin gives us further interesting information in the following passage: "My landlord, having one of his family sick of a fever, asked my book (i.e. bible), as a singular favour, for a few moments. I was not a little surprised at the honest man's request, he being illiterate: and when he told me the reason of it, I was no less amazed, for it was to fan the patient's face with the leaves of the book; and this he did at night. He sought the book next morning, and then again in the evening, and then thanked me for so great a favour: and told me the sick person was much better by it; and thus I understood that they had an ancient custom of fanning the face of the sick with the leaves of the Bible." From a close reading of the work, it seems possible that his "landlord" was McDuffie in Baleromin, with whom he seems to have stayed for a few days.

When Thomas Pennant visited Colonsay in 1772, he made no direct reference to Baileraomainn, but he deprecated the poor productivity and condition of all the farmland in Colonsay, making direct comparison with the excellent results achieved by the energetic tenant of Oransay. He specifically drew attention to the absence of "inclosures", which reminds us that the extensive system of field walls had nowhere in Colonsay been commenced even by that relatively late date. In point of fact, the walls at Baleromindubh and Balerominmòr are largely contemporaneous with the farmhouses themselves, and therefore date only from the nineteenth century.

In 1794, the "Statistical Account of Scotland" mentioned that there were 134 families in Colonsay, and fifteen farms. "There are above 40 souls, at an average, in each of the farms; but some of these being very small, not having above 3 or 4 families, the number of souls in the best inhabited farms is very great." Thus, from a total population of 718, one might assume that about twenty people were resident in each of Baleromindubh and Balerominmòr.

In addition to the above sources, we are very fortunate to have an excellent description of conditions in Baileraomainn on the very cusp of the modern era. Mrs. Frances Murray of Moorepark, Cardross took a holiday let of Oronsay House from the autumn of 1880 until November 1887, and her delightful memoir "*Summer in the Hebrides*" includes a lengthy description of a visit to Baileraomainn in October 1886.

"When we contrast the old days with our own time, one is tempted to wonder whether, after all, the present way of living of the poorer inhabitants is so very different from that of the skin-clad and limpet-sucking dwellers in the caves and dunes. Their ranges of wretched dwellings, scarcely possessing a window or a chimney, the long irregular wave of the roof-tree's curve, and the low walls of rough unplastered stones, are to this day hardly to be distinguished from the hill side…

"(We sail to) Balleraomin Dhu (*sic* – actually Balerominmòr), where on a steep hill side stands a little clachan, a farm house, and Kate McGilvray's cottage, with its back to the hill, and the indispensable stack of peat at the gable end. In spite of a splendid natural drainage, there is in front a fearful and wonderful hole, over which the south-west wind, fresh from the fields of ocean, blows and wafts (thanks, kind wind!) the flavour of limpets, stale fish and other unutterable odours away.

"We enter; a cry of welcome rises from the hut; but nothing can we see, the peat reek is too dense, our eyes smart, we cough and are driven back to the door again. The fire is on the floor: the chimney hole above it, with a stout tarred rope dangling down, to lead up the smoke, and to show where if it had a mind it might find an exit. The walls are black as night, and the rafters are hung with pendants and festoons of shining peat reek.

"They support a covering of turf and bent, bound with heather ropes, which keep out the rain wonderfully well. As to furniture, there is a very small dresser with a little delf, a wee kist, a bed, above which the hens roost, the bedding of which, however, seems clean and white. There is no table, but a little shelf in the window, and such a funny window, a mere hole, with four little panes set in, one broken and stuffed with rags, one with a glass bull's eye, and two filled with pieces of wood. The rest of the furniture consists of two or three stools and two logs of drift-wood on either site of the fire, supported on a few peats by way of legs. Kate's principal chair was made of natural scrub wood twisted by nature into the shape of a seat with arms…

"There was indeed barely room to turn around. In this hut the mother, four children, and two brothers, the latter of whom slept in an unseen recess, lived a healthy and happy life, and here it was that the late Campbell of Islay, heard from a McGilvray now dead, his long-winded story of the "*Knight of the Red Shield*," which you will find in volume second of his most interesting "*Highland Tales.*" … Duncan, whose shaggy white hair, long, curly beard, and coat of many patches, gave him an appearance half vener-able, and half absurd, is a narrator of Gaelic stories only second to his late father…

"Before leaving the little clachan on the hillside, we paid a visit to the other families living there. One of the huts was the dwelling-place of a very aged man, Malcolm Gorm ("Blue"), whose years numbered only two less than the century. For the last eighteen months he has been bed-ridden, and we found him lying in a clean bed with a jug of flowers beside his pillow in a very small room. His face wore a rosy, contented expression in spite of the marks of great age…"

In connection with the "*Knight of the Red Shield*", J.F. Campbell noted that he got the story in July 1860 "from John McGilvray, labourer, Baile Raomainn, Colonsay, aged 72 years. Says he learned it from his father, Farquhar McGilvray, and that he heard him tell it since he remembers anything. Farquhar McGilvray, his father, was a native of Mull, and there learned this tale in his boyhood. He served nine years in the army, in North America, and subsequently settled in Colonsay. He died near about forty years ago, about seventy-five years of age."

In the 1881 census, the McGilvray household gave Catherine as 50 yrs old, and listed Duncan as a 62 yr old "labourer"; her other brother, John, was a 51 yr old "farm servant". They were all unmarried, but looked after 3 nieces and a nephew, ranging at that time from 2 to 16 yrs of age. Their neighbour, Malcolm Blue, gave his own age as 88 years and that of his wife as 77 years. Farquhar McGilvray had baptised a daughter, Mary, on September 10th 1796, and thereby we know that his wife was Annie McLugas. By chance, her name survives, at Baleromindubh, where the ruins of a cottage are still known as Taigh Anna nic Lugais.

There are no listed buildings in Baleromin, but there are six significant monuments listed by RCAHMS:

Cairn, Milbuie NR 387929

This is easily approached from the public road – just pass through the gate to Baleromindubh and strike off to your left up the slope to the summit. It was originally a very substantial cairn and it echoes the one which once existed at Càrn Mòr (see Chapter 5). The remains consist of a circle some 16m in diameter bordered by a stone kerb and in the centre of which there is a recumbent stone slab, surmised by RCAHMS to be perhaps the capstone of a cist.

Standing Stone "Carraig Mhic a' Phi" NR 384914

See under "Pàirc na h'Eaglais (below)

Dùn Cholla ("Colla's Fort") NR 377915

Easily approached from the point at which the the track to Balerominmòr levels off opposite Loch Cholla; it lies about 100m to your right and has an impressive approach. Since it is surrounded by precipitous natural defences, only the entrance required a wall but this has been built on a massive scale. The wall is up to 6m thick and the entrance way is quite narrow, then widens to the left, giving a defender great freedom for swordplay whilst leaving any opponent at a disadvantage. Within the wall, the summit of the dùn is about 54m x 25m and it affords magnificent views, not least as regards the safe landing places provided at An Fhaoghail ("The Ford" – i.e. strand). There are traces of a number of structures with the dùn, which are presumed to date to mediaeval occupation.

Dùn Mara ("Fort of the Sea") NR 37671 90227

RCAHMS accept that this "was probably situated on Beinn Eibhne ("Fair Hill") and mention that by 1881 the rock had eroded to the extent that the only survival was "an arc of wall about 10 feet thick" which included a well-preserved entrance passage. They go on to state that "subsequent erosion has removed all traces". This is an unfortunate error, but it is clear from their suggested map reference that their surveyors were looking in the wrong place. The original statement by William Stevenson in 1881 is worth considering in full: "It has been circular but now only half of it remains. The rock is soft, and a large fall took place one winter lately, which accounts for the disappearance of part of the fort. The entrance to the fort is better seen here than in any remaining one, and goes through a wall about 10 feet thick. On a favourable day there can be seen from this hill Ireland, Islay, Jura, Scarba, Mull, Iona, Tiree, Coll, Dhu Heartach, and on the islands Dun (Eibhinn), Dun Coll, Dun Gallon, Dun Donald, Cairn nan Eoin, &c." The significant feature was that it gave a commanding view of all approaches to An Fhaoghail and line-of-site signalling to the important forts. Thus it was an observation post, not a "fort" as such; in fact, it also gives a clear view of all the three lookout-hills along the east coast of the island (Cnoc na Faire) and also Cnoc an t' Samhla, the signal hill. Dùn Mara simply had to have existed, to provide warning of danger, and William Stevenson's description is entirely accurate. The site is a natural rocky knoll which has been modified to create a flat surface and the rock fall to which he alludes was evidently upon the eastern side, where the natural defence had been slightly improved. Two or three stones remain in position there even now and the "rock fall" was no more than the collapse of some additional loosely-assembled masonry. There seems no reason to suppose that the interior was ever much larger than at present, about 6m in diameter. Any modern "erosion" on the scale which was suggested would not have gone un-noticed, if only by the people who have lived beneath that cliff for the last forty years.

Pairc na h'Eaglais ("Church Field") NR 384914

This survives as a roughly semi-circular enclosure about 22m in diameter, a former burial ground. There are the well-preserved remains of a small oblong building 7m x 3m which RCAHMS identify as being of a domestic nature, presumably post-Reformation.

Inhumations, as far as any hazy tradition survives, were latterly of un-baptised infants. The site is close to a convenient landing-place and is said to have been where Mass was said during the seventeenth century.

An enclosure beside the ruin protects Carraig Mhic a'Phi ("MacPhee's Standing-stone"), which had been broken and was repaired by Ulf Hagman of Sweden in 1977. The stone originally stood upon the low knoll some metres to the east, and was orientated; at some point it had been "Christianised" by a cross which was carved upon it, but the stone was unfortunately inverted when it was re-erected. One can see the base of the shaft of the cross as it disappears into the cement and rubble base; a photograph and sketch made in the late nineteenth century are a little unclear – it is certainly a cross, but uncertain if it could have been a cross of Lorraine (see Chapter 10). In 1623, Malcolm McPhie and four followers were executed here, McPhee himself having been tied to the stone. This also supposedly marks their burial place, as well as that of Donald Ballach McIain ("Poxed Donald") in 1644. This was a Campbell liegeman who had attempted to usurp Colla Ciotach MacDonald's postion, Colla having been captured by Argyll. Donald based himself in Oransay and attempted to impose traditional but outdated taxes, not least by imposing Damph Ursainn (a death-fine) upon a widow of Kilchattan. Colla's son, Angus, abducted the "factor" from Oransay, tied him to the stone and forced his own men to shoot him. He thereupon wrote to Argyll, advising him to keep his distance.

Symington Grieve recorded that, in 1881, he was told by Sir John McNeill that he had observed "a number of men mowing grass near the ruins of the Church at Pairc na h'Eaglais. As it was unusual to see anyone cutting grass there, he asked his attendant what the men were doing. His answer was that they were MacDuffies from Isla, who were shaving the graves of their ancestors. He assured Sir John that a number of MacDuffies had been interred there."

In 1979, another cross-marked stone was discovered, during the excavation of post-holes for the protective enclosure. Like the standing-stone, it is of Torridonian sandstone, but it was only about 1.01m x 0.42m in size. The simple cross had used most of the available field but the shaft is unfinished – it was suggested at the time that perhaps the stone had broken whilst being worked. This cross has been re-buried within the enclosure.

Horizontal Mill, Struthan a' Mhuilinn Duibh ("Black-mill Burn") NR 376908

This is the best-surviving example of such a mill, and may best be approached by following the burn upwards from the links beside the Strand. Such a mill consisted of a transverse wheel on a vertical axle, the mill-stones being supported upon slabs across the stream. The chamber can easily be identified, as can the upper slabs and one half of the socket through which the drive-shaft passed. Further upstream, one can see how the water-flow was regulated. Faint traces of another example can be seen where the Baleromindubh burn enters the sea, just south of Eilean Mhàrtain.

Additional places of interest

The walk described later in this chapter includes a number of sites of interest, some of which are also mentioned here.

Cairns and traces of occupation, Rubha Dubh ("Dark Headland") NR c. 390914

The above list of officially recorded sites of historic interest is surprisingly short. There are no Holy Wells, only one chapel site (dedication unknown) and – most remarkably – no examples of a basic "dùn" or farmstead. This does seem quite extraordinary – this is the most sheltered part of the island, yet there seems to be very little trace of pre-Reformation agricultural habitation. The same may be said for both Garvard and Oransay, but they are rather different in that they both belonged to the Priory and special arrangements may have been made – perhaps insubstantial housing close to the Priory which was redeveloped in the eighteenth century.

There are however some interesting remains in the vicinity of Rubha Dubh at NR c. 390914 which have not been fully examined. The cairns are reminiscent of the one beside the un-named dùn of Ardskenish Glen (see Chapter 10) and this would seem to have been an appropriate and central site for occupation. Very possibly there were earlier habitations sites at both Balerominmòr and Baleromin-dubh which have been obliterated by subsequent development.

Kiln at Meall an Arbhair ("Kiln Bluff") NR 39292 91168

It is unfortunate that the O.S. map has transposed two important place-names, Port a' Chrochaire and Meall an Arbhair (the latter is not, of course "Corn Headland" but is a corruption in reference to an "Àth" or kiln). In the 1980s, John and Pamela Clarke drew attention to a clearly defined roadway running up from the shoreline at Rubha Dubh, for which there was no coherent local explanation. Research revealed that it was once known as Sraid an Aoil ("Lime Road") and led to the discovery of a large and well-preserved kiln at NR 39292 91168. It was noted that Balerominmòr is the only farm on Colonsay devoid of both shell-sand and seaweed, and it then became apparent that an area of limestone lay within its boundary, at the seaward end of Sraid an Aoil. This then led to examination of that area, where it was seen to have been heavily worked. It is not certain how the kiln was fuelled, but coal could be landed at Port a' Chrocaire and this seems to be the most likely method.

Cnoc an t' Samhla ("Reflection Hill") NR 38297 92642
This distinctive name was a puzzle to many people, until Alastair Scouller noticed that there is a hill of the same name on Islay, beside Finlaggan Loch. The two hills are in line-of-site, and the explanation then became very clear – after the Lordship of the Isles became based at a fixed centre, there would be a need for communications between its Council Isle and outlying forts. Various signalling methods were available, including fire, smoke and reflection of polished metal; the name of the hill indicates that it was simply a transmission station.

Hut circle and Cultivation site, Beinn Eibhne NR 37633 90515
There is a well-preserved and unrecorded hut-circle on the shoulder of Beinn Eibhne, in a remarkably good state of preservation. It is at the centre of a plateau which has been comprehensively enclosed by a wall of large boulders. The enclosed area is marked by cultivation ridges and there are a number of rudimentary sgùidean and other structures in the vicinity. The entrance to the hut is from the west, and it is about 6m in internal diameter, within walls 1m thick and standing to a height of 1m, with three full courses of masonry exposed in some parts. The interior of the hut is a jumble of fallen stones, and there is an additional building as an ill-defined annexe on the south side. The annexe entrance was also from the west and it may have been a circular building of about 3m in diameter.

Hut circle nr. Pairc na h'Eaglais NR 38389 91579

There is a hut circle of about 2 m. diameter and standing to about 1 m. in height, not far to the north-east of the point where the path from Carraig Mhic a' Phi joins the track. A later, two-chambered hut has been built against it.

Farmhouse nr. Dùn Cholla NR377915

As one approaches Dùn Cholla from the track, one passes the plain but distinctive remains of a substantial rectangular house.

Suggested Walks

Although the more recent history of these two farms has been reviewed in the opening paragraphs of this chapter, the following topographical description will include some additional details. The farms will be described separately, but there is no difficulty in combining the two walks if a total of about five or six hours can be allowed (total distance a little more than 12 km). The walking is quite varied and can be tiring; waterproof boots are essential.

Baleromindubh Section

There is a convenient parking spot beside the public road, opposite the entrance to the farm. Passing through the gate, follow the track to the highest point, then ascend the hill towards your right, Cnoc an t' Samhla ("Reflection Hill"). In the early mediaeval period, the Lordship of the Isles ceased to be peripatetic and instead developed a fixed centre, at Finlaggan Loch in Islay. Unfortunately, there was no clear line-of-sight communication to connect the lookout centres along the east coast of Colonsay with Dùn Eibhinn, Dùn Cholla and Dùn Domhnuill, nor onwards to Finlaggan. To solve the problem, Cnoc an t' Samhla was selected as a relay-station, and with two additional similarly-named hills in Islay formed just part of a highly-efficient chain of communications which went as far as Rathlin Island and the fortress of Dunluce in Co. Antrim. Within Colonsay, there is line-of-sight from Cnoc an t'Samhla to Dùn Mara, Dùn Cholla, Dùn Gallain and Dùn Eibhinn, also to the look-out posts on at least two of the Cnoc na Faire hills as well as Beinn nan Gùdairean, and commanding views of both An Fhaghoil and Traigh nam Barc.

From the summit of Cnoc an t' Samhla, the visitor enjoys a wonderful view across Linne Tarsuinn ("Crosswise Gulf") towards Loch Tarbert in Jura and the Sound of Islay, whilst closer to hand there is an outstanding opportunity to survey the extensive wetlands for which Baleromin was named. This area is rich in the highly-specialised plants associated with acidic conditions and is well worth visiting in its own right.

Looking towards the northeast, identify the heather-clad hillock to the right of the modern, rather distinctive solar-powered lighthouse at Scalasaig and return across the track to make your way towards it. It is the site of an impressive Bronze-age burial cairn (NR 387929), now a protected historic monument. Although the cairn itself is long-gone, the massive kerb stones remain in place, forming a circle some 16m in diameter. Near the centre of the circle there is a substantial slab, possibly the cover of a cist ("chest") grave. The site of a matching cairn has recently been noticed at Carn Mòr, on the north side of Glassard, both cairns being within plain view of each other.

From the cairn, follow the line of the coast eastwards, out towards Eilean Mhàrtain ("Martin's Island"), which is clearly marked on the Ordnance Survey map. After a short distance, a walled field will become visible ahead of you and lower down – descend to skirt round the corner of this field, leaving it to your right. You will probably notice the slight remains of two or three very old dwellings, and will perhaps raise some snipe and woodcock. Stay on the fairly level patch close to the sea, passing a couple of boat-landings and crossing a burn in the midst of some tussocky ground. As you come within sight of the channel at Eilean Mhàrtain, try to keep about 100 metres inland and approach the headland from behind a low, grassy outcrop (NR39567 92192) – there is a slight notch at its summit, try to keep the notch between you and the Paps of Jura as you approach. Your caution may be handsomely rewarded, as the tide rushes through this channel and creates rich feeding opportunities – from the comfort of the grassy knoll, you will see herons and grey Atlantic seals and, if you are patient, you may have the chance to see an otter. Look out for red-breasted mergansers, great northern divers and, in winter, remember this is a great place for many species of duck.

In due course, turn right to follow the shoreline towards the south; after about 150 metres you will notice the ruin of a boat-shaped structure about 2m x 5m internally, in a sheltered cove. After another 50 metres you will come across a small but enthusi-astic burn, Sruthan a' Mhuilinn Duibh ("Stream of the Black-mill"). There were many such mills in Colonsay at one time, and a good example survives as a listed monument at Balerominmòr (see details above). The wooden paddlewheel of the mill was set on a horizontal axis into a circular chamber, and whenever required could be lowered into the stream by means of a simple lever. The millstones were placed above the wheel, the shaft of which ran through a hole in the nether stone and engaged the upper one. Such a stone was very like a quern stone, but naturally enough without the hole for the wooden peg; a stone of this type may be seen outside the front door of Colonsay Hotel. The chamber of this particular mill can be identified just above the shoreline at NR 39468 92002, and some 20 metres upstream one can see where the mill dam will have been placed, to regulate the flow of water.

After a short distance, the path along the shore is intersected by a magnificent natural dyke (NR 39437 91968), for all the world resembling the handiwork of some giant mason. It is locally believed that this dyke runs below the sea, then re-emerges on the Jura shore at Rubh' an t' Sàilein ("Ocean Point"), dives again under Loch Tarbert and then continues all the way to the summit of Beinn an Oir, the highest of the Paps of Jura. Certainly the distinctive colour and nature of the stone make this a persuasive theory, and one might wonder if the dyke had its origins in the volcanic activity of Ben More in Mull.

Turn right to cross the dyke, after which one descends and passes through a gateway, now that a wall has appeared along the shore; this is the march which divides Baleromindubh from Balerominmòr, but even for those intending to explore these farms in two parts it is too soon to turn back. Pass through the gate, and follow the track which runs alongside the wall but on the seaward side. This track was provided to give access to Baleromindubh from the coast, for at one time heavy goods and livestock were transported by sea. In early times flat-bottomed sailing craft were used, but in the nineteenth century a specialised craft was developed, steam driven and designed to take the beach. Known familiarly as a "Puffer", such a ship was immortalised in Neil Munro's "*Tales of Para Handy*".

The track will quickly lead you onto the magnificent, sheltered, deserted sands of Tràigh Bàn ("White Strand"), an idyllic spot. This is quite a good place to linger for a while, just one hour from the start of your walk, to watch herring gull, shelduck, ringed plover, redshank, dunlin, pipit, pied wagtail etc.

For those who wish to divide Baleromin into two walks, this marks the end of the Baleromindubh section and is the point at which they should retrace their steps along the track and go back through the gate. At that point, they should break away from their original route and instead continue to follow the route of the old track, which will quickly lead them to a position from which they can identify Baleromindubh farmhouse, with a grove of sycamore trees in front of it and steadings to the left. Follow the easiest route up to the farmhouse, then walk back along the main track to regain the starting point. To undertake the second walk, start again below at "Balerominmòr Section".

Baleromindubh continuing through Balerominmòr

Having crossed Tràigh Bàn, one can climb onto a heathery bluff and continue in the same direction for another 250 metres or so, pausing when one's route is crossed by a well-defined gully at NR 39463 91394. This is known as Sràid an Aoil ("Lime Road") and, on closer examination, one can see that a properly constructed roadway has been built along the whole length of this natural declivity. Its very existence had been forgotten, let alone its purpose, until very recently but, looking towards the seaward extremity, it can be seen that a large expanse of rocky foreshore has been quarried away. The geological map reveals that this was the only source of limestone in Balerominmòr, a farm which has no seaweed deposits and only silica sand instead of shell-sand. Clearly the improving lairds of the nineteenth century were prepared to go to extensive lengths to upgrade their land, although lime was also used to purify wells and to disinfect houses that had been visited by disease.

Cross the roadway and continue onwards, bearing slightly to your right as you follow the line of the coast. After a short distance, move up to the summit from which a new and entrancing view will present itself, along the shore of Balerominmòr and towards the dazzling sands of Tràigh a' Mhill Bhàin ("Strand of the White Headland") on Oransay. At almost any time this will be a breezy spot, hence the decision to build the kiln hereabouts. The kiln itself is about 100 metres below the very summit at NR 39292 91168, more-or-less in line with the distant lighthouse of Rubha a' Mhail on Islay, but concealed by bracken in summer. The kiln is boat-shaped and quite substantial, outlined by a wall almost one metre in height; on the western side, one can see a gap or "creep", possibly to give access when the fire was to be lit or perhaps to give access for barrows when the quicklime was to be removed. About 12m to the north-west of the kiln is a substantial walled pit (NR 39293 91184), which one imagines may have been provided to slake the raw product.

Continuing southwards along the coast, keep to the seaward corner of the field that comes into view, to pass through a field gate. Follow the line of the fence and cross to the outside of the fence line at the next gate (c. 40m). This is an excellent field for mushrooms, and in springtime it boasted for many years an expanse of tulips, the vestige of Neil MacNeill's brief post-war experiment in bulb production for the horticultural trade. After a short distance the field slopes towards an attractive land-locked bay and one should pause at the drystane dyke to survey the scene. This sheltered spot is favoured by many birds – curlew, redshank, oyster-catcher, wigeon, teal, ringed plover, mallard, shelduck and, ducking and diving overhead, playful groups of chough.

This sandy natural harbour is Port a' Chrochaire ("Port of the Hanged-man"), one of the most evocative spots in Colonsay; it is a great misfortune that the Ordnance Survey has confused it with Meall an Atha ("Kiln Headland"), some 500 metres to the north. The "hanged man" in question was Colla Ciotach MacDonald, the direct descendant of the Lord of the Isles and the last accredited royalist commander to remain in the field on behalf of King Charles I. Long after Montrose had disbanded his force and fled abroad, even after Huntly had been captured, Alasdair MacCholla continued to hold his ground in Kintyre and to evacuate his forces in an orderly manner. At the very end, Alasdair passed on his commission in Scotland to his ageing father and crossed over to Ireland, as ordered; meanwhile, at the age of 77 years, Colla Ciotach MacDonald mounted a defiant last stand, at Dunivaig in Islay. Within weeks he was captured, and in September 1647 he was hanged at Dunstaffnage; his island home was overrun by the Campbells and the harbour where he had kept his famous birlinn gained its present name. It was, perhaps, a pyrrhic victory – Argyll himself was beheaded in 1661, and indeed his son was subsequently executed (1685) in the aftermath of Monmouth's rebellion. In the meantime, Colla Ciotach's property in Colonsay was restored to his descendants by a grateful monarch, Charles II, and later reconfirmed by James VII.

In more modern times, this harbour was important to the farm of

Balerominmòr and the track that was used can still be traced. In early March, the spirited little meadow-pipit may be seen making his distinctive display on high, before falling steeply and repeating his routine. The links turf along the shore – "fidean" – is a perfect carpet of sea-pinks in May, and an otter may often be seen making his way from the burn out through the rocks and into the sea.

Cross the burn at the head of the sandy inlet and climb up across the dunes, to enjoy the view of Tràigh an Iochdail ("Recess Strand"), now known more popularly as Cable Bay. The pole on the headland is a long-redundant marker post, showing where once an undersea telephone cable came ashore from Islay. This bay provides an idyllic spot for swimming, sunbathing or picnics, as do half-a-dozen more within the next kilometre of coastline. There is a very clear and easily followed pathway leading onwards from the dunes of Tràigh an Iochdail, sometimes dropping down to run along the tideline, sometimes threading its way through the marram grass. The views are magnificent, but keep an eye beside the pathway for the myriad flowers – spring vetch, rue-leaved saxifrage and an interesting selection of some more common species. Perhaps spare a thought for the unknown occupant of "The Sailor's Grave" at NR 38587 90500, which is two hours from the start of the walk.

This is another place to linger, but eventually the coastline will be followed around to the west and the entrance to the strand, opposite the astoundingly beautiful Tràigh a' Mhill Bhàin which borders the Oronsay shore; on the near shore at this point is Sir John's Pool, his favourite picnic spot. As you approach this point, look out for speedwells, wild strawberry, wild pansy and carline thistle. Soon afterwards, the sandy shoreline of Balerominmòr peters out at last and here one should look ahead for guidance – there is a hydroelectric line serving Oronsay, and one should follow the path that leads slightly to the right, towards the pole that breaks the horizon closest to the Colonsay hinterland. Once again there will be chough wheeling and gambolling overhead, whilst fine specimens of crowberry and juniper will be seen beside the path. Looking up to the right you will recognise Uamh nan Gobhar ("Goat Cave") and Dùn Mara, perched upon the nearest craggy peak.

The path will bring you into Bàgh nan Capull ("Mares' Bay"), where high upon the right-hand side there is an isolated, stone-built house in traditional style. Cross the bay and follow the coastline around to the right, bordering the strand. If the tide is low there will be plenty of birdlife; at Rubha Dubh there are excellent wild mussels freely available, but do not be tempted by any oysters – these are waiting to be delivered and belong to the oyster farmer.

On rounding the point, one can see Garvard farmhouse and, soon afterwards, it will be easy enough to identify the "road-end" where the Colonsay road terminates at the strand. The entire area is dominated by the powerful presence of Dùn Cholla, somewhat to the right of the road-end and hogging the skyline. Continuing along the shoreline, a low, rounded natural outcrop of rock can soon by identified, Dùnan na Fidean ("Hillock on the Links"), after which a burn debouches onto the strand. This is marked on the Ordnance Survey map as Sruthan a' Mhuilinn Duibh ("Black-mill Stream") and it is worthwhile to follow the stream back above the shoreline and onwards for about one hundred metres. Here one can see the best surviving example in Colonsay of what is sometimes called a Horizontal Mill; the capstone through which the wheel-shaft ran is still in position, and the wheel-chamber remains clearly defined.

Returning to the shoreline and glancing back towards Rubha Dubh there is a striking landmark, where Am Binnean Crom ("The Crooked Pinnacle") projects dramatically from the cliff. It consists of a beak-like shaft pierced by a natural hole and, perhaps inevitably, has become known to visitors as "Hangman's Rock". Passing onwards, one quickly reaches the public road and can follow it inland for some 500 metres, until (after three hours) a turning to the right indicates the un-metalled track leading up to Balerominmòr farmhouse.

Balerominmòr Section

Note: *for those who have decided to explore Baleromin in two parts, this marks the beginning of the Balerominmòr circuit. Follow the directions until Carragh Mhic a' Phi has been visited, but then* **continue along the track** *until the farm steadings are reached. Go left through the gate behind the steadings, continue onto the ridge, then take a moment to identify the headland to the south of Tràigh Bàn, clearly marked on the Ordnance Survey map as Rubha Dubh ("Dark Headland"). It is easy to walk out to that point and to pick up the walk as has been described (above), rejoining it at Sràid an Aoil. Those who are completing both walks in succession should* **not** *be diverted at Carragh Mhic a' Phi.*

From the main road, follow the track towards Balerominmòr Farmhouse. This is an attractive walk, up a gentle slope. After clearing a rocky knoll to the right, notice a remarkably fine stand of royal fern (at the foot of a hydro-electric pole). Continue up the un-metalled track, keeping an eye open for the flora. Sundew, marsh lousewort, bog asphodel, milkwort, butterwort, bog pimpernel, yellow iris and heath-spotted orchids are easily seen, but it should also be possible to identify lesser butterfly and fragrant orchids and other more elusive plants. Birdlife may include sparrow-hawk and other raptors. After about one kilometre, the track levels off and one has an excellent view across the placid waters of Loch Cholla. Curiously enough there are no fish in this loch, and attempts to introduce them have always failed – possibly the surrounding bogland renders the water too acidic.

Loch Cholla is about 2 hectares in extent, but archaeologists have shown that at one time it was much larger and filled most of the plateau. From pollen analysis, Madeline Solomon has revealed that the loch was surrounded in the Holocene period by a mosaic of vegetative species, predominated by deciduous scrub and woodland – birch-hazel, accompanied by oak, alder and elm. Seemingly the birch-hazel component suffered a significant and prolonged decline ca. 7800-6200 BP, and at the same time there is evidence of encroachment by grasses, sedge, heather and sphagnum moss. The growth and decay of these latter species will have led to the gradual infill of the original loch, leading inexorably to the landscape we see today. It is fascinating to note the proximity of the Mesolithic site at Loch Staosnaig, less than two kilometres to the north, remembering that it has been dated to ca. 8110–7040 BP and that it is charac-terised by remains which suggest exploitation of hazelnuts as a major resource.

Turning right at this point, with one's back to the loch, one can easily ascend a slight slope to reach the summit of Dùn Cholla, one of the most spectacular Iron Age fortresses in Colonsay. Notice the formidable strength of the outer wall, still standing a few courses high and almost 6 metres thick. Approaching the Dùn itself, the entrance is quite narrow and then widens abruptly – at that point any visitors would be in single file and hampered by the constricted passage, thus putting them at the disposal of the gatekeeper. From the summit one can see that this was a truly commanding position, and offered excellent line-of-site communications within the island and to Oransay. It was under the protection of this fortress that St.

Columba is said to have built his first church in Scotland, and to have established his first, tiny monastery of Hinbina (Oronsay).

The origin of the name is uncertain, but the structural remains on the summit are comparatively modern and may well relate to the era of Colla Ciotach MacDonald (1570 – 1647). Although Colla Ciotach established his own household at Kiloran after 1616, his mother and uncle, together with their retinue, had established themselves elsewhere in the island from the 1570s. In view of their rank and position, a location such as this seems probable, close to a sheltered anchorage and affording ready access to Clan Donald interests in Islay and Antrim. Colla would thus have lived longer here than at any other place, and it may be no coincidence that his memory is preserved at the neighbouring harbour and in the deeds enacted at Carragh Mhic a' Phi.

To reach Carragh Mhic a' Phi, return to the main track and turn right. After about 600 metres, a railed enclosure will be noticed on the right-hand side, protecting an erect, heavily-repaired stone slab. This is a Bronze Age standing stone, which originally stood some 10 metres to the east of the present location and which was then orientated. As elsewhere, this pre-Christian site attracted the attention of the early missionaries and a chapel was established nearby. The pagan standing-stone had important connotations and so a cross was carved upon it, to assist in the transformation of the site from mere sun-worship to one of witness. Interestingly, the connotations of both traditions can be seen in the adoption of this site for the public, judicial execution of Malcolm MacPhee and his accomplices in 1623. Colonsay remained Catholic at that date, and it was here that Mass was still celebrated whenever clergy were able to reach the island – no more significant site could have been chosen for the executions.

Eventually the standing stone was toppled and broken, and a descendant of Malcolm MacPhee organised the creation of a small memorial plot, with the re-united stone at its centre. The stone is now inverted, but on the northern face one can still see part of the shaft and boss of the carved cross, the rest of which is hidden by a rubble buttress. This place is known as Pàirc na h' Eaglais ("Field of the Church"), and the boundary bank can still be traced enclosing a semi-circle roughly 22 metres from east to west. The small building to the west of Carragh Mhic a' Phi is said to have been the chapel, although the RCAHMS surveyors regard it as a lay structure;

possibly it served a dual role. An additional cross was discovered by chance in 1979, cut like the Carragh itself from local Torridonian stone, both crosses being very similar in design; this latter stone has been reburied nearby, to protect it from the elements.

Note: *for those who have divided Baleromin into two parts, return to the track, turn right and* **continue along the track** *until the farm steadings are reached. Go left through the gate behind the steadings, continue onto the ridge, then take a moment to identify the headland to the south of Tràigh Bàn, clearly marked on the Ordnance Survey map as Rubha Dubh ("Dark Headland"). It is easy to walk out to that point and to pick up the walk as has been described (above), rejoining it at Sràid an Aoil. Those completing the main route should return to the track and turn right, as follows:*

After about 30 metres, at the bend in the track, break away to the left and follow the firmest of the ground towards the green hillside to the north, Druim na Glaic Mòire ("Ridge of the Big Hollow"). Incidentally, there is a small hut-circle hereabouts, at NR 38389 91579 (roughly opposite the path from Carraig Mhic a' Phi). It is important to proceed with care as this section of the route runs across open bogland, but there should be no difficulty in following an easy route across partially-exposed rock. Do not be tempted to wander aimlessly, and do be careful of bright green patches which often conceal deep pools of standing water – look out for plants that flourish in these very special conditions, especially varieties of sundew.

   Baleromindubh farmhouse and steadings will be clearly visible to the north-east, to the right of a long ridge. As you look ahead to the high ground, identify the right-hand and uppermost of two patches of ivy on the rock, which can be seen between the third and fourth hydro-electric pole counting from the left. This makes a good landmark, and you should aim to the right of that ivy, heading towards the fourth pole – in effect, aim roughly for the mid-point in the length of the rocky bluff. As you reach the halfway point, you should pass between two old iron gate-supports, marking the line of a former pathway. Pass across or through the remains of an old boundary fence and, when you reach the grassy slopes ahead, follow the line of the hydro-electric poles up towards Baleromindubh farmhouse. From here, it is a simple matter to follow the main farm track back towards the public road and your original starting point.

Chapter 12

GARVARD AND TEAMPULL A' GHLINNE

Map: page xvi

This chapter is devoted to a very special part of Colonsay, very closely linked to the memory of St. Columba and one which was historically closely associated with the religious community in Oronsay.

Garvard (*Garbh Aird*, "Rough Promontory") is aptly named as it contains some of the least promising land in Colonsay from a contemporary viewpoint. Although in modern times its boundaries were adjusted to include Ardskenish glen, its traditional limits encompassed instead the links sward which borders the strand, running out to Port Iain Hart and including Rubha Bàgh nan Capull. It may be worth noting that this latter place name, usually translated as "Mares' Bay point", may have its origin as Rubha Bàgh na Caibeal ("Point beside the Bay on the way to the Burial-place"), for it was formerly the crossing point to the sacred island of Oronsay.

The visitor may easily wonder about the origins of a farm such as Garvard, running to about 500 acres but with such a high propor-tion of very rough grazing. Although the footings of a post-mediaeval farmhouse can be traced (NR 36660 91195), Garvard has no obviously ancient dùn or other early habitations and, perhaps fancifully, seems to many to have a special aura which sets it somewhat apart from other places.

Its modern history differs little from the other farms in Colonsay – in 1841, it had six households and a total of 25 inhabitants, none of whom was recorded as a farmer; the farm itself was engrossed in another holding, perhaps that of Oransay. By 1861, the modern farmhouse had been built and an incomer had been established in possession, Donald Currie, born "Kilarow" (Islay), "Farmer of 750 acres" and therefore also in possession of part of an adjoining farm. Interestingly, this 78 year old farmer's household of 11 included only one local individual, 33 year old John McGilvray, "Farm servant", but his six year old daughter, Sarah Currie, had been born in America. From the ages of the other children one can see that

Donald Currie's venture into America had started after 1853 and finished before 1858, reminding us that not every emigration proved to be a great success.

By 1871, Garvard and its associated farm were tenanted by a Colonsay native, Angus McNeill, a 68 yr old widower who "employs 7". By 1881, he had been succeeded by his son Archibald, but the farm had retrenched to just 420 acres, including 32 arable. Archibald was still there in 1901 and in fact there were McNeills or MacNeills in possession almost throughout the twentieth century. In latter years proposed changes in legislation made such tenancies unattractive to landowners throughout Scotland and the farm has therefore reverted to Colonsay Estate's own management. In 2010, the farmhouse is used as a holiday let, and Garvard itself is otherwise completely uninhabited.

The background to the story

The origins of Garvard are shrouded in some obscurity but history, tradition and archaeology give us fascinating glimpses behind the veil. A scattering of Mesolithic flints is remembered at Tom na Saighid ("Bush of the Fairy Shaft"), recalling the belief that such flints were the tips of elfin arrows. On Beinn Arnicil ("Eagle's-cleft Summit") there is a uniquely double-chambered Bronze Age hut circle and associated field system. These and similar field-system remains at Cuirn Mhòra ("Big Cairns") are hard to date with precision, but are likely to originate at some point between c. 2500–600 BC. It is hoped that ongoing research into pollen analysis will help to map climatic change in Colonsay, revealing the period when such sites will have been most attractive to the first farmers.

It is with the advent of the Iron Age that Garvard's history really begins. At this period, from c. 600 BC until c. AD 400, technological and trading developments led to a widespread upsurge of enterprise. By the end of the period the Romans had come and gone from Britain, whilst the Dalriadic Scottii from Ireland had established themselves in the *Ebudae* ("Hebrides") and were eventually to forge the Scottish race. Famously, the Irish based themselves upon Dùnadd, at the heart of the finest agricultural and trading centre of Argyll, but the sea was their highway and they secured it by coherent colonisation. The Firth of Lorn was a vital seaway, the direct link between the kingdom of the Pictii and the ancestral homeland of Dàl Riata, along the coastal fringe of northern Ireland.

Colonsay is the key to the Firth of Lorn – it controls the Sound of Islay and provides easy access to Derry and the Foyle via Loch Gruinard and Loch Indaal in Islay. On a neap tide, a small boat leaving Colonsay at 10 a.m. will be carried by the tides to reach Rathlin before 6 p.m.; leaving Rathlin in the half-light of dawn, the tides will reverse the process. At Colonsay itself, the tidal strand dividing it from Oransay provides a safe and easily defended harbour, with two good entrances. It is hardly surprising that we find the massive strength of Dùn Cholla dominating this strategic harbour, supported by a ring of outlying observation posts. The approaches to the strand itself are watched by Dùn Mara ("Sea Fort") and An Dùnan ("The Little Fort"), and such major strengths as Dùn Èibhinn and Dùn Dòmhnuill are within line-of-sight.

Since Dùn Cholla is in Balerominmòr, the archaeology of that site has been mentioned in Chapter 11, but it is obvious that its strategic situation dominated Garvard and it is in this way that it is so significant to the present chapter. We are very fortunate in that important traditions were recorded by Symington Grieve, an antiquarian who studied Colonsay for more than fifty years. Modern historians would clearly wish to modify many of his theories in the light of new evidence, but it is interesting to see that much of his work has stood the test of time. More to the point, the story that he tells is based upon local lore and has both a cadence and a coherence that are attractive. For these reasons, otherwise unsupported tradition is quoted unashamedly in this and the following chapter, and the reader is invited to form his own opinion. References to works by Symington Grieve and to Richard Sharpe's "*Adomnàn of Iona*" will be found in the bibliography.

Conall mac Comgaill and St. Columba

After earlier and inconclusive settlements from Ireland, "about the beginning of the sixth century, a determined and successful effort was made by the Scots to effect a permanent footing in Alban. Under the joint leadership of Fergus Mór, Lorn, and Angus, the three sons of Erc, the invaders settled on the coast of the modern Argyll and the adjacent islands. From Fergus son of Erc sprang the race of Scottish kings which, in the person of Kenneth MacAlpin, crushed the Pictish monarchy in the ninth century, established the predominance of Scottic power in the whole of Alban, and imposed on the country its modern name of Scotland" (W.C.MacKenzie).

The detailed history of this early kingdom can be extracted if desired from the Annals of the time, suffice here to state that in the fullness of time Conall mac Comgaill, great-grandson of Fergus Mòr, came to the throne, c. 559 AD. He was a direct descendant of Niall Noígiallach, a mighty warrior better known today as Nial of the Nine Hostages and progenitor of many Scottish families. We may assume that Conall's main interests were centred upon Dùnadd, but of course at such an early date all courts were "a moving feast" and Conall will have travelled regularly between his many strengths, one of which was in Colonsay. Very possibly Dùn Eibhinn was the royal stronghold, but Dùn Cholla was of overwhelming strategic importance at that time and will have been the base for Conall's local governor.

Dùn Cholla is said to be named for Colla Uais ("Noble Colla"), an ancient hero of the same lineage, but this is of no particular moment. It is sufficient for us to be aware that the fort protected a vital harbour and was occupied from about 559 AD by the representative and therefore a close relation of Conall, ruler of Dalriada. After Conall's death in 574, the kingship passed to his first cousin, Àedàn mac Gabràin, who was famously consecrated by St. Columba in Iona.

Turning now to St. Columba, we know that he was of royal blood on both sides of his family. His mother, Eithne, was 11th in line of descent from Cathair Mòr, an important king of Leinster (ancestor of clan O'Byrne); and his father, Fedilmid mac Ferguso, was great-grandson of the progenitor of Uí Néill, the powerful "Nial of the Nine Hostages". Thus St. Columba was of outstanding lineage, and was directly related to Conall mac Comgaill.

The laws of tanistry were such that a relationship of third or fourth cousin was very significant in royal circles and it may be taken as certain that Fedilmid mac Ferguso and Conall's father, Comgall, will have been well acquainted. St. Columba, who had been born about 521 AD at Gartan in Co. Donegal, was fostered from an early age with Cruithnechan, the priest who had baptised him. This was not an unusual arrangement, but it had the happy effect of providing a strong spiritual background; his birth and subsequent career had long been prophesied and he displayed his vocation from an early age. In 545 AD he established his first monastery, at Derry ("Oak Grove"), and in the following fifteen years he established some thirty six additional houses.

We will not follow St. Columba's career in detail, but in due course he accepted the challenge of his day and left Ireland in order to preach Christianity in a pagan place. This was not unusual, and it was a way of earning the rewards of "white" martyrdom and eternal salvation. St. Columba, as was appropriate to a man of royal blood, chose to extend the Christian boundaries of Dalriada. In May 563 he set out for Scotland and for the realm of his cousin, Conall mac Comgaill. We know that he actually met Conall that year, although the place of the meeting has not been recorded, and we know that St. Columba and his party continued to an island known at that time as Hinba ("Island of the Inlets"). Hinba was on the direct route between Iona and Ireland, and we are told that it was distinguished by its possession of a "bag-shaped arm of the sea".

In the light of the above, factual, information we turn now to the tradition that has been preserved here in Colonsay; readers must decide for themselves as to its merits, but are reminded that this particular story fits all the known facts and is at least to that extent unique. The long-held belief in Colonsay that "Hinba" was an earlier name for Oransay has now been accepted by modern scholarship, but everything else is a matter for speculation.

As is believed in Colonsay, St. Columba and his party came to this island in 563, having sailed into the strand at high tide and presumably coming from the south-east. They were coming either to meet the king, Conall, or more probably had already met him and were coming under his protection to meet his governor. If they entered An Fhaoghail from the east via Poll Gorm, they will have seen the impressive fortress of Dùn Cholla before they turned into the sheltered water of Tràigh nam Bàrc ("Strand of the Skiffs"). They brought their boat ashore at a creek known to this day as Port na h-Iùbhraich ("Barge Harbour"). *Some readers may wish to note that this has been misidentified on certain maps, and that it will be identified with care in the suggested walk outlined below.*

The party consisted of thirteen individuals, as was no coincidence. There was of course, Columba himself (Calum-cille = "Dove of the Holy Cell"). There were two brothers, "the sons of Brendan", called Baithéne and Cobthach. (Baithéne, also called Cronin, eventually succeeded St. Columba at Iona). There was Ernán, St. Columba's uncle, the future (if short-lived) abbot of Hinba, with his servant Diarmait. And there were two sons of Ruadán, Rus and Fiachnae. A monk called Scandal was "mac Bresail maic Énda main Néill", and another, Carnán, was "mac Branduib maic Meilgi". The party was completed by Lugaid occu Temnae, Eochaid, Tochannu moccu Fir Chete and Grillán. They were clearly individuals of high rank.

It is said that the party made its way on foot around the point of Garvard and up towards Dùn Cholla where they identified themselves and were taken under the protection of the king's governor. They were said to have been given land close at hand, and it is held that the 15th-century chapel known as Teampull na Ghlinne stands upon the site of St. Columba's first foundation in Scotland. There is no evidence for this of course, but no reason to reject it either. The land "close at hand" would have been suitable for cultivation at that time and, curiously enough, aerial investigation seems to support this. The writer has noticed that, from an elevation of about five hundred feet, the evening light appears to reveal a typical Celtic field system in the northwest corner of the modern field nearest to Teampull na Ghlinne (A' Phàirc Bhàn, "The White Field").

The tradition in Colonsay seems to suggest that St. Columba based himself here for about two years before he moved on to Iona, establishing what might be seen as a "forward base" at the end of a secure supply line to Ireland. A short crossing to Islay provided a sheltered and direct route via Loch Gruinart and Loch Indaal to the mouth of the River Foyle and to his beloved Derry, whilst the Sound of Islay provided a convenient route by open sea. He established a small monastery in Oransay under the care of his uncle, Ernán, and this became a place of personal retreat to him in later years. Whilst he was in Colonsay he took steps to Christianise the sacred sites of an earlier time, and the dedications are a roll-call of his era. St. Brigit, St, Catan, St, Catriona, St. Ciaràn, St. Kenneth, Our Lady, St. Oran and St. Maelrubha – a veritable litany, to which we must add the name of St. Columba himself.

Incidentally, it is worth scotching one *canard* that seems to cause great confusion – many people seem to have the impression that St. Columba had rejected Ireland, and that he was forbidden to return. This is completely fallacious – we know that he was in regular communication with his homeland, and there are historical records of no less than ten of his personal visits; indeed, his deathbed bequest was "my soul, to Derry". The notion was coined by Manus O'Donnell in 1532, as a literary device to embellish one such visit to Ireland by St. Columba, accompanied on that occasion by King

Aidan. Subsequently, attention was drawn to certain places known as "Carn cul ri Eireann", which can be translated as "Cairn backing onto Ireland". Strangers tried to interpret this as supporting a rejection of Ireland and suggested that because the saint could see Ireland from Colonsay he built a cairn to commemorate the fact in Oronsay and then moved off to Iona. Such a theory could not, of course, account for other such cairns which exist in Iona itself and in Mull, from which Ireland could never be seen. Fortunately Dr. Richard Sharpe has clarified the matter, explaining that "cul ri Eireann" was a pseudonym for St. Columba himself, and therefore "Carn cul ri Eireann" merely means "St. Columba's Cairn". In a poem attributed to the saint, "Columcille Fecit", the author throws himself into an ecstasy of nature-inspired devotion, praying "that my mystical name might be, I say, Cul ri Erin" (i.e. one who had sought the white martyrdom); naturally those whom he inspired fulfilled his wish.

It seems that the association between Garvard and Hinba was so close that it survived the early years of the Viking occupation and flourished again as the "invaders" adopted Christianity and re-emerged as the Lords of the Isles. Garvard, together with all the islands in the strand, became a pendicle of Oransay and so it remained until after the Reformation. On 9th December 1203, Pope Innocent III confirmed the Benedictine community of Iona in its possession of the church of Colonsay together with the islands of both Colonsay and Oronsay. Subsequently, the (Augustinian) Priory of Oronsay was established by John the Good, and with it went Garvard. All the charters and leases which specify lands in Colonsay carefully enumerate all the farms, but none of them includes Garvard, which remained firmly attached to Oronsay. This fact is borne out even as late as 15 February 1616, when James VI granted "feufarm and quitclaim" to Andrew, Bishop of the Isles. Amongst other lands, he specifies "the island of Oronsay" together with the "16 shillings 8 pence lands of Garvart in Colonsay … which before belonged to the Priory of Oronsay, and never paid dues to the King".

During the eighteenth century, the McNeill lairds obtained clear title to the whole of Colonsay and Oronsay and, as has been seen, created the independent farm of Garvard in the latter half of the nineteenth century. After a union of 1500 years, Garvard was finally divorced from Oransay when that island, together with Garvard's own islands in the strand, was sold to Adam Bergius in the 1970s.

There are six important archaeological sites in Garvard, as listed by RCAHMS:

Standing Stone, Cnoc Eibriginn ("Hill of Arbitration") NR 364912

The prominent standing stone on the summit is 1.75m in height and about 0.6m x 0.2m in girth. Since it fell down in the 1940s and was re-erected about twenty years later, there must be doubt as to its original position. There are initials on the western surface, dating to the Edwardian period.

Dùnan nan Con ("Homestead of the Hounds") NR 377920

Readily accessible from a convenient parking point at the upper end of An Gleann, this structure is on the summit of a low knoll and measures 16m x 11m within a low but very obvious surviving wall. The original entrance was on the north-east side. On an historical note, this dùnan marked the very edge of the portion of Colonsay that belonged to the religious community in Oransay and may well have served as a "porters' lodge".

Hut-circle and Field System, Beinn Arnicil ("Eagle's Cleft") NR 373918

The most obvious feature is the circular field enclosure (30m x 28m) immediately to the east of the summit cairn. One should bear in mind that the low stones we see are not intended to have been stock proof, but were at the core of an earthern bank upon which a hedge would have been planted. There were no rabbits at the time and very few burrowing animals. A smaller enclosure lies to the east of the large one, and there are others to the north-east.

There is an interesting and well-preserved hut some 75m southeast of the summit cairn, in a fairly level gully. The main chamber is 5m in diameter and there are three additional conjoined but smaller chambers, one of which seems to have been a porch. At least two of the chambers seem to have had a connecting doorway, which is quite an unusual feature. In the immediate vicinity one can (in winter) trace numerous sections of walling and, about 10m north-east of the hut, there is another building, possibly another dwelling.

Field-systems and Cairns, Cùirn Mhora ("Many Cairns")
NR 363907

This impressive and complex site lies somewhat to the east of the place-name as indicated by the Ordnance Survey, so the map reference is important. In essence, some 28 cairns range between 2m and 7m in diameter and are mostly about 1m in height; many of them overlap pre-existing ancient field boundaries, in whole or in part. RCAHMS identify stone-cored turf banks, followed by dry-stane dykes and latterly turf banks which are thought to be of comparatively recent date.

Viking Boat Burial, Tràigh nam Bàrc ("Boat Strand")
NR c.358916

It is recorded that a "stone coffin" was once found at the head of the bay, with an iron sword nearby; and there is a tradition of a battle in the vicinity which may mean that there were other burials in the area.

Teampull a' Ghlinne ("The Temple in the Glen")
NR 374917

This chapel stands close beside the road at the foot of An Gleann, within a well-defined garth whose original entrance gate is still in use by visitors. It is orientated and measures 8.0m x 4.2m internally, the main walls being built upon a very obvious foundation wall. The gables have fallen, but the original materials have not been robbed so that one wonders if restoration would be impossible. The doorway and surviving windows are splayed and one can still see the original mortar in many places. An aumbry in the north-west angle is in an unusual location. The chapel belonged to Oransay and was said to have been used in connection with funeral parties making their way to the Priory; RCAHMS suggest a possible 14th-century date, in view of its resemblance to Oransay architecture of that period.

Other sites of interest include Cnoc Eibriginn itself, Sidhean Mór, Port na h-Iùbhraich, An Dùnan, Luba na Eisearan and a kelping-kiln, all of which are to be mentioned in the course of the second walk (below).

Exploring Garvard
This very beautiful part of Colonsay is well worthy of exploration, and two itin-

eraries are suggested. The first one is very easily undertaken and is ideal for every party, including very young children or persons with restricted mobility (1.5 km., 45 mins.). The second one presents no particular hazards but does include some rough going and will bring you into a very remote area – if travelling alone, it would be wise to notify someone of your plans.

Suggested Walk 1: Dùnan nan Con and Teampull na Ghlinne

As the public road enters Garvard, it passes across a cattle grid then runs across the surface of a peat moss. This moss was partially drained after the famine of the 1840s, to allow for the road and thus to create work. The older road, following the ancient funeral route to Oransay, runs on the higher ground about 100 metres to the west and may still be followed with ease. The moss plays host to a range of flowers and insects; notice hares-tails, bog cotton, varieties of sundew, bog myrtle and even cow-vetch along the fringes. About 80 metres after crossing the cattle grid, on the right-hand side of the road, there is a charming display of bog asphodel.

Having crossed the moss, the road seems to pause before it plunges downhill and it is at this point that motorists should park, making use of the small quarry on the right-hand side. You will find that you are at the foot of Dùnan nan Con ("Small Fort of the Hounds"), a small knoll which lies to the west of the modern road as it emerges from the moss. It is a very easy climb, and at the summit there is flat, open space surrounded by the few courses of ancient stonework that survive. It has been suggested that hounds were kept here in ancient times, for use in the chase, but in fact they are more likely to have been employed as watchdogs. Standing on the top of Dùnan nan Con (NR 37743 92028), one can see that it is at the northern apex of Garvard, and therefore of the monastic territory of Oronsay. It commands the ancient trackway, which literally passes the door, and provides, via Dùn Dòmhnuill, a vital link in the signals system between the civil administration at Dùn Éibhinn and the religious community in Oronsay.

On the other side of the ancient trackway, which is clearly visible passing the north side of the dùnan, and about 50 metres to the south-west, there are the substantial foundations of *Bùth Beg* ("Wee Shop"), where one John McInnis lived with his wife and six children in 1841(NR 37697 92018). They were gone by the next census, but the late Para Mór MacAllister said that the shop there had been operated by a grandmother of the late Neil and Ross Darrach and sold such things as meal.

Pass to the left of the lone blackthorn behind the ruins and, from here, it is an easy matter to climb Beinn Arnicil ("Eagle's Cleft") – those who do should notice the interesting prehistoric field enclosures very near the summit (NR 37438 91993), to the south and east of the prominent cairn. About 75m south-east of the cairn, in the mouth of a gully, there is a most interesting and complex hut circle at NR 37454 91945. The main chamber is about 5.5m in diameter, and there are three subsidiary chambers, one of which appears to have served as a lobby. From the lobby, access to the main chamber was gained through an antechamber. The full range of structures on Beinn Arnicil is quite intriguing and has fortunately been surveyed by the Royal Commission on Ancient and Historical Monuments of Scotland (Inventory, Argyll Volume 5).

Whether or not one has chosen to ascend Beinn Arnicil, one will wish to return to the metalled road and to follow its winding descent through the beautiful and sheltered glen. Facing south, this is a well-favoured spot which is full of interesting native flora – being so isolated from the domestic gardens, there are no introduced species to dilute the pristine habitat. To amble here is to experience complete delight – notice grass of Parnassus, three types of St. John's wort, bearberry, primrose, heath-spotted orchid, lesser butterfly orchid, royal fern, tormentil, stonecrop, wood sorrel, bell heather, meadow sweet, yellow iris and a host of other favourites. Crush some leaves of bog-myrtle to enjoy the aroma – or rub it onto the skin, to deter midges.

The late Donald MacNeill farmed Garvard for many years and one of his most beautiful poems was in praise of Sruthan Teampull a' Ghlinne ("The Temple Burn"). The following is just one of his verses, but it captures some of the joy of this place:

Tràth latha anns an t-samhradh tha fàileadh cùbhraidh leum
Bho gach lus ma d'bhruachan, is drùchd a' fàgail fraoich.
Tha 'n uiseag 's i a' seinn dhomh, ag aotromach' mo cheum,
'S measg roiteagach tha snàthainn an damhain-eallaich ghleusd'.

Colonsay resident Alastair Scouller has made a simple and literal translation of much of Donald Garvard's work for non-Gaelic speakers, "as an explanation, not an equivalent"; thus he renders the above as:

> Early on a summer's day a delightful scent leaps
> From every plant around your banks, as the dew rises off the
>   heather.
> The skylark sings her song to me, lightening my step,
> And among the bog-myrtle the clever spider has spun its web.

On the level ground at the foot of the brae, one comes upon *Team-pull a' Ghlinne* itself, "The Temple in the Glen". The word "teampull" is found in the Gaelic name for a number of very early foundations, but may not actually refer to the building, which is properly a "cill" (*cf.* Kiloran, Kilchattan etc.). "Cill", as Columcille, is a word which derives its origin in a cleric's "cell" or hermitage. On the other hand, the biblical word "temple" refers to the "open, or consecrated place" in which worship was conducted, and in which a chapel may well stand. The present structure is perhaps 14th-century in origin but, as has been remarked, it is locally accepted to have been built upon the site of St. Columba's original foundation in Scotland. Interestingly, the north-west window appears to have been modified at some period and – to the lay eye – the courses of the western wall seem to be less "confident" than those of the foundation. Where St. Columba would have built in clay-daubed wattle, the mediaeval church is built of coursed and lime-mortared masonry upon a substantial foundation. The door and windows are lintelled and have been splayed, to maximise both the light and the feeling of warmth and welcome that can be felt, even yet.

   The building is sited within a clearly delineated curtilage of stone and turf, probably originally surmounted by a thorn hedge. This enclosure or "temple" may well pre-date the church itself, and the entrance is by a lych-gate on the northern side, for this was a sanctuary chapel on the funeral-route to Oronsay. Here the body would be rested until the tide was right, and here the mourners would prepare themselves for the final stage of a journey that might have originated many days earlier in some distant corner of Argyll. Beside the chapel itself there is a scatter of funeral cairns – such cairns were erected along the route of a cortege, but of course these may represent actual inhumations. After the Reformation, traditional funeral practices were disrupted and perhaps, in time of difficulty, a burial on the funeral route was seen as an acceptable compromise. Sadly, one of the cairns was vandalised in recent years and, at the time of writing, there is a very real danger that the inertia of our age may fail to protect the structure of the church itself.

In 1772, Thomas Pennant declared of Colonsay that "from the reformation till within the last six years, the sacrament had been only once administered", thus suggesting that from the appointment of Rev. Alexander Hosack in 1766 the situation had improved. It was said that the sacrament was administered hereabouts, and that Glaic a' Phubaill ("Valley of the Tent") commemorates the fact in its name. In those days, the communion service was preceded by some days of prayerful preparation and, although the congregation had no protection from the elements, a small tent was provided to shelter the minister during his lengthy extempore preaching. In 2002, Dr. K. Liddell, a long-term visitor to Colonsay, was fortunate enough to discover a communion token inscribed "JJ COLOSA 1801", which he obtained from an antiquarian source. Since the Parish church was not built until 1802, the token may be a physical link with the days of Glaic a' Phubaill. Of course, in 1801, there was a Preaching House at Machrins, but in the summer of that year Presbytery visited Colonsay and Glaic a Phubaill may have been a more convenient location for a Communion service. The parish minister was Mr Donald McNicol, so the initials JJ are as yet unexplained.

Before concluding this walk, the reader may like to reflect upon another old but unsubstantiated tradition of Colonsay – it is said that Robert the Bruce stayed hereabouts for a day or two in his travels. No doubt this prompted the allusion to the spider in Donald MacNeill's poem, and there is no particular reason to doubt the story. Certainly we know that Angus Òg of Islay was a strong supporter of the Bruce, and we know from the history of the MacKay family of Ugadale that, after a winter in Rathlin, King Robert made his way to Arran by a route that crossed Kintyre. He is said to have reached Kintyre from Jura, where he had sheltered in Uamh an Righ at the entrance to Loch Tarbert in Jura.

Given all of the above, one might suppose that as a fugitive he crossed the relatively untroubled sound between Rathlin and Loch Indaal in Islay, then made his way across that friendly island and re-embarked for the short ferry trip to Oronsay. Crossing with the tide, he would have sheltered at or probably within Teampull na

Ghlinne, before making his onward way via Bailerominmór into
Loch Tarbert and his refuge at Uamh an Righ. If so, we might date
this visit to the very early spring of 1307, barely 9 months after his
coronation at Scone.

Suggested Walk 2: In the footsteps of St. Columba

*This walk of 8 km. will take about three hours; wellington boots might be appro-
priate, and a copy of the Ordnance Survey map is highly desirable. The starting
point is at "the road-end", i.e. where the road to Oransay terminates at the
Strand. Time the walk to avoid encountering high tide at either the beginning or
the end of the excursion.*

Walk out onto the level sand, turning to the west and following a
semi-circular line of stones showing some 30cm above the surface.
Before a modern road was created by Pedie and Carol MacNeill in
the 1980s, access to Garvard farm was governed by the tide and
these stones were a useful guide on a moonless night. There are
plenty of cockles to be seen and they are very tasty – famed for
having given Neil Munro a good line in "*Para Handy Tales*": "The
best cockles in the country iss in Colonsay", said the Captain. "But
the people in Colonsay iss that slow they canna catch them…"

Following the stones, regain the farm track as it leaves the shoreline and passes through a field gate and into an area which is
beloved of geese. Here, according to season, you may see any of
four species, barnacle, white-fronted Greenland, greylag or Canada
geese, and even if you fail to see the birds themselves you will need
to tread warily where they have been. As you come out onto this
level plateau you will see Garvard Farmhouse and steadings to the
north; close at hand there is a bothy and, 80m to its south-west, the
footings of a substantial cottage at NR 36660 91195. The bothy,
known as Gilleasbuig Ruaidh's ("Red-haired Archie" McNeill's),
was re-roofed in recent years to provide a nesting opportunity for
choughs, although as yet they have ignored it.

Make your way to the west, through the gate, and climb the
impressive rocky outcrop, surmounted by a standing stone. Known
as Cnoc Eibriginn ("Hill of Arbitration"), this was said to have been
the place where local disputes were settled. Judgement could only be
given in broad daylight and in plain view of any interested parties,
something that might be regarded as desirable even today. The
standing stone, which had fallen in the 1940s and was re-erected

about 1960, has been somewhat defaced by an inscription, dated 1908. There is a fine view from this point and, looking to the head of the bay which can be seen to the west, one can see a series of grassy mounds in the mouth of Ardskenish Glen. These are known as "sithean" or "fairy knowes" and it said that, at a time when clergy were unavailable, weddings used to be held on the biggest one (Sidhean Mór). A smaller one can be seen to be rather different – like the one mentioned at Kiloran Bay, this was an artificial warren created when rabbits were first introduced to the island.

Turning to the south-west, it will be helpful to identify Loch Breac, which will be approached by a slightly tortuous route. Descend from Cnoc Eibriginn to rejoin the rough track on its westward journey, keeping the hydro-electric poles to your right. Head towards the distant water tank, which can be seen on the Ardskenish peninsula and, after about 400 metres, find the ford which lies to the left of a rocky bluff. Having crossed the ford, follow the scant outline of the track as it turns to the right once more and gains the shoreline of Tràigh nam Bàrc ("Boat Strand").

Turning left along the shoreline, there will be plenty of birds to notice, such as the lapwing, black-backed gull, golden plover, ringed plover, shelduck and oyster-catcher; and along the tideline there will be driftwood in fantastic shapes and possibly exotic nuts or seeds, carried from distant shores. After about 250 metres, just before the first headland, turn left (inland) to approach Loch Breac ("Trout Loch"). This loch, which belonged to the monks in Oronsay, had retained its name but had otherwise lost its significance until recently. Then, c. 1990, when there was a lengthy drought, the water fell to a very low level and Dr Richard Gulliver noticed that a hitherto unknown dam had been exposed. It seems that the community in Oronsay had created or deepened the loch with a view to supplementing their diet, Oronsay having no suitable lochan of its own. There is a garradh or cultivation-enclosure beside the lochan – one wonders if it could have been used to grow flax.

This tiny loch is very beautiful, but please do not approach too closely. There are herons which nest here, also possibly Canada geese, and there is a resident otter – if you keep your distance you will not disturb them and may be rewarded for your patience. When you leave Loch Breac, turn towards the distant gable of Ardskenish farmhouse to rejoin the shore near the prominent lichen-covered rock to the north of Sgeir nam Faoileann ("Seagull Skerry"), and then turn left again. Isolated outcrops of rock litter the sand and there will be a chorus of bird-sounds in the background; after an expanse of bladder-wrack you may have to go over the heather for 50m and will then reach a tiny sickle of shells deposited along the tideline, a likely spot for cowries (NR 35308 90933). This is a useful marker, because after another 200 metres you will reach our objective, Port na h-Iùbhraich, where St. Columba made his landfall. The exact spot is at NR 35267 90800, where a narrow creek leads into a sheltered recess which continues across the headland. Note the modest kelping-kiln at the top of the beach, NR 35264 90772.

To the south-west of the creek there is a fine observation point, An Dùnan, which is a good place to appreciate the lie of the land. An Dùnan, which has clear signs of occupation in antiquity, may well have been the site of a small religious settlement and it is a pity that the Ordnance Survey has marked it some 300 metres to the east of its true location. One can see at least half-a-dozen rudimentary hut-sites, making full use of the natural features e.g. NR 35193 90692, which is 4m in diameter with more than half the circumference protected by a natural feature up to 1m in height. From this vantage point one will notice teal, wigeon, pochard and curlew; close by, to the south of An Dùnan, is a wrecked barge, the remnants of a large structure washed ashore in WWII (NR 35218 90606).

Descending from An Dùnan and continuing across the spit of land, one encounters a large rectangular lagoon, divided into three sections by low walls, e.g. at NR 35299 90572. This is Luba na Eisearan ("Oyster Pool"), where an attempt to cultivate native oysters was made soon after Lord Strathcona purchased the island in 1904. That attempt was unsuccessful, but in the 1970s a further attempt was made, elsewhere in the strand, which has proved very successful. The present enterprise was established by Andrew Abrahams, a pioneer of Scottish acquaculture, and is based upon non-native species which do not breed naturally in these waters but which thrive in the rich feeding of our powerful tides. It is extraordinary to notice how significant an industry has grown so quickly in Scotland, based entirely upon the ingenuity and application of a handful of risk-takers.

Making your way to the margin of the tide-mark, turn left along the strand. We are now following quite literally in the footsteps of St. Columba and his companions, and it is pleasant to reflect upon how little the scene will have changed. Somewhere hereabouts St. Fergnae had his cell. He had lived "for many years in obedience among the brethren" of Hinba, and then "for a further twelve years he withdrew to live in isolation at the place of the anchorites in Muirbolc Már ("The Great Sea-bay", i.e. An Fhaoghail). We have no way to identify the exact sites, but surely the anchorites will have had no location more suited to their purpose than this area, the point of Garvard? Somewhere like the shelter at NR 35652 90561 might fit, but one can identify any number of likely nooks and crannies.

The shoreline here has many curiosities – the tripe-like ganglia of the kelp wrack, the aptly named and rather dreadful "dead man's fingers", the egg-sacks known as "mermaid's purses" and the strange patterns in the sand created by seaweed anchor-stones, drifting on the tide. Further along the shore, there will be examples of remarkable lichens, including one which is of a most distinctive brick-like colour.

Looking westward, towards the open Atlantic, there are the big skerries of Eilean Mhugaig ("Whale Island") and Leac Bhuidhe ("Yellow Flagstone"). From time immemorial, the grey Atlantic seals which thrive here have been a valuable resource, providing leather, grease, oil and meat for the taking; and in more recent centuries, the rich harvest of the seaweed has provided hard work for the kelpers and staggering wealth for their landlords. As we pass along the shoreline, Tigh na Cealpairean ("Kelper's Cottage") is the name for a tiny cave-like shelter amongst a jumble of rocks, hidden now above a fringe of brambles (NR 35797 90562). Perhaps, in former times, it was home for one of the anchorites – in more recent times it provided a bothy, so that the kelpers could take full advantage of suitable spring tides.

Once the kelp was cut, it was rafted together on a rising tide and dragged into the shelter of a south-facing bay, just beyond Rubha nan Ròn ("Seal-point"). You will know you are approaching the landing beach if you keep an eye open for some rusted corrugated iron, covering the collapsed roof of an old boathouse. Here the weed could be spread to try, turned and turned again as it was slowly worked up the slope towards the kiln. Such kilns are not easily found after more than 150 years of disuse, but this one is very much more substantial than most and can easily be identified in the middle of the sloping ground, about 50 metres from the high-water mark at NR 36171 90467.

Further up this slope and to the right, there are traces of a very ancient field system, overlaid in places with an extensive array of cairns. This is Cuirn Mhòra (NR 363907), now a protected historic monument; (to avoid confusion, note that the Ordnance map locates the site some 200 metres too far to the west). In recent years the cairns have become less obvious, so a precise reference to NR 36399 90719 should identify at least one circular structure, 5m in diameter and 1m in height. It has been suggested that the cairns represent field-clearance mounds, although this might be refuted by anybody with practical experience of tillage. As at Ardskenish, Balnahard and in Oronsay, it seems at least possible that these are burial cairns, as was first mooted by John Gray, who farmed Oronsay in the 1980s. One could imagine that at a time of plague, affected persons would be sent to live apart from the community on the raised beaches, where they could easily bury the dead and survive until such time as the epidemic was over.

From this bay one has a choice of route, either along the shore-line or following the old kelper's path behind Rubha na Dearg Sgeir ("Red-skerry Headland"). The latter is the shorter way, and is full of sheltered nooks and hollows, carpeted with sphagnum moss and cross-leaved heath, interspersed by clumps of goat-willow. On regaining the shoreline, it will be easy to identify the starting point at the "road-end" and walk back across the sand towards it.

There is a remarkably attractive pillar-stone on your route across the sand which is highly reminiscent of a petrified tree, but it has no ancient significance. It was in fact erected as a warning against quicksand nearby; some cattle were lost in the vicinity many years ago and the area is known to be very unsuitable for wheeled vehicles. There is no known danger to pedestrians, although it might be best to skirt the area after heavy rain. The setting has been adorned in recent years by an attractive whorl-pattern of stones, an appropriately mystical touch at the conclusion of this particular walk.

Chapter 13

ORANSAY AND ITS PRIORY

Map: page xvi

Oransay – the recent past

Although the visitor will be struck by the ethereal qualities of this remarkable place, it might be useful to provide some mundane facts as background. The island extends to some 1417 acres (586ha), of which 1317 (538ha) are devoted to rough grazing and about 100 (40ha) to hay or silage. Modern methods of farming and the special characteristics of a wildlife-friendly regime make current statistics less valuable, but figures from 1972 show that Oransay supported 10% of the Colonsay cattle and 18% of the adult sheep, together with 20% of all the lambs. Currently, 2010, it is stocked with 50 breeding pedigree Luing cattle and 600 sheep including 100 Hebridean ewes. Knowing that Oransay represents about 15% of Colonsay's acreage, it is clear that it can easily hold its own in stocking rates. More significant however has been the quality of the stock – it is very warm land, affording surprisingly good shelter and an excellent quality and range of grazing. In former days it was remarkable for the fact that the farmer did not need to attend the market – stock from Oransay which was produced by the late Andrew MacNeill could sell itself, and at a premium price. Very little has changed – nowadays livestock is managed in a different way, but even the casual observer will note that the animals have an air of contentment and a striking gloss to their condition.

The human population seems just as contented, comprising just two households. There is an estate management couple who are responsible for the property on behalf of its owner, also a manager and his wife, together with an assistant warden and residential volunteers all of whom work for the farming tenant, the Royal Society for the Protection of Birds. The RSPB uses its tenancy to pursue environmentally-friendly farming methods; the aim is to preserve the existing habitat and encourage species diversity, not least in respect of birds especially corncrake and red-billed chough. The RSPB staff manage the farm in addition to ornithological monitoring and other scientific activities. Visitors are particularly requested to assist in this work by keeping close control of any dogs and by avoiding any nesting sites or special habitats which might be indicated. It is worth noting that the present owners of Oransay have devoted many years to an ongoing programme of restoration and conservation. All of the telephone cable and much of the electricity cable has been buried, all of the domestic and agricultural buildings have been thoroughly upgraded and in the last 15 years the RSPB has renovated most of the drystone dykes. The important collection of mediaeval gravestones has been properly protected and made available for study, and in 2003 a programme of conservation work was started in the Priory itself, in conjunction with Historic Scotland.

The modern history of Oransay may be said to have commenced in the early eighteenth century, when the McNeill lairds allocated the farm to a junior branch. Alexander McNeill was the second son of Malcolm McNeill, who died in 1742, and was made tacksman of Oransay. He married a daughter of Alexander McDougall of Dunollie, a noted agriculturist, and in the fullness of time became factor of the entire Colonsay estate on behalf of his nephew, Archibald. It was Alexander McNeill who built Oransay House in 1772, but it suffered a serious fire in 1784 as is described in a letter to Patrick McDougall. "Colonsay [i.e. Archibald McNeill] was sleeping alone at his Uncle's house at Oronsay. The house took fire in the dead hour of night, and the flames proceeded so far before he awaked, that he hardly had time to tye the sheet on his bed to a chair which he put cross the window, and bring himself to the Ground by the end of it. I am told the house is totally demolished."

Fortunately the house was insured and it was quickly rebuilt. It was subjected to further considerable modification in 1830, when Alexander's grandson married Anne Elizabeth Carstairs, the daughter of a successful businessman. Family records reveal that a second staircase was certainly installed, and construction evidence suggests that the entire western wing was built at the same time.

Alexander McNeill of Oransay ensured that his eldest son, John, was fully instructed in the very latest agricultural techniques and by 1805 the tacksman's son had bought out his cousin Archibald and became laird in his own right. Naturally enough, John McNeill (the "Old Laird") removed himself to Kiloran House and his former home in Oransay became peripheral to his interests. Despite the upgrading in 1830, the family seems to have spent much of its time elsewhere and the house began a gentle slide into an honourable decay which was only finally arrested in recent years.

In the census of 1841, there were 43 individuals recorded in Oransay, in four households. The census was taken in June and Ann McNeill, of "Independent" means, was in residence together with her six children and their tutor plus an assortment of domestic staff. This was Anne-Elizabeth Carstairs, daughter-in-law of the "Old Laird", whose husband had inherited the whole estate in 1846; but he sold it soon afterwards to his brother, Duncan. Anne and her husband, together with two of their daughters, were to be drowned in 1850 in the wreck of the "*Orion*" at Portpatrick, on passage from Liverpool to Greenock. The ship ran onto rocks and started to sink immediately – the crew panicked – the ship's boat was swamped – the boiler exploded; our eye-witness, Rev. J. Clarke, climbed onto the upper bulwarks, where he saw "clinging to one of the davits a young girl, having no covering over her shoulders, being evidently as she had just risen from her bed, and to all appearance waiting calmly and quietly for what was to follow". Within fifteen minutes the ship was sunk, some 400 metres from the shore – the eyewitness was rescued, and next morning visited the disused former Custom House: "Oh I can never forget that room! ... the FLOOR! How shall I describe what we saw! I cannot dwell on so sad a sight! I would rather close the door and leave those *twenty-five* bodies lying there, without one further remark. Is that the result of last night's catastrophe!! The intelligent countenances – the manly step – the cheerful intercourse – aye and the bright-beaming looks and merry laugh of lovlier forms; – are they all thrown aside for an appearance too shocking to behold!"

Even from the 1841 census, we can see that the big house was already divided, being partly in use as a holiday home and partly as the farmhouse. The farm manager was Malcolm McNeill, assisted by about half-a-dozen labourers and two or three dairy maids. This was the "Calum Ruadh" McNeill, now aged 50, who had incurred the wrath of the "Old Laird" when he converted to the Baptist Faith c. 1826 and was baptised in Loch Fada. He was consequently compelled to leave the island when the laird refused him any sort of employment, but two of the laird's own daughters were themselves converted. Malcolm was eventually recalled to the island "and made Manager of Oronsay, a position he retained till the Laird died 20 years later".

Unsurprisingly, after the tragic death of Alexander and his wife and daughters, Oransay seems to have meant rather less to the McNeill lairds and it became subject to erratic management. In the 1851 census the three remaining households totalled 22 souls, including two dairy maids and ten agricultural labourers; at this time the farm was evidently being managed as an out-farm of Kiloran. By 1861, there came a significant change – a mainland tenant had been installed, one Walter B MacNeill of Glendaruel, and he had brought his own labourers. Only three Colonsay people were employed, all labouring youngsters, but a Colonsay lobster fisherman had moved into a vacant cottage.

The incomer did not last long and by 1871 the tenancy had been assigned to the non-resident "Col. A.C. McNeill", who installed a full team of Colonsay workers under the supervision of one of their own, Malcolm McKinnon. Colonel McNeill employed a small domestic staff and about eight agricultural workers, but his initiative proved to be equally short-lived. By 1881, the only inhabited house was occupied by yet another stranger and his family, William Griffin from Mochram, a shepherd. He may have been running the farm as a sheep-walk for the McNeill lairds, but the appointment was not a success as one Neil McNeill is recorded as farm manager before July 1882. It was during this period that the main house became available as a holiday let and for six years from 1880 it was occupied throughout the summer months by the Murray family of Moore Park, Cardross. We are fortunate that Mrs. Frances Murray wrote a delightful account of her experiences as "*Summer in The Hebrides*", and that she "resolved to make a summer home in an old mansion, so long disused as to be partly ruinous, but which, under ingenious hands, and with little but the roughest material, soon wore a cheerful aspect."

The next census is rather more encouraging, for in 1891 we find that the Colosach, Neil McNeill, continues in post as farm manager and that two households are recorded with a total of 23 residents. In addition to two housewives, twelve children and a schoolteacher, there are no less than four rabbit trappers on the roll. Neil McNeill remained in post as farm manager until at least 1913, although by 1901 the population of Oransay was down to just twelve persons in two households, including two rabbit trappers, both sons of Neil McNeill. Neil was eventually succeeded by his son Malcolm, and in due course Malcolm's daughter Flora and her husband Andrew

MacNeill took over the tenancy and held it until the estate was broken up in the mid-1970s. Thus the family of Neil McNeill provided a century of farming continuity as an element of stability in a somewhat fractured history. Whilst it is probably fair to say that, after the death of Alexander McNeill in 1850, almost 150 years were to elapse before there would be serious investment devoted to either the buildings or the land, the situation has now changed. The present owners have worked tirelessly on restoration, and have been helped by the fact that limited but significant conservation work was carried out at the Priory about one hundred years ago.

The historical background

The archaeological remains in Oransay are so significant as to have been closely studied and published in depth. The RCAHMS published an excellent and inexpensive volume which was an essential purchase for any visitor, "*Colonsay & Oronsay, An Inventory of the Monuments Extracted from Argyll Volume 5*"; currently out of print but it is being urged to permit a reprint. Details of the Mesolithic sites will be found in "*Excavations on Oronsay*" by Paul Mellars (EUP 1987). A first-rate introduction to the mediaeval background is "*The Lords of the Isles*" by Ronald Williams, and much pleasure will be derived from "*Summer in the Hebrides*" by Mrs. Murray, which is available locally in a facsimile edition.

Dùn Dòmhnuill ("Donald's Fort") NR 534890

This fort is a prominent feature which may be clearly seen from Colonsay; it is on the right-hand side of the public road about 400 m before reaching the Priory. The entrance is on the northern side and clearly defined – approaching the summit, the access had been contrived to put a right-handed individual at a disadvantage. The summit measures 69m x 24m within a wall up to 3.5m in thickness, surrounded by vertical faces up to 30m high (RCAHMS). With the exception of the footings of two oval huts which post-date the main wall, the interior is almost featureless. There is, however, a basin of about 0.5m in diameter and 0.3m depth which has been cut into the living rock, and which is widely believed to have been connected with the inauguration ceremonies of the Lords of the Isles.

Hut-circle, Field-system and Cairns, Druim Mòr ("Great Ridge") NR 3587

This is a very extensive and complex monument which is fully described by RCAHMS. In essence, archaeologists believe that the earliest features are some of the obvious banks, which form part of a prehistoric field system. In the centre of the array, there is a hut-circle, 6m in diameter within an earth-and-stone bank 0.75m high and with its entrance to the south-east; it is felt that this may be of the same date as the field system. The cairns, of which almost sixty have been enumerated, in many cases partially intrude upon the banks, suggesting that they are of later date. RCAHMS suggest that some, at least, are funeral cairns and one can imagine that it might be convenient to place a corpse beside a pre-existing bank before building the cairn, so as to minimise the work.

Viking Burials

Three sites are recorded, as follows:

1. Càrn a'Bharraich ("The Barra-man's Cairn")
NR 360883

Excavations in 1891 and 1913 revealed three burials of Viking date and a layer of carbon which contained boat rivets. In the 1891 excavation, two long stones were discovered which were confidently declared to have fallen from upright positions, in view of the footings that were revealed. Various grave goods were discovered, including two bronze brooches and a ringed pin. The brooches are believed to have been made "from the strap terminals of a portable shrine", suggesting perhaps that it had been pillaged.

2. Druim Arstail ("Crosswise Ridge") NR 364889

Several items, including a bronze ringed pin of Viking date, were discovered due to erosion by M. Buchanan in 1912; the surviving items are preserved in the Hunterian Museum, Glasgow. About 100m to the north-east "several hundred" boat rivets were also discovered.

3. Lochan Chille Mòire ("Lochan at Our Lady's Chapel")
NR c.361889

"Six teeth from an individual of between about twenty-five and thirty years of age, one iron rivet and a number of fragments representing at least nine others, three iron strips or plates and some fragments of wood, which are probably oak" came from this site and are preserved in the National Museum of Antiquities (RCAHMS).

Chapel, Cill Mhoire ("Our Lady's Chapel") NR 360888

Situated about 80m east of the public road, where it makes a sharp turn at the foot of a brae as one approaches the Priory, the chapel is roughly in line between the left-hand gate-pier and the northern tip of Eilean Ghaoideamal. It is orientated, 5.5m x 3.5m within walls 1m thick and surviving to 0.35m height. A grave is marked beside the north-west corner.

MacDuffie Cairn and Cross NR c.356884

This cross, mentioned elsewhere, was said to have been of outstanding beauty and marked a resting place for funeral parties before reaching the Priory. The stone is described as *in situ* in 1695 by Martin Martin and again in 1772, when Pennant says: "Nearer the shore in the east side of the island, is a large conic tumulus [i.e. Caisteal nan Gillean]; and on the same plain, a small cross placed, where a Mac-dufie's corps is said to have rested". The cross is said to have been buried at some later date in order to protect it, at the south-west edge of Pàirc na Croise ("Field of the Cross"). The specific threat is not recorded, but a Presbyterian ministry commenced in Colonsay at the latter end of the eighteenth century, and a furore raged as to the position of the glebe. According to the legal evidence presented by the then minister, the Colonsay glebe should properly have been the island of Oransay; this claim was vigorously resisted. At about this time, when the tenant of Oransay, John McNeill, became owner of the entire estate, he removed to Kiloran. Perhaps the tenantry or some of the MacPhee family feared that his removal presaged the arrival of a Presbyterian minister who might have been a threat to the cross? There is no tradition of it ever having been retrieved from its place of concealment.

Oronsay Priory

Please refer to RCAHMS "*Inventory Volume 5*" and to "*Late Medieval Monumental Sculpture in the West Highlands*", K A Steer & J W M Bannerman, RCAHMS 1977 for detailed information. It is enough to mention here a few details, and a brief descriptive guide to the monument will be given in the main text. One prominent feature is the McNeill mortuary chapel, containing amongst others the memorial to Sir John Carstairs McNeill, Equerry to Queen Victoria and the last of the McNeill lairds. He was awarded a Victoria Cross in the New Zealand war but his military career was blighted through a disastrous error in the Sudan. During his duties at Osborne House he was rash enough to insult the queen's favourite, John Brown, who is said to have had him subsequently barred from the royal presence. Fortunately he retained good relations with her son and King Edward VII made a point of visiting Colonsay during his inaugural tour. On his death, Sir John's funeral was at St. James' Palace and the royal family was represented at the final interment in Oransay.

Within the main church one of very few Scottish pre-Reformation high altars survives; in certain lights it is possible to identify the consecration crosses on the upper surface. A recess behind the altar is now an ossuary for remains that have come to the surface and at one time will have contained holy relics. In the Middle Ages, Oransay Priory is said to have housed the remains of "St. Buono Bardus". The writer suggests that this is a Latin form of a Gaelic name, "St. Buo, the priest" and that it may commemorate an Irish evangelist who worked in Iceland and who died about 900 AD. The feast day of St. Buo is January 5th, but Oransay was dedicated to St. Columba who is remembered on June 9th. The Priory is a later foundation, supposedly of about 1350 AD by John of the Isles, dedicated to St. Augustine of Hippo (354–430; patron saint of brewers), whose feast day is August 28th. One might imagine that the relics of St. Buo were "inherited" by the Augustinian monks. The small chamber built into the south-east corner of the church is the "Sacrament House" – what would nowadays be known as the Tabernacle. Here the sacred vessels would be kept; very probably it will have been so arranged as to house a concealed inner chamber, for the additional protection of the most important items. Such an arrangement predates the Tridentine (1545-63) arrangements for a standardised liturgy, with the tabernacle mounted upon the altar.

Those who followed the Rule of St. Augustine were normally Canons Regular (i.e. ordained priests), and they were not normally seen as reclusive – witness the extreme case of Martin Luther. The Rule was formally established in 1243 and was admittedly to "organise" alleged hermits, but "could be adapted for community life in a wide range of circumstances … as Canons Regular… their priestly duties took them to places where they could provide pastoral care for the laity, so they had precisely the opposite attitude to the world from the Cistercians. They sought out newly developing towns; they planted their houses beside the castles and homes of the wealthy, often taking over existing large churches whose community life was in disarray... they gave tangible benefits to the communities around them; they served in parishes or hospitals as priests." ("*A History of Christianity*", D MacCulloch 2009). Since there seems to have been no lay novitiate, it seems that the agricultural and labouring work of Oransay (and Garvard, the out-farm) will have been undertaken by direct labour, resident outwith the main Priory buildings.

It seems almost perverse that John "the Good" established Cistercians at Saddell Abbey yet chose to seat Augustinians at Oransay, but this does appear to be the accepted fact. (Incidentally, Iona was Benedictine; and the Franciscan missionaries who visited Oransay in 1623 made no mention, merely noted that "*Insula haec satis amaena egregium habet monasterium per S. Columbam olim exstructum, cuius modo exstantes parietes cum chori et tecti partibus, aedificium persuadent quondam fuisse pulcherrimum*". "This attractive island has the ruins of a monastery founded long-ago by St. Columba, of which only the walls and parts of the choir and roof survive, a building which one can believe was once very beautiful." It is interesting that they judged the former beauty of the Priory by the walls and "parts of the choir and roof" that survived – the Reformation was barely 50 years old and had not yet reached Oransay, yet the Priory was already in ruins. Nonetheless, as recently as 1555 Queen Mary had been in correspondence with the Pope concerning the appointment of a new prior and in 1592 King James VI had presented "the patronage and vicarage" of Oransay to "Donaldus Dufacius"; indeed, it was not until 1616 that King James had disposed of the Priory's patrimony to Andrew, supposed Bishop of the Isles (the "*pseudoepiscipus*" who harassed the Franciscan missionaries and whose agents were hotly opposed by Colla Ciotach).

To one side of the church, a side-chapel is associated with Clan McPhee, the family which governed Colonsay for centuries on behalf of the Lords of the Isles, which provided many of the Priors of Oransay and which commissioned the High Cross and many of Oransay's monumental gravestones. From the north side of the church one can enter the cloister, a sheltered quadrangle provided for contemplative purposes; here the monks would have read their daily Office, free from external distractions. One of the pillars bears the inscription: +MA/ELSEAC/HLA(I)ND / SAER O/CUIND / FECIT I/STUD O/PUS i.e. "Malachy O'Quinn, mason, made this work"; O'Quinn is a widespread name in Ireland, with important branches in both Tyrone and Antrim.

Directly to the north and a metre or so above the level of the cloisters is the refectory building, although many people believe that this may have been the original location of the priory church. At the eastern end of the refectory is the small building known as "The Prior's Chapel", possibly on the site of the original Sanctuary of the earlier church. There is an old story that, hidden below the grass, there is a gravestone covering the remains of someone who was buried face down …

A few paces north of the Prior's Chapel is the substantial building known today as The Prior's House, which was probably at one time a monastic granary. Here tithes would be garnered, and very possibly the seed-corn for the entire island too, protected by the Church against the depredations of the MacLeans and other marauding groups. Today, the important mediaeval gravestones of Oransay are gathered in this building, safely protected from the elements. Descriptive material is provided, but visitors might like to know that one of the two recumbent effigies is that of Sir Alexander MacDonald of Lochalsh, who was murdered in this very building in 1497. He was tracked down by John MacIan of Ardnamurchan, acting for King James IV, and probably with the connivance of his sister Mariota. Her tombstone is also to be seen, a lady below a canopy with a book in one hand and a rosary in the other, lap dogs nestling in her cloak: HIC IACET …/… [MAR]IOTA ALEX/ANDRI IOHA[NN]IS MACEAIN i.e. "Here lies … Mariota, daughter of Alexander, son of John MacIan". At the far end of the room, one can see openings in the wall through which running water was once led, no doubt a great convenience in its day.

Leaving the Prior's House one can skirt behind the cloisters to reach the Oransay Cross. This stands in its original socket upon a tiered pedestal base and consists of a single slab, delicately thin, 3.67 metres high. The stone was quarried at Loch Sween and the quality of the craftsmanship is quite breathtaking. Both sides are carved with interlacing foliage and the west side features a passionate representation of the Crucifixion in high relief. Inscriptions reveal that the mason was Malachy O'Quinn and that the work was commissioned by Malcolm MacDuffie, chief of clan McPhee 1490–1520 and husband of the Mariota MacIan mentioned above.

The main entrance to the Priory Church is close beside Oransay Cross and it is interesting to note that work seems to have commenced here upon the unfinished construction of a tower. The work may well have been interrupted by the Reformation, although monumental gravestones continued to be made in Oransay as late as 1539. We have no information as to the specific dissolution of the Priory and can only speculate as to what became of the members of the community. It is worth noting that many people have commented upon the ground-plan of the Priory as being unusual, yet a cursory examination will show that it echoes that of Iona quite precisely, although upon a smaller scale.

Other Sites of Interest

Oransay was exploited by hunter-gatherers of the Mesolithic period and the surviving archaeological evidence makes it a very important site. The island was rather smaller in the Mesolithic period (less than four square kilometres) due to the higher sea level, and the period of occupation is said to have lasted for between 600 and 700 years (from c.6100 to 5400 BP). Despite the small size of the island, the Mesolithic inhabitants had no less than five occupation sites, all of which were beside the then-existing shoreline, and they moved between them with the seasons, so as to maximise the benefit of the available resources. In his definitive study, *"Excavations on Oransay"*, Prof. Paul Mellars identified the sites and seasons as follows:

1. Priory Midden, 80m from the northeast corner of Port na Luinge – the winter site. This site was first noticed by the farmer, the late Andrew MacNeill, and is described as "a relatively well-defined mound, rising some 1.5m above the level of the adjacent ground, and forming a clearly visible landmark when viewed from the south and west" (Mellars).

2. Caisteal Nan Gillean ("Lads' Castle"), behind Seal Cottage – early summer occupation. Note that there are two sites here, NR 3582 8797 and NR 3586 8800, which stand about 50m. apart. The first of these is very prominent and easily identified – it still stands to about 17.7m above sea-level, although it lost about 2m during Victorian excavation of the site.

3. Cnoc Sligeach ("Shell-mound") at NR 3728 8909 – high summer occupation. This site is very easily identified, standing out as bright green (due to the midden material) and very evenly conical.

4. Cnoc Coig (? "Cock-hill"), near Cill Moire at NR 3605 8857 – autumn occupation. This was at the core of Prof. Mellars study and was excavated to almost 75% of the total deposits. "Visually, Coc Coig is the least impressive of all the Oronsay middens. At present the site appears as a relatively low and irregular mound, rising no more than 1–2m above the level of the adjacent ground" (Mellars).

Seal Cottage NR 3618 8805
A former boat-house which was initially converted to a romantic bower by a former laid (possibly 2nd Baron Strathcona?) and more comprehensively enhanced by the present proprietor. About 200 m to the north there is the ruin of Tigh Guail ("The Coal-house"), which is where puffers used to be beached to allow cargo to be discharged. There is a very fine well close at hand, with a stainless-steel cup, a gift from the late David and Jane Todd, long-term enthusiasts for the "Honourable Council of Colonsian Thiefs".

Shell Craters NR c. 342885
Hereabouts one can identify shell-craters, created when the Royal Navy tested new guns from a position near the north end of Jura. During the trials, the inhabitants of Oronsay joined the official observers, including the First Lord of the Admiralty, all of whom were positioned on the summit of Beinn Oronsay. These craters are an interesting reminder of a remarkable story.

It will be recalled that "Hugh of the Glen" was gifted with second-sight, and an example of this has been mentioned in Chapter 10. He lived in the early nineteenth century and, in one of his visions, he foresaw a large-scale military funeral in Colonsay. Loder mentions a route from Garvard, whereas the late Para Mòr MacAllister described the tradition of the cortege going "across the golf course", but both versions suggested a procession over a mile in length, in which Hugh saw men in strange uniforms with guns reversed.

Many years later the Royal Navy developed powerful new guns, with a range of 25 miles, and trials took place in September 1913, in the presence of Winston Churchill, first Lord of the Admiralty. The fleet had been on station for weeks on end and the sailors were becoming disenchanted. Then an unfortunate accident occurred, in which a relatively humble crew member was killed in an explosion, and it was decided to give him a full scale naval funeral so as to occupy the men and raise morale. In this way, Hugh's vision came to be fulfilled.

Some details were recorded in the "*Naval Gazette*" and additional information has been obtained from the family of the deceased: "Richard Prior was a master gunner in the Royal Marine detachment aboard the battleship "*King Edward VII*" which was part of the fleet off Colonsay to test a new gun. So important was the exercise that the First Lord of the Admiralty Mr. Winston Churchill and Mrs. Churchill were watching the exercise from Colonsay, and they were quartered aboard the battleship HMS "*Enchantress*". According to the "*Chatham Express*" (Richard came from Chatham) a shell stuck in the breech and, as Richard was trying to clear it, the shell exploded, killing him and injuring three others. I have a letter from the Captain of the ship, Captain Heaton Ellis, to my Great Grandmother, dated September 18th 1912 *(from which I give)* the following extract:

'The accident happened during night practice at 10.15pm on September 16th when a shell exploded in the breech of the gun. Part of the shell struck your son ... killing him instantly, we are quite sure that he could not have suffered.

'Your son has been laid to rest in the cemetery at this beautiful place with all the impressiveness of a naval funeral and the solemnity of that beautiful Service. The First Lord of the Admiralty attended the service as did Admiral Burney, myself and representatives of all the officers' messes.' "

Richard was 31 years old and unmarried, the eldest of seven boys in the one household. Five more of them were to perish in the Great War:

James Prior, killed at sea 22 September 1914
Charles Prior killed in Belgium 23 December 1914

Harry Prior killed on the Somme 7 October 1916
Archibald Prior killed at Arras 3 May 1917
Herbert Prior killed at sea 30 October 1918

The correspondent went on to say that "I am intrigued to hear that his grave is not commemorated since, in his letter of 18 September 1912, the Captain of "*King Edward VII*" wrote that the shipmates of Richard had collected enough money for a headstone to be erected." This omission has now been rectified and a suitable memorial has been provided in Kilchattan graveyard.

Leab' Fhalaich Mhic a' Phi ("MacPhee's Hiding-place")
The hunt for Malcolm MacPhee led from north to south and came to an end when he was discovered hiding under some seaweed at the furthest extremity of Eilean nan Ròn ("Seal Island"). Looking southwest from Oronsay Priory, one can identify Eilean nan Ròn by the three gables of a roofless bothy.

   Whilst actually within the Priory church one can identify another Leab' Fhalaich Mhic a' Phi by entering the "sacristy" on the north side of the altar and looking upwards to the flagged roof. Malcolm is said to have concealed himself in the roof valley above those flag-stones.

Visiting Oronsay
Oransay is separated from the rest of Colonsay at high tide by a navigable channel and is therefore regarded as an island in its own right. Nonetheless, it is in no way independent of its parent, and is often mentioned locally as "the best farm in Colonsay". The tidal flat between the islands is nowadays known as "The Strand", but is properly An Fhaoghail ("The Fording-place"). Although barely 100 metres separates the two islands at the narrowest part there is very deep water at that point and the visitor should follow the conventional route of almost 1.9 kilometres, clearly marked upon all maps. The following section gives information which is commonly sought by first-time visitors – other readers, please ignore.

Crossing the Strand
In pre-planning a visit, it may be useful to know that there are two tidal cycles per day in Colonsay, each of roughly twelve hours and with a maximum range of about four metres. The maximum range occurs during a Spring Tide, whilst the minimum range is a Neap

Tide. Spring tides are the best for crossing to Oransay, and these occur about two days after a Full Moon or New Moon; any normal diary will give these phases of the moon.

More precise details are available locally, from the post office, shop, hotel or pier office, all of which have a Tide Table to hand. As a rule of thumb, a window of up to five hours exists at Springs, falling away to virtually nothing at Neaps. The obvious plan is to follow the tide out at Springs, noting the time and comparing it with dead Low-water as obtained from a Tide Table; if one can cross (say) 2 hours before Low-water, one should plan to be leaving the Oransay shore for the return journey no more than 2 hours after Low-water. It is also possible to cross at Low-water neaps, remain in Oransay for the day and then return c. 12 hours later, at the next Low-water. A further possibility is to make use of a boat for one or other leg of the crossing, although no licensed commercial vessel operates in 2010.

Although it is possible to drive across the Strand, this is not recommended. The traveller on foot will experience a sense of pilgrimage and achievement which is denied to the motorist, and will also enjoy a surprising diversity of stimuli from the natural environment – the wind in the hair, the sand underfoot, the smell of the tangle, the cries of the seabirds.

There will, of course, be those who are obliged to drive because of infirmity or special circumstances and they are well-advised to seek the help of a local guide. If you must make the trip without assistance, begin by making quite sure that you have correctly calculated the tidal window. At the Colonsay "road end" stop your car, establish your bearings, engage first gear and make your way at walking speed or less towards Rubha Dubh (the headland due south, 750 metres). At no point should the vehicle be allowed to come to rest on the Strand, but be aware that the shingle shore at Rubha Dubh provides a point of refuge if you do need to stop. As you approach Rubha Dubh, you will make a dog-leg turn of about forty degrees towards the south-west, heading for the nearest headland on the Oransay shore (c. 600 metres). As you approach the Oransay shore, you will cross the deepest part of the channel which should not be more than (say) 15 cm. deep for a modern car travelling very slowly – if in doubt, turn in a circle and return to Rubha Dubh, but do not stop or attempt to reverse.

On reaching the Oransay shore, you will be slightly to the east of a tiny island with a (modern) pillar stone prominently sited upon it; there is hard shingle between the island and the shore, providing another point of refuge if you need to stop. From this point, the route heads westwards, hugging the Oransay shore but there is a choice of two tracks. The one marked upon the map goes outside the tiny island and along the surface of the Strand – it used to be in common use, but requires care due to some very deep lagoons, hidden rocks etc. One might prefer to take "The High Road", which runs between the island and the Oransay shore, then threads its way along the rocky foreshore and through a narrow pass before rejoining the usual track for the final 100 metres.

Caveats: Those of a nervous disposition will be disturbed to know that one or two vehicles come to grief on this crossing nearly every year, although it is slightly reassuring to know that the maximum depth on the route is barely 3 metres at high tide; thus *in extremis*, one should theoretically be safe enough standing on the roof until the tide goes down! Driving at walking speed or more can do almost as much damage to your vehicle as total submersion, straying from the approved track will almost certainly result in total submersion, and total submersion always leads to an escape of fuel and consequent environmental damage. Because of the environmental damage, whoever can be subsequently persuaded to remove the affected vehicle is likely to be far from sympathetic.

On the other hand, people do cross and re-cross this route on a daily basis; just stick to the correct time, speed and route and there will be no problem.

A Suggested Walk in Oronsay

The most obvious reason to visit Oronsay is to see the Priory and, since so much authoritative information is readily available, no useful purpose would be served by attempting a detailed description here. Instead, the reader is invited to take a notional ramble through the island, affording the opportunity to take things as they come. Please note that the route to be followed is deliberately loose – most visitors to the island will happily content themselves with a trip to the Priory, others will be deterred by some of the terrain. More importantly, at certain times of the year sections of this route may be unsuitable due to wildlife considerations – please do be ready to comply with any request to modify your route. If you wish to reach a specific objective and have any doubts as to an acceptable route, feel free to ask advice of the Estate Manager or the RSPB Staff. The route described is 15.7 km in total and takes a minimum of 4 hours to complete – it is suggested that a first-time visitor should allow between 5 and 6 hours.

In crossing the Strand, one normally passes a few metres to the east of the Prostrate Cross which lies at NR 36971 90322 midway between Rubha na Dearg Sgeir ("Red Skerry Point") and Rubha Dubh ("Dark Point"); this marks the outer limit of the sanctuary provided by the Priory in mediaeval times. In those days, a criminal could be "put to the horn" and thus deprived of all rights and property, a prey to one and all; such a person could seek sanctuary in a monastic house, conform to their Rule and subsequently be restored to normal society. A neighbouring upright cross known as Crois an Tearmaid ("Sanctuary Cross") seems to have slipped below the sand and awaits recovery – from old photographs, it used to stand about 80 metres further to the east. (Something like a rubble foundation was noted at NR 37042 90305 on 6 March 2010).

On reaching the Oransay shore at NR 36712 89800, the track skirts the tiny island of Eilean a Chraobh Chaorainn ("Rowan Tree Island"); the Rowan is regarded as a protection against evil, and to this day will be seen planted beside many a gate in the Highlands. This was always the "entrance" to Oransay, although in former days the funeral route continued along a more easterly route than the modern track which we now follow along the shoreline to the south-west. After 250 metres, the track passes through a narrow defile in the living rock, then drops down onto the seabed once more; at this point look to the left to see the aptly-named "Elephant's Trunk", a natural arch. Properly known as A' Chloich Thuill ("The Pierced Stone"), it was at one time believed that three clockwise circuits of the pillar would give protection against tuberculosis. No doubt this arose from a folk memory of such devotional approaches to the Priory itself, and it reflects the helplessness of the people when the causes and cure of such a crippling disease were as yet unknown. It underlines the special importance of Colonsay's own Dr. Roger McNeill, whose life's work did so much to eradicate this scourge throughout the nation.

Leaving the shore, one might think of St. Fergnae and the other anchorites who lived along the shores of the Strand some 1,500 years ago, wondering if some hint of their memory survives in the name of this gentle slope, Bruthach an t-Aoradh, leading to an attractive, level hillock just at the summit, Cnoc an t-Aorach ("Worship Hill"), NR 35951 89207. The writer wonders if this might not be the site of St. Columba's original foundation in Hinba, one with very open views and in line of site from the protecting power in Dùn Cholla. At all events it is a peaceful spot, little changed since St. Columba's day, and very close to the actual spot described by St. Adomnàn in the following incident:

"On another occasion, when this eminent man [i.e. St. Columba] was staying in the Hinba island, he saw, on a certain night, in a mental ecstasy, an angel sent to him from heaven, and holding in his hand a book of glass, regarding the appointment of kings. Having received the book from the hand of the angel, the venerable man, at his command, began to read it; and when he was reluctant to appoint Aidan king, as the book directed, because he had a greater affection for Iogenan his brother, the angel, suddenly stretching forth his hand, struck the saint with a scourge, the livid marks of which remained in his side all the days of his life. And he added these words: "O know for certain," said he, "that I am sent to thee by God with the book of glass, that in accordance with the words thou hast read therein, thou mayest inaugurate Aidan into the kingdom; but if thou refuse to obey this command, I will strike thee again." When therefore this angel of the Lord had appeared for three successive nights, having the same book of glass in his hand, and had repeated the same commands of the Lord regarding the appointment of the same king, the saint, in obedience to the command of the Lord, sailed across to the Iouan island (i.e. Iona), and there ordained, as he had been commanded, Aidan to be king, who had arrived at the same time as the saint. During the words of consecration, the saint declared the future regarding the children, grandchildren and great- grandchildren of Aidan, and laying his hand upon his head, he consecrated and blessed him."

Although most readers will continue along the road, our notional route leads us to turn right at this point, picking our way across a boggy plateau so as to able to approach Beinn Oransay by its north-eastern slope. (Please note that at certain times of year you will be asked to avoid this route to avoid disturbance to breeding birds –

look out for relevant notices). At the summit (93 metres) one is rewarded by an excellent view of Oransay House and Priory, as well as an overview of the whole island. Here one stands in the footprints of St. Columba, at Carn Cul ri Eireann (NR 35154 89195), but there are other literary references to the site which might be of interest. Martin Martin, writing in the days of the first McNeill laird, described a mysterious island that seems subsequently to have disappeared:

> Mr. Mack-Swen, present Minister of the Isle Jura, gave me the following account of it, which he had from the Master of an English vessel that happened to anchor at that little Isle, and came afterwards to Jura; which is thus:
>
> "As I was sailing some thirty leagues to the southwest of Islay, I was becalmed near a little isle; where I dropped anchor and went ashore. I found it covered all over with long grass; there were abundance of seals lying on the rocks, and on the shore; there is likewise a multitude of sea-fowls in it. There is a river in the middle, and on each side of it I found great heaps of fish-bones of many sorts. There are many planks and boards cast up upon the coast of the isle, and it being all plain, and almost level with the sea, I caused my men (being then idle) to erect a heap of wood about two stories high; and that with a design to make the island more conspicuous to sea-faring men. This isle (*is*) of four English miles in length, and one in breadth. I was about thirteen hours sailing between this isle and Jura."
>
> "Mr. John Mack-Swen above-mentioned, having gone to the Isle of Colonsay some few days after, was told by the inhabitants that from an eminence near the Monastery, in a fair day, they saw as it were the top of a little mountain in the southwest sea, and that they doubted not but it was land, tho' they never observed it before. Mr. Mack-Swen was confirmed in this opinion by the account above-mentioned; but when the summer was over, they never saw this little hill, as they called it, any more. The reason of which is supposed to be this, that the high winds, in all probability, had cast down the pile of wood that forty seamen had erected the preceding year in that island; which by reason of the description above recited, we may aptly enough call the Green Island."

There is little that one can add to the above, save to confirm that

Rev. McSwine was the Episcopalian incumbent of Gigha, Jura and Colonsay during the suppression of the Presbyterian Church, and that he remained in office until November 1697 or later. Ruairidh MacIlleathain, witing in the *West Highland Free Press*, has suggested that the island may have been the one known in tradition as Rocabarra. It is said that this island has appeared twice above the surface of the Minch, and twice it has submerged again. According to that same tradition, it will appear for the third time at the Day of Doom. Curiously enough, grey Atlantic seals from Oransay and elsewhere have been tracked by radio-transmission in recent years and many of them seem to spend a great deal of time in the exact area which is indicated in this tale.

It is suggested by a later writer that a structure existed on Beinn Orasa which would have given a slightly higher viewpoint than at present. Thomas Pennant visited the site in the 1770s and left a description: "Ascend the very hill that the Saint did. Lofty and craggy, inhabited by red billed choughs, and stares (i.e.starlings). On the top is a retreat of the old inhabitants, protected by a strong stone dike and advanced works". Not a vestige of this "retreat" is visible to the casual observer today, and one wonders exactly when it can have been removed. It sounds very similar to one which survives at Beinn Bheag, Balnahard, unless perhaps the reference is to the neighbouring Dùn Domhnuill.

Leaving the summit one can descend towards the south-east, threading one's way through rocky outcrops toward Dùn Domhnuill ("Donald's Fort"). This powerful Iron Age fort was re-utilised by the Lords of the Isles and the rock-cut basin on the summit at NR 35419 89028 is said to have featured in their peripatetic inauguration ceremonies. It is not known when such ceremonies ceased, and when the Lordship became based upon a fixed, central powerbase at Finlaggan in Islay, but a Colonsay tradition suggests a date. According to the tradition, this fort is named for Donald, who was Lord of the Isles from 1207 until c. 1270, the progenitor of Clan Donald and a fairly warlike individual. The story is that Donald re-fortified this ancient dùn, despite the fact that it had been a place of sanctity since the time of St. Columba. Subsequently, overcome with remorse, he made his way to Rome, accompanied by seven priests, in order to make a personal apology to the Pope. He said that he would accept any penance that was given him, even to the extent of swallowing molten lead, but the Holy Father imposed a much stricter penalty and forbade him ever to return again to Oransay. Because of this, Donald was constrained to adopt a more settled life, and so established himself and his court on an island in Finlaggan Loch in Islay.

Despite the above, it should be noted that a document survives from August 1st 1492 in which John, Lord of the Isles, granted certain rights in Tiree, whilst he was in Oransay. This was just a year before the Forfeiture of the Lordship and one wonders if he was a guest of the Priory community rather than encamped upon the ancient dùn.

Romantic visitors may like to look out across the fields below, tracing the ancient funeral route. The cortege wound past the tiny chapel of Cill Moire, southwest of the eponymous lochan. From there, the remains were carried on a route that lay almost parallel with the modern road, but about 300 metres to the south, so as to approach the priory along the formal wall-lined avenue that has been preserved to the present day. The field closest to Cill Moire is known as Pairc na Croise ("The Field of the Cross"), and contained the final resting place for the pallbearers. The cross in question is said to have been of inordinate beauty, and by tradition was especially associated with Clan MacPhee (a.k.a. MacDuffie). Items of such craftsmanship were at great risk from iconoclasts following the Reformation and, in order to protect it, the cross is said to have been eventually taken down and buried nearby. It seems to have been seen by Martin Martin about 1695: "About a quarter of a mile on the south side of the church there is a carne, in which there is a stone cross fixed called Macduffie's Cross, for when any of the heads of their family were to be interred their corps was laid on this cross for some moments in their way towards the church". Funerals continued for a while in the normal manner, pausing now at the bare site of the buried cross, and so the patch of ground became hallowed in its own right. The cross seems to have been buried in or around 1800 and, as recently as the 1970s, the then farmer could identify the spot, which was never ploughed nor harvested.

On leaving Dùn Domhnuill, the easiest route is to depart by the original entrance on the north side, then turn left and descend along the hillside to reach the road somewhere before the cattle-grid, then continue to the Priory (350 metres).

Oransay Priory

A very brief but useful late Victorian description is worthy of reproduction here, from vol. iii. of MacGibbon and Ross's "*Ecclesiastical Architecture of Scotland*". It is concise and helpful, but be aware that it was written more than 100 years ago, when some additional original features survived and when, for example, the ground level within the church was 0.5m higher than it is today. To use it as your guide, make your way towards the main entrance (close to the High Cross), rather than to the McNeill Mortuary Chapel:

"The general arrangement of the buildings is peculiar. The ground slopes rapidly from north to south, necessarily carrying the drainage with it; yet, contrary to the usual custom, the cloisters and residential buildings were placed to the north of the church. Exclusive of the projections at the north-east and south-west angles, and a mortuary chapel on the south, the structures occupy a parallelogram about 87 feet from north to south, by 65 feet from east to west. The latter length is also that of the church proper, which occupies the south side of the square, but has at the west end a narthex about 15 feet square internally, which projects beyond the general range of the buildings. The walls of the narthex are now level with those of the church, but as there are roughly hewn corbel stones for carrying a floor overhead, it is probable this is only the lower stage of a bell-tower, of which the upper part has been long since demolished. The greater thickness of the walls, and two sadly injured freestone buttresses on its south face, favour this idea.

"Entrance is obtained by a doorway with a plain pointed freestone arch, having a hood moulding close to the westmost buttress. The church is, internally, nearly 18 feet in width; and at the right hand, on entering, there remains the solid foundation of a stone stair leading to a tribune or organ-gallery, recesses for the ends of massive beams to carry it being still visible, together with rough rubble corbelling on either side.

"On the left is a narrow doorway, neatly formed with thin schist stones, leading to the cloisters. Internally, the church is entirely devoid of architectural decoration; but an extensive range of stalls, of which traces still exist, and other wood-work, including an open roof, must have redeemed an otherwise bald interior, into which very little light can have been admitted. The principal source of light was a 5 feet wide window at the east end, divided by mullions, into three lanciform lights, the pointed arch-heads of which run up to the main arch. The other gable is modern, and forms the entrance porch to what may have formerly been the chapter-house, but which has been appropriated in recent times as a burial-place by the proprietor of the island. Apart from this there were only three windows in the nave, two very small, and another rather longer with a cusped head, all formed in freestone, and on the extreme east end of the south wall near the altar, a square-headed window with slab lintel and sill. Between these windows a plain schist doorway gives access to the mortuary chapel of the M'Duffies or M'Fies, which is about 25 feet long by 12 feet wide over the walls. These are unbonded into the south wall of the church, and were covered with a plain lean-to roof, in which there was evidently a priest's apartment. The chapel is lit from the south by two small windows, and in a recess on the north side is the burial-place of Abbot M'Duffie, covered with a carved slab, representing the abbot fully vested, with his right hand raised in benediction, and a pastoral staff in his left. Pennant says : ' In the same place is a stone enriched with foliage, a stag surrounded with dogs, and ship with full sail ; round which is inscribed, "Hie jacet Murchardus Macdufie de Collonsa, A.D. 1539, Mense Mart. Ora me ille, Ammen."

"Beyond this chapel, at the south-east angle of the church is a singularly massive buttress, at the bottom of which, on the level of the floor, and accessible by a narrow opening from the interior of the church, is a curious ambry, about 3 feet cube, strongly lintelled overhead, and designed, no doubt, for the safe keeping of the church treasure, but is now desecrated as a ' bone-hole.' The altar still remains built of freestone, evidently re-used from some previous building.

"On the north side of the chancel the arrangement is very peculiar, an opening about 8 feet wide, with a plain pointed free-stone arch resting on schist impost caps, gives access to a kind of trance or passage, having an ambry at the ground level on the left, and a blocked up window on the right. It is formed between the north wall of the church and the south end of the chapter-house, which is gabled independently of the church. Its only apparent use may have been as a sacristy. It is roofed in by large

flat stones, with a rapid slope to the east. The east range of buildings is pretty complete, except on the north, where the gable fell
some years ago. On the ground floor a large apartment, 19 feet 6
inches long, by 15 feet 4 inches wide, with a doorway entering on
the east cloister-walk, was no doubt the chapter-house.

"The range of domestic buildings on the north has been sadly
ruined, this having been the point where entry was obtained in
recent times, for the removal of materials, and thus of the north
and south walls only fragments remain. A massive wall, still
happily intact, encloses the cloister on the west. The internal area
is rather over 41 feet square, with cloister-walks about 7 feet
broad, and the arcading presents some very singular features.
The south arcade, which is evidently the most ancient, is
composed of five low narrow arches with circular heads, very
neatly turned with thin schist slabs, without any freestone or
architectural dressing of any kind. The other three arcades were
evidently part of a later restoration, and the peculiar form in
which they were constructed is evidently due to the nature of the
materials employed, viz. Schist slabs of the same quality as that
used for the sculptured slabs.

"The north range of the buildings, which no doubt contained
the refectory and dormitories, has been too much dilapidated to
admit of any intelligible description. In a line with it, however,
and extending eastward beyond the priory square there is a small
chapel of very early character, built entirely in rubble, without
any freestone dressings. It is 17 feet over the walls, and 33 feet in
breadth ; but for no apparent reason the west gable is slewed
round to the south, making an inequality of 2 feet in the length of
the sides. There has been a wide window in the east gable, but
owing to the demolition of the wall its character cannot be
judged. There are two small windows in the north side and one in
the south, mere slits with no provisions for frames or glazing.
There is an entrance doorway on the south side at the west end,
and a priest's door at the east. On the north side there is a very
small door, nearly opposite that of the entrance on the south.

"The foundations of the altar still remain, and a line of stones
still indicates the position of the chancel rail. The base of the
pulpit remains on the north side, and at the west end there has
been a tribune or organ gallery, which has been accessible by a
door in the east gable of the priory buildings. In this gable, on the

ground floor, an archway has been formed 6 feet 8 inches in width, with a plain pointed rubble arch, which seems to have been subsequently filled in, and a square-headed doorway of much smaller size substituted.

"Immediately to the north of this chapel, and separated from it by an 8 foot wide passage, is a most interesting example of a monastic barn and byre, 39 feet in length, by 22 feet in breadth. It is an excellent specimen of rubble building, with freestone dressings in the windows, &c., in the same style as the church, and may be coeval with the later restoration. The windows are small, and on the north side close to the ground are openings for the discharge of refuse from the byre. In the south-east angle a small chamber has been formed for the herd, with a little eyelet and ambry, and it would no doubt be cut off by partitioning from the other occupants. At the south- west angle there is a small door opening inwards, and some indications that a chamber had been formed between the building itself and the north wall of the priory. At the south wall head (internally) there has been inserted a 4 or 5 foot long schist slab, with a quaint human head carved in the centre.

"It serves no purpose where it is, and must evidently have been a relic of some older structure. There can be no doubt there was a doorway to the west, but, if so, the present entrance shows no traces of it. The building is still roofed, and in use."

The Crosses

Cross 1. "In the graveyard close to the south-west angle of the narthex, stands the Great Oronsay Cross. It is a monolith, 12 feet 2 inches high, by 1 foot 6 inches wide, and 4 to 5 inches thick, and is socketted into a thick slab, about 3 feet 3 inches square, which rests on a pedestal of masonry nearly 4 feet high. On the west face of the cross is a crucifix, sculptured in high relief, with a back ground of irregular interlacing ornament. This cross is supposed to have been erected to the memory of Colin, a prior, who died in 1510; as it bears the inscription, + Hec est Crux Colini Filii Cristini M(eic)Dufaci ["This is the cross of Colinus, son of Cristinus MacDuffie"]. On the socket-stone there is a much-worn inscription [+ Maelseachlaind Saer Ocuinn Fecit Istam Crucem "Mael-Sech-lainn Ó Cuinn, mason, made this cross"].

Cross 2. "Standing in a pile of masonry at the north-east of the priory buildings is the lower stone of the shaft of another cross, 3 feet 3 inches high, one of its faces worn smooth, the other covered with intertwining scrollwork of stems, terminating in broad-leaved foliage. This stone is surmounted by a disc which did not belong to it originally, judging from the character of its sculpturing (we are informed that some years ago it lay in the graveyard). The disc or head of the cross has a recess or cusped niche sunk in one of its faces, within which is sculptured in bas-relief the figure of an ecclesiastic curiously robed [St. John the Evangelist, driving venom from a poisoned chalice]."

Do bear in mind the fact that the above description is over one hundred years old and is only intended to assist one to navigate the site; considerable scholarship has been devoted to the subject since that time and authoritative information may readily be obtained from a variety of published sources.

In recent years an attractive and sympathetic garden has been created behind the Priory, where once the monks will have cultivated vegetables and medicinal herbs. The garden was especially designed by Penelope Hobhouse and is an exciting response to the challenge of a very demanding environment. Although the garden is not open to the public, it is good to know that it exists and that it is just one of the many hidden facets of the isle.

Leaving the Priory, one might follow the avenue towards the south, leading towards a stone dedicated to the memory of Ike Colburn (1924-92), the celebrated American architect and late owner of Oransay. The route leads along behind a lengthy and beautiful sandy beach, and then to a rocky gully and a tiny house at NR 35085 87907, An Taigh Cearc ("The Hen House"), a well-preserved example of a type of dwelling common in eighteenth-century Colonsay. The footings of similar houses can be traced in many locations, but no other example has survived in the round.

Passing through a gateway, one is still heading south and by keeping close to the sea can identify two small sandy inlets along a rocky shoreline. This rocky shore supports the growth of seaweed known as kelp, which was a most valuable resource during the Napoleonic wars. The industrial revolution had created an enormous demand for potash, but the conflict prevented its importation from natural deposits in North Africa. Fortunately, although by horrendous labour, it could be obtained from kelp which was harvested, hauled ashore, dried and then burned to produce the desired residue. In a slight hollow beyond the second sandy beach a diligent observer will be able to identify an excellent example of a kelping kiln, boat shaped and kerbed in stone at NR 34796 87347. Other examples survive in Colonsay, but this is probably one of the best-preserved; nonetheless, even within the last thirty years, its outline is becoming less distinct – it is about 50 metres inland from a fairly prominent upright stone. The stone is only there by chance, but it has been in place for over a decade and may well remain a little longer.

Turning now towards the east, one can cross Druim Mòr ("Great Ridge"), heading straight towards the distant Paps of Jura, and on passing the summit will become aware of numerous stone cairns. All told there are about sixty such cairns and it has been suggested that they might have been built during a time of plague or famine. A tiny lochan to the northeast of the area is called Lochan na Cealltrach ("Little Loch at the Burial-ground").

The view to the east now includes a group of small islets, the largest of which is Eilean Ghaoideamal ("Island of the Stolen Rent"), a name which is very possibly a Gaelic pun. From old maps it seems originally to have had a similar-sounding Norse name, meaning "Goat Field", but in 1686 there was a nasty incident involving Sarah MacDonald's factor: "Archibald Campbell... with twenty men in arms, with swords, pistols and hagbuts, invaded the saide Donalde MacDonald while he was uplifting the rents of the lands of Oronsay", assaulted him and deprived him of the rents. It seems that by a subtle change, the name of Eilean Ghaoideamal now commemorates the affair.

Turn left, passing through marram grass and eventually crossing a ruinous wall, in line with the southern end of Eilean Ghaoideamal. Looking a little towards your left and with help from the Ordnance Survey map, it is easy to identify and approach Caisteal nan Gillean ("The Lads Castle") at NR 35833 87972. This is the most famous and most southerly of Oransay's numerous Mesolithic shell mounds, but there is another just 50 metres to the northeast, at NR 3586 8800. These mounds all consist of midden material from seasonal occupation by hunter-gatherer communities more than 6,000 years ago. Originally excavated in the nineteenth century by

Symington Grieve, the shell mounds have been the subject of
detailed examination in the 1970s by Prof. Paul Mellars and have
revealed much detailed information about the lifestyle and capabilities of Scotland's early inhabitants.

From the summit of the first Caisteal nan Gillean one can identify the chimney pots and roof of Seal Cottage. A grass track runs
vaguely towards it and one can ramble northwards over easy
terrain, following whatever route is most appealing, remembering to
bear left so as to regain the public road beside the tiny Lochan
Chille-moire ("Small Loch beside Our Lady's Chapel"). The chapel
itself is on a slight rise, about 80 metres short of the road, being
about 6m by 4m in size and orientated in the traditional manner.
The walls survive to no more than 0.35m in height and one or two
graves are marked nearby with unassuming stones at the head and
foot. Some items in the National Museum of Antiquities, including
a rivet and some pieces of iron and wood, are labelled "From Viking
Burial Lochan Kill Mhor Oronsay 1891" but have no more detailed
provenance. Perhaps this enigmatic note is an appropriate one on
which to end. Here one rejoins the road and turns one's face for
home, reflecting on the history and allure of this very special place.

Appendix

THE "MASSIF CENTRAL"

There does not seem to be a distinct name for the hilly area within Colonsay's circle of habitation, but the area is worthy of exploration. This is a straightforward walk of only 6.5km, but it does involve two fences and you should allow about 3 or 4 hours. Leave your car at the graveyard and walk up the hill, then turn right into the clachan at Seaview. Follow the track behind the houses, pass through a gate and then turn off to the right and climb the grassy slope to reach An Diollaid ("The Saddle"), crossing a burn to do so.

The path now runs along a marshy glen towards the prominent hill ahead of you, Carn Mòr ("Great Cairn"). After a short distance (30 metres or so) there is an interesting exposure of a rare ouachitite dyke on your right-hand side (a small wooden peg beside the path marks the spot). Please do not be tempted to take a sample – sadly, there has been wanton damage to this site in the very recent past, as can be seen where the rock has been hacked away. The rock, which is faintly radio-active, is remarkable for the large discs of mica that it contains.

Continue along the little glen until the ground starts to rise – at this point, follow the faint track through the rising ground on your right, aiming to pass to the right of Carn Mòr along an obvious gully. You will now encounter two sets of stone assemblages, at NR 37081 94788 and NR 37101 94799. The second of these is known as Uaigh an Fhomhair ("The Giant's Grave") and it was for many years considered to be a possible passage-grave; in recent years it has been identified instead as a habitation-site of undetermined age.

Continue along the clearly defined route of the pathway, up the rising gully. In former times this was a main route across the island and will have been well-trodden. Near the top of the slope, identify the old, broken wall to your left and climb up through the gap to reach the summit of Carn Mòr. There are two cairns here and an excellent viewpoint. Coll, Tiree, the Treshnish Isles and the Torran Rocks are all visible, and possibly Donegal on a good day. Close at hand, there are good views of the Dubh Loch ("Black Loch") and the smaller Fionn Loch ("White Loch"). There is said to be the foot-print of a mythical fellow called Lusbirdan upon this summit, and there is a matching one behind the crofthouse at Mull Dubh, on the other side of Loch Fada.

Leaving the highest of the two cairns, identify The Monument at Scalasaig and head somewhat to its right (directly towards the north side of Loch Tarbert on Jura) to follow the line of an inviting, if narrow, descending glen. About 150 metres into that glen, you will come across structures at NR 37421 94615 and NR 37417 94598. The first grouping consists of two conjoined circular huts, of which the walls survive to 0.8m. The larger one is 3m internal diameter, with a cunningly contrived doorway leading indirectly into the house so as to mitigate the full force of the westerly wind. The smaller hut is of 2m internal diameter with a doorway facing to the southwest, and beside it there is an oblong structure of 2m x 1.5m internal dimension. The second O.S. reference is to a substantial structure surviving to more than 1m in height in its main section and which may originally have been a hut of about 2.5m internal diameter. As it stands, it is about 4m internally along one axis and it is unclear if this is due to a collapse of masonry or to some degree of deliberate modification. The original doorway faces to the south-east.

Turn now to identify Carn na Cainnle ("Candle Cairn") and make your way towards it, keeping to the right of a marshy plateau. After about 250 metres, you will be passing a thriving holly tree in a sheltered gully, a relatively uncommon species to survive in Colonsay. The holly will be below you, on your left, if you have gone through the heather on the higher ground, but it will be on your right if you have chosen to follow the line of a boggy glen. In the latter case, climb up onto the higher ground when you are passing the holly – you will find that it is reasonably short from this point onwards. Soon after this you will reach a fence-line, which can easily be crossed at NR 37889 94388, slightly to the right of another marshy hollow (an agile dog will be able to slither underneath this fence). Continue towards the right-hand shoulder of Carn na Cainnle, keeping the marshy area on your left and ascending a slight slope to regain a view of The Monument and the sea behind. You will skirt around Carn na Cainnle, perhaps noticing a stone circle of 4m diameter at NR 38021 94422 and a square foundation 2m x 2m at NR 38094 94347.

As you round the shoulder of Carn na Cainnle, following the obvious and original pathway, you will be rewarded by the sudden appearance of Dùn Eibhinn, very close at hand. From this angle it is very easy to recognise the two occupation levels and to appreciate that it must have presented a most impressive appearance in its heyday. Doubtless you will pause to visit the Dùn, the entrance to which is in its north-east corner.

Descending from the entrance to the Dùn, make your way towards Loch na Sgùid ("Shelter Loch"), and identify the eponymous "sgùid" or rock overhang which will have been the habitation site. There is a large, prostrate slab in front of it with a circular depression in its upper surface – this may perhaps be a cup-mark and would suggest a connection with the Bronze Age.

Just above and behind the "sgùid" there are traces of cultivation and, near at hand, the remains of Tobhta Donnchaidh an Oir ("Duncan of the Gold's Home"). Turn left, following the line of the loch but at a slight elevation – you are now following the path taken by the school-children of Scalasaig. You will be able to see the school straight ahead of you, originally built by the Scottish Society for the Propagation of Christian Knowledge and to a design by Thomas Telford. If you look closely, you will see that the short driveway leading from the school to the public road continues in a straight line through the rushy fields and towards the loch. There were stepping stones in the loch for use in summer – but do not be tempted to use them, even if you can find them, as there are some very dangerous pitfalls on the other side. Of course, in time of flood or bad weather, the direct route was too dangerous, so the children followed a different path, leading down across the slope of An Gleann ("The Glen") and towards the western end of Loch Fada.

This is the way that you will need to follow as well – there are no great hazards until you reach the burn, which runs between deep banks and is difficult to cross for much of its length. As you approach it, notice a bend in its course surrounded by thickets of goat-willow, brambles and birch, which should be kept a little below you. Thus you will reach the burn at the foot of a slight waterfall, at NR 38008 95009, which is the correct place to cross it.

From here, you will need to pick the best route you can – there are paths through the bracken and the going is easier than through the rank heather. Head towards the left hand end of whatever houses you see across the loch, perhaps noticing a small hut at NR

37960 95086 (1.2m wall height with 2m internal diameter).

Do not lose too much height – try to keep in line with the loch but below the worst of the heather and near the upper margin of the bracken; in due course you will reach a fence, which has a stone stile about 150m inland from the loch shore at NR 37681 95155. If you have a dog, climb up to your left to the right-angle of the fence-line, where you will find that it should be possible to squeeze through behind the corner-post.

From here on, it is easy to follow the line of the path, which will lead through an old gateway in an ancient wall and down through broken rocks to the loch-side. As you follow the shoreline, you will notice exposed tree-roots, stumps and boles above the surface – these are part of Colonsay's ancient forest and have been dated to 4,300 (± 300) years old. Despite the fact that this is a protected Site of Special Scientific Interest, the loch has been drained to such an extent in recent years that more than fifty per cent of the water has gone and these timbers have been exposed to decay.

It is particularly unfortunate that a small group of crannogs (artificial islands) have also suffered from the same catastrophic intervention. When you reach the very head of the loch you may still be able to identify the sites of two of the group, a small one at the water's edge and a slightly larger one to its west, with a tiny hummock between. It seems that in ancient times a walkway linked the three crannogs that have been identified, and the hummock was one of the intermediate staging posts for the walkway. Until recently, the water was about 0.6 m. deeper than at present, so the crannogs were protected from decay and, in times of flood, were perfectly silhouetted and easily recognisable.

Whilst one might regret the damage to this specific SSSI, it is worth remembering that most of Colonsay and Oronsay have been placed under official protection orders of one kind or another. One imagines that such orders will not readily be rescinded and that in fullness of time some competent supervisory body will be empowered to enforce them.

Make your way westwards, remaining on the east side of the rushy area until you come close to the enclosed fields of Seaview croft ahead of you, then turn right to regain the main road. Turn left on the main road and, after 1 km, regain your starting-point at the graveyard.

BIBLIOGRAPHY

Note: This is not an exhaustive bibliography, but some attempt has been made to list the main reference sources in the order in which they were consulted.

Introduction: "Lonely Colonsay"
History of the Western Highlands of Scotland, Donald Gregory, Tait, Edinburgh 1836
History of the Western Highlands of Scotland, Donald Gregory, Morison, Glasgow 1881 (2nd edition)
The Book of Colonsay and Oronsay (2 vols.), Symington Grieve, 1923, Oliver and Boyd
The Orkneying Saga, Joseph Anderson, 1981, James Thin, Edinburgh
Professor Donald Mackinnon and Doctor Roger McNeill, Gaelic 'Lads o' Pairts' from Colonsay, Prof. John W. Sheets, 1999, unpublished mss.
Colkitto! A Celebration of Clan Donald of Colonsay, Kevin Byrne, 1997, House of Lochar, Colonsay
Colonsay and Oronsay in the Isles of Argyll, John de Vere Loder, Colonsay Press 1995 edition
Colonsay & Oronsay, An Inventory of the Monuments, extracted from Argyll Volume 5, RCAHMS, 1994

Author's Foreword: Names and Naming
Jura, Island of Deer, Peter Youngson, 2001
Adomnan of Iona: Life of St. Columba, Trans. Richard Sharpe, Penguin 1995
Lands of the Lordship, 1976, Donald MacEachern
Nya Lidköpings-Tidningen, Sweden, June 19 1995, article on p. 8

Chapter 1: Prehistoric Colonsay
Colonsay, Ordnance Survey Sheet: NR 38/39/49 1:25000
Colonsay, Geological Survey of Great Britain, Sheet 35, 1968 ed.
Port Askaig, (Oronsay section) Geological Survey of Great Britain, Sheet 27, 1967 ed.
Placenames of Colonsay and Oransay, Kevin Byrne, Colonsay Books 1993
A Guide to the Geology of Colonsay, Alex Maltman, n.d.
Colonsay, One of the Hebrides, Murdoch McNeill, House of Lochar, 2001

facsimile edition

Colonsay and Oronsay, Norman Newton, David & Charles, 1990

The Geology of Colonsay and Oronsay with Part of the Ross of Mull, Craig, Wright & Bailey, HMSO, 1911

Excavations on Oronsay – Prehistoric Human Ecology on a Small Island, Paul Mellars, EUP, 1987

Hunter Gatherer Landscape Archaeology – The Southern Hebrides Mesolithic Project 1988–98 Steven Mithen (Editor), McDonald Institute Monographs 2000

After the Ice, A Global Human History, 20,000–5,000 B.C., Steven Mithen, Orion Publishing 2003

Plants & People in Ancient Scotland, C Dickson & J Dickson, Tempus, 2000

Boulder Survey, Proceedings of the Royal Society of Edinburgh, Session 1880-81, pp 263-266

Chapter 2: Historic Times – at a canter

Popular Tales of the West Highlands, J.F. Campbell, 2 vols. Birlinn, 1994

The Lordship of the Isles, I.F. Grant, James Thin, 1982

Late Medieval Monumental Sculpture in the West Highlands, K A Steer & J W M Bannerman, RCAHMS 1977

Celtic Britain, Lloyd Laing, Paladin, 1987

Acts of the Lords of the Isles 1336–1493, Scottish History Society, 1986

Lord Strathcona, a biography of Donald Alexander Smith, Donna McDonald, Dundurn, 1996

Graveyard Inscriptions of Colonsay and Oronsay, Kevin Byrne, privately published in digital form, 1996

Clan Donald, Donald J Macdonald, Macdonald, 1978

Sea-Road of the Saints – Celtic Holy Men in the Hebrides, John Marsden, Floris, 1995

Chapter 3: Natural History

"*Choughs feeding on Miner Bee* Colletes succinctus *larvae on Colonsay*, J & PM Clarke, Bird Study (1995) 42, pp 253–254

Natural Environment of the Inner Hebrides, J M Boyd (Editor), Royal Society of Edinburgh, 1983

The Birds of Colonsay and Oronsay, D. Alexander 1978, updated by J & PM Clarke 1996, updated by J. How 2000, further updated by M. Peacock 2002, www.colonsay.org.uk

European Eel: decline of a highly migratory fish, S. Ringuet, Traffic Dispatches Number 16, March 2001

A Tour in Scotland and Voyage to the Hebrides 1772, T Pennant, Chester 1774

Chapter 4: Scalasaig

The Rev. Dr. John Walkers "Report on the Hebrides" of 1764 and 1771, Margaret M. McKay (editor), John Donald, 1980

The Western Gàidhealtachd after the Statutes of Iona 1609, Dr. Domhnall Stiùbhart, speech published in "The Corncrake" issue # 40–44, 2001

Ben Odhran House, a description of re-cycled fragments of The Monument used as quoins; Kevin Byrne, privately published 1996

Colonsay's Fallen, Alan Davis, 2004

Chapter 5: Riasg Buidhe and Balavetchy

Colonsay, The Old Parish Register Transcribed, Kevin Byrne, private digital edition

Colonsay, Transcribed Census of 1841, 1851, 1861, 1871, 1881, 1891, 1901, Kevin Byrne, private digital edition

Colonsay and Oronsay: A Survey of Two Islands in the Inner Hebrides, J. E. Harvey, unpublished thesis, Dept. of Geography, University of Manchester 1973

The Physician, Roger McNeill (posthumous, private publication).

"Argyll Colony Plus", *Journal of the North Carolina Scottish Heritage Society*, Volume 6

The Island of Colonsay in Argyll: aspects of its social, economic and cultural life since the nineteenth century, Mary Campbell Carmichael, thesis for M. Litt., University of Edinburgh 1985

The Hebrides, A Natural History, J.M. Boyd & I.L.Boyd, Collins 1990

Natural History in the Highlands and Islands, F. Fraser Darling, Collins 1947

Chapter 6: Balnahard

Dwelly's Illustrated Gaelic to English Dictionary, Gairm 1977

A Dictionary of the Gaelic Language, Rev. Dr. Norman MacLeod and Rev Dr. Daniel Dewar; McPhun (Glasgow), 1871

Scandinavian Scotland, Barbara E. Crawford, Leicester U.P., 1987

Prose Writings of Donald MacKinnon, Lachlan Mackinnon, ed., Scottish Gaelic Texts Society, Edinburgh, 1956

Notes on the Antiquities of the Islands of Colonsay and Oransay, William Stevenson (re-printed from *Proceedings of Society of Antiquaries of Scotland 1880–1881*), Colonsay books n.d.

The MacMillans and the MacNeills who emigrated in 1806 from the Isle of Colonsay, Argyllshire, to Prince Edward Island, Canada on the ship "Spencer" and settled in Wood Islands, Douglas C. MacMillan, privately published, 2nd edition 1991

Chapter 7: Colonsay House and Gardens

A Description of the Western Islands of Scotland, Martin Martin, Mercat Press 1981 (facsimile of 1716 edition)

John Oliver, Mrs. Marylin L. Tusher, personal communication; documentary information provided by Mrs. Tusher is archived at Homefield, Colonsay

The McNeills of Colonsay and Oronsay, facsimile of mss. family pedigree, archived at Homefield, Colonsay

Report of Whale Strandings 1919 and 1920, page 17, Sidney Harmer, British Museum.

Jawbone and other parts of the Blue Whale still surviving in Colonsay were identified in 2002 by Nicholas Redman, personal communication.

Whales' Bones, Nicholas Redman, 2004

Summer in the Hebrides, Sketches in Colonsay and Oronsay, Frances Murray, Glasgow 1887

Lord Strathcona, Donna MacDonald, Toronto 1996

Citation: John J. McCusker, *Comparing the Purchasing Power of Money in Great Britain from 1264 to Any Other Year Including the Present*, Economic History Services, 2001, URL http://www.eh.net/hmit/ppowerbp/

Colonsay map by Ordnance Survey 1st and 2nd Edition 1878 and 1899

Colonsay & Oronsay map by David Wilson "from an actual survey made in 1804"

Chart 2418, corrected to 1962, based upon 1855 survey for Hydrographer Royal

"On the status of *Arcitalitrus dorrieni* (Crustacea: Amphipoda) on the island of Colonsay, Inner Hebrides", P.G. Moore and J.I. Spicer, *Journal of Natural History*, vol. 20 issue 3, 1986

Chapter 8: Kiloran Bay, Uragaig and Loch an Sgoltaire

The Birds of Colonsay and Oransay, D.C. Jardine, House of Lochar 2002

Gravestone Inscriptions of Colonsay and Oransay, transcribed by Kevin and Christa Byrne, updated to 2007, private digital publication.

Chapter 9: Upper and Lower Kilchattan, with Baile Iochdrach

Go Listen to the Crofters, A.D.Cameron, 1990 edition, Acair

The Discovery of the Hebrides, Voyagers to the Western Isles 1745–1883, Elizabeth Bray, Collins 1986

The History of Elderslie Township 1851–1977, editor Gordon Reid, 1977, Elderslie Historical Society, Ontario

Hopefield and its Families 1856–1989, Catherine Fraser, n.d. Privately published, P.E.I.

History of the Baptists in Scotland, Ed. Rev. Geo. Yuille, 1926, Baptist Union

Baptist Church in Colonsay, John McNeill, Edinburgh 1914 (from the library of Mrs. Eleanor McNeill, Colonsay).

Memoir of Sir John McNeill, G.C.B., by his Granddaughter, F.M., 1910

The Highland House Transformed, Daniel Maudlin, 2009

Argyll & Bute, F. A. Walker, 2000

Chapter 10: Machrins and Ardskenish

Gloomy Memories, Donald McLeod, facsimile of 1892 edition, n.d., B. Jain, New Delhi.

"Excavations at Machrins", J.N. Graham Ritchie, 1981 *Proc Soc Antiq Scot*

Physical changes brought about by the floating power of seaweed, Symington Grieve, 1929

Chapter 11: Baleromindubh and Balerominmòr

"Wetland Development of Woodland Disturbance – A Pollen and Microscopic Charcoal Analysis of an Apparent Woodland Decline at Loch Cholla, Colonsay, Scotland ca. 7800 BP", Madeline Solomon, paper submitted to University of Sheffield, April 2000

"Further Placenames of Colonsay and Oronsay", Kevin Byrne, unpublished notes 1978–2003

Chapter 12: Garvard and Teampull a' Ghlinne

The Highlands and Isles of Scotland, W.G. MacKenzie, 1937

Moch is Anmoch, Donald A. MacNeill, (Alastair MacNeill Scouller, ed.) House of Lochar, 1998

Saint Columba of Iona, Lucy Menzies, JMF books (1992 Facsimile edition).

The Bruce, John Barbour – prose translation by George Eyre-Todd,

Mercat 1996

Argyll, The Enduring Heartland, Marion Campbell, House of Lochar 2001

Further Wanderings, Mainly in Argyll, M.E.M. Donaldson, Gardner 1926

Columba, Ian Fraser, Richard Drew Publishing, 1990

Life of St. Columba, Founder of Hy, Adomnàn, Llanerch Press 1988

Adomnàn of Iona: Life of St. Columba, Trans. Richard Sharpe, Penguin 1995

Chambers Biographical Dictionary, 1986 Edition

Para Handy Tales, Neil Munro, Pan 1973

Chapter 13: Oransay and its Priory

Highland Postbag, Jean MacDougall, Shepheard-Walwyn 1984

Oransay and its Monastery: Iona's Rival, F.C.E. McNeill c. 1882

The Wreck of the 'Orion', Rev J. Clarke 1851

The Mythology, Traditions and History of MacDhubhsith – MacDuffie Clan – The Lands of Our Fathers, Volume VI, Earle Douglas MacPhee, 1975, privately published, Vancouver

The Great Auk, Errol Fuller, Harry N. Abrams Inc., 1999

A History of Christianity, Diarmaid MacCulloch, 2009

Irish Franciscan Mission to Scotland 1619–1646, Cathaldus Giblin, 1964

Origines Parochiales Scotiae, Cosmo Innes (Google Books)